THIRD EDITION

research
METHODOLOGY

WELMAN • KRUGER • MITCHELL

OXFORD
UNIVERSITY PRESS

OXFORD
UNIVERSITY PRESS

Southern Africa

Oxford University Press Southern Africa (Pty) Ltd

Vasco Boulevard, Goodwood, Cape Town, Republic of South Africa
P O Box 12119, N1 City, 7463, Cape Town, Republic of South Africa

Oxford University Press Southern Africa (Pty) Ltd is a wholly-owned subsidiary of
Oxford University Press, Great Clarendon Street, Oxford OX2 6DP.

The Press, a department of the University of Oxford, furthers the University's
objective of excellence in research, scholarship, and education by publishing
worldwide in Oxford, New York

Auckland Dar es Salaam Hong Kong Karachi
Kuala Lumpur Madrid Melbourne Mexico City Nairobi
New Delhi Shanghai Taipei Tokyo Toronto

With offices in
Argentina Austria Brazil Chile Czech Republic France Greece
Guatemala Hungary Italy Japan Poland Portugal Singapore South Korea
Switzerland Turkey Ukraine Vietnam

Oxford is a registered trade mark of Oxford University Press
in the UK and certain other countries

Published in South Africa
by Oxford University Press Southern Africa (Pty) Ltd, Cape Town

Research Methodology 3rd edition
ISBN 978 0195789010

First published 1994 by Southern Book Publishers (Pty) Ltd
Second edition published by Oxford University Press Southern Africa 2001
Reprinted 2002
Third edition published 2005
Third impression 2007

Publishing manager: Marion Griffon
Editor: Aimeé van Rooyen
Designer: Oswald Kurten
Cover design: Oswald Kurten
Illustrator: Rassie Erasmus
Indexer: Ethné Clarke

Published by Oxford University Press Southern Africa
PO Box 12119, N1 City, 7463, Cape Town, South Africa

Set in 10.5 pt on 12.5 pt Chaparral Pro by John Bennett
Cover photo: Getty images
Cover reproduction by The Image Bureau
Printed and bound by Clyson Printers, Cape Town

The authors and publishers gratefully acknowledge permission to reproduce material in this book.
Every effort has been made to acknowledge copyright holders, but where this has proved impossible, the
publishers would be grateful for information that would enable them to amend any omissions in
future editions.

The cartoons/drawings on pp. 5, 8, 58, 61, and 284 were sourced from the study guide for
Research Methodology published by Technikon SA.

Contents

Chapter 6 Validity of conclusions *105*

**Chapter 9   Data analysis and
               interpretation of
               results   209**

Preface

The main purpose of *Research Methodology* is to explain the nature and process of research in order to enable readers to conduct their own research to find answers to their specific research problems. This aim is achieved by providing practical guidelines, exercises, examples relating to all the relevant fields of study, and activities with case studies. The book is therefore essential to undergraduate as well as graduate students who need to conduct research. It can be used by researchers and students dealing with individuals, groups of people, organisations, products or systems, activities or events. As the principles of scientific research are the same for almost all fields of study, the book can be used by students and researchers conducting studies in the following fields:

▶ management and business administration
▶ correctional services and policing
▶ cost and management accounting
▶ credit management
▶ human resource management
▶ information technology
▶ internal auditing
▶ library and information studies
▶ public management
▶ real estate
▶ safety management
▶ taxation
▶ banking
▶ marketing, and
▶ human behavioural sciences (e.g. sociological, social psychological, and industrial psychological research).

The book is organised according to the different stages of research:

▶ Chapter 1: Establish the aim of your research.
▶ Chapter 2: State the problem to be investigated and formulate hypotheses.
▶ Chapter 3: Do a literature review in order to establish which problems and answers other researchers have encountered in their research.
▶ Chapters 4 and 5: Decide on a specific research design, based on the outcome of the literature review.
▶ Chapter 6: Investigate all the factors that may influence the sampling method and the validity of your conclusions.
▶ Chapters 7 and/or 8: Collect the data.
▶ Chapter 9: Analyse and interpret the data.
▶ Chapter 10: Write a report in which you draw conclusions about the value and significance of addressing the specific research problem.
▶ Chapter 11: This chapter provides guidelines on writing a research proposal with reference to relevant sections in the rest of the book for those researchers and students who are required to write one.

The contents of this book can be adapted according to the requirements of a specific course or type of research. If your research problem lends itself to be studied by a **quantitative approach**, we recommend that you read Chapters 1, 2, 3, 4, 5, 6, 7, 9, and 10. For those whose research problem lends itself to be studied by a **qualitative approach**, we recommend that you read Chapters 1, 2, 3, 8, 9, and 10. If you need to submit only a literature review for partial fulfilment of a degree or for an assignment, we recommend that you read the first three chapters. Then proceed with your study keeping the guidelines in Chapter 6 in mind. Before finishing, you may find the recommendations in Chapter 10 in conjunction with your own academic institution's regulations helpful. Chapter 11 provides guidelines to students on how to prepare a research proposal.

In the light of the increasing importance of the electronic media in research, we also include information on using the Internet as a research tool. A list of useful web sites appears in Appendix B. Also included is a CD-ROM containing *MoonStats*, a statistical software program. This program provides the tools for data exploration and description. It enables students of statistics and research to gain a solid foundation in statistics, and allows them to manage basic statistics confidently.

Welman, Kruger, and Mitchell

The aims of research

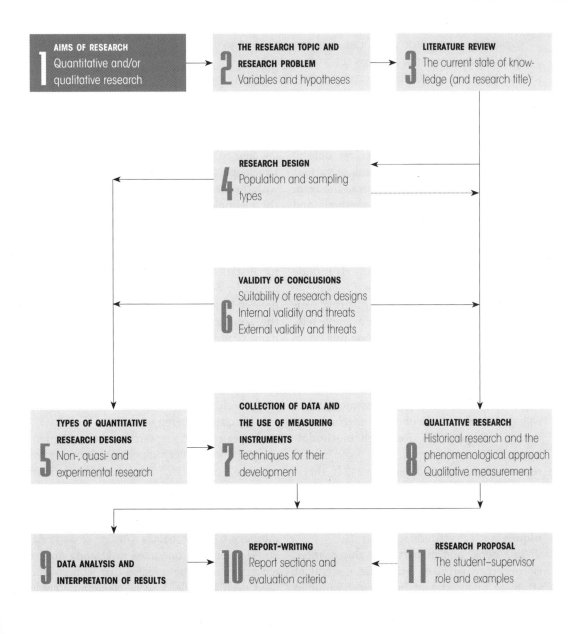

1 AIMS OF RESEARCH
Quantitative and/or qualitative research

2 THE RESEARCH TOPIC AND RESEARCH PROBLEM
Variables and hypotheses

3 LITERATURE REVIEW
The current state of knowledge (and research title)

4 RESEARCH DESIGN
Population and sampling types

6 VALIDITY OF CONCLUSIONS
Suitability of research designs
Internal validity and threats
External validity and threats

5 TYPES OF QUANTITATIVE RESEARCH DESIGNS
Non-, quasi- and experimental research

7 COLLECTION OF DATA AND THE USE OF MEASURING INSTRUMENTS
Techniques for their development

8 QUALITATIVE RESEARCH
Historical research and the phenomenological approach
Qualitative measurement

9 DATA ANALYSIS AND INTERPRETATION OF RESULTS

10 REPORT-WRITING
Report sections and evaluation criteria

11 RESEARCH PROPOSAL
The student–supervisor role and examples

LEARNING OUTCOMES

In this chapter we define the basic terminology with regards to research. This includes the terms *quantitative* and *qualitative*. In any research that is planned, the first stage involves determining the aims of the specific research study. This is a very important step as the aims of the research directly influence the choice between qualitative and quantitative research methodologies.

After studying this chapter, you will be able to:
- differentiate between research methodology as opposed to research methods and techniques
- name the three key characteristics (core features) of scientific knowledge that differentiate it from common human inquiry
- explain how research produces scientific knowledge
- illustrate the research process diagrammatically
- briefly describe the differences between the qualitative and quantitative approaches.

1.1 Introduction: What is research?

Research is a process that involves obtaining scientific knowledge by means of various objective methods and procedures. The term **objective** indicates that these methods and procedures do not rely on personal feelings or opinions, and that specific methods are used at each stage of the research process (see the figure on page 1). These methods include procedures for drawing a sample (for example stratified random sampling), measuring variables, collecting information (for example telephone interviewing), and analysing this information (for example calculating the product moment correlation coefficient). There are various methods and techniques available and, in general, the aim of a specific research project will determine which of these methods are the most appropriate. **Research methodology** considers and explains the logic behind research methods and techniques. It therefore has a much wider scope than **research methods** (such as opinion polls) which, in turn, have a wider scope than **research techniques** (such as attitude scales).

This book, and in particular this chapter, is concerned with the **scientific** method of attaining knowledge of human behaviour in a variety of contexts. This type of knowledge differs in important respects from a naive, or lay, person's knowledge of human behaviour. Lay people usually associate the idea of science with the medical and natural sciences, and with the technological achievements connected to these disciplines. Examples of such achievements range from heart transplants to the Katse dam at the Lesotho Highlands Project, for instance. This stereotype is further reinforced by advertisements in which a person, dressed in a white laboratory overcoat, claims the superiority of some well-known brand name of washing powder, toothpaste or motor oil over other brand names. However, the term *scientific* is not restricted to knowledge in certain fields of study only, and many fields of study besides physics, chemistry, and surgery may lay claim to being scientific.

Proper scientific research and the methodology applied are very important. Consider, for instance, the research conducted in southern Africa as well as America on the effectiveness of Nevirapine. This drug is used in poor countries to prevent the spread of HIV from mothers to their babies (Ancer & Sapa-AP, 2004). Research conducted in Uganda on the efficacy of the drug revealed that women who used even a single dose of Nevirapine could develop a resistance to the drug. This meant that these women would not be able to use Nevirapine or any similar drug when their health deteriorated as a result of the AIDS virus. However, as the initial research was "so riddled with sloppy record keeping" (Africa research on AIDS "hides flaws", 2004), these results were withheld. As a result, warnings regarding the toxicity and resistance associated with the drug were ignored until these initial research results were eventually brought to light. Further research has since been conducted and research in South Africa revealed that "80 per cent of women with HIV who receive a single dose of Nevirapine develop resistance [to the drug] – double what was initially believed" (Green, 2005). This new research revealed that the problems associated with the drug are serious enough to warrant further research into other ways of preventing transmission of the disease to newborns. Proper scientific research using the correct methodology is therefore of crucial importance as it can often mean the difference between life and death.

In this book we will use the concept of **research** to refer to the process of using scientific methods to expand knowledge in a particular field of study.

1.2 Scientific as opposed to non-scientific knowledge

1.2.1 Sources of non-scientific knowledge

There are five sources of non-scientific knowledge: authority, opinions of peers, traditions, debating, and accidental observation.

1.2.1.1 AUTHORITY

Non-scientific knowledge is often merely accepted on the basis of the **authority** of some or other source. According to the scientific approach, however, we should check the way in which findings are acquired and not accept them merely because they originate from a so-called expert. This means that we must examine the evidence on which a claim is based.

FOR EXAMPLE In 1610, with the aid of his newly invented telescope, the Italian physicist Galileo discovered that there were spots on the sun. His colleagues, however, rejected his finding because it was not in accordance with the prevailing opinion that was based on the authority of Aristotle, a fourth century Greek philosopher, who stated that the sun was spotless.

This example clearly illustrates the acceptance of non-scientific knowledge based on the authority of a specific person.

1.2.1.2 OPINIONS OF PEERS

Non-scientific knowledge can also be acquired by asking the **opinion of peers**. Instead of calling on the opinions of experts, we may turn to our friends to obtain knowledge.

FOR EXAMPLE Front-line factory managers do not ask only personnel practitioners for advice when they want to promote some of their workers, but also their fellow front-line managers, who have already promoted their workers. Similarly, students who have already completed a course may be consulted by their fellow students on whether it is better to prepare for the final examinations by studying regularly through the semester or studying shortly before the examinations.

1.2.1.3 TRADITIONS

Another source of non-scientific knowledge is that which is carried over from one generation to the next.

FOR EXAMPLE Consider the commonly held beliefs that women are less capable of thinking logically than men, and that fat people are always happy. Such traditional beliefs are often reflected in idiomatic expressions such as the following:
- Birds of a feather flock together.
- Like father like son.
- A leopard cannot change its spots.

1.2.1.4 DEBATING

People often attempt to obtain knowledge and insight by arguing in a seemingly logical manner. This method appeals to the intellect rather than to experience and also constitutes a source of non-scientific knowledge.

FOR EXAMPLE Some students may argue that it is not worth the trouble to start revising early in the semester, as that would leave more time before the exam in which to forget what they have learnt. Others, however, may argue with as much conviction that they should begin revising well in advance so that they will have enough time to study everything thoroughly. Similarly, politicians often act as if they have access to seemingly scientific knowledge through debating.

Figure 1.1 *Methods of "logical" reasoning*

However, research (Feather, 1964) suggests that people are inclined to judge illogical arguments that correspond with their own attitudes and convictions as logical, whereas they judge those that are logical but do not correspond with their own attitudes and convictions as illogical. It is therefore not unusual for advocates and adversaries of a specific issue to reach diametrically opposed conclusions by means of their methods of reasoning. They often reason logically but from a false premise, so that the ultimate conclusions are flawed.

1.2.1.5 ACCIDENTAL OBSERVATION

If we notice something happening in one situation, but do not investigate the phenomenon in a systematic and planned manner, we may come to incorrect conclusions about what really happened.

FOR EXAMPLE A supervisor may observe that trainees who started studying a week before the course examination the previous year and who were successful, used the correct learning method. Somebody else, however, might remember examples of trainees who prepared well in advance yet failed hopelessly.

In our everyday dealings we naturally come into contact with only a small group of people and we cannot therefore necessarily elevate our perceptions (such as in the above-mentioned example) to become generally accepted rules. The same bias that was apparent in the previous source of non-scientific knowledge (debating) also applies here: we are inclined to observe that which fits in with our preconceptions or prejudices and to ignore that which differs. This is called **selective observation**.

RESEARCH EXAMPLE I   DISTRIBUTED VERSUS MASSED LEARNING

The objective is to obtain scientific knowledge about the relative effectiveness of distributed learning (i.e. regularly mastering study material in more than one session) versus the practice of massed learning (i.e. trying to learn all the study material in one session). This will require a study to be conducted in which we compare:
- the performance of one group of apprentices who learned in a distributed fashion; with
- the performance of another, comparable group who studied the same material by means of massed learning.

1.2.2 Scientific knowledge

The focus of this book is the expansion of scientific knowledge. At this early stage it is impossible to describe the process fully; instead, we will describe three core features of scientific knowledge.

These features reflect a critical predisposition towards claims based on any non-scientific sources of information, as well as claims which may even appear to be quite convincing.

1.2.2.1 SYSTEMATIC OBSERVATION

Firstly, we should obtain scientific knowledge by means of **systematic observation**, not selective observation. When we make use of selective observations, we pay attention only to information that supports our presumptions and we ignore that which does not support our presumptions. Accidental observations, for instance, tend to be selective rather than systematic.

Let us consider the example provided in **Research Example I**: instead of merely debating which learning method is the most effective, the scientific approach requires that we plan an investigation in which we use the results of two groups that have actually applied these methods strictly. Using such a systematic method of observation, we will be able to make valid conclusions.

Figure 1.2 *Obtaining knowledge in a controlled manned (eliminating alternatives systematically)*

1.2.2.2 CONTROL

Secondly, we should obtain scientific knowledge in a **controlled** manner. By control we mean that alternative explanations for the obtained results should be eliminated systematically. In **Research Example I**, for instance, scientific research would require that we eliminate the following alternative explanations for the superior performance of, for instance, the group that studied regularly:

▶ they studied a greater number of hours in total
▶ they were more familiar with the study material from the start
▶ they were more intelligent than the other group.

1.2.2.3 REPLICATION

Thirdly, the manner in which we obtain scientific knowledge must be **replicable**, that is, it must be possible to replicate the research results. By this we mean that similar results should be obtained by other researchers, involving other research participants in other circumstances. This should be independent of the original research yet must still be compatible with the same theory.

The expansion of scientific knowledge is therefore not a private matter. Rather, the manner in which scientists reach their conclusions is put before the scientific community for thorough inspection. (Read Chapters 3 and 10 concerning the publication of a research report.) The research is thus open to critical evaluation, and anybody who cares to do so may replicate, or repeat, the procedures used to determine whether comparable results are obtained.

The scientific community generally consists of people who, according to certain goals and rules, recognise the scientific method of creating knowledge. The products of this method should be rewarded by accepting such scientific information to be published in credible and accredited academic journals (Chapter 3), and so on.

The development of scientific knowledge is a democratic process. The most humble student and the most famous scientist have equal access to arriving at scientific claims. At this stage we may formulate the following principle of public scrutiny that applies to the scientific expansion of knowledge:

The procedures of scientific research should be submitted to the careful and critical evaluation of other members of the scientific community. These procedures include the arguments, choice of data, collection and analysis of data, interpretation of results, conclusions, and so on, and will be addressed in the following chapters (also see the figure on page 1).

1.3 **Qualitative and quantitative research cycles**

There are two main approaches to research. On the one hand we have the **positivist** approach which is based on a philosophical approach known as logical positivism. The positivist approach underlies the natural-scientific method in human behavioural research and holds that research must be limited to what we can observe and measure objectively, that is, that which exists independently of the feelings and opinions of individuals. The natural-scientific approach strives to formulate laws that apply to populations (that is, are universally valid – see p. 52) and that explain the causes of objectively observable and measurable behaviour. The term **objective** implies that people other than the researcher should agree on what is being observed, such as the score that the observation should register on a measuring instrument (see Chapter 7).

FOR EXAMPLE Botanists must agree (be "objective") that mealies will grow to 1,45 m in height within a specific number of days after planting if they have been planted in a specific type of soil and have received specified amounts of fertiliser as well as water.

The positivist approach to research is also known as the **quantitative** approach.

The positivist approach is opposed by the **anti-positivists** who share a resistance to upholding the natural-scientific method as the norm in human behavioural research. According to the anti-positivists, it is inappropriate to follow strict natural-scientific methods when collecting and interpreting data. They hold that the natural-scientific method is designed for studying molecules or organisms and is therefore not applicable to the phenomena being studied in the human behavioural sciences. In Chapter 8 you will see that, according to the phenomenologists (a sub-group of the anti-positivists), human experience, which is the object of behavioural research, cannot be separated from the person who is experiencing it. The phenomenologists oppose the way in which, for example, researchers in the business and administrative sciences try to imitate the natural-science researchers by distancing themselves from the phenomena they are studying. These researchers attempt like a fly on the wall to research another fly (struggling along in, for instance, a plate of soup) in an objective and detached way (see Figure 1.3). The anti-positivist approach to research is also known as the **qualitative** approach.

Figure 1.3 *The positivist and anti-positivist views*

The different points of view held by the positivists and anti-positivists are reflected in their definitions of their fields of study and their quantitative versus qualitative research aims (see Section 8.3). The positivists define their approach as the study of observable human behaviour, while the anti-positivists focus their research on the experiencing of human behaviour. While the positivists aim to uncover general laws of relationships and/or causality that apply to all people and at all times, phenomenologists are concerned with understanding human behaviour from the perspectives of the people involved. Therefore, phenomenologists are not concerned with the description of phenomena, but with their experience of these phenomena.

FOR EXAMPLE While the positivist researcher attempts to develop and test theories and models whereby, for example, leadership can be explained and predicted, the phenomenological researcher will attempt to understand how leaders in South Africa experience their transactional role as opposed to leaders in other countries.

Essentially, the anti-positivists claim that the positivists have absolutised the natural-scientific method of studying objects which do not interpret events. This method cannot be applied with equal success in fields of study in which humans are studied.

Although the approaches with which we deal in Chapter 8 conceptually fit in better with the qualitative approach, it would be incorrect to maintain that, by definition, all such approaches are anti-positivist in nature. As a result, it does not mean that those considering using these methods should first make an anti-positivist confession.

One should also guard against viewing qualitative research approaches as easier substitutes for quantitative approaches. The quantitative methods have built up an extensive arsenal of checks and balances which may aid researchers in averting unjustified conclusions (Chapter 6).

In the qualitative approach which we will describe in Chapter 8, by contrast, the *qualitative researcher* constitutes the primary research instrument. In a sense, the researcher must take over the function of the control group to rule out counter explanations, observe without affecting that which is being observed, and keep his or her expectations under control.

FOR EXAMPLE Suppose a researcher wants to investigate the nature of prison gangs and the reasons why people become involved with them. The researcher would probably not get much cooperation from the prisoners if he or she asked them to complete a questionnaire, for example. Instead, in order to get close to the subjects, the researcher could to try to be accepted as a member of one of the gangs. In this way, the researcher would be able to collect data concerning the reasons why prisoners form gangs. However, there is the danger of the researcher becoming involved with the gang to such an extent that the scientific community would question his or her objectivity.

It therefore requires a seasoned and mature researcher with both a sound knowledge of these threats and complete self-insight to be detached from, yet so involved with his or her object of study. The reason for this is that in the final analysis, qualitative researchers, to the same degree as quantitative researchers, have to defend their conclusions before the critically disposed scrutiny of their colleagues. If qualitative researchers believe that they have obtained new insights which cannot withstand the test of scrutiny, such supposed knowledge is no different from everyday observation and idle speculation.

1.4 Differences between quantitative and qualitative research methodologies

According to Denzin and Lincoln (1994, p. 4), "the word qualitative implies an emphasis on processes and meanings that are not rigorously examined, or measured (if measured at all)

in terms of quantity, amount, intensity or frequency". Therefore, according to these authors, the aims of qualitative research methods are to establish the socially constructed nature of reality, to stress the relationship between the researcher and the object of study, as well as to emphasise the value-laden nature of the inquiry. On the other hand, quantitative research methods do not involve the investigation of processes but emphasise the measurement and analysis of causal relationships between variables within a value-free context (Denzin & Lincoln, 1994). Stainback and Stainback (1984) summarise the direct contrast between the quantitative and qualitative methodologies as follows:

▶ The purpose of quantitative research is to evaluate **objective data** consisting of numbers while qualitative research deals with **subjective data** that are produced by the minds of respondents or interviewees (i.e. human beings). Qualitative data are presented in language instead of numbers. The researcher tries to understand the significance which respondents attach to their environment.

▶ As a result of dealing with numbers, quantitative researchers use a process of analysis that is based on **complex structured methods** to confirm or disprove hypotheses (see Section 2.4). Flexibility is limited to prevent any form of bias in presenting the results. On the other hand, qualitative research is based on **flexible and explorative methods** because it enables the researcher to change the data progressively so that a deeper understanding of what is being investigated can be achieved.

▶ The purpose of quantitative research is not to deal directly with everyday life, but rather with an **abstraction of reality**. "They seek a nomothetic or ethic science based on probabilities derived from the study of large numbers of randomly selected cases" (Denzin & Lincoln, 1994, p. 5). In contrast, qualitative researchers investigate only the constraints of day-to-day events and base their results on the daily events and behaviour of people.

▶ Quantitative researchers try to understand the facts of a research investigation from an **outsider's perspective**. Therefore it is important for quantitative research to keep to a detached, objective view of the facts as that will keep the research process, hypothetically, free from bias. On the other hand, qualitative researchers try to achieve an **insider's view** by talking to subjects or observing their behaviour in a subjective way; they believe that first-hand experience of the object under investigation produces the best data.

▶ Quantitative researchers try to keep the research process as **stable** as possible. They focus on the causal aspects of behaviour and the collection of facts that won't change easily. In contrast, qualitative researchers work with the **dynamic and changeable** nature of reality.

▶ Quantitative researchers control the investigation and structure of the research situation in order to identify and isolate variables. Specific measurement instruments are used to collect data. Their approach is therefore described as **particularistic**. In contrast, qualitative researchers make use of a **holistic** approach, that is, they collect a wide array of data, for example documents, records, photos, observations, interviews, and case studies.

▶ Stainback and Stainback (1984) allege that both quantitative and qualitative researchers aim at reliable and valid results. Quantitative researchers, however, focus more on **reliability**, that is, consistent and stable measurement of data as well as replicability. As far as qualitative data is concerned, **validity** is considered as more important because the objective of the study must be representative of what the researcher is investigating.

▶ Quantitative research usually aims for **larger numbers** of cases and the analysis of results is usually based on statistical significance. Qualitative research, on the other hand, involves **small samples** of people, studied by means of in-depth methods (Miles & Huberman, 1994).

In conclusion we can say that the purpose of both quantitative and qualitative research is to try to understand the subject's point of view. Quantitative researchers do it by means of controlling the situation and using remote, empirical, and inferential methods. Qualitative researchers, on the other hand, use unstructured interviewing and detailed observation processes to gain better information about the views of the subject.

SUMMARY

The process of scientific research involves several stages as set out in the figure on page 1. By using scientific methods and procedures in each of these stages, we acquire "knowledge" which explains the mystery of certain phenomena. Scientific knowledge has three core features: it is obtained by means of systematic observation, control is exercised in the process of obtaining the information, and the results can be replicated. Non-scientific knowledge, on the other hand, is obtained by means of authority, opinions of peers, traditions, debating, and accidental observations. We can distinguish between two methodologies – the quantitative and qualitative methodologies. These research methodologies allow us the means to explore unexplained phenomena as well as those which were previously explained but misunderstood. Through the use of methods and techniques that are scientifically defendable, we may come to conclusions that are valid and reliable. Quantitative research uses structured methods to evaluate objective data, whereas quantitative research uses more flexible methods to investigate subjective data.

TEST YOURSELF

Question 1: Multiple-choice questions

Only one of the answers for each question is correct. Identify and mark the correct one. (Answers appear in Appendix A on page 299.)

1.1 Methodology can best be described as
   a) the logical step of science
   b) the science of knowing
   c) the discovery of reality through experience
   d) the discovery of the truth through scientific methods.

1.2 Scientific enquiry, in comparison to non-scientific inquiry,
   a) should guard against certain scientific errors
   b) does not view the ordinary citizen's opinion as valuable
   c) takes special precaution to avoid error
   d) is less concerned about making mistakes.

1.3 Something which helps us organise and interpret the world is referred to as a
   a) paradigm
   b) theory
   c) hypothesis
   d) concept.

1.4 The essential features of science are
   a) counter-intuitive and definite findings
   b) didactic rules of evidence and quantification
   c) intuition, inference, and experimentation
   d) systematic observation, control, and replication.

Question 2: Self-evaluation questions

(Some answers appear in Appendix A on page 299.)

2.1 Suppose it occurs to a group of people travelling through South Africa that the most cases of reckless driving which they have encountered involved cars with Gauteng (GP) registration numbers. They come to the conclusion that drivers with GP registration numbers are the most reckless drivers in the country. Are we dealing here with a source of:
   a) non-scientific knowledge, or
   b) scientific knowledge?
   If (a), identify the particular source of non-scientific knowledge as one of the following:
   • authority
   • opinions of peers
   • tradition
   • debating
   • accidental observation.

2.2 Suppose school children regularly eat apples because their teacher taught them that this habit promotes healthy teeth. Are we dealing here with a source of:
   a) non-scientific knowledge, or
   b) scientific knowledge?
   If (a), identify the particular source of non-scientific knowledge as one of the following:
   • authority
   • opinions of peers
   • tradition
   • debating
   • accidental observation.

The research topic, project title, and research problem

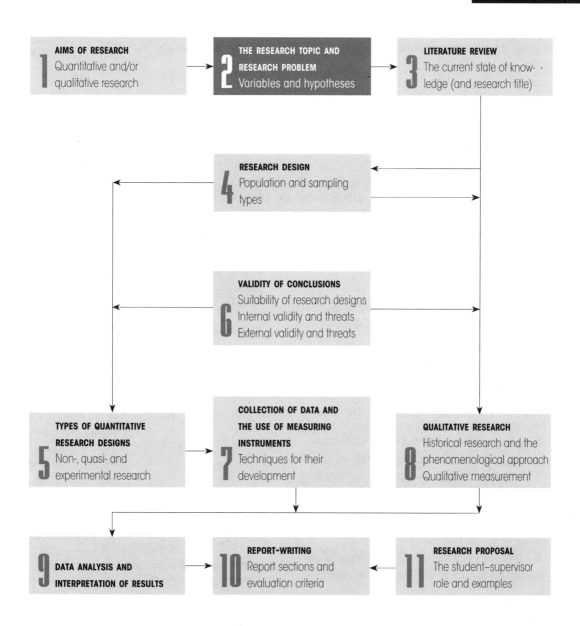

1 AIMS OF RESEARCH
Quantitative and/or
qualitative research

2 THE RESEARCH TOPIC AND
RESEARCH PROBLEM
Variables and hypotheses

3 LITERATURE REVIEW
The current state of knowledge (and research title)

4 RESEARCH DESIGN
Population and sampling
types

6 VALIDITY OF CONCLUSIONS
Suitability of research designs
Internal validity and threats
External validity and threats

5 TYPES OF QUANTITATIVE
RESEARCH DESIGNS
Non-, quasi- and
experimental research

7 COLLECTION OF DATA AND
THE USE OF MEASURING
INSTRUMENTS
Techniques for their
development

8 QUALITATIVE RESEARCH
Historical research and the
phenomenological approach
Qualitative measurement

9 DATA ANALYSIS AND
INTERPRETATION OF RESULTS

10 REPORT-WRITING
Report sections and
evaluation criteria

11 RESEARCH PROPOSAL
The student–supervisor
role and examples

LEARNING OUTCOMES

In this chapter we look at the second step of the research process which involves the statement of the research problem. Once you have decided what the topic of your research is going to be, you have to develop a question which you are going to investigate. This question should express the relationship between the relevant variables in such a way that it can be tested. Based on this question, the null and alternative hypotheses are then used to express the relationship between the dependent and independent variables more precisely.

After studying this chapter, you will be able to:
- list four typical examples of research topics appropriate to your field of study
- explain the role of theory in scientific research
- illustrate some basic purposes of doing research by means of an example
- discuss the six basic steps of the research process
- explain the importance of identifying the purpose of an investigation before starting the research
- explain what the statement of the research problem entails
- understand the difference between a conceptual and an operational definition
- differentiate between the independent and the dependent variables
- define and explain the different types of hypotheses
- distinguish between deductive and inductive research
- explain briefly why applied research instead of basic research will typically be done in industry and commerce, and describe two examples of applied research
- explain briefly why action research will typically be done in industry and commerce.

2.1 Introduction

The first concrete step in the scientific research process is to formulate the specific problem that is to be examined clearly. If, for instance, the objective of our research project is to test hypotheses stemming from some theory, we should then state this theory and indicate explicitly the manner in which the proposed hypotheses are implied by the theory. It is important that we define the following terms:

▶ A **hypothesis** is a tentative assumption or preliminary statement about the relationship between two or more things that needs to be examined. In other words, a hypothesis is a tentative solution or explanation of a research problem and the task of research is to investigate it.

▶ A **theory** is a group of logical, related statements that is presented as an explana-

tion of a phenomenon. A theory therefore encompasses one or more hypotheses.

2.2 The research process

We will briefly elaborate on the various stages before we consider the statement of the research problem in detail.

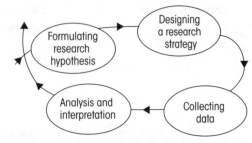

Figure 2.1 *The deductive, empirical cycle in the scientific expansion of knowledge (Source: Huysamen, 1994, p. 10.)*

2.2.1 Identifying a research topic

We may find that a research topic suggests itself as a result of our course work, job, interests or general experience.

FOR EXAMPLE We may be interested in the employment problems of minority groups in society, the difficulties of funding small businesses, what makes managers successful, or the commercial sponsorship of sport – the possibilities are endless.

Having **identified** a research topic which is of general interest to us, we can continue to the next stage.

2.2.2 Defining the research problem

Defining the research problem involves narrowing down our general interest in a research topic in order to focus on a particular research problem which is small enough to be investigated. This process leads to the setting of the research questions. In academic research the classic way to identify a research problem is to consider the literature and identify any gaps. These gaps indicate original areas to research.

FOR EXAMPLE In our reading of the literature on strategic management, we might realise that there is a lack of research in a certain context (Africa), or certain industries (for instance mining). This would therefore trigger us to do some research to fill this "research gap".

If a student has already conducted an undergraduate dissertation, that subject area may lead to his or her master's or doctorate research questions. Alternatively, management consultancy or commissioned research may suggest research questions.

2.2.3 Determining how to conduct the study

Our general approach to the research is known as our **research paradigm**. The term *paradigm* refers to the progress of scientific practice based on people's philosophies and assumptions about the world and the nature of knowledge. In this context, the term refers to the way in which research should be conducted.

FOR EXAMPLE If we have a positivist approach to research, we might tend to rely on questionnaires to collect data. However, if we are more anti-positivist in view, we might approach research in a more qualitative manner, and rely on case studies or interviews to collect data.

Our approach to the entire process of the research study is known as our **research methodology** (see Chapter 1, Section 1.1). Although, in part, this is determined by our research problem, the assumptions we use in our research and the way we define our research problems will influence the way in which we conduct the study.

2.2.4 Collecting the research data

There are various ways in which we can collect our research data and we will discuss the main data collection methods in Chapters 7 and 8. If we follow a **quantitative methodology**, we will be attempting to measure variables or count occurrences of a phenomenon. On the other hand, if we follow a **qualitative methodology**, we will emphasise meanings and experiences related to the phenomena (see Chapter 1, Section 1.3).

2.2.5 Analysing and interpreting the research data

The **analysis** and **interpretation** of our research data form the major part of our research project. The tools of analysis that we will use depend on whether we collected qualitative or quantitative data. An introduction to the various methods and techniques of analysis is presented in Chapter 9.

2.2.6 Writing the report

This is the culmination of the research process. It is important to start writing up the research in draft as soon as the project is started, continuing to do so until it is completed. In this way, we will have a thorough report containing all the necessary information.

2.3 Statement of the research problem

In the process of scientifically investigating research problems we may distinguish between different, successive stages called the **empirical cycle**. These stages are common to all science-based investigations whatever type of research is adopted, and are represented in Figure 2.1. The first stage in any research project is to choose a research area or a general topic. This process also requires the delineation of a problem area and the description of one or more research problems.

Consider the following research problems (research questions) that are relevant to various fields of study:

- Which factors play a role in the incidence of fraud?
- Does exposure to aggressive role model behaviour encourage aggressiveness among security company workers?
- Does the number of bystanders have an effect on the probability that assistance will be given to someone in distress?
- Why does poverty appear more often in some societies than in others?
- Which programmes are likely to promote socio-economic development?
- What are the causes of violence in township areas?
- How can our organisational system be made compatible for the year 2010 by using our existing computer technology?
- Is a police presence required to a greater extent around household driveways than at shopping centres to prevent the hijacking of motor vehicles in suburban areas?

- Will specialists familiar with computer languages such as Cobol be better equipped to make large mainframe computer programs compliant with requirements than those specialists not familiar with Cobol?
- Does the publication of the expectations of major private employment organisations in South Africa regarding a decrease in employment levels decrease the level of union initiated strikes?
- Why were the secret operations of the South African Police Force during the "total onslaught" years not revealed by journalists who knew about them?
- Has the legislation introduced over the last two years criminalised money laundering in South Africa?
- Will the idea of a mega-city combine the best elements of the existing system with the single-city model in Gauteng?
- Will the South African tax collection system be enhanced by requiring taxpayers to do their own assessment when they file their tax returns, as is the case in Namibia?
- How heavy should the penalties imposed by the Receiver of Revenue be for under-assessment by taxpayers filing their tax returns?
- What measures must be taken to advance the convergence of information technology and telecommunications in southern Africa?
- Will a company's customer relationships be improved by providing "call centres" to ensure that requests are acted upon without the necessity for endless telephone calls?

A **research problem** refers to some difficulty that the researcher experiences in the context of either a theoretical or practical situation and to which he or she wants to obtain a solution.

NOTE: Exploratory research does not start with a specific problem – the approach of such a study is to find a problem or a hypothesis to be tested (typical of qualitative research – see Section 1.3).

To define a problem correctly, the researcher must know what a problem is. To answer (solve) a research problem, the researcher must be able to answer the following two questions:

▶ What is the problem?
▶ What is the best way to solve the problem?

Although these questions seem trivial, they are, in fact, of vital importance. Answering the first question implies that the researcher clearly knows what he or she wants to investigate. A common mistake is to go ahead with data collection and other "practical" activities before knowing the actual problem. Such an approach often ends up in a situation where "a bunch of data is searching for a problem" and wastes time and resources. However, this does not mean that we should not make any observations prior to the research. It is very often useful to explore and to become acquainted with the phenomenon (problem) in order to arrive at the actual research question.

A useful strategy which can be used to identify the research problem involves asking questions. Good questions have the following characteristics:

▶ they express relationship(s) between two (or more) variables
▶ they are clear, that is, what is asked is understood.

The advantage of expressing relationships between variables is that they can be tested.

FOR EXAMPLE A marketing manager wonders whether the marketing effort should be directed towards large or small households, depending on where the propensity to purchase the firm's product is the highest. A possible question could be: "Is there a relationship between household size and propensity to purchase?" More specifically: "Are large households more likely to buy than smaller households?"

NOTE: In the example the following two concepts are included: household size and propensity to purchase. The questions therefore express a relationship between two variables in a clear way. The relationship between the two concepts is a **hypothesis** (see Section 2.4).

The researcher should therefore **rephrase a research problem** to put it in terms that are as specific as possible. This will make the problem operationally viable (see Section 2.4.2) and help with the development of hypotheses.

We can illustrate the technique of defining a problem by considering another example of a research problem stated in broad general terms:

Why is productivity in Japan so much higher than in South Africa?

In this form the question or statement is much too general and there are several ambiguities such as the following:

▶ To which type of productivity is reference made?
▶ Which industries are involved?
▶ To what time period of productivity is reference made?

We can narrow down the research problem to the following:

What factors were responsible for the higher labour productivity of Japan's manufacturing industries during the decade 1991 to 2000 in comparison to South Africa's manufacturing industries?

This version of the research problem is an improvement on the first one, but we can rethink it further and rephrase into an even better one:

To what extent did labour productivity from 1991 to 2000 in Japan exceed that of South Africa in respect of 15 selected manufacturing industries, and what factors were responsible for the productivity difference between the two countries?

Now we have a well-defined research problem that is meaningful from an **operational point of view** and which may pave the way for the **development of hypotheses** (see Section 2.4) and solving of the problem itself.

Implicit in each research question (research problem) is the view that **some variables are the causes of other variables** and, *vice versa*, that the latter are the effects or consequences of the former.

FOR EHAMPLE The main aim of a diamond mining company such as Ocean Diamond Mining Holdings is to retrieve diamonds from the sea successfully and profitably. Therefore at least two variables are important, namely:

- diamond retrieving (which may be called diamond production);
- the price paid to the company for its products (diamonds).

When we move from the conceptual to the empirical level in research, concepts are converted into variables by mapping them into a set of values. For example, assigning numbers to objects involves the mapping of a set of objects into a set of numbers. A **variable** is a property that takes two or more values and is subject to change while a **constant** has one value only. For example, the concepts of "height" and "gender" can be mapped into specific values in the following way:

Construct	Variable
Height	150 cm; 180 cm; …
Gender	1 = female
	0 = male

A variable is therefore a **characteristic** or an **attribute** of the study object. The study object may be individuals, groups, organisations, human products and events, or the conditions to which they are exposed. These conditions are not the same for all the study objects within the spectrum of the business and administrative sciences.

The price of diamonds varies (some diamonds may fetch a high price and others a low price on the diamond market), as does the number of diamonds retrieved (for example one day only 100 diamonds may be retrieved and the next day 2 000). As a result, these are called variables.

A variable such as *weather conditions* will most definitely play a major role in the achievement of the company's aim. Fortunately, variables such as *technological progress* and *improved ships* diminish the role of bad weather conditions in retrieving diamonds from the sea.

In the case of an experiment (see Section 5.2), our aim is to determine whether one or more specifically chosen variables, known as the **independent variables**, affect another variable, referred to as the **dependent variable**. The dependent variable is the one that we eventually have to measure to determine whether the research participants (study objects) in the various levels of the independent variable differ in terms of it. Consider the following example while you read the definitions below:

FOR EHAMPLE In an organisational setting, we might want to measure if the driving skills (dependent variable) of drivers improve after they attended a driving course (independent variable).

▶ The **independent variable** (*X*) is that factor which the researcher selects and manipulates in order to determine its effect on the observed phenomenon (the problem that is being investigated).

This variable is considered to be independent because the researcher is interested in how it affects the other variable(s) being studied. In other words, the researcher seeks to find a cause and a resultant effect relationship, if it is present. By definition, the independent variable must have at least two levels in order to qualify as a variable. In the example above the independent variable had two levels –

attending a driving course and not attending a driving course.

▶ The **dependent variable (Y)** is that factor which the researcher observes and measures to determine how it was affected by the independent variable. It is therefore the factor which appears, disappears, or varies as the researcher introduces, removes, or varies the levels of the independent variable. The dependent variable changes as a result of variations in the independent variable and it is considered to be dependent because its value is assumed to depend upon the values of the levels of the independent variable. In terms of our example above, the skills of the drivers depend on whether they attended the course or not.

> **EXAMPLE   DEPENDENT AND INDEPENDENT VARIABLES**
>
> We can differentiate between the independent variable and the dependent variable as follows:
>
> Fire (independent) causes smoke (dependent)
> – the more a fire rages on a piece of land, the more smoke will occur. It can be illustrated as follows:
>
> Fire ⎯⎯⎯⎯⎯⎯→ Smoke
> Independent   Dependent
> Variable (X)   Variable (Y)

In Research Example II the independent variable is the *management style*, or *role model behaviour*, of the supervisors. It has two levels, namely an *iron-fisted style* and an *approachable style*. The dependent variable is the *management style of the trainee supervisors*. The independent variable is the level that the researcher purposefully chooses and in terms of which he or she divides the research participants into groups.

RESEARCH EXAMPLE II   THE TRANSMISSION OF MANAGEMENT STYLE

In 1999 researchers working for a big company randomly assigned (Section 6.2.7) 48 male and 48 female trainee supervisors to two main groups of 24 males and 24 females each. Half of the first group (12 males and 12 females) individually watched a video of a female supervisor's rude behaviour towards one of her subordinates, called Bobo. Bobo had interrupted the supervisor by calling her while she had been taking her tea break. The supervisor's iron-fisted management style was relatively unique. For example, she pointed her finger and said rude things such as "I will punch you in the nose" and "I will kick you". The remainder of the first group watched the same behaviour, but performed by a male supervisor.

Half of the second group (also 12 males and 12 females) watched the same female supervisor as the first group. This time the female supervisor showed an approachable management style, being friendly and willing to listen to her subordinate. The remainder of the second group watched the same male supervisor as before, but this time showing a friendly willingness to listen to the subordinate who had called him during his tea break.

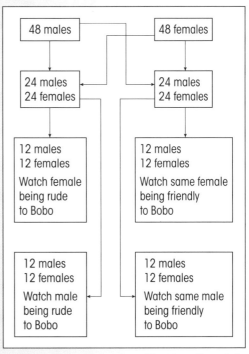

Compare Figure 5.2(b) on page 80 and see Figure 2.2.

After watching the behaviour of the supervisors, the trainee supervisors were allowed individually to participate in recreational activities during their tea break. Once they were engrossed in these activities (typically within two minutes), they were impolitely called on by the subordinate (Bobo) to rouse their frustration.

The researchers recorded the number of times a trainee supervisor repeated the behaviour of one of the supervisors (called a tally – see Section 7.7.6 and Chapter 9). The groups who had watched the iron-fisted supervisors displayed a management style significantly more similar to that manifested by the supervisor than did the other group. The males exhibited more iron-fisted responses than did the females.

Figure 2.2 *Exposure to an iron-fisted role model and its effect on a trainee supervisor's behaviour towards a subordinate (called Bobo)*

ACTIVITY 2.1

Read the following problem statement and answer the question. Compare your answer with the one given.

PROBLEM STATEMENT

A manager believes that good supervision and training will increase the production level of the workers.

QUESTION

What are the dependent and independent variables in this case? Give brief reasons for your answer.

ANSWER

Supervision and *training* are the independent variables. *Output* (production) is the dependent variable. The reason for this answer is as follows: the manager wants to ascribe the differences in output (also called production levels) to, or explain them according to, the influence of the level of supervision (for example strict control versus the absence of control) and the level of training (for example memory learning versus knowledge of application).

If the manager regards strict control and knowledge of application as aspects of good supervision and training respectively, he or she would want to prove through research that the output level of the workers was increased by these factors rather than, for example, poor control and rote learning.

ACTIVITY 2.2
Next, read Case Study F in Appendix D on page 306.

QUESTION

Write down the two most important variables in the case study and indicate whether they are dependent or independent variables. Briefly provide a reason for your answer.

ANSWER

Business people (entrepreneurs/managers) is the independent variable, and *innovative problem-solving style* is the dependent variable. The reason for this answer is as follows: it appears from the literature in the introduction of the case study that people who are entrepreneurs or managers differ in terms of the extent (level) to which they use innovative problem-solving. Using an innovative problem-solving style to a certain extent therefore seems to depend on whether a business person is an entrepreneur or a manager of a large business in South Africa.

2.3.1 The origin of research problems

We could view the following as typical sources of research problems:
- practical problems
- previous research
- theories.

2.3.1.1 PRACTICAL PROBLEMS

Let us have a look at South African society with its wealth of practical problems caused by rapid political, social, and economical changes. These include for instance:
- the high population growth that is out of all proportion to what is economically sustainable
- the excessive culture of violence
- the increase in the incidence of AIDS and its effect on group life assurance policies
- the prejudices between different population groups that need each other so that South Africa can become internationally more competitive
- the appointment of unqualified managers to provide for the increase in the numbers of vacant black advancement posts.

Only smaller aspects of these problems could, in fact, be examined in a single research project (a dissertation or thesis for academic degree purposes), for example, or even in a bigger project conducted by a national research organisation such as the National Research Foundation (NRF).

EXAMPLE

National Conference: Police officials as victims of trauma and crisis.
Media release 25 and 26 February 1998 at Technikon SA: Conference Centre, Johannesburg.

Not enough is being done to equip police officers with the tools to operate in the violent, fast-changing, and high-stress environment that characterises South Africa today. Unacceptably high levels of crime and violence are taking their toll on members of the police service, who are increasingly displaying symptoms of severe stress and trauma.

This emerged at a ground-breaking conference hosted last week by Technikon SA, where police officers, academics, psychologists, social workers, and international experts gathered to find ways of dealing with what is becoming a growing crisis for the South African Police Services (SAPS) – the dangerously high stress levels of many of their members and the fact that they lack the necessary life skills to deal with them.

The failure to respond adequately to the reality that police too are victims of crime and violence is leading to growing incidences of suicide, absenteeism, resignation, depression, alcohol abuse, violence, and other problems within the SAPS. In the past two years, 269 police officials committed suicide, with the rate escalating rapidly last year. High levels of stress and depression are reflected in absenteeism (as many as 10 000 police officers are absent on any given day), under-performance, and resignations (an average of 450 members leave the SAPS each month).

Delegates adopted a resolution at the end of the two-day conference to elicit the support of top management in helping police to cope better with the psychological traumas of the job. A task team was also set up to "maintain the momentum of the conference" by organising follow-up skills-building workshops, identifying crucial areas of research, and developing links between various people in the field.

2.3.1.2 PREVIOUS RESEARCH

Significant research has usually already been conducted on most topics and new research proceeds from such existing research.

The results of previous research projects can be found in books, journal articles, congress papers, and unpublished research reports. In the section of a research report (see Section 10.1) in which we record our results, we usually have to point out the problems, shortcomings, and contradictions that have arisen from our research. It is not unusual for a research project to generate more new questions than it originally set out to answer, especially when the results of one study conflict with the results of another study or theory. The researcher may then suggest ways in which this apparent contradiction may be solved.

2.3.1.3 THEORIES

We should preferably associate a research project with a specific theory. In order to understand this fully, we need to define two important terms.

Concepts are the building blocks of any theoretical model. A concept is an abstraction representing an object, a property or a certain phenomenon.

FOR EXAMPLE *Cost, income, market share*, and *business strategy* are all examples of common concepts in business administration.

Concepts are crucial in the researcher's toolbag and serve a number of purposes:

- Concepts are the **foundation of communication**; without a set of agreed concepts, meaningful communication is impossible.
- Concepts introduce a **perspective**, a way of looking at the empirical world.
- Concepts are a means of **classification** and **generalisation**.
- Concepts serve as **components of theories** (models) and thus of explanations and predictions.

Concepts are the most critical element in any theory (model), because they direct that which is captured.

FOR EXAMPLE The concepts *cognitive* and *dissonance* direct the theory of cognitive dissonance, and *supply* and *demand* are key concepts in economic theory.

Even though many concepts used in everyday life are ambiguous (for example *democracy* and *influence*), they must be clear and agreed upon to be useful in research. Clarification and precision of concepts are achieved through **definitions**. Here we will distinguish between two types of definitions, conceptual and operational.

Definitions that describe concepts by using other concepts are **conceptual definitions**.

FOR EXAMPLE The concept of *market* is defined in marketing literature as *all the potential customers sharing a need or want who might be willing and able to engage in exchange to satisfy that need or want.* In this definition *customers* and *need/want* are among the concepts used to define the concept of *market* (Kotler, 1997). Good definitions use concepts that:

- point out **unique attributes** or **qualities** of whatever is defined
- are **not circular**, that is, do not contain any part of the thing being defined; for instance, defining "market exchange" as "exchange taking place in the market" does not enhance clarity in the definition
- are **stated positively**, that is, contain the properties of the concept defined
- use **clear terms**.

A **theory** may be viewed as a system which orders concepts in a way that produces understanding or insights. A theory includes more than one concept and links the concepts together. For the purposes of this discussion, we define a theory (see Section 2.1) as follows:

*A **theory** is a statement or a collection of statements that specify the relationships between variables with a view to explaining phenomena such as human behaviour (for example, producing machines, organising an event, formulating a policy) in some or other population (universum).*

There are four important aspects that we need to point out here:

▶ Firstly, theories and research problems deal with the relationships between variables (as defined in Section 2.3).

FOR EXAMPLE In Research Example II (page 17), the two variables were *management style role model behaviour* and *management styles of trainee supervisors.*

Some, if not the majority, of the variables in human behavioural theories and research problems qualify as constructs.

A **construct** is an abstract concept that is deliberately created to represent a col-

lection of concrete forms of behaviour. The concrete behaviours thus qualify as indicators of the construct.

Important constructs in the human behavioural sciences include attitudes, management style, problem-solving, socio-economic status, and so on.

Each of these constructs does not have a self-evident meaning as do, for example, body height or eye colour, but is deliberately conceived to represent a divergent collection of concrete behaviours.

FOR EXAMPLE Under *management style* we may understand the ability to motivate people in organisations, such as schools, hospitals, churches, retail and manufacturing stores, security departments, local and state government agencies, to achieve goals, as well as the ability to devise solutions to practical problems, and so on.

▶ Secondly, theories and research problems are concerned with the relationships between variables.

FOR EXAMPLE Research Example II (page 17) involved an implication of a theory about the relationship between the exposure to management style role model behaviour and management styles among company trainee supervisors.

We will see in Section 5.2.2 that such relationships may be either causal or correlational in nature.

Relationships between variables:

- One variable is regarded as the direct **cause** of another if the former precedes the latter in time and if changes in the latter can be related to changes to only the former (and not to any other variables).
- A **correlational** relationship means that changes to one variable are accompanied by, or associated with, changes to the other, but that the one is not necessarily the cause of the other.

A causal relationship between variables X and Y necessarily also implies a correlational relationship between them. However, a correlational relationship between variables X and Y is not necessarily an indication of a causal relationship between them.

FOR EXAMPLE In Research Example II (page 17), a causal relationship is suggested: the more iron-fisted the role model management style (X), the more iron-fisted the management style of the company trainee supervisors (Y) exposed to it tends to be.

▶ Thirdly, theories and research problems are not concerned with the behaviour of individual units such as Lindiwe, Anna, Bongani or Johnny, as displayed in a few situations, but with the **behaviour of a particular population of individuals under a universe of settings** (see Section 4.2).

By definition, a theory cannot apply to a few individuals or organisations only (see Section 6.3.2). If a separate theory were to be applicable to each and every different individual person or company, the concept of a theory would lose its appeal and value.

A population (for example all South African women, or all companies listed on the Johannesburg Stock Exchange) encompasses the entire collection of cases (or units) about which we wish to make conclusions. In Research Example II (page 17), it involves company trainee supervisors.

▶ Fourthly, a theory applies not only to specific situations (for example the tax policy in one province) but to **universes of circumstances** (for example South Africa as a whole) (see Section 6.3.3).

FOR EXAMPLE A theory about role model behaviour as a factor contributing to aggressive reactions should be applicable to all role models rather than to a specific supervisor, and to behaviour in a variety of situations (for example workplace, tea rooms, and at home), not the workplace only, for instance.

A theory can therefore be defined as a *set of interrelated concepts, definitions, and propositions that present a systematic view of specifying relations among variables with the purpose of explaining and predicting phenomena* (Kerlinger, 1979, p. 64).

It is important to note the purposes of theory, that is, whether it aims to improve understanding or to predict.

FOR EXAMPLE A researcher holds a theory of how "advertising works" which is based on a prediction of an outcome resulting from the spending of advertising money. He then uses this theory to allocate the firm's advertising budget. Also note the notion of "proposition", that is, an assumed relationship between two concepts, for example, between "performance" and "satisfaction".

A theory should furthermore present a systematic view in order to enhance explanation and prediction, that is, the concepts and relationships involved should represent a coherent "whole".

It is important to notice that theories focus on specific aspects of the phenomena or problems studied. This is done to capture the actual problem, and (hopefully) understand (solve) it more satisfactorily. On the other hand, some aspects are left out. This is done because human beings have limited cognitive capacity, making it almost impossible to take everything into account at the same time.

2.3.2 The purpose of research

The purpose of research is threefold:
▶ to describe **how** things are, that is, define the nature of the study object
▶ to explain **why** things are the way they are. It may be so because one thing has caused another to change. We also like to explain what this relationship between things is.

▶ to **predict** phenomena, such as human behaviour in the workplace, with the aim of using this information, for example, to screen job applicants.

NOTE: The purpose of exploratory research is to determine whether or not a phenomenon exists, and to gain familiarity with such a phenomenon; not to compare it with other phenomena.

We can therefore say that the purpose of conducting research into theories and other research problems is to define, explain and, consequently, predict and even modify or control, human behaviour, its organisations, products, and/or events.

FOR EXAMPLE

• To **describe**, or define, the levels of production staff turnover figures and the average level of job satisfaction, a researcher could undertake a study to describe the major characteristics of a successful front-line manager in a manufacturing company in Gauteng. A successful manager may be found to have a certain leadership style.

• To **explain** why production remains at a certain level, why employees resign, why they are dissatisfied, and so on, the researcher may state that "authoritarian individuals are successful leaders because the nature of the job requires the leader to tell the employee what to do and when to do it".

• To **predict** which employees will be productive, who will be the most likely to resign, and who will be dissatisfied, the researcher may state that "authoritarian individuals in manufacturing companies in Gauteng will be successful leaders".

It is quite possible that, due to the lack of knowledge of research methods, the purpose of your first research study will be to describe something. However, although descriptive research may appear to be less demanding than other types of research, this is often far from the case.

A census, such as the one conducted during 2001 in South Africa which cost about R632 million is a form of descriptive research. Here the purpose was to count and describe the characteristics of an entire population. By using **descriptive methods** we try to understand the way things are; by using **experimental methods** we try to understand the way things could be if we changed and manipulated them.

Descriptive research has two goals: explaining phenomena and predicting behaviour:

▶ Firstly, the goal of research is to **explain phenomena** such as human behaviour in the business and administrative sciences by indicating how variables (see Section 2.3) are related to one another and in what manner one variable affects another.

FOR EXAMPLE

• Research on crime is descriptive when it defines the kind of crime by stating when, where, by whom, and how often it is committed. However, we would also want to explain why the crime rate is higher in Gauteng than in the Northern Province.

• Learning theory provides an explanation for the incidence of management style among trainee supervisors. By describing the relationship between two variables, we are actually defining the one variable in terms of the other. In Research Example II (page 17), we defined the management style of trainee supervisors in terms of the management styles of role models.

▶ Secondly, the possibility of explaining and **predicting human behaviour** may enable us to change or control it. (This, however, is not the same as prediction studies – see Section 5.4.4.)

FOR EXAMPLE

- On the basis of our findings we would like to predict in what way the type of crime committed will influence decisions made by the police. This could include, for example, why drug-sniffing dogs will be deployed in Gauteng where there is a problem with drug smuggling, but power vehicles, such as 4x4 vehicles, will be bought to patrol the

green hills in KwaZulu-Natal where there may be a problem with weapon smuggling.
- In Research Example II (page 17), senior supervisors could be trained not to act in an iron-fisted manner. This would in turn prevent trainee supervisors from emulating or copying such a management style.

ACTIVITY 2.3

Read Case Studies A, B, C, D, and F in Appendix D on page 306.

QUESTION

Describe the investigation in each case study in terms of whether it is a descriptive, explanatory or predictive study. Briefly explain your answers.

ANSWER

Case Study A is a **descriptive study** because one variable, *attitudes towards AIDS,* is defined in terms of the other variables, *knowledge of AIDS* and *attitudes towards prostitution.* The purpose of the study was only to describe the phenomenon *attitudes towards AIDS* in the sample, indicating the state of affairs amongst the medical staff of that hospital at that moment.

Case Study B is a **predictive study** because, on the basis of the results of the investigation, the researcher hopes to predict that implementing the role induction procedure will help goldsmith apprentices experience supervision as less stressful in the future and so reduce their period of adaptation.

Case Study C is a **predictive study** because the researcher wishes, on the basis of the (expected positive) results of the investigation, to predict that there will

be a significant increase in the knowledge of management principles of all current first-line supervisors (as well as other newcomers) who will attend the training course.

Case Study D is a **descriptive study** because *speech quality* is defined in terms of *preparation time* and *anxiety.* It is a description of the relationship between the variables occurring at a specific time between the groups of technikon students, and no attempt is made to explain it.

Case Study F entails a **descriptive study** because the researcher only wants to establish whether or not a difference in innovative problem-solving styles already exists between entrepreneurs and managers. The question "why" there may be a difference is not addressed by the study and it is therefore not an explanatory or predictive study.

2.3.3 The purpose of other forms of research (See Chapter 8)

2.3.3.1 HISTORICAL RESEARCH (RECORDS)

In **historical research** the sources that have recorded past happenings or preserved them in some or other way are located and evaluated. The evaluated sources are then synthesised and interpreted with a view to suggesting causal explanations (Section 5.2.2) for events or practices. By "past" we do not mean only the

distant past, but also the more recent past as in the case of corporate law.

The central thesis or main theme of this type of research concerns the investigation of specific events that took place with the purpose of establishing a set of propositions about it and postulating that the phenomena may be occurring universally. Historical research (as part of analytical research) therefore is not concerned so much with collecting new information, as with finding new explanations for, or interpretations of, existing information.

The first step in historical research is the **problem statement**. This includes explanations or interpretations which are not tested as research hypotheses but which may, rather, be described as the central thesis or main theme of such a study.

EXAMPLE

We cite Rhoodie's (1986) explanatory study (which may be classified as analytic research) of white-black conflict as well as the development of revolutionary movements in South Africa in terms of Galtung's theory about revolutionary aggression.

Galtung identifies eight social and political factors which, in markedly stratified societies, give rise to revolutionary movements. According to him, the impetus for revolution is relative deprivation that is introduced into a social system when all members of a particular stratum or segment of the population do not occupy either the top or the bottom in respect of all the various criteria of ranking (for example income, educational level, political power, and so on).

During the eighties, Rhoodie came to the conclusion that the South African situation met these conditions and that apartheid society was practically and structurally programmed for revolution.

2.3.3.2 CASE STUDY RESEARCH

We saw that hypothesis-testing research deals with the general and the regular. In **case study research** (see Section 8.4.1) the opposite happens and research is directed at understanding the uniqueness and idiosyncrasy of a particular case in all its complexity. The objective is usually to investigate the dynamics of some single bounded system, typically of a social nature, such as a family, group, community, participants in a project, institution and practice (for example the testing of drug usage at schools).

2.3.3.3 ACTION RESEARCH

Action research (Section 8.4.5.1) is conducted with a view to finding a solution for a particular practical problem situation in a specific, applied setting. It therefore corresponds to case study research (see Section 8.4.1) in the sense that the case in question refers to a problem situation. Unlike the typical case study, however, it is not directed simply at describing the case involved, but also at searching for a solution (to the problem situation).

FOR EXAMPLE Lazarus (1985) helped develop and evaluate an alternative educational programme supported by a church community organisation and in which pupils who had left the traditional school set-up ("Bantu education system") in the early eighties participated.

Thus, in action research there is no theory from which one or more hypotheses (see Section 2.4) have been inferred and which are to be subjected to empirical research and testing (see Section 2.5). A theory may indeed exist that suggests particular solutions for the problem situation. However, the purpose of action research is not to test such a theory, but to provide a solution to a problem.

It is important to note that **applied research** in industry has several features that distinguish it from basic research at a university:

▶ Firstly, the need for research in industry develops as a result of **organisational problems**. Problems arise, for example, with excessive absence of employees, staff turnover, and job dissatisfaction, and this could be the beginning of a research study that is designed to reduce the seriousness of the problems. Research in industry is virtually never used simply "to test a theory" or to satisfy intellectual curiosity.

Secondly, the goal of research in industry is **to improve the effectiveness of an organisation**. This usually means an increase in profitability. For example, research is used to determine consumers' preferences regarding new products and services, to identify methods of reducing waste material, or to utilise human talent better in an organisation.

Thirdly, the **participants** in research in industry are typically **employees** or job applicants.

Fourthly, if the **results** of research in industry are positive and usable, the research unit of the organisation where the research is done will attempt to have the conclusions of the study accepted and **implemented** by the rest of the organisation. For example, if it is found that a brief, realistic overview of the organisation given to job applicants for administrative posts leads to reduced staff turnover, the researchers will try to convince the rest of the organisation to use such procedures during the recruitment of new employees in other divisions. If the results are negative, the organisation will attempt to use secondary, but valuable ideas obtained from the study.

2.4 Research hypotheses

We will have to test hypotheses (of which some are derived from theory) during the research process.

FOR EXAMPLE Theory: People will try to balance their input (work) and their output (payments). Employees will do only as much work as they think is justified for the remuneration they receive.

According to this theory, we can therefore predict that a worker who feels that he or she is underpaid according to a piece-work system (for example stitching the shirt collar in a shirt manufacturing factory), will increase the quantity of each item produced, but will reduce the quality of items produced.

The purpose of this research is to test whether a prediction (hypothesis) such as this holds true.

In the natural sciences as well as in some areas of social sciences, it is common to test hypotheses. A **hypothesis** is a statement or proposition that can be tested by reference to the empirical study.

FOR EXAMPLE A research question might be:
What is the relationship between advertising expenditure and income?
A hypothesis dealing with the same question could be:
There is a positive relationship between advertising expenditure and level of income.
The hypothesis can be shown to be true or false as a result of empirical research.

A research question differs from a hypothesis in that the *research question* is always expressed as a *question*, while the *hypothesis* is expressed as a *statement*. The question format lends itself more to descriptive and inductive research, while the hypothesis is more appropriate for explanatory and deductive research.

Hypotheses are usually stated in a form that predicts a difference between two groups regarding some variable.

FOR EXAMPLE
There is a difference between the organisational commitment of male employees and female employees.
or
There is a relationship between job satisfaction and salary level.

These hypotheses are called **non-directional hypotheses** because they do not predict the direction of the difference or relationship.

Directional hypotheses are used if the researcher is more confident about the direction of the difference or relationship, or if the literature reports that previous studies found differences to be in a particular direction. In such cases, the researcher might propose the research hypothesis as a directional hypothesis.

Female employees have a higher level of organisational commitment than male employees.

or

There is a positive relationship between job satisfaction and salary level.

In each of the hypotheses above, the direction of the difference or relationship being studied is predicted by the hypothesis; that is, a higher level of commitment and a positive relationship.

A **null hypothesis** states that there is no difference between two groups in relation to some variable, or that there is no relationship between two variables.

There is no difference between the organisational commitment of male employees and female employees.

or

There is no relationship between job satisfaction and salary level.

A null hypothesis is usually indicated by the symbol H_0. The alternative hypothesis to the null hypothesis is indicated by the symbol H_1. For example,

H_0: There is no relationship between job satisfaction and salary level (null).

H_1: There is a positive relationship between job satisfaction and salary level (alternative).

While it is usually easier to think about research questions and hypotheses in terms of relationships and differences among variables (the alternative hypothesis), the null hypothesis is useful when a researcher is seeking to prove or disprove a proposition using statistical analysis.

The researcher can accept the null hypothesis if the statistical differences between groups or the strength of relationships are absent, or small and insignificant. Alternatively, the researcher can reject the null hypothesis if the differences between the groups, or the strength of relationships, are large enough to be significant. It is important to note that a researcher can never actually prove that an alternative hypothesis is true (Kerlinger, 1973: 21) because of the many potential errors, known or unknown, involved in the measurement of variables and the selection of research subjects. The researcher therefore usually tests whether the null hypothesis is probably true or probably false, and whether it is probably false to accept the alternative hypothesis as the logical alternative.

The use and application of hypotheses in the context of statistical analysis are discussed further in Chapter 9.

2.4.1 Formulating the research hypothesis

Where possible, we should translate the research problem (see Section 2.3) into a research hypothesis that states:

‣ a **relationship**
‣ between **two or more variables**
‣ in one (or more) **population(s)** (see Chapter 4).

We can use the following approach to **develop** a hypothesis:

‣ Discuss the problem, its origin, and the objectives in seeking a solution (see Section 8.4.3) with experts.
‣ Examine data and records concerning the problem (this is called secondary data collection) for possible trends and clues (see Sections 3.3.2 & 8.2).
‣ Review similar studies (this is called a literature review – see Chapter 3).
‣ Interview interested parties and individuals on a limited scale to gain greater insight into the practical aspects of the problem (see Section 7.7.4.4).

A theory is a general statement which applies to a population of individuals under a universe of circumstances (see Sections 2.1 & 2.3.1.3). From this theory we can derive conclusions or hypotheses as to what should be observed in certain circumstances. To derive an implication deductively from a theory means to formulate a statement that must be valid if the theory is valid. The validity of the theory is then examined indirectly by testing whether these hypotheses hold good.

If we investigate an implication of a specific theory (see Section 2.3.1.3), we **deductively** infer the research hypothesis from the theory (see Figure 2.4).

Deductive research therefore refers to research in which a conceptual and theoretical structure is developed and then tested by empirical observation; thus, particular instances are deduced from general inferences. For this reason, the deductive method is referred to as *moving from the general to the particular*.

FOR EXAMPLE We may have read about theories of motivation and wish to test them in our own workplace. Having studied a specific theory, for example Maslow's Hierachy of Needs Theory, we might conduct research to actually test this established theory.

Although a research hypothesis is normally formulated in accordance with an implication which is deduced from a theory, a **counter hypothesis**, which amounts to the opposite of the research hypothesis, is usually subjected to testing.

FOR EXAMPLE In Research Example II (page 17), the counter hypothesis will be that there is no difference in management style between trainee supervisors who observed an iron-fisted management style role model and trainee supervisors who observed an approachable management style role model.

If we want to investigate the research problem or question in the most economical manner, we must formulate it in the form of a research hypothesis that we can test on the basis of observable data and reject, if necessary. To serve this purpose, we should formalise the research hypothesis in terms of **operationalised constructs** (see also Section 2.3.1.3).

2.4.2 Formalising the research hypothesis in terms of operationalised constructs

An **operationalised construct** represents an attempt to define/understand an abstract construct by means of concrete variables.

NOTE: The meaning of concepts such as *the freedom of the individual, indoctrination, affirmative action, and sexual harassment in the workplace*, cannot be as readily defined as, for instance, the mass of an object weighing 80 kg.

The definition (conceptual or operational) of constructs and their relationships thus precedes their empirical testing. A **conceptual analysis** of constructs must be done before data are collected (Chapters 7 and 8) to test research hypotheses. This means that constructs (concepts) and their relationships (as postulated by a theory) must be analysed carefully. The implications of constructs must be carefully spelled out, possible inconsistencies between their definitions pointed out, and modifications to the construct must be proposed. In this way constructs are defined in terms of concrete, observable behaviour or the products of human behaviour. As a result, others may understand exactly what we mean by such a definition. Such a definition, known as an **operational definition**, describes a set of procedures that describe the activities to be performed to establish empirically the existence or degree of existence of what is described by a concept. Operational definitions are crucial in measurement. They tell the researcher what to do and what to observe in order to bring the phenomenon defined within the range of the researcher's experience.

FOR EXAMPLE *Market share* may be defined operationally in the following way (Ghauri & Gronhaug, 2002):

$$market\ share\ =\ \frac{a\ company's\ sales\ of\ products\ in\ category\ X\ in\ area\ A\ during\ time\ t}{total\ sales\ per\ product\ category\ X\ in\ area\ A\ during\ time\ t}$$

This definition also requires specifications of "sales", product category *X*, area, and time period.

Note that the value defined differs depending on whether sales are measured in volume (i.e. number of units), or value (i.e. in Rands) and, when measured in value, whether in cost or sales.

In order to operationalise the independent variable, we should carefully define it in the light of the theory in which it appears. This definition should provide clear guidelines about the concrete procedures and manipulations for producing/generating/developing the independent variable (see Section 2.3). However, we must be careful that we do not compile an operational definition that bears little relation to the conceptual variable that it was supposed to create. The **construct validity** (see Section 7.4.1) of the independent variable (see Section 2.3) refers to the degree to which the independent variable as implemented represents the independent variable as conceptualised.

FOR EXAMPLE In Research Example II (page 17) the exact manner in which the role model supervisors were to act to generate a management style in the trainees was clearly specified.

Usually we should first investigate how the independent variable was generated in previous research (see Chapter 3) and consider whether such procedures will be adequate for operationalising the independent variable (see Section 6.2.3) in the proposed research project (see Chapter 11).

The experimental manipulations required for creating a treatment factor (see Section 5.2) are often dictated to some degree by the research hypothesis. If the research hypothesis states that one method for increasing achievement motivation is more effective than another, these two methods are already defined to a greater or lesser degree. An operational definition of these methods will then require the researcher to describe the materials and procedures for their application clearly. It is often difficult to operationalise independent variables, especially those in the social sciences.

FOR EXAMPLE In Research Example II (page 17), an iron-fisted role model management style was created by having a supervisor treat a subordinate in a verbally rough manner. The subordinate frustrated the trainee supervisors by calling them from their tea break.

Operational definitions do not guarantee accuracy or "truth", but enable researchers to communicate with one another. By always clearly defining constructs operationally, other researchers are in a position to evaluate the appropriateness of these definitions. Moreover, such definitions enable them to **repeat the procedures** contained in such definitions to establish whether they obtain comparable results. This requirement again focuses attention on the principle of public scrutiny in the scientific expansion of knowledge that we have mentioned (see Section 1.2.2.3).

The procedure and components involved in testing an implication of a theory in this manner may be represented diagrammatically as in Figure 2.3 on page 30.

The oval shapes in Figure 2.3 represent **constructs**, such as *iron-fisted management style of role model* and *iron-fisted management style of trainee supervisors*, while the rectangles symbolise indicators of these constructs. Naturally, we can make the theory more complex by including constructs such as hereditary rude behaviour and socio-economic status.

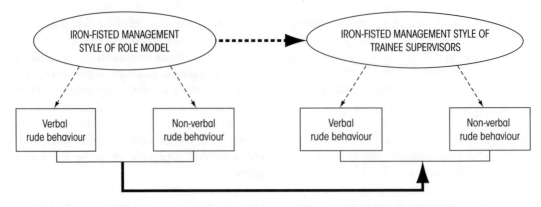

Figure 2.3 *Testing the relationship between constructs in terms of observable variables (Source: from Huysamen, 1994, p. 12.)*

The dark dotted line between the two constructs represents a **constitutive definition**, that is, a definition of management style displayed by trainee supervisors in terms of exposure to a role model's iron-fisted management style. Since this dotted line also constitutes a one-directional arrow, it implies a causal (instead of merely a correlational) relationship.

The light dotted lines symbolise **operational definitions**.

FOR EXAMPLE In Research Example II (page 17) a role model's "iron-fisted management style" is defined operationally in terms of verbal behaviour, such as uttering, "I will kick you" and "I will punch you in the nose".

The uninterrupted one-directional arrow between the rectangles at the bottom of Figure 2.3 (denoting the four observable variables) represents the **relationship** posed by the research hypothesis.

Thus, in practice, an implication from a theory or any research problem, symbolised in Figure 2.3 by the dark dotted one-directional arrow at the top, is investigated by means of a research hypothesis.

A research hypothesis is a positive statement about the relationship between operationalised variables.

In a sense, the operational definitions (the light, dotted arrows in Figure 2.3) also represent hypotheses that may be investigated (in what is known as psychometric research), but typically the operational definitions are accepted as valid. If the results obtained support the research hypothesis, both the constitutive definition (the dark dotted-line arrow) and the operational definitions (light dotted lines) are provisionally confirmed.

FOR EXAMPLE In Research Example II (page 17), the research hypothesis may be formulated as follows:

Trainee supervisors who watch supervisors exhibiting an iron-fisted management style behaviour towards a subordinate, will afterwards display more iron-fisted management style reactions towards subordinates than comparable trainees who have not watched such behaviour in the supervisor.

In this example:
(i)   a causal relationship is postulated between
(ii) operationally defined variables
(iii) in an identified population (Chapter 4).

As far as (ii) is concerned, the researchers working for the company described exactly how the role model should behave to give the appearance of iron-fisted management style behaviour and how the management styles of the trainee supervisors should be measured (Research Example II, page 17).

2.4.3 The construct validity of the operationalisation of the independent variable and of the measurement of the dependent variable

The independent and dependent variables as we define them can be represented by x and y respectively. Specific constructs (X and Y) underlie these variables. If we want to achieve **construct validity**, our findings must not only be applicable to the x embodied in our dependent variable and the y that we have measured. Ideally our findings should be applicable to the constructs X and Y underlying the variables x and y.

FOR EXAMPLE Consider Research Example II (page 17) and, in particular, the group that watched the rude behaviour. If the greater number of reactions considered to be indices of iron-fisted management style is to be attributed to the exposure to the simulated iron-fisted role model management style, we would like to interpret this finding as meaning that an iron-fisted role model management style promotes iron-fisted management style behaviour among trainee supervisors.

It is firstly required that x, the operations performed, should create X, the independent variable as defined (and not something else). In other words, the square boxes representing iron-fisted management style role model behaviour in Figure 2.3 must provide a complete realisation of the oval shapes that represent the corresponding construct (iron-fistedness).

FOR EXAMPLE In Research Example II (page 17), if the trainee supervisors were to view the actions of the role model as being comical rather than iron-fisted, it would mean that the operationalisation of the independent variable did not bring about the intended level of the independent variable (that is, iron-fisted role model management style).

The construct validity of the operationalisation of the independent variable would then be **unsatisfactory**. This requirement is discussed further in Section 6.2.4.

By the same token, the square box on the right-hand side at the bottom of Figure 2.3 should represent the corresponding cigar shape on the right-hand side at the top. If y, the trainees' reactions that were recorded, did not reflect Y (iron-fistedness) but excitement, for instance, it would mean that what was measured represented a different variable than the construct in which we were interested.

NOTE: This requirement is known as the construct validity of the measurement of the dependent variable and we will discuss it further in Section 7.4.1.

ACTIVITY 2.4

Read the following problem statement and answer the questions. Compare your answers with the given answers.

PROBLEM STATEMENT

The manager of TABOK Company observes that the morale of her employees is low. She thinks that their morale will improve if the working conditions, pay scales, and leave benefits of the employees are improved. She doubts, however, that increasing the pay scales is going to raise the morale of all employees. Her guess is that those who have good side incomes (by doing other work in their own time) will not be motivated by higher pay.

QUESTIONS

1. Define the research problem for this situation.
2. Develop four different research hypotheses for the situation.

ANSWERS

1. Will an improvement of the working conditions, pay scales, and leave benefits improve the morale of all employees?
2. Combinations of these given research hypotheses are correct.
   a) When the working conditions improve, the morale of all employees will improve.
   b) Better leave benefits will improve the morale of all employees.
   c) An improvement of the working conditions and leave benefits will improve the morale of all the employees.
   d) The morale of employees who do not have good side incomes will improve if their pay scales (and working conditions and leave benefits) improve.

ACTIVITY 2.5

Read Case Studies A, B, C, D, E, F, and G in Appendix D on page 306.

QUESTIONS

In your own words, formulate the research hypothesis (hypotheses) or research question(s) in each case study.

ANSWERS

case study a

Amongst a group of medical staff members at a specific hospital, there is a high correlation between their attitudes towards AIDS, their knowledge of AIDS, and their attitudes towards prostitution.

case study b

Participation by goldsmith apprentices in a role induction procedure causes them to experience supervision more positively than before participation.

case study c

The knowledge of management principles of first-line supervisors at a South African agricultural corporation will be significantly more after attending a training course than before, while there is no difference in the pre- and post-measurement of the knowledge of management principles of first-line supervisors who did not attend the course.

case study d

There is a significantly high positive relation/correlation between the speech quality and total preparation time of a group of speech-making students at a technikon.

AND

There is a significantly high negative relation/correlation between the speech quality and speech anxiety of a group of speech-making students at a technikon.

case study e

Bankrupt small businesses have exceeded their bank overdraft limits with significantly greater amounts per month and experienced more cash flow problems than non-bankrupt small businesses during the past two years.

case study f

Entrepreneurs will be significantly more innovative in their problem-solving style (obtain a significantly higher mean score on the KAI scale) than managers of big businesses.

case study g

(a) What are the attitudes of nurses towards HIV/AIDS patients? (b) Is there a difference between the attitudes of older and younger nurses towards HIV/AIDS patients?

2.5 The cyclic progress of the scientific expansion of knowledge

We have already referred to the important role that testing hypotheses deduced from theories (see Section 2.4) plays in the scientific expansion of knowledge.

We have defined a theory as a general statement (see Section 2.1 & 2.3.1.3). From a satisfactory theory, which is supposed to apply to a population of individuals under a universe of circumstances (see Section 2.3.1.3), we can always **deductively infer** conclusions or hypotheses as to what should be observed in certain circumstances (see Section 2.4.1).

In Research Example II (page 17) this deductive order of thought (see Section 2.4.1) was approximately as follows:

Company trainee supervisor workers are inclined to imitate the behaviour of role models.

Therefore, trainees who have been exposed to specific management styles (for example pointing a finger at a subordinate) in their role models, will more often display similar iron-fisted management style behaviour when compared to trainees who observed an approachable management style in their role models.

A more complete rendering of the deductive thinking (see Section 2.4.1) involved would be as follows:

▶ Trainee supervisors are inclined to imitate the behaviour of their role models.
▶ Trainee supervisors are more inclined to imitate the behaviour of role models of their own sex than the behaviour of role models of the opposite sex.
▶ Iron-fisted management style is a highly masculine-typed behaviour.

Therefore, males will be more inclined than females to imitate iron-fisted management style behaviour and this tendency will be most pronounced in those who are exposed to an iron-fisted management style male role model.

The information that is collected in terms of a research design (see Chapter 5) often eliminates beforehand any counter hypotheses which ascribe the differences to factors other than those implied by the theory.

FOR EXAMPLE In the research design in Research Example II (page 17), we took the counter hypothesis (that the trainee supervisors who observed an iron-fisted role model management style were probably more inclined to show iron-fisted management style behaviour than those in the other group) into account from the very start.

There is always the possibility that someone may come up with other counter hypotheses or explanations (called **rival hypotheses**) that will explain our obtained results equally well, if not better. Although it is not possible to prove that a theory is correct, it may be falsified by failing to refute counter hypotheses. According to this **falsification principle**, our confidence in a theory grows to the extent that implications and hypotheses in conflict with the theory are eliminated by research.

Our present confidence in the tenability of a theory is limited insofar as it has **survived** counter hypotheses suggesting alternative explanations for the obtained results and no new ones are envisaged. If support is found for the counter hypotheses, we should consider possibly modifying the original theory. Hypotheses that are then deduced from such a modified theory must be subjected to empirical testing afresh.

Until now we assumed that a specific theory (for example balance theory) must be examined. By starting with such a theory and by subjecting research hypotheses that have been deduced from it to testing, we are proceeding deductively (from the broad and general to the specific – see Section 2.4.1). To **infer deductively** therefore means to begin with one (or more) statement(s) that are accepted as true and that may be used to conclude one logical true statement. We may say that deduction means "testing theory" and concerns mainly quantitative research (see Section 1.3).

The explanation of the process of testing one or other implication of a theory represents one segment in the scientific expansion of knowledge. Often, however, we enter an area about which little knowledge and insight exist (for example the issue of cloning mammals). In such circumstances researchers should first observe and systematically describe the phenomenon being studied and attempt gradually to unravel relationships and patterns in order to eventually formulate a theory. In this regard **sociologists** refer to **grounded theories**.

Researchers in such areas proceed **inductively**. They therefore begin with an individual case or cases and then proceed to a general theory. This is done in order to generalise to all cases based on the conclusions reached from observing one or more cases. The inductive method is therefore the reverse of the deductive method. Since it involves moving from individual observation to statements of general patterns or laws, it is referred to as *moving from the specific to general*.

Inductive research is research in which theory is developed from the observation of empirical reality; thus, general inferences are induced from particular instances.

FOR EXAMPLE We may have observed from factory records in our company that production levels decrease after two hours of the shift; we therefore conclude that production levels vary with length of time worked.

These researchers are also more inclined to study an individual case carefully (also known as **ideographic** research) rather than study the average tendencies of large groups (as is the case in **nomothetic** research). We may say that induction has to do with building theory and the collection of **qualitative data** (see Section 1.3).

FOR EXAMPLE Inductive reasoning:
- Trainee supervisor 1 (was observed to) have an iron-fisted management style.
- Trainee supervisor 2 (was observed to) have an iron-fisted management style.

- Trainee supervisor 3 (was observed to) have an iron-fisted management style.
- All trainee supervisors (were observed to) have an iron-fisted management style.

The inductive approach is concerned with generating theories and hypotheses on the basis of studying **specific cases**, whereas the deductive course of action seeks to **test hypotheses** in terms of the data obtained. This process is illustrated in Figure 2.4.

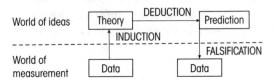

Figure 2.4 *The three main steps in the research process*

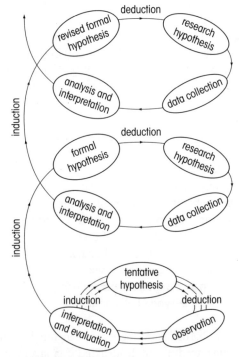

Figure 2.5 *A sequence of qualitative and quantitative research cycles (Adapted from Huysamen, 1997.)*

According to Figure 2.4, we should use facts and observations during induction to make a theoretical statement that explains the observations and facts. Through deduction we can determine whether such a theory is a reliable version of reality. A prediction of a theory is made through logic to determine what can be expected in certain circumstances and specific conditions. The validity of the prediction is then determined through falsification – and the suitability of the basic theory is determined.

This is done by collecting new data and checking whether the prediction(s) is/are thereby substantiated. If the prediction(s) is/are not supported, and it is assumed that the research methods and deductive logic are correct, we can assume that the theory on which the prediction was based must be adapted or changed. The process is depicted in Figure 2.5.

SUMMARY

In order to specify the topic of the research problem, we need to develop a research question which expresses the relationship between two or more variables. A variable refers to a characteristic of something (for example the age of people, the profit of a business in rands, the number of criminals convicted) that may differ from one instance to the next (called the "unit of analysis" – see Chapter 4). One employee may be 18 years of age and the next employee that we study may be 47 years of age. Therefore, the variable "age" can be presented by various numbers.

The concepts used for the research question should be clearly defined in order to avoid any confusion.

The next step involves expressing the relationship between the independent and dependent variables in the form of two hypotheses – the alternative and null hypotheses. Research hypotheses are statements about the relationship between variables. Research hypotheses arise from theory and/or findings from earlier research, from practical problems, or from accidental observation (for example that married older females are more efficient secretaries than any other group of secretaries). A research hypothesis is similar to an expressed expectation of what the answer/solution/explanation for a problem is. Deductive research involves moving from the general to the particular, whereas inductive research moves from the specific to the general. Historical research, case study research, and action research are further examples of research which arise in specific situations in order to satisfy specific requirements.

TEST YOURSELF

Question 1: Multiple-choice questions

Only one of the answers for each question is correct. Identify and mark the correct one. (Answers appear in Appendix A on page 299.)

1.1 Which of the following are variables?
   a) female, Jewish, 21 years old
   b) plumber, professor, dentist
   c) occupation, age, type of risk
   d) dishonest, violent, conservative.

1.2 An independent variable is a
   a) theoretical concept
   b) variable influencing other variables
   c) variable influenced by other variables
   d) set of attributes.

1.3 The factors that are controlled (or manipulated) by a researcher in order to establish their effects are called the
   a) potential variables
   b) dependent variables
   c) intervening variables
   d) independent variables.

1.4 A research report was entitled "Determinants of electrical power". The dependent variable was
   a) determinants
   b) electrical power
   c) either (a) or (b), depending on the researcher's theory
   d) there is no dependent variable.
1.5 If a researcher wanted to know why there was a noticeable increase in the number of electrical power failures in the Northern Cape during 1999, the researcher would design a(n)
   a) descriptive study
   b) explanatory study
   c) panel study
   d) exploratory study.
1.6 If a researcher makes systematic observations of a single dependent variable in circumstances at one point in time, it may be described as a scientific method of
   a) explanation
   b) prediction
   c) exploration
   d) description.
1.7 If a researcher wanted to conduct research in a specific context to see whether it supports an established theory, the researcher would conduct
   a) deductive research
   b) exploratory research
   c) case studies
   d) inductive research.

Question 2: True/false questions

Indicate whether the following statements are true (T) or false (F). (Answers appear in Appendix A on page 299.)
2.1 Variables are empirical whereas concepts are abstract.
2.2 The independent variable must occur later in time than the dependent variable.
2.3 Scientific inquiry is a process involving an alternation of deduction and induction.
2.4 In deduction we start from observed data and develop a generalisation that explains the relationship between the observed concepts.

Question 3: Self-evaluation questions

(Some answers appear in Appendix A on page 299.)
3.1 Provide some alternative explanations for the conclusion to which the researcher travelling through Gauteng arrived (see Chapter 1 – Test yourself question 2.1 on page 10).
3.2 A few years ago, the principal of a South African university pointed out that the mean number of students per thousand of the population was 29,2 for whites; 19,8 for Asians; 4,7 for coloureds; and 2,2 for blacks in South Africa as compared to 7,5 in the United Kingdom and 11 in Australia.

   On the basis of these figures he came to the conclusion that the whites in South Africa either must be much more intelligent than the citizens of other countries, or that they are occupying very favourable positions. Point out possible alternative explanations for the statistics quoted above.
3.3 Identify and list (a) the hypothesis, (b) independent variable, and (c) dependent variable in Research Example II (page 17).
3.4 A researcher sent false application forms of (fictitious) prospective students who differed in terms of gender, race, and ability to each of 12 randomly assigned groups of 20 undergraduate universities. (Some applicants were male, white, and highly intelligent; others were female, black, and highly intelligent; and so on.) If an "applicant" was accepted with encouragement, it was scored 5; if he or she was merely accepted, it was scored 4; and so on; those who were unsuccessful obtained a score of 1.

   Identify and list (a) the independent variables, and (b) the dependent variable.

Literature review

3

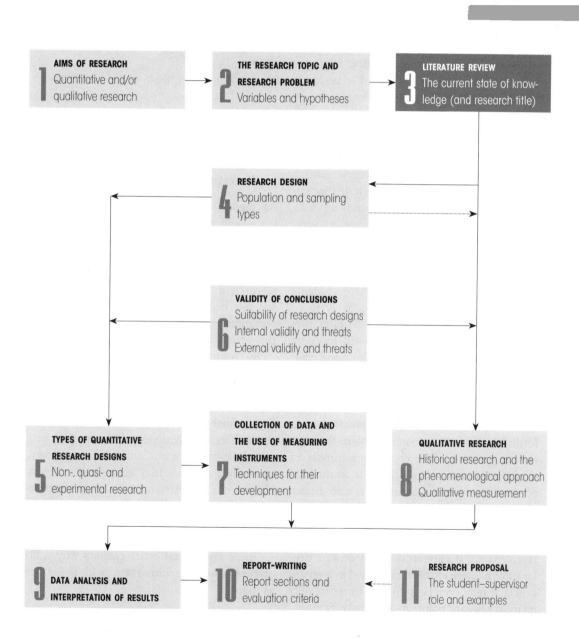

1 AIMS OF RESEARCH Quantitative and/or qualitative research	**2 THE RESEARCH TOPIC AND RESEARCH PROBLEM** Variables and hypotheses	**3 LITERATURE REVIEW** The current state of knowledge (and research title)
	4 RESEARCH DESIGN Population and sampling types	
	6 VALIDITY OF CONCLUSIONS Suitability of research designs Internal validity and threats External validity and threats	
5 TYPES OF QUANTITATIVE RESEARCH DESIGNS Non-, quasi- and experimental research	**7 COLLECTION OF DATA AND THE USE OF MEASURING INSTRUMENTS** Techniques for their development	**8 QUALITATIVE RESEARCH** Historical research and the phenomenological approach Qualitative measurement
9 DATA ANALYSIS AND INTERPRETATION OF RESULTS	**10 REPORT-WRITING** Report sections and evaluation criteria	**11 RESEARCH PROPOSAL** The student–supervisor role and examples

LEARNING OUTCOMES

In this chapter we focus on a few themes to which we should attend before we may start a particular project in earnest, whether for degree purposes or as an integral part of our daily activities. The first concrete step in the scientific research process is the formulation, however incomplete or tentative, of the problem which should be investigated (see Section 2.4). Until we know what the problem is, we cannot begin to investigate it systematically. Consequently, finding a topic for a dissertation or thesis often represents one of the most frustrating problems (if not the most frustrating) for graduate students.

After studying this chapter, you will be able to:
- use the necessary library facilities
- do a literature search on a chosen topic
- compile a literature review and reference system
- advise a novice on the steps to be followed in preparing to write a review of literature relevant to a specific topic.

3.1 Introduction

In Section 2.3.1 we mentioned that in academic research the classic way to identify a research problem is to do a literature search. In discussing their findings (in their research reports), previous researchers may have suggested ways of eliminating inconsistencies between their findings and those of other studies or a theory. With this in mind, the appropriate starting point for prospective graduate students in their search for a topic is probably to go through professional journals (see Literature and electronic sources on page 49) to check what research has already been done and what still needs to be done.

We usually begin the literature review section by reviewing the literature dealing with our chosen topic. This will set the scene for a clear formulation of the research problem (hypothesis or question). The comprehensiveness of the literature review again depends on the kind of research report. Dissertations and theses require a more extensive review than a journal article in which reference is made to previous research directly related to the proposed research only. If a literature survey on a particular topic has already been published in a review article, it may even be sufficient to reflect only its most relevant points in a journal article.

3.2 Literature searches

3.2.1 Significance of reviewing related literature

As mentioned before, prospective researchers should acquaint themselves with previous research (see Section 2.3.1) on a particular topic before they start planning their own research. Of course, it will be of little use to research a topic on which general consensus has been reached unless, of course, the researcher intends to provide a new perspective on it.

By compiling a review of research findings on a particular topic that have already been published, researchers may become aware of inconsistencies and gaps that may justify further research. Such a review enables researchers to indicate exactly where their proposed research fits in. Considered on its own, someone's research may elicit little interest. However, if its relation to the body of knowledge is evident, it achieves greater importance and may even persuade other researchers to do research on the particular topic as well.

There are several other reasons why a literature search is important and these are as follows:

1. A review of related literature can provide the researcher with important facts and background information about the subject under study.
2. Such a review also enables the researcher to avoid duplicating previous research.
3. If a study on the same topic has been conducted before, a review provides the researcher with information about aspects of the problem which have not been investigated or explored before.
4. A review can also help a researcher develop various parts of the study.
5. Insights regarding the weaknesses and problems of previous studies can be gained.
6. The researcher can get ideas on how to proceed with the investigation.
7. In relational and exploratory studies, the review provides the researcher with a basis in order to determine variable relationships, types of relationships, and measurement.
8. Findings and conclusions of past studies can be accessed which the researcher can relate to his own findings and conclusions.
9. Lastly, a review often provides motivation.

3.2.2 Tracing and recording relevant literature

The first step to take in tracing relevant literature on a particular topic, is to list the headings or **key words** under which it may be classified in a library catalogue or in a computer retrieval system. Nowadays university libraries usually have staff available to assist researchers in conducting a computer search for references on relevant research on the basis of such a list of key words. If such key words are too specific, relevant references may possibly be excluded; however, if they are too general, you may be swamped with irrelevant references.

Until such time as the topic is delineated more clearly, it may be worthwhile for you to read widely rather than too narrowly. You should preferably summarise any article, book, dissertation, or other source that has relevance to the topic and that may possibly be included in the literature survey. Pay particular attention to the most important conclusions and implications and note these. It is not helpful to merely keep photocopies of these sources, as this would require you to read the same source repeatedly in order to determine its relevance.

Not only should you summarise these sources, but you should also indicate any shortcomings in the reported research. Summarise each separate article or any other source of information on a separate index card (or as separate files in a directory on your computer) and indicate its complete reference as it should appear in the list of references (see Section 10.3.9). Remember to include page numbers if material is quoted directly. By following this approach, you can change the order of the index cards quite easily, for example, to group those dealing with the same aspect together. When you reach the stage where you must compile the list of references, you can readily rearrange the cards in alphabetical order. Of course, all these tasks become much easier if you have access to a personal computer.

Libraries are no longer the only source of information. The development of the Internet and electronic publishing has had an enormous impact on research supervision, peer review of publications, and general communications capabilities, and have changed the way in which researchers work. Information from the Internet is considered less reliable than that of printed sources because web pages can be updated and changed on a daily basis. A printed hard copy of an Internet source should therefore be included with your research paper as an appendix. This will ensure that factual information used cannot be contested at a later stage.

FOR EXAMPLE

Research and Knowledge Networking Database
is published with the Nexus Database System and is very useful. It contains biographical profiles of individual researchers in South Africa, including their fields of interest and areas of specialisation in the social sciences and the humanities. If you have access to the Internet, you should visit the following web site: http://stardata.nrf.ac.za. This will provide you with access to research conducted on various topics as well as information about specific researchers. Information on monetary issues around the world can be found at the following web sites:

- http:www.imf.org/
- http://www.mbendi.co.za
- http://www.busrep.co.za
- http://www.dti.gov.za
- http://www.thestar.co.za
- http://www.brain.org.za.

3.2.3 Planning the literature search

It is important that you plan this search carefully to ensure that you locate relevant and up-to-date literature. Most students find literature searching a time-consuming process, which takes far longer than expected. Fortunately, time spent on planning will be repaid in time saved when searching for literature. As you start to plan your search, you need to be aware of information overload. You therefore need to clearly define your research questions and objectives, and have an outline of your proposal. Before starting with your search, it is suggested that you plan further by doing the following:

▶ **Define the parameters of your search.**
For most research questions and objectives you will have a good idea of which subject matter is going to be relevant. A researcher however, needs to be clear about the following issues:

- Language of publication (for example English)
- Subject area (for example sociology)
- Business sector (for example finance)

- Geographical area (for example Africa)
- Publication period (for example 1995–2005)
- Literature type (for example refereed journals).

▶ **Generate key words and search terms.** The identification of **key words** or **search terms** is the most important part of planning your search for literature. These key words are the basic terms that describe your research question(s) and objectives, and will be used to search the literature. Key words can be identified using several techniques, including the following: discussion with colleagues, supervisor, and librarians; initial reading; dictionaries, thesaurus, encyclopaedias, and handbooks; and brainstorming. In order to maximise your results, you should ensure that your key words are correct. The following is a very useful checklist to help you in this regard (Saunders, Lewis & Thornhill, 2003, p. 63):

1. Is the spelling incorrect?
2. Is the language incorrect?
3. Are you using incorrect terminology?
4. Are you using acronyms and abbreviations?
5. Are you using jargon rather than accepted terminology?
6. Are you using a word that is not in the controlled index language?

▶ **Discuss your ideas as widely as possible.** Any researcher should take every opportunity to **discuss** his or her research. In discussing your work with others, whether face-to-face, by email, or by letter, you will be sharing your ideas, receiving feedback, and obtaining new ideas and approaches.

3.3 Compiling a literature review

3.3.1 Integrating the studies

The literature review should not consist of a mere compilation of separate, isolated summaries of the individual studies of previous researchers. You should clearly show how these studies relate to one another and how the proposed research ties in with them. For example, you should group together those studies that are in agreement and refer to this agreement by using words like "similarly" when moving from one to the next.

The most glaring blunder in this regard is to present the opinions or findings of different authors, who basically are in agreement but who have expressed themselves in different ways, as different contributions. If you cite contradictory findings, you should point out this discrepancy – even if you only do this by means of phrases such as "on the other hand" or "by contrast".

3.3.2 Sources for literature searches

The literature sources available to help you to develop a good understanding of and insight into previous research can be divided into three categories: primary, secondary, and tertiary. These categories represent the flow of information from the original source. Often, as information flows from primary to secondary to tertiary sources, it becomes less detailed and authoritative but more easily accessible.

▸ **Primary literature sources** are the first occurrence of a piece of work. They include published sources such as reports and some central and local government publications such as White Papers and planning documents. They also include unpublished manuscripts such as letters, memos, and committee minutes that may be analysed as data in their own right.

FOR EXAMPLE *Hansard*, the written report of what was said by politicians in parliament, may be regarded as a primary (documentary) source of events in parliament.

▸ **Secondary literature sources** such as books and journals constitute the subsequent publications of primary literature. These publications are aimed at a wider audience and are easier to locate than

primary literature as they are covered more thoroughly by the tertiary literature.

FOR EXAMPLE *Whereas Hansard may serve as a primary source of parliamentary proceedings, newspaper reports of these proceedings based on interviews with members of parliament (who were indeed present) represent a secondary source.*

▸ **Tertiary literature sources** are designed either to help locate primary and secondary literature or to introduce a topic. They therefore include indexes and abstracts as well as encyclopaedias and bibliographies.

3.3.3 Searches using computers: CD-ROM databases

A CD-ROM contains permanent, digitally encoded information on a large scale which may represent text, graphics, images, or data and can be accessed very quickly. The contents of a CD-ROM cannot be altered or erased. CD-ROMs are expensive, but once subscriptions are paid, they are available for unlimited use. Check your library to see what is available. Table 3.1 shows a small selection of CD-ROM databases available in the business and management field.

Table 3.1 Examples of CD-ROM databases

Example	Description
ABI/INFORM	Covers every aspect of business and management theory and practice including accounting, computers, human resources, marketing, and organisational behaviour.
Anbar	Includes subjects such as accounting and finance, information management and technology, management and technology, management services and production, marketing and distribution, personnel and training, and top management.
ECONLIT	Covers industrial relations, business finance, monetary theory, and financial institutions.

Example	Description
Helecon	Collection of European databases; searching is conducted in English; many databases contain a key word in English; many articles are in European languages.
Institute of Management International Database (IMID)	Series of databases which include references to and information on audio-visual materials, books, IM publications, company practices, short courses, training packages, and working papers.

3.3.4 Using the Internet

Searching the Internet can consume significant amounts of time and the serious researcher can find the final results disappointing. If you know the address of the relevant web site, you can go there directly; alternatively you will need to use a search engine. The following search engines are very useful:

▶ www.google.com
▶ www.altavista.com
▶ www.askjeeves.com
▶ www.dogpile.com.

Although you might prefer a specific search engine, your research strategy always stays the same: remain as focused on your own research question as possible. The more general or common the keyword you use, the more precisely you will need to explain or delimit it. For the most effective searches it is recommended that you use **Boolean operators** such as those set out in Table 3.2.

Table 3.2 Boolean operators

Operator	Example	Result
+	entrepreneur+women	The search engine will locate documents that contain all those terms.
OR	stress OR anxiety	The search engine will locate web sites containing either of these terms.
NEAR	labour NEAR absenteeism	The search result will find documents where the terms are just a few words apart.
NOT	stress+entrepreneurs NOT managers	The term after NOT should not appear in the results. For example, it will produce documents with only the word 'stress' and 'entrepreneurs' in them.
FAR	book FAR keeping	This search will locate documents in which the two terms are at least 25 words apart.
ADJ	overtime ADJ working	This search will find terms that are directly adjacent to one another regardless of the order.
BEFORE	hard BEFORE working	This search should contain both terms in the order given.
INURL	corporate+strategy INURL:*.pdf	This search will generate results with specific words or file specifications in the web address. Using the example, the search will result in sites that are in Acrobat PDF file format. This is helpful if you are searching for articles or documents. You can also use other file extensions such as doc (Microsoft Word) or xls (Microsoft Excel).

3.3.5 Quotations

With the exception of direct quotations, the entire research report should be presented in the author's own words, that is, without paraphrasing or patching together pieces from other sources. Use direct quotations sparingly as they are actually only permitted when something is expressed so eloquently or in such an original way that you feel something will be lost in the process of reformulating it.

The following are general guidelines for using quotes in research reports:

▶ Incorporate quotations of up to (and not longer than) about 30 words into the text.
▶ Enclose the quoted material in double quotation marks.
   FOR EXAMPLE A quotation from Bem (1986, p. 430) relating to Section 10.1, likens the findings of a report to a jewel which is being cut and polished to get the very best out of it:

   "Good report writing is largely a matter of good judgement; despite the standardized format, it is not a mechanical process."

▶ Indent longer quotations as an independent block. This means the script should start about four spaces from the left of the page border, without any quotation marks:
   FOR EXAMPLE Kerlinger (1986, p. 11) eloquently expresses the effect of the principle of public scrutiny on report writing as follows:

   Every scientist writing a research report has other scientists reading what he writes while he writes it. Though it is easy to err, to exaggerate, to over-generalise when writing up one's own work, it is not easy to escape the feeling of scientific eyes constantly peering over one's shoulder.

   This chapter deals with the sections of a research report, ...

▶ Apart from the surname of the author and the year of publication, all quotations should also be accompanied by the page number on which the material appears in the quoted source, as shown in the following example:

FOR EXAMPLE According to the above two examples, Bem (1986, p. 430) and Kerlinger (1986, p. 11) ...

▶ If the first letter of a quotation is a capital letter that has to be changed to a small letter to incorporate the quotation into a sentence (in the report), put the modified letter between parentheses:
   FOR EXAMPLE B.F. Skinner (1904–1990), the famous psychological researcher, suggests as one of his "unformalized principles of science", that "(w)hen you run into something interesting, drop everything else and study it" (Bachrach, 1981, p. 6).

3.3.6 Evaluating the relevance of literature

In order to ensure that the literature which you consult is relevant, you should consider the following points (Saunders *et al.*, 2003, p. 71):

1. How recent is the item?
2. Is the item likely to have been superseded?
3. Is the context sufficiently different to make it marginal to your research question(s) and objectives?
4. Have you seen references to this item (or its author) in other items that were useful? If the answer to this question is yes, then one may assume that the information from the source is reliable.
5. Does the item support or contradict your arguments? For either it will probably be worth reading and could add value to the external validity of the study.
6. Does the item appear to be biased? Even if it is, it may still be relevant to your critical review.
7. What are the methodological omissions within the work? Even if there are many, it may still be of relevance.
8. Is the precision sufficient? Even if it is imprecise, it may be the only item you can find and therefore still of relevance.

3.4 The reference system

In this section we will discuss the reference system required by the **South African Journal of Psychology (SAJP)**. The main concern regarding the use of a specific reference method is that it must enable the reader of your research report to locate the information sources we referred to if so needed. The reader may want to read more about the issue from the information source to which we referred in our research paper.

There are minute differences between the method of referencing (according to the SAJP) described here and the more broadly used Harvard method. For example, references in the text of a research proposal/report are the same as indicated in Section 3.4.1, but also include specific pages as in "Strauss (1990: 34)" where the number "(... 34)" is the page from where the researcher read about the reported issue even if no text was directly quoted (compare the previous guidelines mentioned in Section 3.3.5).

As far as the reference list is concerned, the Harvard method differs little from the SAJP method which we will describe. For more information in this regard, you can visit the following web site:

▶ http://www.lib.uct.ac.za/infolit/ bibharvard.htm.

3.4.1 References in the text

▶ If you refer to theories, research findings, or any other contribution previously reported, you should give the sources involved due credit. Give the surname(s) of the author(s), followed immediately by the year of publication between parentheses.
  FOR EXAMPLE In a well-designed experiment, Strauss (1990) found that ...

▶ You may not list a string of references that are not appropriate in the context in which you cite them. It is not permissible to cite sources without identifying their relevance.

For example, it should be clear whether it is a finding or an opinion that has been obtained from the source.

▶ If you refer to the same source more than once in the same paragraph, the date should accompany only the first reference.

▶ If a source has more than two authors, you should list them all the first time it appears in the report.
  FOR EXAMPLE Plug, Meyer, Louw and Gouws (1987)

  In all subsequent references only the surname of the first author is provided, followed by "*et al.*" (which is the Latin for "and others").
  FOR EXAMPLE Plug *et al.* (1987) ...

▶ If there is more than one source with several authors, and they have the first two authors and the same date in common, give the first three surnames plus "*et al.*" (for the remaining authors) in further references to distinguish between them.
  FOR EXAMPLE The following references occurred in the text:
  Smith, Jones, Botha and Tiffin (1990) ... and later also ... Smith, Jones, De Beer, and Zwane (1990). Further references to the same authors must be made in the following way:
  Smith, Jones and Botha *et al.* (1990) ... and ... Smith, Jones and De Beer *et al.* (1990).

The above principle is extended in similar fashion to situations in which various sources have more than the first two authors and the same date in common: give as many authors (plus "*et al.*") as may be necessary to distinguish between the different groups of authors and add "*et al.*".

▶ When more than one reference appears between brackets, put a comma between the author(s)' surname(s) and the date, and a semicolon (;) between the different references (source plus date). Note that when sources with two or more authors appear between brackets, the "and" between the last author and the author before the last is replaced by an "&".

FOR EXAMPLE

> (Bachrach, 1981; Jordaan & Buthelezi, 1995;
>   Plug, Meyer, Louw & Gouws, 1987) ...

Note that in a reference list (Section 10.3.9) the &
appears as follows:

> Plug, C., Meyer, W.F., Louw, D.A. & Gouws,
>   L.A. (1987) ...

▶ To distinguish between different publications of the same author published in the
same year, alphabetise them according to
their titles and affix the letters a, b, c, and
so on to these dates.

FOR EXAMPLE Suppose the publications of the
same author are mentioned in the reference list
(Section 10.3.9) as follows:

> Kolb, D.A. (1976a). Management and the learning
>   process. *California Management Review,* **18**(3),
>   21–31.
> Kolb, D.A. (1976b). *Learning style inventory:*
>   *Technical Manual.* Boston: McBer.

In the text you would refer to these as follows:

> ... Kolb (1976a) ... Kolb (1976b) ...

▶ Distinguish between different authors
with the same surname by providing their
respective initials together with their
(common) surname.

FOR EXAMPLE

> J.J. Zuma (1990) ... S.M. Zuma (1990) ...

instead of

> Zuma (1990) ... Zuma (1990) ...

▶ References to institutions are done with
minimum identification or description.

FOR EXAMPLE

> *(Human Sciences Research Council, 2002,
>   p. 60)...*

▶ When a reference is made to a quotation
found in a secondary source, it is cited in
the text as follows:

FOR EXAMPLE

> ... (Smith, as quoted by Khoza & Du Preez, 2000,
>   p. 56).

▶ When the date of publication of a source is
unknown, it is cited as follows:

FOR EXAMPLE

> According to Ryan and Bernard (n.d.) ....

3.4.2 Alphabetical order of sources in the reference list

Arrange references alphabetically in terms of
the surname of the first author.

FOR EXAMPLE

Nel, T.J. appears before Nelson, A.M. even though **S** (in
Nelson) alphabetically precedes **T** (in Nel, T.J.).

> Also note that Cronbach, L.J. (1980) appears before
> Cronbach, L.J. & Furby, L. (1970), and that MacPherson
> precedes McArthur.

Arrange sources with the same first author but
with different co-authors alphabetically according to the surname of the second author. The
same principle applies when there is more than
one collection of authors of which the first
two, or first three, and so on are the same.

FOR EXAMPLE

Smith, J.C. & Erikson, M. (1989) ...
Smith, J.C. & Fromm, S. (1990) ...
Smith, J.C. & Green, S. (1980) ...
or
Smith, J.C., Jones, D. & Erikson, M. (1989) ...
Smith, J.C., Jones, D. & Fromm, S. (1990) ...
Smith, J.C., Jones, D. & Green, S. (1980) ...

If the same author or collection of authors has
different publications, list them chronologically according to the date of publication.

FOR EXAMPLE

Khoza, R. & Mafumane, T. (1989). *The influence of ...*
Khoza, R. & Mafumane, T. (1990). *Woman in manage-*
ment ...
Khoza, R. & Mafumane, T. (1995). *Affirmative action ...*

3.4.3 Language of reference

You should provide all the information in
a list of references in the language of the
source and not the language in which the
report is written. An English translation of a
non-English title should be given in brackets

immediately following the original title. Words appearing in the title should be presented as they appear. For example, the American spelling of "labor" and "center" should not be changed to the British spelling "labour" and "centre", respectively.

3.4.4 Journal articles in the list of references

To master any system of references, it is advisable to study examples in appropriate journals carefully. The following example provides a reference to a journal article with one author, followed by an example with more than one author:

FOR EXAMPLE

Eberhard, H. (1990). Induction guidance – what do the novices want? *South African Journal of Psychology*, **22**, 210–225.

Nieuwoudt, J.M., Plug, C. & Mynhardt, J.C. (1997). White ethnic attitudes after Soweto: A field experiment. *South African Journal of Psychology*, **16**(2), 1–12.

You should note the following about this example:

▶ Above, the figures 22 and 16 that appear in the first and second references respectively, are the volume numbers of the journal and appear in bold.

▶ Usually each year has a new number. For example, if the volume number of 1990 was 10, for 2001 it would be 21.

▶ If the numbering system of the pages of each edition of a journal starts with (page number) 1, the number of the edition should also appear between brackets immediately after the volume number.

▶ You must note the following with regard to using capital letters in the titles of the article and the journal: only the first letter of the article title and, of course, proper names are capitalised, but both the first letter and every important word in the journal title are capitalised.

▶ The name of the journal title appears in *italics* (or is <u>underlined</u>).

3.4.5 Books and chapters in books

Similar to journals, the name of a book appears in *italics* (or is <u>underlined</u>). Only the first letter of the first word of the book title (and of any proper names) is **capitalised**:

FOR EXAMPLE

Du Preez, P. (1991). *A science of mind: The quest for psychological reality*. London: Academic Press.

If you refer to a chapter in a book, the surname(s) of the author(s) of the book are followed by their initials.

FOR EXAMPLE

Valle, R.S., King, M. & Halling, S. (1989). An introduction to existential-phenomenological thought in psychology. In R.S. Valle & S. Halling (Eds), *Existential-phenomenological perspectives in psychology* (pp. 3–16). New York: Plenum.

NOTE: You will note that "Editor" is abbreviated to "Ed.", but "Editors" to "Eds" (that is, without a full stop because both end in the same letters).

When the author and the publisher of a book are the same organisation or body, the full name of the organisation, followed by its abbreviation, appears in the position of the author and only the abbreviation in the position of the publisher.

3.4.6 Other sources

The following are a few other kinds of references as well as the surname (of the author) that may be looked up in the list of references (see pp. 334–336) to check the corresponding kind of reference.

▶ **Dissertation or thesis**
   FOR EXAMPLE
   Botha, M.P. (1990). *Television exposure and aggressiveness among high-school pupils: A follow-up study over five years*. Unpublished doctoral thesis, University of the Free State, Bloemfontein.

▶ **Book review**
FOR EXAMPLE

Haertel, E.H. (1987). Review of "Foundations of behavioral research" (3rd ed.) by F.N. Kerlinger. *Contemporary Psychology*, **32**, 249–250.

▶ **Unpublished paper delivered at a meeting**
FOR EXAMPLE

Strümpfer, D.J.W. (1980, September). *One hundred and one years after Wundt.* Paper presented at the National Psychological Congress, Johannesburg.

▶ **Article in a newspaper**
FOR EXAMPLE

Botha, J. (1988, 1 Apr.). Worst USA TV series also broadcast here. *The Star*, p. 10.

▶ **Article in a newspaper without any author indicated**
FOR EXAMPLE

Too much beer leads to temporary impotence. (1991, 7 Jan.). *The Citizen*, p. 5.

▶ **Letter to a newspaper editor**
FOR EXAMPLE

Mathibela, J. (1996, 1 Apr.). The stars in black management [Letter to the editor]. *Sowetan*, p.12.

▶ **Reference to an Internet source**
FOR EXAMPLE

Department of Labour. (2000). *Employment Equity Act.* http://www.labour.gov.za/ docs/legislation/eea/forms/eea3-eng.htm (date when document was accessed).

▶ **Reference to a CD-ROM**
FOR EXAMPLE

20th World Conference on Open Learning and Distance Education. (2001). [CD-ROM] Fern Universität Hagen, Germany.

3.4.7 Date of publication unknown

If the date of publication of a source is unknown, it is cited in the reference list as follows:

FOR EXAMPLE

Ryan, G.W. & Bernard, H.R. (n.d.). *Techniques to Identify Themes in Qualitative Data.* http://www.analytictech.com/mb870 (12/01/2003).

3.4.8 Managing references

It is important to keep track of all the references used. You can choose to do this manually by means of index cards or a computerised list. Bibliographic software, such as Endnote or Reference Manager for Windows, is available as well.

ACTIVITY 3.1

The aim of this exercise is for you to visit a library and to become familiar with the procedures (such as catalogue systems and inter-library loans) required to gather secondary sources (see Section 3.3.2). It is not meant to create extra work for the librarian at the library you visit.

ASSIGNMENT

Compile a literature review (with references) for research on a topic relevant to your field of study. In the review you should consult most of the following sources of information and present them in a reference list, correctly according to a particular reference system (see Section 3.4):

- recent academic books (published during the past three years)
- academic journal articles
- research reports/studies of master's/doctoral degrees
- practice-oriented (popular) journal articles (such as *People Dynamics* or *Servamus*)
- articles from newspapers and/or ordinary magazines.

Remember to write down your literature research review topic first (see Section 11.1) and underline it before you
▼ start the literature review.

SOME POINTERS TO HELP YOU WITH ACTIVITY 3.1

In order to evaluate your literature review, you should use the following three criteria as basis:

1. Your answer should relate to your chosen topic and the information sources you listed in the list of references (see Sections 3.4.4, 3.4.5, 3.4.6 & 10.3.9).
2. You have to start documenting the information obtained from the sources listed broadly and later narrow it down to make it more specific to your chosen topic (see Sections 10.3.3, 10.3.4 & 10.3.5).
3. Your references to sources in your text must be correct and consistent according to a specific reference system, as described in Sections 3.4.1, 3.4.2, and 3.4.3.

The introductory paragraph on page 265 and the list of references on pages 271–272 of the article by Welman and Basson may serve as an example of what a literature review should look like.

If you choose to use a library to help you with this exercise, you should keep the following guidelines in mind:

1. Write down your chosen research topic (see Section 2.3).
2. Write down the key terms – the most important variables (see Section 2.3).
3. Use the library catalogue to find the sources containing information on your research topic. A library catalogue usually offers three ways of locating information, namely by authors, by titles, and by subjects.

FOR EXAMPLE Suppose we had to search the title of the textbook prescribed for the subject "Research Methodology". You will therefore search "methodology" or "research" in the title catalogue.

4. Use the classification number provided on the card or computer screen (for example 001.4) regarding the topic "research" according to the Dewey Decimal System. The Dewey Decimal System uses three-digit numbers ranging from 000 to 999. Each group of 100 numbers refers to a different broad academic discipline, for example 300–399 is social sciences.
5. Use the group of numbers concerning your topic/subject to choose a specific information source.

FOR EXAMPLE For a book on assessment for learning in higher education, the specific classification number is 378.1664 ASS.

6. Now proceed to find the book you are looking for on the library shelves. To find a specific article in a journal, follow steps 1 and 2 and ask the librarian for a Journal Index. Then proceed with steps 3 to 6.

If your library has limited resources on your chosen topic, write down the names of articles and important books relevant to your topic from the bibliographies and reference lists at the back of standard textbooks. Try to find these identified information sources through an inter-library loan.

ACTIVITY 3.2

Read Case Study F in Appendix D on page 306.

QUESTION

Briefly criticise the list of references in the case study.

ANSWER

a) The names of the authors are not in alphabetical order.
b) The source Swayne & Tucker, 1973 is outdated.

c) Although there is reference to Kirton, 1987 in the text, it is not mentioned in the reference list.

3.5 **Literature and electronic sources**

Many journals are available electronically and can be accessed on the Internet. The following two web sites offer access to journals from all over the world:

▶ http://www.sabinet.co.za/journals/onlinejournals.html

▶ http://www.e-journals.org/.

For further sources, you can also consult the library at any university. UNISA's library collection can be accessed at http://www.oasis.unisa.ac.za.

You can also visit the following web sites for further reading material:

▶ The **African Digital Library** provides access to close to 8 000 full text on-line books to people living in Africa, at http://www.AfricaEducation.org/adl/.

▶ **Sabinet Online** provides access to a variety of high quality databases. The web site is http://www.sabinet.co.za.

SUMMARY

In order to develop an understanding of, and insight into previous research findings that may be helpful to your own research question/problem, a critical review of the literature relating to your research topic is crucial. Such a literature review will help you to recognise and identify variables that may hamper or influence the results of your own study even before the empirical research starts.

By presenting the findings of other studies relating to your research topic broadly at the start of the literature review, you are familiarising the reader of the research report with the background of your investigation. As you progress with your literature review, you should narrow its focus to references relating as specifically as possible to your own situation and circumstances in which your empirical research is going to take place. In this way the reader of your report is prepared for the research hypothesis/es (usually presented in the next chapter of the research report).

TEST YOURSELF

Question 1: Multiple-choice questions

Only one of the answers at each question is correct. Identify and mark the correct one. (Answers appear in Appendix A on page 299.)

1.1 Documents in which one may obtain the most scientifically scrutinised findings or information on a specific topic are:
   a) recent academic books (published in the past three years)
   b) academic journal articles
   c) research reports/studies of master's/doctoral degrees
   d) practice-oriented (popular) journal articles
   e) articles from newspapers and ordinary magazines.

1.2 Documenting large sections of another researcher's written work as your own, is called:
   a) misrepresentation
   b) illegal citation
   c) wrongful referencing
   d) plagiarism.

1.3 A published academic book that discusses work of another original academic book is called a(n)
   a) alternative source
   b) secondary source
   c) derived source
   d) primary source.

1.4 When making reference in a research paper to an original source that one has not read, one should:
a) cite the original source
b) mention that the original source was found in another source
c) cite the secondary source in which the original source was found
d) mention only the name of the author of the original source.

1.5 Which of the following evaluations may be used as criteria to determine whether a research report is scientifically unbiased?
a) the reputation of the researcher writing the report
b) the precision of the reported data
c) verification of the scientific value by more than one peer researcher
d) an accepted scientist that generally approves the scientific merits of the report.

Population and sampling types 4

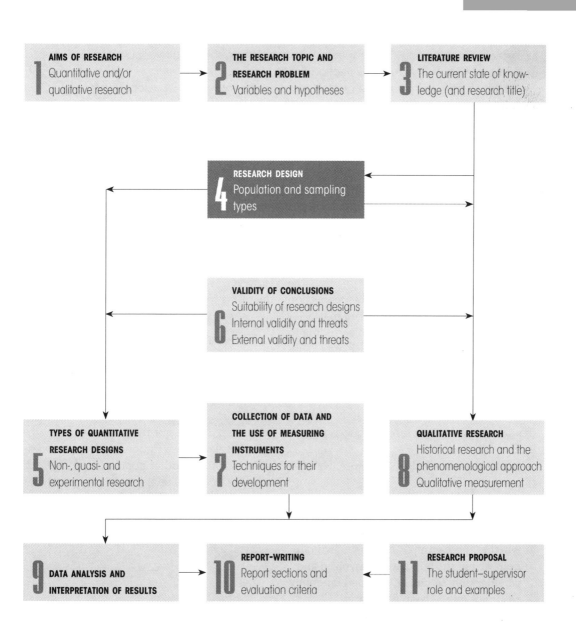

LEARNING OUTCOMES

In this chapter we look at the issues involved in the selection of a sample. Once the research topic has been clearly defined and delineated, the next step involves drawing a sample from the relevant population. In this chapter we define all the basic concepts and we explain the various ways of obtaining a sample.

After studying this chapter, you will be able to:
- differentiate between populations, sampling frames, and samples
- list the five basic types of units of analysis found in the human behavioural sciences and illustrate them by way of examples
- list the different types of sampling as well as their advantages and disadvantages in terms of their predictive power (see Section 2.3.2)
- explain why we should be cautious when making generalisations about the results of samples of populations (see Section 2.4.3)
- list the steps in using a table of random numbers to draw a representative sample from its population.

4.1 Introduction

When we conduct research to investigate a research hypothesis or a research question (see Sections 2.3 & 2.4), we collect data from the objects of our enquiry in order to solve the problem concerned. The results we eventually obtain should therefore shed light on the tenability of the hypothesis and it should give an indication whether to accept or reject the hypothesis. A crucial element in this connection is the research design that we intend to use.

A **research design** is the plan according to which we obtain research participants (subjects) and collect information from them. In it we describe what we are going to do with the participants, with a view to reaching conclusions about the research problem (research hypothesis or research question – see Section 2.4).

In the research design, therefore, we have to specify:
- the number of groups that should be used (this is necessary to decide which statistical technique to use – see Chapter 9)
- whether these groups are to be drawn randomly from the populations involved and whether they should be assigned randomly to groups (see Section 6.2.7) and

- what exactly should be done with them in the case of experimental research (see Section 5.2.1).

In this chapter we deal with the sampling requirements of research designs. These requirements serve as criteria for the evaluation of research reports (see Section 10.3). However, we first need to define and explain the terms "population" and "sample".

4.2 Population and sample

The population is the study object and consists of individuals (see Figure 4.1), groups, organisations, human products and events, or the conditions to which they are exposed. In Section 2.4 we saw that a research hypothesis postulates the relationship between variables in some or other population. A research problem therefore relates to a specific population and the **population** encompasses the total collection of all **units of analysis** about which the researcher wishes to make specific conclusions.

FOR EXAMPLE In Research Example II (see Section 2.3, page 17), the research hypothesis deals with the (causal) relationship between the exposure of a population of trainee supervisors to an iron-fisted management style and these trainee supervisors' subsequent management style. Conceptually, each member of the population has a score on each of these two variables and the researcher wishes to draw conclusions about the relationship between these variables for the entire population (that is, all trainee supervisors). Here the units of analysis are the trainee supervisors.

A population is the full set of cases from which a sample is taken. In sampling, the term "population" is not used in its normal sense, as the full set of cases need not necessarily be people.

FOR EXAMPLE For research to discover relative levels of service in a restaurant throughout the country, the population from which you would select your sample would be all the restaurants in the country. Alternatively, you might need to establish the average "life" of long-life batteries produced over the past month by a particular manufacturer. Here the population would be all the long-life batteries produced over the past month by that manufacturer.

We indicate the size of a population by **N**.

FOR EXAMPLE If the size of the population is 1 000, we write it as $N = 1\,000$.

NOTE: We refer to the members or elements of the population as the **units of analysis** (see Figure 4.2). In the human behavioural sciences, units of analysis typically refer to:

- humans
- groups (for example couples married in a particular year; households in a particular geographic region; homosexual clubs; gangs; crime syndicates; and so on)
- organisations or institutions (for example schools; classes; congregations; hospitals; political parties; companies; and so on)
- human products or outputs (for example houses; paintings; articles published in a particular journal in a particular period; dramas; and so on)
- events (for example elections; riots; court cases; and so on). (See Section 7.7.6 for time sampling methods.)

44 white women
6 black women

44 white men
6 black men

Figure 4.1 *The population of 100 South African multimillionaires (N = 100) (Adapted from Babbie & Mouton, 2001, p. 169. Used with permission.)*

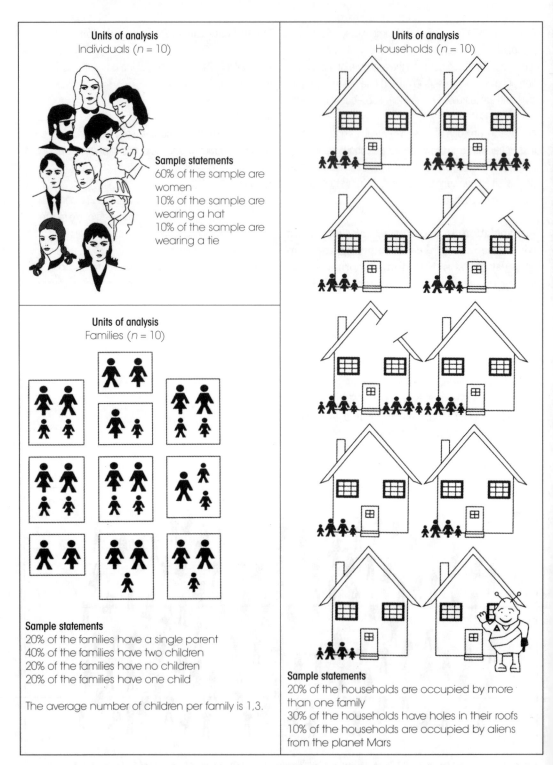

Units of analysis
Individuals (*n* = 10)

Sample statements
60% of the sample are women
10% of the sample are wearing a hat
10% of the sample are wearing a tie

Units of analysis
Families (*n* = 10)

Sample statements
20% of the families have a single parent
40% of the families have two children
20% of the families have no children
20% of the families have one child

The average number of children per family is 1,3.

Units of analysis
Households (*n* = 10)

Sample statements
20% of the households are occupied by more than one family
30% of the households have holes in their roofs
10% of the households are occupied by aliens from the planet Mars

Figure 4.2 *Illustrations of units of analysis (Adapted from Babbie & Mouton, 2001, p. 91. Used with permission.)*

It is impractical and uneconomical to involve all the members of the population in a research project; usually the populations that interest human behavioural scientists are so large that, from a practical point of view, it is simply impossible to conduct research on all of them. The census conducted in 2001, for instance, cost ±R632 million and the size of the population was 44,8 million people (Statistics SA web site, 5 August 2005). Consequently, we have to rely on the data obtained for a sample of the population (compare p. 22 – theories). We indicate the size of the sample by **n**.

The selection of the sample, however, is a very important stage. A population is a group of potential participants to whom you want to generalise the results of a study. This aspect of generalisability is extremely important: it is only when the results can be generalised from a sample to a population that the results of research have meaning beyond the limited setting in which they were originally obtained. When results are not generalisable (when the sample selected is not an accurate representation of the population), the results are applicable only to the people in the same sample who participated in the original research, not to others. In order for results to be generalisable, the sample must therefore be **representative**. By "representative" we imply that the sample has the exact properties in the exact same proportions as the population from which it was drawn, but in smaller numbers. Consequently, a representative sample is a miniature image, or likeness, of the population (see Figure 4.3).

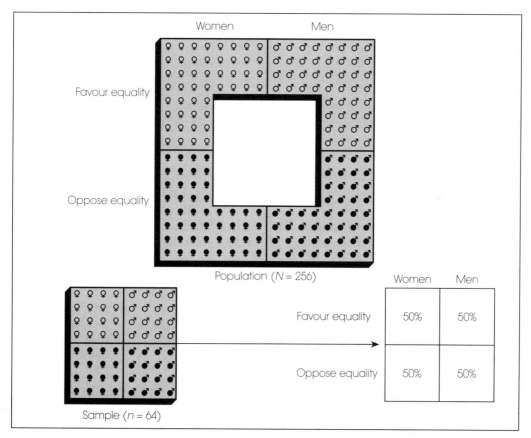

Figure 4.3 *A representative sample (Source: Babbie & Mouton, 2001, p. 478. Used with permission.)*

ACTIVITY 4.1

Read Case Studies A to G in Appendix D on page 306.

QUESTION

What is the unit of analysis for each case study? Explain your answer.

ANSWER

case study a

The unit of analysis is individual people, that is, health care professionals, namely *nursing sisters and doctors* who serve mainly white and coloured population groups at a general hospital. These people completed the questionnaire used in the investigation.

case study b

The unit of analysis is a group of people (not individuals), namely *goldsmith apprentices*, who all receive the same type of training and supervision and whose attitudes the intervention (role induction procedure) is intended to affect.

case study c

The unit of analysis is people, namely *first-line supervisors* employed at agricultural corporations in four of the provinces in South Africa. These are the people who attended the training course and had to write the three-hour test.

case study d

The unit of analysis refers to a group of people at four technikons, namely *students in public speech-making* who all received the same type of training and whose speech preparation time, speech performance, and speech anxiety were investigated.

case study e

The unit of analysis refers to *a group of small businesses* in Tshwane (formerly Pretoria), namely small businesses (between 40 and 60 employees) whose owners agreed to participate in the research project.

case study f

The unit of analysis is *business people* (entrepreneurs and managers).

case study g

The unit of analysis is individual people, that is, *nurses from a public hospital* in South Africa who take care of HIV/AIDS patients.

4.3 Sampling

We can distinguish between **probability samples** and **non-probability samples**.

- Examples of probability samples are:
  - simple random samples
  - stratified random samples
  - systematic samples
  - cluster samples.
- Examples of non-probability samples are:
  - accidental or incidental samples
  - quota samples
  - purposive samples
  - snowball samples
  - self-selection samples
  - convenience samples.

In the case of **probability sampling**, we can determine the probability that any element or member of the population will be included in the sample. In **non-probability sampling**, by contrast, we cannot specify this probability. Elements which have a chance of being included have a probability that exceeds zero. In some examples of non-probability samples some elements have no chance (that is, a probability of zero) of being included.

The advantage of probability sampling is that it enables us to indicate the probability with which sample results (for example sample means) deviate in differing degrees from the corresponding population values (for example population means). Unlike non-probability sampling, probability sampling enables us to estimate **sampling error** (see Section 4.3.7). This is a statistical term that relates to the **unrepresentativeness** of a sample (see Figure 4.4). Nevertheless, non-probability sampling is frequently used for reasons of convenience and economy.

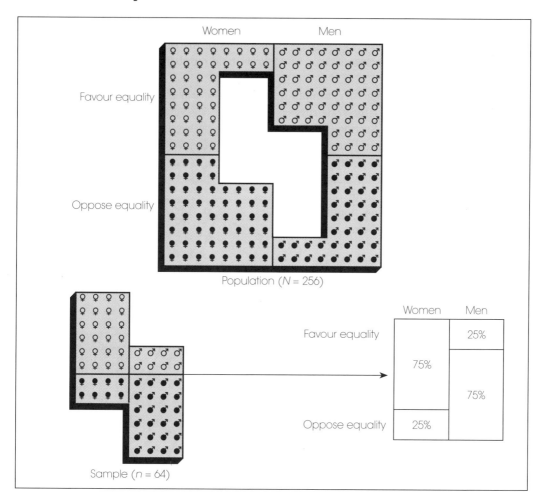

Figure 4.4 *An unrepresentative sample (Source: Babbie & Mouton, 2001, p. 479. Used with permission.)*

4.3.1 **The sampling frame**

Before researchers draw a sample of the population for analysis, they should obtain clarity about the population, or units of analysis, to which their research hypotheses apply. This involves compiling a sampling frame. A **sampling frame** is a complete list in which each unit of analysis is mentioned only once. Unless such a sampling frame is borne in mind, it is impossible to judge the representativeness of the obtained sample properly. The sample should be representative of the sampling frame, which ideally is the same as the population, but which often differs due to practical problems relating to the availability of information.

FOR EXAMPLE If the population actually involves all people who are entitled to vote, but we refrain from explicitly identifying it as such, we may easily settle for a sample obtained from our immediate vicinity, for example our residential area, hostel or workplace. An explicit specification of the sampling frame before commencing the research may prevent us from regarding such a sample as being representative of the relevant population.

The compilation of a satisfactory sampling frame presents problems in large-scale survey research in particular (see Section 5.4.5). A list that is comprehensive and accurate for a particular population at a specific point in time is frequently simply not available. On a daily basis people relocate from one region to another, change from one population to another (for example from being wealthy to bankrupt, and *vice versa*), and even die. Lists that we could possibly consider to be sampling frames in some instances include telephone directories, mailing lists of municipal ratepayers, lists of students registered at a university, and lists of television licence holders.

If we use a list that does not contain all relevant units of analysis, and if the missing units differ in a systematic manner from those on the list, the resulting sample would not be representative of the population. Consequently we could eventually draw incorrect conclusions in our research.

FOR EXAMPLE Suppose the population in question involves all voters in a city and we use the telephone directory for that city as our sampling frame. If a large proportion of the adults do not have telephones, and these people are exclusively from a particular socio-economic group, our sampling frame is deficient because it systematically excludes individuals who do not have telephones.

Under these circumstances it is, of course, impossible for a telephone survey (see Section 7.7.4) to yield a representative picture of the entire population of voters.

If we were to use the numbers listed in a telephone directory as a sampling frame for the population with telephones, the occurrence of unlisted numbers may present a problem. To overcome this problem, we could dial numbers randomly without using a telephone book (directory). A drawback of this procedure, however, is that we could dial business numbers or discontinued numbers instead of household numbers.

NOTE: To obtain a random sample of telephone numbers from a telephone directory (see Section 4.3.2), one could do the following: select every number that appears at a specific point (e.g. 4 cm measured with a ruler) from the top (or bottom) of each page in every second column of the following page in the telephone directory.

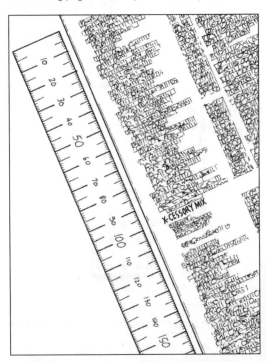

Figure 4.5 *How to sample randomly from a telephone directory*

In order to compile an appropriate sampling frame, we should bear the following checklist in mind (Saunders *et al.*, 2003, p. 154):

▶ Are the cases listed in the sampling frame relevant to your research topic? For example, are they current?

▶ Does the sampling frame include all cases, in other words, is it complete?

▶ Does the sampling frame exclude irrelevant cases, in other words, is it precise?

▶ (For purchased lists) Can you establish and control precisely how the sample will be selected?

4.3.2 Random sampling

Conceptually, random sampling is the most attractive type of probability sampling. We must distinguish between **simple random sampling** and **stratified random sampling**.

4.3.2.1 SIMPLE RANDOM SAMPLING

In the simplest case of random sampling, each member of the population has the same chance of being included in the sample and each sample of a particular size has the same probability of being chosen (see Figure 4.6).

FOR EXAMPLE In a random sample of, for example, 50 multimillionaires from the population of all multimillionaires in South Africa, each multimillionaire, irrespective of sex, race, age, region, and so on, will have an equal chance of being included.

Suppose we wish to draw a random sample of three units of analysis ($n = 3$) from a population of five units of analysis ($N = 5$), A, B, C, D, and E. In such a case each of the following 10 samples will have the same chance of being the randomly selected sample:

ABC   ABD   ABE   ACD   ACE
ADE   BCD   BCE   BDE   CDE

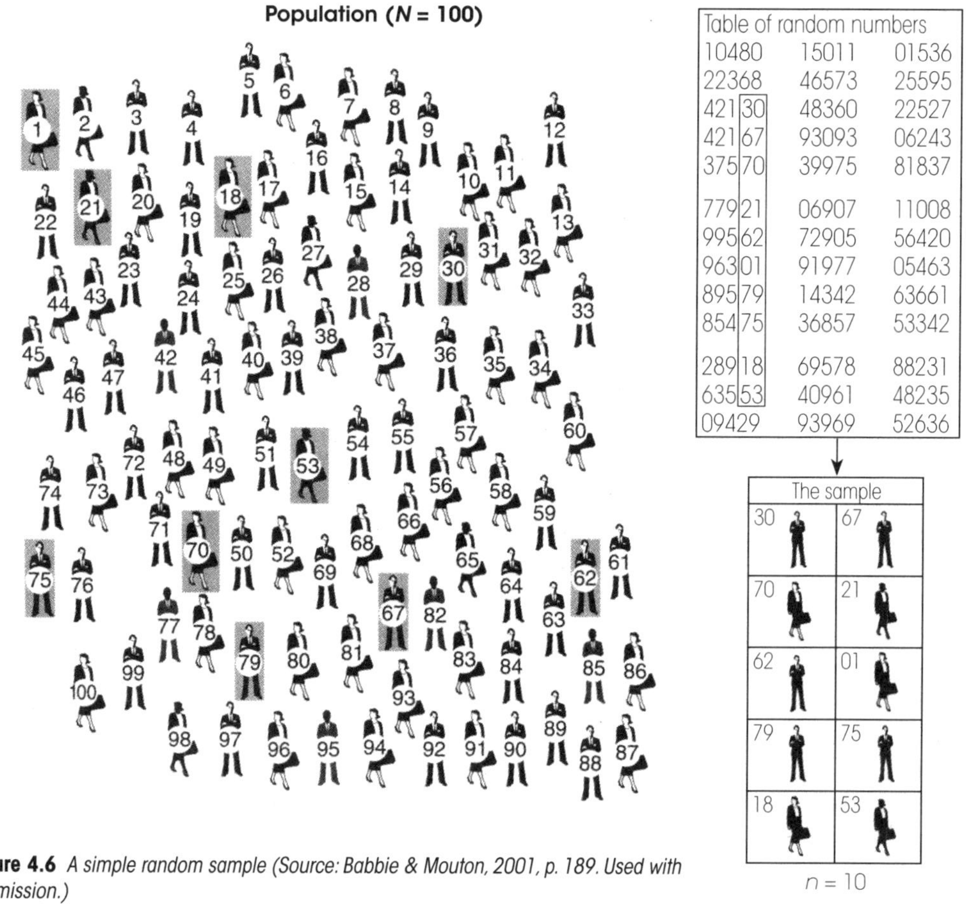

Figure 4.6 *A simple random sample (Source: Babbie & Mouton, 2001, p. 189. Used with permission.)*

Two steps are necessary to draw a random sample:

▶ Firstly, we should identify all the units of analysis in the sampling frame and give them consecutive numbers (for example 001, 002, 003, and so on).

▶ Secondly, the mechanism we use to choose the units of analysis should ensure that each number has an equal chance of being selected. We can do this by means of a table of random numbers (see Appendix C, page 305) or a computer program.

4.3.2.2 HOW TO USE A TABLE OF RANDOM NUMBERS

The numbers listed in a table of random numbers (see Figure 4.6 and Appendix C) show no order, irrespective of whether you proceed along its columns or its rows. In other words, if you start at any given number, there is no way of predicting the value of the next number (whether it is the one to the left or right of it, or the one above or below it).

You start at any arbitrarily chosen number, for example, by blindly making a mark with a pencil on the table and selecting the number closest to the pencil mark. Next, you write down the numbers assigned to the units of analysis that you encounter as you move from that point along the row or column. You must ignore a number if it appears for a second (or third, and so on) time. Similarly, you must ignore a number that is greater than the highest number assigned to units of analysis in the sampling frame. Continue in this fashion until you have written down a collection of numbers equal to the size of the desired sample. This collection represents the numbers of the members of the randomly chosen sample.

In Figure 4.7 you can see that the pencil tip is placed randomly on the table and the number 73 is closest to the pencil tip. You can now move in any direction to the next number, that is, up, down, across or diagonally to the left or right.

Suppose you move upwards from the number 73; the following numbers are 26, 51, 43, and so on, and you continue to move until you have drawn the required number for the sample. Of course, this will depend on the size of the sample that was chosen. If you reach the top of the column, you can simply continue at the top or bottom of the following column – as long as you apply the chosen method consistently.

Suppose you want to draw a sample of 80 people from a sample frame of 400; a number with three figures would have to be considered. In other words, 373 is the number closest to the pencil tip (the 3 of the column to the left of 73 is also taken into consideration), and when you move the pencil upwards, the numbers 326, 451, 243, 745, 342, 063, and so on, follow. You will therefore use the units of analysis to which you assigned the above numbers during the composition of the sample frame to compose the sample. Of course, you will ignore the numbers 451 and 745 because they are greater than the size of the sample frame, which is 400 in this case.

If any unit is chosen in this way, it will mean that each unit ultimately included in the sample has had the same chance of being selected.

The advantage of a simple random sample is that it is representative of the population in the sense that it does not favour one unit of analysis (individual or subpopulation) over another. Consider the sample drawn in Figure 4.6: the chances that the sample taken in this example will include females only, for example, is remote and the chance of this happening can be determined.

If large samples and populations are involved, access to computer facilities is required to draw random samples. As indicated, one of the prerequisites for drawing a random sample is the availability of a sampling frame, that is, a list of all the elements of which the population is composed. It may be very difficult, if not impossible (in terms of time and costs), to compile such a list especially if a very large population is involved.

Figure 4.7 *An example of using a table of random numbers (see Appendix C)*

4.3.2.3 STRATIFIED RANDOM SAMPLING

Suppose the population is composed of various clearly recognisable, non-overlapping subpopulations (which we may call **strata** [singular stratum]) that differ from one another in terms of a specific variable (see Section 2.3). Each subpopulation is a **stratum**. The division into groups may be based on a single variable such as gender (so that there are two strata: men and women). It may also involve a combination of more than one variable, for example gender and age (so that there are strata such as young adult males, young adult females, middle-aged males, middle-aged females, and so on).

The members of a particular stratum will thus be more alike or homogeneous than the population at large. Put differently, the variation within any particular stratum will be smaller than the variation among the respective strata. As it may be unwise to ignore

the differences among such clearly discernible populations, we have to include them when we draw a random sample.

FOR EXAMPLE Suppose heart attacks occur four times more frequently among men than women. If, in a single random sample of an equal number of men and women, the proportion of heart-attack patients is not separately determined for these two groups, the incidence of heart attacks will be seriously underestimated among men and seriously overestimated among women.

In order to draw a representative stratified random sample, the following two aspects must be kept in mind:

▶ Firstly, we should identify the various strata according to one or more variables.

FOR EXAMPLE Naturally, in a stratified random sample approach, the researcher is required to be aware of the stratification variables, that is, the variables in terms of which the population may be divided into homogeneous strata, such as tax level; organisation authority level; industrial or commercial sector; crime type; technological generation order; and so on.

▶ Secondly, we should draw a random sample from each separate stratum.

Using this method, we can be more certain of obtaining a representative sample from a population with clearly distinguishable strata than with simple random sampling.

FOR EXAMPLE In Figure 4.6 we obtained a sample of five white male, three white female, and two black female multimillionaires by using simple random sampling. There was no black male in our sample, even though we know from Figure 4.1 that male black multimillionaires make up 6% of the population and that black multimillionaires (male and female) make up 12% of the population. If we had drawn a random sample according to such strata, white versus black, there would have been a probability of 0,5 (50%) of a black male being included in our sample of 10 (see Sections 4.3.2.1 & 4.3.4 for an explanation) and the sample would have been more representative.

61

4.3.2.4 THE ADVANTAGES OF A STRATIFIED RANDOM SAMPLE

Stratified random sampling has two important advantages:

▶ In a random sample from a normal population that is stratified in terms of gender, the probability of a sample consisting of members of one gender only is zero. On the other hand, while there is a very small probability that a simple random sample from a small population of 50 cancer patients, for example 25 men and 25 women, will be composed of men only, such a possibility does exist.

▶ In order to ensure that important strata are represented in the sample, stratified random sampling requires a smaller sample (involving less time and money) than simple random sampling. The probability that a simple random sample will include, for example, men and women in the appropriate proportions, increases as the size of the sample increases. Stratified random sampling requires smaller samples than simple random sampling in order to obtain valid results.

NOTE: With a stratified random sample we are ensured of a sample's representativeness, irrespective of sample size, because it has been built into the sampling strategy right from the very beginning (see Figure 4.8).

A. Some men and women who either favour (=) gender equality or do not (≠) favour it.

Population (*N* = 20)

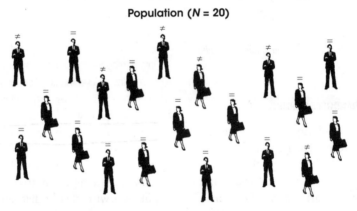

B. Separate the men and the women (the independent variable).

Women (*n* = 10)   Men (*n* = 10)

Figure 4.8 *Proportions and strata (Source: Babbie & Mouton, 2001, p. 432. Used with permission.)*

C. Within each gender group, separate those who favour equality from those who do not (the dependent variable).

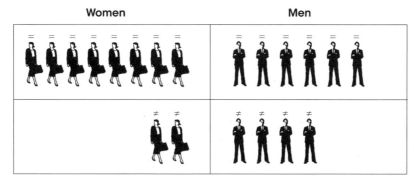

D. Count the numbers in each cell of the table.

E. What percentage of the women favours equality?

F. What percentage of the men favours equality?

G. Conclusions:
While a majority of both men and women favoured gender equality, women were more likely than men to do so.
   Thus, gender appears to be one of the causes of attitudes toward gender equality.

	Women	Men
Favour equality	80%	60%
Do not favour equality	20%	40%
Total	100%	100%

Figure 4.8 *Proportions and strata (continued)*

4.3.3 Other types of probability sampling

Systematic sampling and cluster sampling are simpler and more convenient than random sampling, especially when we want to obtain a representative sample from the entire population, as in large-scale opinion polls (see Section 5.4.5). These sampling methods may be used in combination with each other or with simple or stratified random sampling.

4.3.3.1 SYSTEMATIC SAMPLING

Suppose we need to obtain a sample of n members from a population of N elements (units of analysis) that are numbered from 1 to N. In **systematic sampling**, we include every N/nth element (where $\frac{N}{n}$ is an integer, that is, a whole number) (see Figure 4.9).

FOR EXAMPLE (see Figure 4.9): Suppose we need to select a systematic sample of 10 multimillionaires from a total population of 100 in South Africa. In this instance, $\frac{N}{n} = \frac{100}{10} = 10$. To obtain a systematic sample, we first draw an element (multimillionaire) randomly (see Section 4.3.2.1) from the first 10 on the list. From there onwards we choose every tenth element of the residue of 100.

Suppose the number of the first element we draw is 3. The numbers of the elements that we subsequently select are 13 (obtained by 3 + 10), 23, 33, and so on, up to 93. Once we determine the number of the first element, the numbers of all n elements are fixed. Therefore, if we do not determine the first number randomly, the sample obtained is a non-probability sample (see Section 4.3.4).

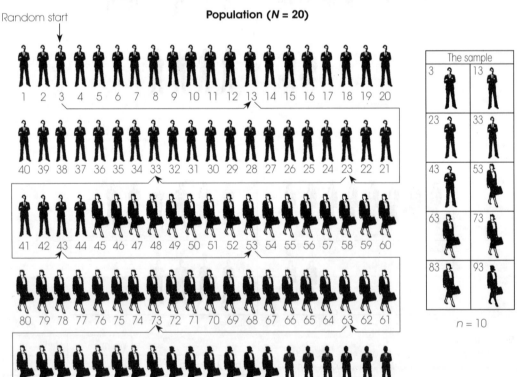

Figure 4.9 *A stratified, systematic sample with a random start (Source: Babbie & Mouton, 2001, p. 198. Used with permission.)*

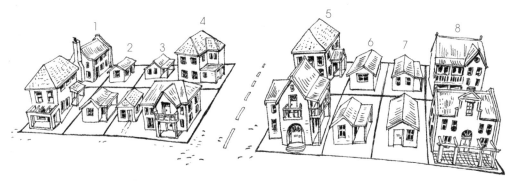

Figure 4.10 *A regular pattern in the sampling frame related to financial strata*

Figure 4.9 illustrates the example by combining systematic sampling and stratified sampling (where the different strata are grouped together – see Section 4.3.2.3). In the case of systematic sampling, we should bear in mind the possibility of any cyclical order or regular pattern in the sampling frame (see Chapter 6) which is related to clearly distinguishable strata.

FOR EXAMPLE (see Figure 4.10): Suppose a residential area is laid out in such a manner that each block contains eight stands, and the first and fourth stands of each block are corner stands. If, in such a case, we select stands at intervals of four, and the first stand number we choose randomly is two, there will be no corner stand included in our sample. In contrast, if we use the same interval (that is, four) and the number of the first stand is four, we will select corner stands only. Now, if the households of corner stands differ from the others in respect of a variable (see Section 2.3) that is related to our research (for example financial position), none of these systematic samples will be representative of the population of all households. For instance, suppose the corner stands are larger and more expensive than the others, and their occupants are financially better off than the others, then a variable such as *financial position* will have a bearing on our research and systematic sampling may very well affect our results.

NOTE: If there is such a systematic pattern in the numbers assigned to the members of the population, the most obvious solution is either to randomise the entire list prior to the assignment of numbers, or to rather use simple random sampling (see Section 4.3.2.1).

Because systematic sampling requires less time and is cheaper than simple random sampling, it is more practical. However, since simple random sampling ensures greater accuracy, we may consider systematic sampling to be more practical than, yet similar to, random sampling.

4.3.3.2 CLUSTER SAMPLING

In large-scale surveys (see Sections 5.4.1, 5.4.5 & 7.7.3.1) it is usually difficult, if not impossible, to obtain lists of all the members (units of analysis – see Section 4.3.1) of the population as would be required for drawing random or systematic samples. In the case of cluster sampling, we first draw (or stratify randomly – see Section 4.3.2) pre-existing, heterogeneous groups, called **clusters**. All the members of the selected clusters, or a simple random sample or a stratified random sample drawn from these clusters, constitute the eventual sample.

FOR EXAMPLE Suppose we have to draw a sample from the population of all the farm workers in South Africa. According to cluster sampling, we first draw a sample of, for example, all the farms in South Africa (for example big and small; crop and cattle; and so on) and within each of these categories we obtain a random sample of farm workers.

We can perform cluster sampling in more than one phase.

FOR EXAMPLE Suppose we wish to conduct an opinion survey on an issue such as reinstating the death penalty for the whole of South Africa. We can:

- first draw a sample from the nine provinces or regions within South Africa;
- then draw a number of townships and cities within each region;
- next, select a few street blocks within each of these townships and cities; and
- finally, draw a sample of individuals randomly within these street blocks.

Because we do cluster sampling in phases, we do not have to list all the members of the population initially (see Sections 4.3.2.1 & 4.3.2), but only those who appear in the selected clusters. Even in cases in which a complete list of all members of the relevant population (units of analysis) is available, and a random sample of names or codes may readily be drawn (as is the case with simple random sampling – see Section 4.3.2.1), it may be impossible for practical reasons to rèach all these individual units for research purposes.

Especially when the members of the relevant population are scattered across the country, it may require a great deal of time and money to reach one or two individual units in remote areas who have been selected by a random sampling procedure. The greater the distance between the selected individual units, the higher the travelling expenses become, the more time is wasted travelling across the country, and the more difficult it becomes to collect the information (such as the opinions of people).

In contrast to simple random sampling, in cluster sampling fewer locations have to be visited but more than one or two individual units must be included at each such location.

The advantage of cluster sampling is that there is a considerable saving in time and costs when compared to simple random sampling.

However, when some clusters are homogeneous (similar) in terms of the variables of interest, cluster sampling may lead to **biased samples**. By biased samples we mean samples that tend or lean towards a particular factor of the research topic.

FOR EXAMPLE Suppose the relevant population (for example personal computer users) includes more or less the same number of men and women. However, if several of the clusters that are drawn consisted of men only (for example from the motor parts distributors sector), the eventual sample may include a disproportionately large number of men.

Thus, the disadvantage of cluster sampling is that there is a possibility of such bias in each phase. This means that in any phase we could draw a sample that is not representative (see Section 4.3) of the population. Even if all the clusters we draw during the first phase are representative of the population, the members we select during the second phase need not necessarily be representative of the various clusters. We should therefore be mindful of the sample size (see Section 4.3.5) and the accuracy of sampling during each phase in cluster sampling. To attain the desired sample size, there should also be a balance between the sample sizes in the successive phases so that the initial samples are not too large and the eventual samples too small, or *vice versa*. The influence of various factors on the probability sampling techniques discussed are summarised in Table 4.1.

Table 4.1 Impact of various factors on choice of probability sampling techniques (Source: Saunders *et al.*, 2003, p. 160.)

Sampling technique	Sampling frame required	Size of sample needed	Geographical area suited	Relative cost	Easy to explain to support workers	Advantages compared to simple random sampling
Simple random	Accurate and easily accessible	Better with a sample size of over a few hundred	Concentrated if face-to-face contact required, otherwise does not matter	High if sample size is large or if sampling frame is not computerised	Relatively difficult to explain	
Systematic	Accurate, easily accessible, and not containing periodic patterns; actual list not always needed	Suitable for all sizes	Concentrated if face-to-face contact required, otherwise does not matter	Low	Relatively easy to explain	Normally no difference
Stratified Random	Accurate, easily accessible, divisible into relevant strata	See comments for simple random and systematic as appropriate	Concentrated if face-to-face contact required, otherwise does not matter	Low, provided that lists of relevant strata are available	Relatively difficult to explain (once strata decided see comments for simple random and systematic as appropriate)	Better comparison across strata; differential response rates may necessitate re-weighing
Cluster	Accurate, easily accessible, relates to relevant clusters not individual population members	As large as practicable	Dispersed if face-to-face contact is required and geographically-based clusters are used	Low, provided that lists of relevant clusters are available	Relatively difficult to explain until clusters selected	Quick but precision is reduced

4.3.4 **Non-probability sampling**

The probability that any element (unit of analysis) will be included in a non-probability sample cannot be specified. In some instances, certain members may have no chance at all of being included in such a sample (see Figure 4.11).

FOR EXAMPLE If we use non-probability sampling to determine whether the majority (for example 80%) of South African citizens are in favour of reinstating the death penalty, we may never be certain that the results we obtain are nearly as accurate as those we may have obtained with probability sampling. This means that we may not be as confident about our conclusions.

The advantage of non-probability samples is that they are less complicated and more economical (in terms of time and financial expenses) than probability samples. Non-probability samples may be especially useful in pilot studies (see Section 7.6) in which a preliminary form of a questionnaire has to be tested.

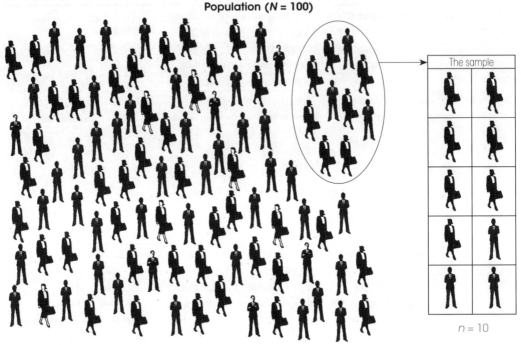

Figure 4.11 *Accidental sample example (Source: Babbie & Mouton, 2001, p. 170. Used with permission.)*

4.3.4.1 ACCIDENTAL SAMPLING (INCIDENTAL SAMPLING)

An **accidental sample** is the most convenient collection of members of the population (units of analysis) that are near and readily available for research purposes (see Figure 4.11).

FOR EXAMPLE Students who have registered for a particular course and show up at class on a particular day (this is also an example of what is referred to as a *captive audience*); the people who happen to be at a particular shopping centre at a particular time when the researcher is conducting interviews; the organisations that are close to the researcher's home.

NOTE: Researchers should consider using accidental samples only if they have no other option. Insofar as the conclusions obtained inductively are based on accidental samples, they need not necessarily be typical of the relevant population of individuals and universe of circumstances. Such conclusions could thus be seen as hypotheses that will have to be examined deductively according to the procedure in Section 2.4.1.

4.3.4.2 QUOTA SAMPLING

In the case of **quota sampling**, we make an effort to have the same proportions (see Figure 4.7) of units of analysis in important strata (see Section 4.3.2.3) such as gender, age, and so on as are in the population. However, we obtain the units of analysis in any particular stratum accidentally (this is also called **segmentation**).

FOR EXAMPLE Suppose we know that of the population of top managers (*N* = 1 000) 80% are men (800) and 20% are women (200). In a quota sample (*n* = 100) of the population of top managers we will see to it that 80% are men (80) and 20% are women (20). However, we obtain both these groups in an accidental fashion as explained before.

We may find that a quota sample yields quite satisfactory results under certain circumstances.

▶ Firstly, we should know the important strata according to which the population is composed and their respective proportions with a reasonable degree of accuracy, or be able to estimate them (see Figure 4.9).

▶ Secondly, we should include enough cases (at least 15, but preferably more than 25) of each stratum in the sample.

4.3.4.3 PURPOSIVE SAMPLING

This is the most important type of non-probability sampling. Researchers rely on their experience, ingenuity and/or previous research findings (see Section 3.2) to deliberately obtain units of analysis in such a manner that the sample they obtain may be regarded as being representative of the relevant population (see Section 4.3.1).

FOR EXAMPLE If a minister of foreign affairs of another country wishes to assess the opinions of a broad spectrum of the South African public in 2001, he or she may decide to interview only a sample of opinion-makers. Such a sample, which may include, for instance, the state president and the leaders of the ANC, DA, IFP, PAC, and UDM, would be an example of a purposive sample.

The problem with this kind of sampling is that different researchers may proceed in different ways to obtain such a sample. It is therefore impossible to evaluate the extent to which such samples are representative of the relevant population.

4.3.4.4 SNOWBALL SAMPLING

In the first phase of **snowball sampling**, we approach a few individuals from the relevant population. These individuals then act as informants and identify other members (for example acquaintances or friends) from the same population for inclusion in the sample. The latter may, in turn, identify a further set of relevant individuals so that the sample, like a rolling snowball, grows in size till saturated.

FOR EXAMPLE An executive director of a well-known South African company, who obtained her academic qualifications during the sixties at Oxford University, may identify someone else with the same academic background, who in turn may put us in contact with another similar individual, and so on.

4.3.4.5 SELF-SELECTION SAMPLING

Self-selection sampling occurs when we allow a case, usually an individual, to identify their desire to take part in the research. We therefore do the following:

▶ Publicise our need for cases, either by advertising through appropriate media or by asking them to take part.

▶ Collect data from those who respond.

Cases that self-select often do so due to their feelings or opinions about the research question(s) or stated objectives. In some instances, this is exactly what the researcher may want.

4.3.4.6 CONVENIENCE SAMPLING

Convenience or haphazard sampling involves selecting haphazardly those cases that are easiest to obtain for our sample, such as the person interviewed at random in a shopping centre for a television programme. The sample selection process is continued until we reach the required sample size. Although this technique of sampling is used widely, it is prone to bias and influences that are beyond our control due to the fact that the cases appear in the sample because they were easy to obtain. Often the sample is intended to represent the total population. In such instances the choice of sample is likely to be biased, meaning that subsequent generalisations are likely to be flawed at best. These problems are less important where there is little variation in the population, and such samples often serve as pilots to studies using more structured samples. The influence of various factors on the non-probability sampling techniques discussed are summarised in Table 4.2.

Table 4.2 Impact of various factors on choice of non-probability sample techniques (Source: Saunders *et al.*, 2003, p. 172.)

Sample type	Likelihood of sample being representative	Types of research in which useful	Relative costs	Control over sample contents
Accidental (incidental)	Very low	When performing explorative research. When you do not expect to generalise findings	Low	Low
Quota	Reasonable to high, although dependent on selection of quota variables	Where costs are constrained or data needed very quickly so that an alternative to probability sampling is needed	Moderately high to reasonable	Relatively high
Purposive	Low, although dependent on researcher's choices: Extreme case Heterogeneous Homogeneous Critical case Typical case	Where working with very small samples Focus: unusual or special Focus: key themes Focus: in-depth Focus: importance of case Focus: illustrative	Reasonable	Reasonable
Snowball	Low, but cases will have characteristics desired	Where difficulties in identifying cases	Reasonable	Quite low
Self-selection	Low, but cases self-selected	Where exploratory research needed	Low	Low
Convenience	Very low	Where very little variation in population	Low	Low

4.3.5 Sample size (*n*)

Generalisations about populations from data collected using any probability sample are based on probability. The larger our sample size, the lower the likely error in generalising to the population. Probability sampling is therefore a compromise between the accuracy of our findings and the amount of time and money we invest in collecting, checking, and analysing the data. Our choice of sample size within this compromise is governed by:

▶ the confidence we need to have in our data – that is, the level of certainty that the characteristics of the data collected will represent the characteristics of the total population

▶ the margin of error that we can tolerate – that is, the accuracy we require for any estimates made for our sample

▶ the types of analyses we are going to undertake – in particular the number of categories into which we wish to subdivide our data, as many statistical techniques

have a minimum threshold of data cases for each variable
▶ the size of the total population from which our sample is being drawn.

NOTE: As a general rule, we should not use any sample with less than 15 units of analysis, but preferably one with more than 25 units of analysis (Huysamen, 1991). If the population size is 500, then the sample size should be 200. If random sampling is done, it is not necessary to use a sample size larger than 500 units of analysis, no matter what the size of the population may be (see Section 5.2.1.2).

When we determine sample size, the following four factors should be kept in mind:
▶ Firstly, when we determine the size of the sample (n), we should bear in mind the size of the population (N). In general, it holds that the smaller the total population, the relatively larger the sample should be to ensure satisfactory results.

FOR EXAMPLE If one population of 100 000 requires a sample of 1 000 (1%), it does not mean that a population of 1 000 may be equally satisfactorily represented by a sample of 10 people only (also 1%). As a matter of fact, if the population consists of only 10 cases (for example the population of small business enterprises in a particular city that have doubled their taxable income within one year of establishing the business), it may be advisable to include all of them in the sample.

The influence of absolute sample size (n) instead of proportion ($\frac{N}{n}$) to the size of the population (N) is related to the **standard error of the mean**. Therefore, the number of units (n) involved in our sample is more important than the percentage of the total population which they represent. This is illustrated in Table 4.3.

Table 4.3 The effect of sample size on the standard error of the mean for a population of 10 000

Sample size (n)	Standard error
20	2,24
50	1,40
100	0,99
250	0,62
500	0,44
1 000	0,30
2 500	0,17
5 000	0,10

$N = 10\ 000$

An increase in the sample size, in proportion to the size of the population from which the sample is drawn, results in a decrease in the standard error. Therefore, although we must try to draw the largest possible sample, it is not necessary to draw a sample larger than 500 as it will have little effect in decreasing the standard error and margin of error.
▶ Secondly, the desired sample size does not depend on the size of the population only but also on the variance (heterogeneity) of the variable. As a general rule, the larger the variance of the variable, the larger the sample which is required. The sampling error may be estimated in the case of random samples. (Compare the formula in Chapter 7 of Babbie & Mouton, 2001.)

FOR EXAMPLE Suppose we expect the proportion of "yes" and "no" votes in a nationwide referendum to be closer to each other (say 45 :55) in one region than in another. The variance is therefore larger in the former region. As a result, we should draw a relatively larger sample from the former region than from the latter. On the other hand, if there were only a very few "no" votes in one region, it would be important to represent this group in the sample as well.

▶ Thirdly, if each stratum of a highly heterogeneous population is relatively homogeneous, a relatively smaller stratified sample than that required for a random sample may be sufficient. If the strata differ in size and heterogeneity, we should adjust the size of the respective samples we take from them accordingly – the smaller the stratum and/or the more heterogeneous it is, the larger the sample that we should draw from it.

FOR EXAMPLE If the 10 000 students at a particular technikon or university are composed of 8 000 undergraduate, 1 000 fourth year, 800 master's, and 200 doctoral students, we should obviously select a much higher proportion of doctoral students than undergraduates. (All students would therefore not have the same chance of being included in the sample.)

Much larger samples are normally used in large-scale surveys than in experimental research (see Section 5.2). An example of a large-scale survey would be an opinion poll (see Section 5.4.5), in which we intend to assess the position of the entire population on a particular variable. Although these samples seldom exceed several thousand, samples of this magnitude may still yield quite accurate estimates of the responses of a population of several million.

FOR EXAMPLE Almost two months prior to the referendum on a new constitutional dispensation in South Africa in 1983, Mark- en Meningsopnames (a survey research company) predicted, on the basis of a sample of fewer than 2 000 voters, that 67,4% would vote yes. Eventually 66,3% of the more than two million votes were recorded in this category (Perold, 1983).

▶ Fourthly, in determining sample size, we should also bear in mind that the number of units of analysis from which we eventually obtain usable data may be much smaller than the number that we drew originally. It may not be possible to trace some individuals, others may refuse to participate in the research, while still more may not provide all the necessary information or may not complete their questionnaires, so that their information will have to be discarded. Therefore, it is usually advisable to draw a larger sample than the one for which complete data is desired in the end.

FOR EXAMPLE If we need the completed postal questionnaires of a sample of 100 respondents, we would probably have to mail the questionnaire to 300 people or organisations (called response rate – see Section 4.3.6).

ACTIVITY 4.2
Read Case Studies A to G in Appendix D on page 306.

QUESTION
What type of sampling was used in the research in each case study? Briefly explain your answer.

ANSWER
case study a

Non-probability sampling was used as certain nursing sisters and doctors who work with AIDS patients did not have the chance to serve as sample members. Because it was convenient to use the group of nursing sisters and doctors of just one general hospital, for which permission had been granted, the specific type of sampling used was *accidental sampling*.

case study b

Non-probability sampling was used as goldsmith apprentices who do the same course with other jewellery firms did not have the chance to take part as sample members. The specific type of sampling used was *accidental sampling*, because it was convenient and economical to use the group of goldsmith apprentices at just one large jewellery firm.

case study c
Simple random sampling was used because each of the 60 first-line supervisors employed at agricultural corporations in South Africa had an equal chance of serving as subjects.

case study d
Purposive non-probability sampling was used because the data concerning public speech-making students at only four technikons who had already completed seven assignments, were used.

case study e
Accidental sampling was used because the units of analysis were bankrupt small businesses in Tshwane

(formerly Pretoria) whose owners were willing to participate in the project. The units of analysis were therefore not randomly sampled from all bankrupt small businesses in South Africa.

case study f
A *self-selecting sample* was used because the respondents (business people) were conveniently available from Gauteng and the Western Cape – those who agreed to participate in the project.

case study g
Non-probability sampling, in particular *purposive sampling*, was used because the other nurses did not have a chance to serve as sample members. Researchers usually obtain respondents with whom to conduct unstructured interviews by means of purposive or snowball sampling (see Section 4.3.4). In this investigation, purposive sample was used to select 20 nurses on account of their experience (two years' experience in the care of HIV/AIDS patients).

4.3.6 Response rate

The most important aspect of a probability sample is that it represents the population. A perfectly representative sample is one that exactly represents the population from which it is taken. If 60% of our sample were small service sector companies, we would expect 60% of the population to be small service sector companies. We therefore need to obtain as high a response rate as possible to ensure a representative sample.

Non-responses are likely to occur. Non-respondents are different from the rest of the population because they have refused to be involved in the research for various reasons. Consequently, the respondents will not be representative of the total population and the data collected may be biased. In addition, any non-responses will necessitate extra respondents being found to reach the required sample size, thereby increasing the cost of the study.

It is therefore important to analyse the refusals to respond to both individual questions and entire surveys in order to check for bias. Non-response is due to four inter-related problems:
▶ refusal to respond
▶ ineligibility to respond
▶ inability to locate respondent
▶ respondent located but unable to make contact.

The most common reason for non-response is that the respondent **refuses to answer** all the questions or to be involved in our research, but without a reason. This type of non-response can be minimised by paying careful attention to the methods used to collect the data. Alternatively, some of the selected respondents may not meet our research requirements and will therefore be **ineligible** to respond. **Non-location** and **non-contact** create further problems – the fact that these respondents are unreachable means they will not be represented in the data collected.

We need to include the response rate as part of the research report. Neumann (2000) suggests that we should include all eligible respondents when calculating the total response rate. The **total response rate** is obtained by dividing the total number of respondents by the total number of ineligible respondents in the sample:

$$\text{Total response rate} = \frac{\text{total number of respondents}}{\text{total number in sample (ineligible)}}$$

A more common way of calculating a response rate excludes ineligible respondents as well as those who, despite repeated attempts, were unreachable. This is known as the **active response rate** and this is calculated by dividing the total number of responses by the sample size minus the number of respondents who are ineligible or unreachable:

$$\text{Active response rate} = \frac{\text{total number of responses}}{\text{total number in sample} - (\text{ineligible} + \text{unreachable})}$$

Even after ineligible and unreachable respondents have been excluded, we will probably still have some non-responses. It is therefore important to assess to what extent the data are representative of the population. It is also very important to allow for the impact of non-response in the calculations of sample size.

4.3.7 Sampling errors

No matter how hard a researcher tries, it is impossible to select a sample that perfectly represents the population. The researcher could, of course, select the entire population as the sample, but that defeats the purpose of sampling, that is, making an inference about a population based on a smaller sample.

Sampling error expresses the lack of fit between the sample and the population. It can be defined as the difference between the characteristics of the sample and the characteristics of the population from which the sample was selected.

FOR EXAMPLE The average height of 10 000 Grade Seven students is 40 inches. If we take 25 samples of 100 Grade Seven students and compute the average height for each set of 100 children, we will have an average height for each group, or 25 averages. If all these averages are exactly 40 inches, there is no sampling error at all. This result, however, is highly unlikely as the selection of samples is not perfect. Instead, we would find the average values for the samples to be, for example, 40,3 inches, 41,2 inches, 38,9 inches, and so on.

The amount of **variability** or the spread of these average values gives us some idea of the amount of sampling error. The larger the diversity of sample values, the larger the error, the less precise and representative the sample is.

SUMMARY

In each hypothesis one or more populations are implied (for example all businesses in the Northern Province with fewer than 30 staff members). In this example, the population may be defined as the total collection of individual businesses who are potentially available for observation and who have the characteristic to which the research hypothesis refers ("fewer than 30 staff members"), in common. If it is not possible to involve all the members of the population, the researcher has to rely on a sample of the population, which is a relatively small subgroup of individual units from the population (for instance "males", instead of males as well as females; in such a case, "gender" cannot be considered a variable – it is held constant – and "male" is the unit of analysis).

In selecting a sample, the sampling frame plays a very important role. There are various ways of drawing probability as well as non-probability samples, each with their own advantages and disadvantages. Simple random samples, stratified random samples, systematic samples, and cluster samples are examples of probability samples. The class of non-probability samples consists of accidental samples, purposive samples, quota samples, snowball samples, self-selection samples, and convenience samples. The issue of non-response can influence the degree to which the sample is representative of the population and should also be considered in the selection of a sample.

TEST YOURSELF

Question 1: Multiple-choice questions

Only one of the answers to each question is correct. Identify and mark the correct one. (Answers appear in Appendix A on page 299.)

1.1 The main purpose of sampling is to be able to select:
   a) a sample whose statistics will accurately portray a known population parameter
   b) a sample whose statistics will accurately portray an unknown population parameter
   c) a sample whose unknown statistics will accurately portray a known parameter
   d) simple random samples.

1.2 In a study where a researcher examined newspaper editorials from small South African towns that dealt with news on the topic of electrical power failures, the unit of analysis was:
   a) electrical power failures
   b) small towns
   c) newspaper editorials
   d) electricity.

1.3 In sampling, the complete list of the units of analysis of a population is called a:
   a) population list
   b) target list
   c) sampling frame
   d) sample list.

1.4 When the overriding factor used in selecting the units of analysis is mainly due to their availability, the resulting sample is called:
   a) a cluster sample
   b) a convenience sample
   c) a snowball sample
   d) an accidental sample.

1.5 To be able to generalise from a sample to the population depends on the following characteristic of the sample:
   a) distinctiveness
   b) power
   c) representiveness
   d) variability.

1.6 In general, as sample size increases:
   a) the standard error fluctuates in size
   b) the standard error is constant
   c) the standard error decreases in size
   d) the standard error increases in size.

1.7 We call the measure used to estimate the difference between the true population value and the results of the sample the:
   a) sampling index
   b) margin of error
   c) discrepancy error
   d) population equation.

Question 2: True/false questions

Indicate whether the following statements are true (T) or false (F). (Answers appear in Appendix A on page 299.)

2.1 Generally, the more heterogeneous the population, the more beneficial it is to use stratified sampling.

2.2 Cluster sampling is a useful sampling procedure for large populations that are geographically scattered.

2.3 Cluster sampling requires a complete listing of all the primary sampling units.

Question 3: Self-evaluation questions

(Some answers appear in Appendix A on page 299.)

3.1 What is the unit of analysis in the research problems listed under Section 2.3?

3.2 What is the main feature of probability sampling that distinguishes it from non-probability sampling?

3.3 Mention and briefly explain the two requirements that should be met for drawing a simple random sample from a particular population.

3.4 What should the researcher bear in mind when he or she considers drawing (a) systematic samples, and (b) cluster samples?

3.5 Indicate the similarity and the difference between stratified random sampling and quota sampling.

Types of quantitative research designs

5

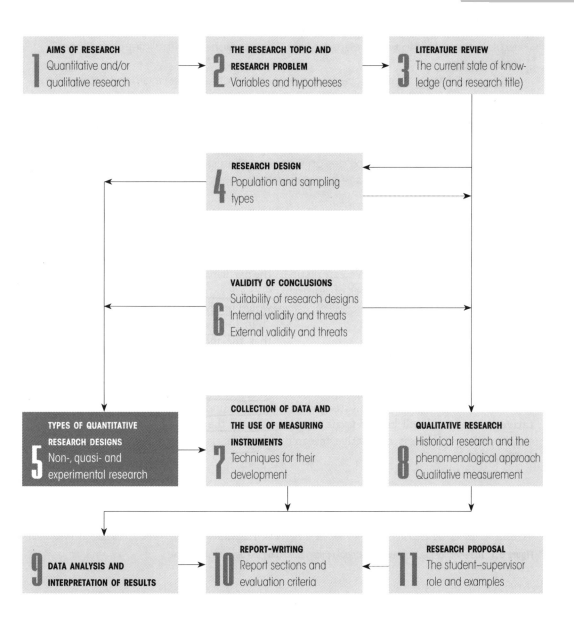

AIMS OF RESEARCH
1
Quantitative and/or
qualitative research

**THE RESEARCH TOPIC AND
RESEARCH PROBLEM**
2
Variables and hypotheses

LITERATURE REVIEW
3
The current state of knowledge (and research title)

RESEARCH DESIGN
4
Population and sampling
types

VALIDITY OF CONCLUSIONS
6
Suitability of research designs
Internal validity and threats
External validity and threats

**TYPES OF QUANTITATIVE
RESEARCH DESIGNS**
5
Non-, quasi- and
experimental research

**COLLECTION OF DATA AND
THE USE OF MEASURING
INSTRUMENTS**
7
Techniques for their
development

QUALITATIVE RESEARCH
8
Historical research and the
phenomenological approach
Qualitative measurement

**DATA ANALYSIS AND
INTERPRETATION OF RESULTS**
9

REPORT-WRITING
10
Report sections and
evaluation criteria

RESEARCH PROPOSAL
11
The student–supervisor
role and examples

LEARNING OUTCOMES

In this chapter we look at the various types of quantitative designs that are used. Some of these designs require random sampling whereas others do not. The decision to use a specific design is therefore closely tied to the issue of sampling, as discussed in the previous chapter. The degree to which causality can be inferred also varies from one design to the other and the choice of design therefore influences the interpretation of the results obtained.

After studying this chapter, you will be able to:

- illustrate with examples the three important components of the classical experiment
- list and illustrate the prerequisites for establishing causality
- explain why it is difficult to do random sampling in field research
- explain the extent to which causality can be researched by the interrupted time-series design
- explain briefly why mainly non-experimental research is done and non-random sampling is used in organisations, and explain what field investigations involve
- explain why relationships (correlations), but not causality, can be researched by non-experimental research designs
- compare cross-sectional and longitudinal designs
- compare the criterion-groups design with prediction studies
- discuss the two major issues of any research design.

5.1 Introduction

We generally structure and execute our research in a different way, depending on the specific research design used. We can distinguish between four different types of research design:

▶ experimental research
▶ quasi-experimental research
▶ non-experimental research
▶ qualitative research.

The first three categories constitute **quantitative** research and will be our focus in this chapter. We will address qualitative research in Chapter 8.

5.2 Experimental research

All types of experimental research involve some form of **intervention**. In other words, the participants (units of analysis – see Section 4.2) are exposed to something to which they would not have been subjected otherwise.

In the hypothesis we express the influence that the independent variable is expected to have on the dependent variable and it is this influence that we measure in the experiment. We therefore measure the extent to which the intervention (independent variable) has changed or affected the units of analysis (dependent variable). This is shown in Figure 5.1.

Figure 5.1 *The effect of the independent variable (intervention) on the dependent variable*

The measurement of the dependent variable before the intervention is called **premeasurement**, and the measurement after the intervention is called **postmeasurement**.

In a research design where one group is involved, we refer to a **premeasurement and a postmeasurement single-group design** (see Section 6.2.3).

When we work with one group only, the possibility exists that considerable changes (in the dependent variable) could have occurred without the intervention (independent variable). We can therefore not be 100% certain that the intervention or independent variable alone is responsible for any changes we observe. We therefore need a **control group** that is not exposed to the experimental intervention to which we can compare the group that was exposed to the intervention. (In Section 5.2.2 we deal with an important principle involved here, namely causality.)

A **control group**, as its name indicates, therefore is a group that does not receive the intervention, but serves to exercise control over the **nuisance variables** (see Sections 5.2.1.3, 6.2.3.3, 6.2.8.2 & 9.3.2.3).

FOR EXAMPLE Suppose we expose the trainee supervisors of one mining company to aggressive supervisor behaviour towards a subordinate, and the trainee supervisors of another company to neutral behaviour by the same supervisor.

Subsequently, we measure the aggressive behaviour of both groups in the same manner. We therefore have two groups: the experimental group (the group who observed the aggressive supervisor behaviour) and the control group (the group who did not observe the aggressive supervisor behaviour). Our aim here is to attribute differences in the aggressiveness measured in the two groups to the influence of the independent variable (the aggressive supervisor behaviour).

The design used in this example is an **intact-group design**. Any intact groups (for example,

the residents of two hostels, the students in two classes, the workers in two particular mining companies, and so on) may be **self-selected** in terms of the dependent variable or other variables related to it.

In terms of the way in which we decide which of the participants we should subject to which intervention, we may distinguish between the following types of research:

- pre-experimental research (see Section 6.2.2)
- true experimental research
- quasi-experimental research (see Section 5.3).

In the next section we focus on true experimental research. The distinguishing feature of this type of research is that the experimenter has optimal control over the research situation.

5.2.1 **Characteristics of true experimental research**

True experimental research has three distinct characteristics: control over the independent variable, random assignment of units of analysis to groups, and nuisance variables.

5.2.1.1 CONTROL OVER THE INDEPENDENT VARIABLE

Having full **control** over the independent variable (see Section 2.3) means that we may determine which levels of the variable we should use.

FOR EXAMPLE If we wish to investigate the relative effectiveness of distributed learning as opposed to massed learning as in Research Example I (see Section 1.2.1), we are dealing with two levels of the independent variable *learning*. In order to determine the effects of these two levels, we need to define distributed and massed learning in terms of the number of hours each involves as well as the period of time over which learning takes place.

5.2.1.2 RANDOM ASSIGNMENT OF UNITS OF ANALYSIS TO GROUPS

Although all types of experimental research have some or other intervention in common, the distinguishing feature of true experimental research is that the different groups (exposed to the different levels of the independent variable) are formed by means of **random assignment** (see Section 6.2.7). The term *random* refers to the way in which the groups are assigned to the different levels of the independent variable (see Section 2.3) and not to the way in which we obtain the participants (see Section 4.3.2).

There are various ways in which we can randomly assign individuals to groups, for example by tossing a coin, or by using a table of random numbers (see Section 4.3.2.2, Appendix C, and CD-ROM). If we use a table of random numbers, we can place those with even numbers in one group and those with uneven numbers in the other. This assignment results in a 50/50 chance of any particular individual being assigned to Group 1 rather than Group 2.

FOR EXAMPLE In Research Example II (see Section 2.3, page 17) a sample of trainee supervisors was randomly assigned to two main groups that subsequently observed iron-fisted and approachable role model management style behaviour respectively.

NOTE: We call the design that is generated by assigning individuals randomly to groups in this manner, a **randomised groups design**. This design represents the simplest example of a true experimental design (see Section 9.3.2.3 for a more complex design, namely the randomised-block design).

Figure 5.2 shows three types of randomised designs, namely the randomised two-group design, the randomised multigroup design, and the randomised pre-test and post-test design. We will focus on the first two designs. Consult Huysamen (1994, pp. 59–61) for an explanation of the randomised pre-test and post-test design, where Y_1 is a point in time before Y_2 (later).

It is generally advisable to assign not fewer than 30 elements/individuals to a group.

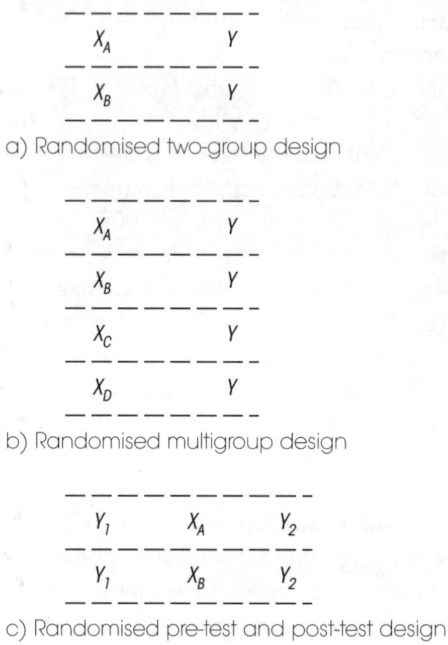

X_A	Y
X_B	Y

a) Randomised two-group design

X_A	Y
X_B	Y
X_C	Y
X_D	Y

b) Randomised multigroup design

Y_1	X_A	Y_2
Y_1	X_B	Y_2

c) Randomised pre-test and post-test design

Figure 5.2 *Diagrammatic representations of randomised groups designs (Source: Huysamen, 1994, p. 58.)*

(a) Randomised two-group design

In the simplest example of a randomised group design, participants are randomly assigned (see Section 6.2.7) to two groups that are subsequently subjected to two different levels of the independent variable (X_A and X_B). We may therefore view the groups as being matched (see Sections 6.2.3 & 6.2.8).

Figure 5.2(a) is a diagrammatic representation of the randomised two-group design. The dotted lines represent the boundaries of the two groups and symbolise the fact that individuals are randomly assigned to the different groups and that the treatments are assigned randomly to these groups. The symbol X represents the independent variable (see Section 2.3), and X_A and X_B the different levels of this variable (see Section 2.3) (or groups A and B). The symbol *Y* represents the measurement of the dependent variable. *X* appears in front of *Y*, meaning that the experimental intervention (independent variable) takes place before the measurement of the dependent variable (*Y*).

FOR EXAMPLE Suppose our aim is to determine whether government loans or subsidies have the largest positive effect on small farming practices. In terms of our diagrammatic representation, the small farming practices form the dependent variable (*Y*), while loans (X_A) and subsidies (X_B) are the two levels of the independent variable *financial aids*.

(b) Randomised multigroup design
If the treatment factor (independent variable) has more than two levels, the research participants (units of analysis – see Section 4.2) are randomly assigned (see Section 6.2.7) to as many groups as there are levels, and the levels are randomly assigned to these groups. The resulting **randomised multigroup design** is simply an extension of the randomised two-group design described above.

Figure 5.2(b) gives a diagrammatic representation of this design. In this representation the independent variable *X* has four levels, namely X_A, X_B, X_C, and X_D, and the dependent variable is represented by *Y*. (Compare Research Example II on page 17.)

5.2.1.3 NUISANCE VARIABLES

In true experimental research, we have considerable control over irrelevant variables, also called **nuisance variables** (or third variables).

A nuisance variable is any variable which was not mentioned in the research hypothesis (see Section 2.4) that may influence the dependent variable (see Section 2.3). It is important to control the effect of these variables (see Sections 6.2.3.3, 6.2.8.2 & 9.3.2.3).

As a matter of fact, the basic purpose of experimental research is to control nuisance variables to such an extent that the various

groups differ only in terms of the levels of the independent variable in question. (To the extent that the experimenter succeeds in achieving this, we may confidently attribute changes in the dependent variable (see Section 2.3), to the independent variable.)

There are various ways of controlling the influence of nuisance variables:
- We can determine the speculated effect of nuisance variables by doing a proper literature review (see Section 3.2). In this way, nuisance variables documented in earlier research findings (see Section 3.2.1) can be identified and controlled.
- In a few cases it may be possible to eliminate the effect of the nuisance variable completely.

  FOR EXAMPLE If *noise* constitutes the nuisance variable, we can perform the experiment in a noise-proof room.

  If the nuisance variable refers to some or other attribute of the research participants, we can eliminate its effect by using only subjects who are as far as possible alike or homogeneous in terms of this characteristic. The disadvantage of this way of controlling nuisance variables is that the results we obtain will be applicable only to that level of the nuisance variable that we have used in the study.

  Suppose *gender* is the nuisance variable. We can eliminate its effect by using either males or females as research participants. For example, if males and females react differently to television violence, we could use only males in an investigation into the effects of television violence. If we then find that the most frequent viewers exhibit the most aggression, this relationship could not have been affected by the gender of the participants as only one gender (males) was involved. However, the relationship between television-viewing and aggression would be applicable only to males and could not be generalised to all people of both genders (males and females).
- A more efficient way of controlling such a nuisance variable is to build it into the design as an additional independent variable (see Section 9.3.2.3).

Another way of controlling nuisance variables is to purposely form the various groups so that they are as similar as possible in terms of all variables except the independent variable. Instead of completely eliminating such nuisance variables, we attempt to keep their effects the same for all groups or, put differently, to hold them constant for all groups (see Section 6.2.8.2).

As we will indicate in Section 6.2.7, the most practically feasible way of holding nuisance variables constant for all groups is to assign individuals randomly to the groups that are to receive the various levels of the independent variable (the intervention to which the participants are exposed).

This control that researchers have over the assignment of subjects to the various levels of the independent variable demonstrates in particular their control over the experimental situation. We can apply this to Research Example I (see Section 1.2.1.5, page 4) in the following way:

EXAMPLE

To obtain scientific knowledge on the relative effectiveness of the practice of distributed learning (mastering study material in more than one session) versus massed learning (mastering all the study material in one session) in Research Example I, we will have to conduct a study in which the performance of:

- one group of apprentices who learned in a distributed fashion is compared with
- another, comparable group who studied the same material by means of the massed procedure.

By merely drawing lots, we may determine whether any particular apprentice (subject) will be assigned to the group that is to learn according to the distributed method rather than the massed one.

Say we then find differences in the dependent variable (examination results) between the two groups following these interventions (distributed and massed

---

learning method). We might infer that these differences are due to the effect of the independent variable (distributed and massed learning method) rather than any other variable. This is because the groups were the same in terms of all other possible nuisance variables.

5.2.2 Causality in the human behavioural sciences

The purpose of science is to explain phenomena and, in particular, the causes of these phenomena (see Section 2.3.2). Philosophers of science have devoted much attention to the issue of causality, and we will discuss this topic very briefly in this section.

Any variable X may be regarded as a (sufficient or necessary and sufficient) cause of another variable Y if each of the following three conditions is met:

- there must be a correlation between the variables
- the cause must precede the effect
- the third variable must be controlled (see Section 6.2.3).

5.2.2.1 CORRELATION BETWEEN VARIABLES

A **correlational association** between X and Y exists when Y tends to appear in association with X.

FOR EXAMPLE If there is a correlation between the number of hours that mine workers spend watching violent films on television and their scores on a questionnaire of aggressiveness, the number of hours they spend watching violent films on television does not necessarily cause the scores on a questionnaire of aggressiveness. The higher aggressiveness of some mine workers may make them more inclined to watch violent films, which may further reinforce their aggressiveness. This would be an example of a mutual relationship (between television watching and aggressiveness).

Therefore, the existence of a correlational relationship (even if it were perfect) would not necessarily be an indication that X causes Y. A correlation between variables X and Y may be the result of either a mutual relationship between X and Y, or of a third variable Z, which may cause both X and Y (see Section 9.4.2.3).

A **mutual relationship** means that one variable (X) plays a role in the occurrence of another (Y) which, in turn, affects the former so that there is a mutual relationship between them.

FOR EXAMPLE We may expect to find a high, positive correlation (see Section 9.4.2.3) between the number of churches (Y) in towns and cities and the incidence of crime (X). However, this correlation may be attributed to a third variable (see Section 6.2.3.3), namely the number of people (Z) living in the towns and cities. The size of the population of the towns and cities has an effect on both the number of churches and the incidence of crime (see Figure 5.5).

5.2.2.2 CAUSE MUST PRECEDE THE EFFECT

If we want to infer a causal relationship, it is necessary for the **cause to precede the effect**. In the human behavioural sciences it is often difficult, if not impossible, to meet this requirement. Often, causal factors are not events that take place and are concluded at some or other identifiable point in time because of a mutual relationship between the variables.

FOR EXAMPLE Motivation plays a role in academic achievement, which subsequently raises motivation. This, in turn, further promotes academic achievement. In this case it is not clear which of the two variables (*motivation* or *academic achievement*) qualifies as the cause and which one as the effect.

In the discussion of causality we often encounter a distinction between necessary and sufficient causes.

A variable, or event X, is considered to be a **necessary cause** of Y if Y cannot occur in the absence of X (see Figure 5.3).

FOR EXAMPLE Consider the irrigation of a lawn in a desert area. It requires a water supply (for example a borehole or a reservoir somewhere in a neighbouring rainfall area). The water supply X is therefore a necessary cause of wetness on the lawn. However, the presence of such a water supply does not guarantee a wet lawn. Some type of functional irrigation system has to be connected to the water supply. The presence of a water supply is thus a necessary but not a sufficient condition or cause of a wet lawn.

A variable, or event, X is a **sufficient** cause of Y if the presence of X necessarily results in the occurrence of Y (see Figure 5.4).

FOR EXAMPLE Consider the same irrigation problem. We may regard the connection of a functional irrigation system to the water supply as a sufficient cause of a wet lawn. If such an irrigation system were to be switched on, it would necessarily lead to wetness on the lawn. However, the incidence of a wet lawn is not proof of the presence of a programmed irrigation system, because the lawn could also have been watered manually with a watering-can. The availability of an irrigation system would thus be a sufficient but not a necessary condition or cause of a wet lawn.

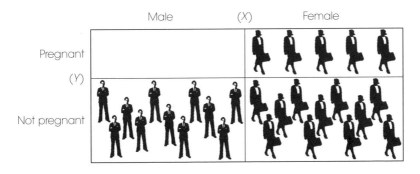

Figure 5.3 *Necessary cause (Source: Babbie & Mouton, 2001, p. 84. Used with permission.)*

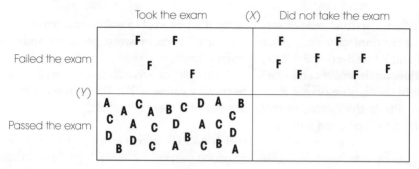

Figure 5.4 *Sufficient cause (Source: Babbie & Mouton, 2001, p. 84. Used with permission.)*

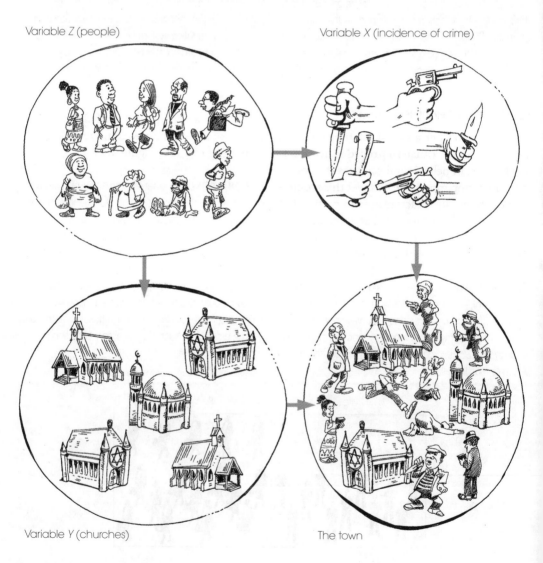

Figure 5.5 *Causality and the role of the third variable*

5.2.2.3 CONTROL OF THE THIRD VARIABLE

In the previous example, a wet lawn was not necessarily evidence of one particular type of irrigation. The existence of a correlation between X and Y, and X's precedence over Y in time are not sufficient to conclude that X causes Y. Therefore, there is a third condition for inferring causality: there should not be a **third variable** Z to which the effect in X could be attributed.

FOR EXAMPLE Only if we could show that there were no hosepipes, watering-cans, or other means of irrigation, and that weather conditions made dew or rain impossible, could we attribute the wet lawn to a sprinkler irrigation system.

Consider the example regarding the increase of crime and the increase in the number of churches (see Section 5.2.2.1 and Figure 5.5): the positive correlation between the number of churches (Y) in towns and cities and the incidence of crime (X) satisfies the first condition for X to be the cause of Y. However, an increase in crime cannot be ascribed to an increase in the number of churches because the role of the third variable, that is, *population size* (Z) (number of people) has not been ruled out.

The principle that all other factors except the one whose effect is being investigated, have to be excluded, is referred to in science and law by means of the Latin phrase *ceteris paribus*, which means *everything else being the same* (see Sections 5.3 & 6.2.1).

The *ceteris paribus* principle brings us back to the falsification principle (see Section 2.5), namely that knowledge in the human behavioural sciences, as in the business and administrative sciences, accumulates through the elimination of rival hypotheses or alternative explanations of behaviour.

Unfortunately, matters are not as simple in the human behavioural sciences as in the natural sciences, where the presence of a sufficient cause necessarily leads to a particular effect.

FOR EXAMPLE In the above example regarding the irrigation of a lawn in a desert area, rain would always be followed by a wet lawn (provided that there is a lawn, of course).

We could liken the situation in the human behavioural sciences to one in which the same amount of rain would wash away the lawn of one person and leave his neighbour's lawn bone-dry. This illustrates the fact that in the human behavioural sciences the concept of absolute causality is not often found. The regularity notion about causality (which was addressed at the beginning of this section) thus presents an oversimplified construction of human behaviour.

What makes matters in the business and administrative sciences so complicated is that there are seldom only one or two variables that we may identify as the causal factors. Any phenomenon tends to be dependent on a number of different factors. To investigate its effect with only one supposed independent variable would imply a negation of reality and an oversimplification of the problem.

FOR EXAMPLE To perform well financially, not only a particular level of trading skill may be required, but also the necessary motivation, social support, physical facilities, practice, and so on, of the small business entrepreneur. Various factors besides trading skill therefore play a role.

5.2.3 Laboratory versus field studies

Depending on whether we do research in a laboratory or under natural circumstances, we distinguish between laboratory and field studies. The environment in which research is carried out actually constitutes a continuum, with laboratories at the one extreme and natural environments at the other.

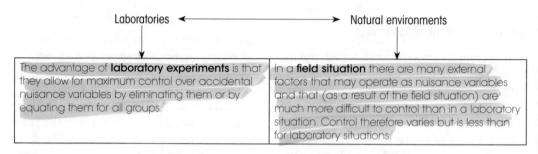

Figure 5.6 *Control in laboratory and field studies*

In the business and administrative sciences, a laboratory does not necessarily mean a room with burning gas cylinders, glass apparatus, and people wearing white overcoats.

Any venue (place or even the environment) that is specially equipped for the purpose of studying a particular phenomenon, such as individual or group behaviour; the products of such behaviour; or the nature of a material, qualifies as a **laboratory**. To a greater or lesser extent such a laboratory may be characterised by artificiality in comparison with the real world situation.

Research Example II (see Section 2.3, page 17) represents an instance in which experimental research was carried out in a laboratory situation. The training centre in which the trainee supervisors' management styles could be observed, qualified as a laboratory. This is because it was equipped with the necessary apparatus for the demonstration of their reaction to the subordinate Bobo (video machines, recreation facilities, and equipment to make tea) and for the observation of their behaviour (one-way mirrors).

Some problems (for example taxi wars) cannot be studied in a laboratory situation. Even if this were possible, the artificiality of the situation would probably change the very behaviour that was being studied. Many research problems in the business and administrative sciences lend themselves to field studies as they could be investigated only with great difficulty in laboratory situations.

FOR EXAMPLE It will not be possible to study the relationship between the level of inflation in a country and the price of oil over a period of, for instance, 10 years by means of a laboratory study. Another example might be research on management styles and the effect this has on job satisfaction. This type of study would be suited to field studies.

Field studies are conducted in the actual environment in which a phenomenon was observed originally. In such studies, we randomly assign subjects to the experimental and control groups, and the experimental intervention is effected in a natural, everyday environment.

FOR EXAMPLE To investigate the research problem in Research Example II (see Section 2.3, page 17) in a field situation, we might be required to observe the management styles of the trainee supervisors at their work stations with their own recreational facilities. However, different trainee supervisors are exposed to different work situations at their stations and not all of them have a subordinate at a given time to demonstrate Bobo's behaviour or that of the role model supervisor. Moreover, some visitor (for example a company director) who has an inhibiting effect, may pay an unscheduled visit so that an iron-fisted management style could possibly be impeded.

Although field researchers are careful to minimise such nuisance variables (see Section 5.2.1.3), there is always the possibility that **uncontrolled nuisance variables** may complicate their research. In this regard, the chances that something similar may happen in a laboratory situation are relatively slim.

ACTIVITY 5.1

Read the following problem statement and answer the question. Compare your answer with the given answer.

PROBLEM STATEMENT

A machine operator thinks that fumes emitted in the workshops play a role in the low efficiency of the operators. He would like to prove this to his supervisor by doing a research study.

QUESTION

What would the study situation be: laboratory experiment or field experiment? Give brief reasons for your answer.

ANSWER

The study situation would be a field experiment, because the research occurs in a natural, familiar environment (in a workshop) and not in a specially-designed environment (laboratory). The investiga-tion contains an experiment as an attempt is made to control/check the amount or levels of fumes as opposed to pure air in a workshop.

ACTIVITY 5.2

Read Case Studies B and C in Appendix D on page 306.

QUESTION

Will the study situation in each case study involve a laboratory experiment or a field experiment? Give brief reasons for your answers.

ANSWER

case study b

The investigation involves a field experiment rather than a laboratory experiment because the experiment (on the influence of the role induction procedure on attitudes) is carried out in the natural, everyday setting where the goldsmith apprentices receive their training – the ordinary scheduled practical meetings.

case study c

The investigation involves a laboratory experiment rather than a field experiment because the experiment (the training course) was most probably carried out in a classroom situation where the hour-long written test was completed. The classroom situation functions artificially from the natural, everyday environment in which first-line supervisors at an agricultural corporation work.

5.3 Quasi-experimental research

We have indicated that the critical feature of true experimental research is the random assignment of subjects to different treatment groups (see Section 5.2.1.2). The purpose of such assignment is to equate the groups in terms of all known and unknown nuisance variables (see Section 5.1.2.3). To the extent that we have achieved this, we then have to attribute the observed differences between the groups to the various levels of the independent variable (see Section 2.3) rather than to any nuisance variables.

It is often impossible or undesirable to assign subjects randomly to different groups and/or to bring about certain interventions and thus to effect the control that is characteristic of true experiments (see Section 5.2.1). The effect of earthquakes, the introduction of a new education system, and the repeal of influx control represent a few examples of problems that we cannot investigate along these lines.

Furthermore, it is often necessary to carry out research in natural environments such as classrooms, workplaces, or circumstances where the researcher does not have control over the intervention that takes place (by itself) or the particular intervention any particular individual may receive. In the case of several important problems in the business and administrative sciences, true experimental research is simply impossible. In such circumstances, however, quasi-experimental research may be considered.

Quasi-experimental research differs from true experimental research in that the researcher cannot randomly assign subjects to the different groups. These groups may therefore differ from one another in terms of nuisance variables as well as the independent variable (see also Section 5.2.1.2). Although quasi-experimental research usually enables us to make conclusions about causal relationships (see Section 5.2.2) with less conviction than in true experimental research, it nonetheless allows us to draw conclusions about such relationships with much more confidence than in pre-experimental research (see Section 6.2.2).

To meet the *ceteris paribus* requirement (see Section 5.2.2), attempts are made to take known threats to internal validity (see Section 6.2) into consideration in several other ways. Quasi-experimental research therefore presents a second best alternative to eliminating known nuisance variables (see Section 5.2.1.3) as far as possible, and the corresponding rival hypotheses (see Sections 2.4

& 9.3.2.1) on logical grounds. We can distinguish between two types of quasi experimental research: the non-equivalent control group design and the interrupted time series design.

5.3.1 The non-equivalent control group design

In the **non-equivalent control group design** we use **two pre-existing groups** as an experimental and a control group respectively (see Figure 5.7). Spector (1981) calls such a design an **ex post facto design**. The threat of group differences that may already have been present prior to the start of the experimental intervention (see Section 6.2.6) is taken into account by measuring both groups on the dependent variable (see Section 2.3) prior to the experimental intervention. However, the groups may differ in respect of a variable which has not been detected by the premeasure but which does affect performance on the postmeasure (see Section 6.2.4).

If the experimental and control groups do not differ in terms of the premeasure but do differ on the postmeasure, we can ascribe the difference in the postmeasure with some certainty to the difference in intervention that they have received (see Section 6.2.5). Threats such as historical events (see Section 6.2.3.1), spontaneous development (see Section 6.2.3.2) (in one or both groups), measurement reactivity (see Section 6.2.5.1), instrumentation (see Section 6.2.5.2) and statistical regression may, however, be in operation.

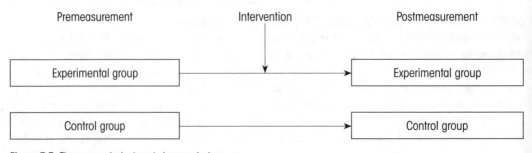

Figure 5.7 *The non-equivalent control group design*

QUESTION

Does the research in Case Study C involve an interrupted time-series design or a non-equivalent control group design? Provide brief reasons for your answer.

ANSWER

In Case Study C the evaluation of a training course in management principles for first-line supervisors at a South African agricultural corporation was studied and the intervention consisted of training the experimental group in management principles. The evaluation of the knowledge of management principles of the experimental and control groups was carried out before and after the course was offered to the experimental group. Therefore, the research in Case Study C involves a **non-equivalent control group design** (ex post facto design), because two pre-existing groups were used as an experimental and a control group respectively.

5.3.2 The interrupted time-series design

The interrupted time-series design represents an improvement on the premeasurement and postmeasurement design in that it keeps some of the above-mentioned threats at bay. In the interrupted time-series design **more than one** **measurement** of the dependent variable is obtained, with equal intervals both before and after the intervention. It can be considered as an expansion of the premeasurement and post-measurement single-group design (see Section 5.2). Figures 5.8, 5.9, and 5.10 are schematic representations of this design.

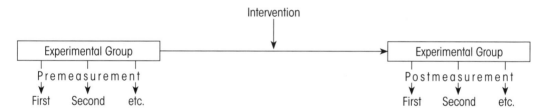

Figure 5.8 *The interrupted time-series design*

Spector (1981) is of the opinion that there should preferably be an equal number of measurements before and after the intervention. The researcher may plan the intervention, or it may be an unplanned event (for example an earthquake or the collapse of the stock market) in which case archival records (see Section 7.7.2.3) may be considered as a measure of the dependent variable.

FOR EXAMPLE Campbell and Ross (1968) analysed the traffic fatalities in the American state of Connecticut during the fifties and sixties. In reaction to a record number of traffic deaths of 324 in this state in 1955, its governor introduced extremely severe penalties for speeding violations. When the number of traffic deaths declined by 12,3% (to 284) the following year, the governor took this reduction as evidence of the success of his crackdown on speeding (see Figure 5.9).

However, the mere comparison of the traffic deaths before and after the intervention corresponds to the use of a premeasurement and postmeasurement single group design (see Section 5.2). Such a design does not take into consideration the following factors (with which we will deal in Sections 6.2.3 & 6.2.6):

▶ historical events beyond the control of the researcher (more traffic accidents could have occurred because of the weather in 1955 than in 1956)

▶ spontaneous development (there could have been a gradual decline in traffic accidents countrywide as a result of the general realisation of the economic implications it has)

▶ statistical regression and accidental fluctuations (traffic accidents could possibly fluctuate naturally from one year to the next)

▶ the interaction of selection and regression (maybe the decline in 1956 partially resulted from the shock of the high death figure for 1955).

Taking the possible threats to internal validity mentioned above into account, Campbell and Ross (1968) traced the number of traffic deaths for the four years before, and the three years after the introduction of the severe penalties. They then produced an interrupted time-series design. (The data which they obtained according to a premeasurement and postmeasurement single group design are indicated in the small block in Figure 5.9.)

NOTE: Cook and Campbell (1979), and Glass, Willson and Gottman (1975) describe statistical procedures to analyse the data obtained in an interrupted time-series design.

In terms of the single group design it would appear that the campaign did indeed have an effect on the number of traffic deaths. However, if we inspect the results of the interrupted time-series design, it is clear that we could not ignore the possible role of regression and accidental fluctuations. Compare, for instance, the decline in the number of traffic deaths from 1951 to 1952 and 1953 to 1954.

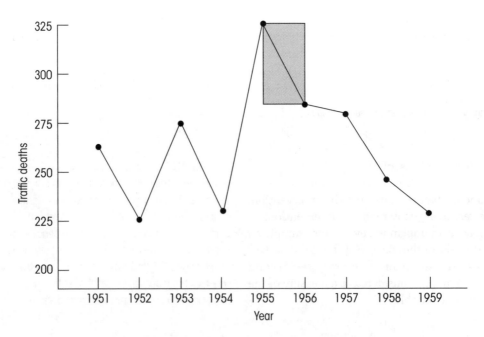

Figure 5.9 *Traffic deaths in an interrupted time-series design (Source: Huysamen, 1994, p. 90.)*

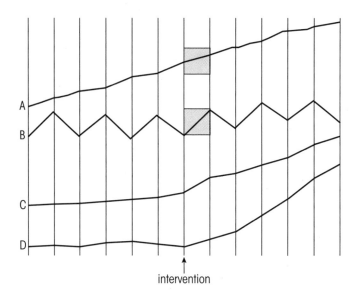

intervention

Figure 5.10 *Possible results in an interrupted time-series design (Source: Huysamen, 1994, p. 90.)*

NOTE: The value of the time-series design is that it enables us to determine whether changes taking place at the same time as the intervention represent a **temporary fluctuation** or the **onset of a sustained change**. In the case of graphs A and B in Figure 5.10, it appears as if the change at the time of the intervention would have occurred in any case as part of an established, ongoing pattern of change, while those in graphs C and D suggest a sustained, enduring effect.

If only a single measurement (premeasurement and postmeasurement single group design – see Section 5.2) was obtained both before and after the intervention and the results resembled those in the shaded blocks in A and B in Figure 5.10, it would have been impossible to distinguish between a real effect and the continuation of a tendency that was not related to the intervention.

The interrupted time-series design **eliminates the influence of spontaneous development** (see Section 6.2.3.2); that is, that there could have been a gradual decline in traffic accidents countrywide as a result of the general realisation of its economic implications. However, it does not eliminate the influence of historical events (see Section 6.2.3.1)

beyond the control of the experimenter, for example more traffic accidents could have occurred because of the weather in 1955 than in 1956.

FOR EXAMPLE If there had been fewer traffic deaths countrywide as a result of better weather conditions at the same time as the governor's introduction of the penalties, or a drastic increase in the price of petrol kept motorists off the road, this design would possibly lead to incorrect conclusions.

In order to compensate for the effects of historical events, the researcher may systematically check news reports of the particular period to determine whether any such events occurred at the same time as the intervention.

Such threats can also be eliminated by means of debating (see Section 1.2.1.4). These processes, however, do not necessarily guarantee conclusions that are as foolproof as those that are obtained with true experimental research (see Section 5.2.1). If someone else should convincingly argue that there were indeed historical events that might have led to the decline in traffic deaths, it would cast doubt on the researcher's conclusion.

ACTIVITY 5.4

Read Case Study B in Appendix D on page 306.

QUESTION

Does the research in Case Study B involve an interrupted time-series design? Give brief reasons for your answer.

ANSWER

In Case Study B the change being studied is a change in the attitude of the apprentices towards supervision, and the intervention is the participation in the role induction procedure.

It appears that the research in Case Study B does indeed involve an **interrupted time-series design**. The attitudes of the sample members were measured on three occasions (instead of two, as in the case of the pre-test/post-test, single-group design), namely at the start of the training period, immediately before the role induction, and one week after the role induction. It would perhaps have been better to make more meas-

urements before and after the intervention (the role induction procedure) as a single angry outburst by one of the supervisors, for example, could easily have upset at least half (10) of the apprentices, bringing about negative scores on their attitude questionnaires and therefore having a substantial impact on the results of the study. If six measurements were taken, for example, such a solitary event would have a smaller influence (as third variable) on the results, and it would prevent the researchers from coming to an incorrect conclusion. This example also demonstrates the negative effect that small sample sizes can have on results.

5.4 **Non-experimental research**

Neither random assignment (see Section 5.2.1.2), nor any planned intervention occurs in **non-experimental research**. In this type of research one or more variables (see Section 2.3), apart from the independent variable in question, could be the actual source of observed variation in the dependent variable(s). It is therefore generally accepted that conclusions about causal relationships (see Section 5.2.2) may be made with greater confidence by means of true experimental research (see Section 5.2.1) than non-experimental research. Random assignment of subjects to the levels of the independent variable does not occur as subjects cannot be equated in terms of all other variables (see Section 5.2.1.2).

FOR EXAMPLE Almost all our modern knowledge about astronomy has been obtained by non-experimental means because we cannot manipulate the stars – not yet!

If there is a great degree of regularity and orderliness in the phenomenon being studied, we may obtain highly satisfactory results by

means of non-experimental research. It is important for us to be thoroughly familiar with the nature of the variables (see Section 2.3) in the field of research and the statistical methods (see Chapter 9) that are available in order to disentangle the relationships among them.

In Section 5.2.3 we distinguished between laboratory and field studies. Both experimental (see Section 5.2) and non-experimental research can be conducted in either of these settings. As a result, there are four basic types of research design:

▶ laboratory experiments
▶ field experiments
▶ laboratory surveys
▶ field studies (or field surveys).

Although we may collect data for non-experimental research in laboratory surveys, it is typically done in natural environments or field studies. Research Example III falls into this category. Because there is no planned intervention and the data are collected in a field situation, this design is supposed to show the greatest similarity to real life.

RESEARCH EXAMPLE III   **PREFERENCE FOR TELEVISION PROGRAMMES AND AGGRESSIVENESS OF PRISONERS**

A measure of both the level of violence of their favourite television programmes and their own aggressiveness (behaviour) was obtained for each of 644 male and 567 female prisoners. The prison warders were asked in individual interviews to list these prisoners' three most popular television programmes. Independent raters familiar with the contents of these programmes classified them as either violent or non-violent. At the same time, the aggressiveness (behaviour) of the prisoners was rated by their fellow prisoners. A strong relationship (statistically significant, positive correlation – see Section 9.4.2.3) was found between the violence ratings of the prisoners' favourite programmes and their aggressiveness ratings (see Section 5.4.2.1).

5.4.1 Survey designs (relationships between variables)

Although it is unsatisfactory to describe one type of research as being opposite to another, there does not appear to be a satisfactory umbrella term for non-experimental hypothesis-testing research at present. The most satisfactory candidate for this purpose appears to be survey research, although this term tends to be associated mainly with opinion surveys. However, non-experimental hypothesis-testing research covers a wider spectrum than opinion polls (see Section 5.4.5). It includes such surveys as counting traffic at a road intersection or crossing; counting and searching a library collection; recording the repair activities and interaction between computer service stations and the computer users; and so on.

In **non-experimental, hypothesis-testing research** there is **no planned intervention** and **no random assignment** of research participants to groups (see Section 5.2.1.2) consisting of different levels of the independent variable(s) (see Section 2.3). In this type of research we examine the relationships that occur between two or more variables (see Section 9.4.2.3) without any planned intervention.

Variables such as *age, gender, socio-economic status, manufacturing sector,* and so on are of great importance, especially to non-experimental research in the business and administrative sciences, and it is impossible to assign participants (see Section 5.2.1.2) who are already members of the various levels of such variables, to these randomly.

There are often many variables that **covary**, in other words, they occur together and mutually influence one another. It is therefore inappropriate to refer to a single independent variable influencing a single dependent variable (see Section 2.3).

FOR EXAMPLE When we examine the influence of a variable such as *home language* (independent variable) on the *understanding* (dependent variable) of work instructions being communicated in English only, the culture of the units of analysis (see Section 4.2) may also influence the understanding of the work instruction. This variable *culture* thus covaries as an independent variable.

ACTIVITY 5.5

Read Case Studies A, D, E, and F in Appendix D on page 306.

QUESTION

Does the investigation in each case study involve an experimental research design or a survey research design? Give brief reasons for your answer.

ANSWER

case study a

The investigation involves a *survey research design* because it investigates the existence of a relationship between the variables. The influence (causality) of one variable on another (effect) which is typical of experimental research is not investigated.

case study d

The investigation involves a *survey research design* because it investigates the existence of a relationship between the variables; the influence (causality) of one variable on another (result) which is typical of experimental research is not investigated.

case study e

The investigation involves a *survey research design* rather than an experimental research design because the participants in the study are not randomly assigned to the groups bankrupt/non-bankrupt. Furthermore, a group of small business owners was not told to exceed their bank overdraft limits and purposefully given a lot of cash flow problems in order to see what the effect would be – such manipulations are typical of experimental research.

case study f

The investigation involves a *generic survey research design* rather than experimental research. The study investigates only whether a difference already exists in the innovative problem-solving styles of entrepreneurs and managers. The participants in the study were not randomly assigned with regard to being an entrepreneur or a manager in order to see what the effect on their innovative problem-solving styles would be. In other words, the researcher did not manipulate a variable to see the effects of such a change (an intervention). Such manipulations are typical of experimental research to determine the influence of one variable on another (called causality).

5.4.2 Non-experimental research designs involving measurements at a single time

There are three non-experimental research designs which involve measurements at a **single time**, namely the correlational design, the criterion-groups design, and the cross-sectional design.

5.4.2.1 CORRELATIONAL DESIGN

In the simplest non-experimental design, namely the **correlational design**, a single group of units of analysis (see Section 4.2) is obtained preferably randomly (see Section 4.3.2). Each individual is measured on two or more variables (see Section 2.3) at more or less the same time. The relationship (correlations) between these variables is then analysed (see Section 9.4.2.3).

FOR EXAMPLE In Research Example III (page 93) the violence ratings (done by independent raters) of prisoners' favourite television programmes were correlated with ratings of their aggressiveness by fellow prisoners. This study thus concerns the relationship between two variables (see Section 2.3) in a single population (see Section 4.2).

NOTE: The fact that this type of research design is called *correlational* does not indicate that only correlational techniques are used to analyse the data – other statistical techniques can also be used for the analysis.

5.4.2.2 THE CRITERION-GROUPS DESIGN

In the **criterion-groups design**, samples (the criterion groups) are drawn randomly (see Section 4.3.2) from the populations representing the different levels of the independent variable (see Section 2.3). This variable therefore qualifies as a classification factor. The intention is to investigate whether these groups differ in terms of the dependent variable.

NOTE: Both the correlational (see Section 5.4.2.1) and the criterion-groups designs concern the correlational relationship between variables.

FOR EXAMPLE When we use the correlational design (see Section 5.4.2.1), we may draw a random sample of individuals who have been found guilty of shoplifting, then record each person's gender as well as his or her highest educational qualification, and examine the relationship between these two variables.

We could investigate the same problem in a criterion-groups design by first drawing a random sample of men and a random sample of women from the population of shoplifters and by recording each person's highest educational qualification. If we found that women have, on average (see Section 9.4.2.2), a higher qualification than men, this finding would boil down to a relationship between the variables *gender* and *educational qualification of shoplifters*.

5.4.2.3 CROSS-SECTIONAL DESIGN

The **cross-sectional design** is a special case of the criterion-groups design. In the cross-sectional design the criterion groups typically comprise different age groups (such as technikon, university or organisational year groups), known as **cohorts**. These cohorts are examined in terms of one or more variables (see Section 2.3) at approximately the same time.

FOR EXAMPLE To investigate age-related changes in racial prejudice, 18-, 21-, 24-, and 27-year olds may be measured in terms of this phenomenon at about the same time.

The problem with this type of analysis, however, is that the participants may differ in terms of other variables apart from age, which may have a greater relationship with the variable *racial prejudice*. For example, we do not have any guarantee that the racial prejudice of the present 18-year-old group was comparable three years ago (at the age of 15) with that of the present 15-year olds, or that in three years' time (when they will be 21) they will correspond with the present 21-year olds.

Furthermore, apart from various threats to internal validity, for instance history in the present example (see Section 6.2.3.1), any one of the groups may possibly not be sufficiently representative (see Section 4.3) of its age group.

5.4.3 Longitudinal designs

A **longitudinal design** may be used instead of a cross-sectional design. This design involves examining the **same group at different time intervals**.

FOR EXAMPLE To investigate the above-mentioned problem longitudinally, the racial prejudice of the same group will have to be measured at the ages of 15, 18, 21 and 24 (that is, up to nine years after the initial measurement).

A longitudinal design is relevant when we want to investigate changes due to the passage of time. This time period may extend from weeks to years, and the accompanying events (such as the screening of television programmes) thus represent the independent variable (see Section 2.3).

FOR EXAMPLE Suppose we want to investigate how the attitudes (see Section 7.7.3.3) of whites towards the ANC have changed from 1985 to 2005 (that is, before and after the organisation came to power in South Africa). In this case a longitudinal design is the appropriate design to use. If we want to investigate how the attitudes of parents to Outcomes-Based Education have changed every five years since the implementation stage, a longitudinal design would also be appropriate.

Typically, the dependent variable (see Section 2.3) involves the attitudes towards some or other topic but it could be any other subject variable such as values, products, promotional methods, and so on. For example, Research Example IV deals with a longitudinal investigation of the influence of the introduction of television in South Africa on the aggressiveness of teenagers.

One disadvantage of longitudinal designs is that they are time-consuming and expensive undertakings. We may distinguish between at least three types of longitudinal designs (see Figure 5.11):

▶ panel designs
▶ cohort designs
▶ trend designs.

5.4.3.1 PANEL DESIGNS

In a **panel design** a sample is drawn that is more or less **representative of the relevant population** (see Section 4.2). Measurements are then obtained at different points in time on one or more dependent variable(s) (see Section 2.3) for this sample (see Section 4.3).

FOR EHAMPLE In terms of our earlier example of the attitudes of whites to the ANC, we could have obtained the telephone numbers of a random sample (see Section 4.3.2) of white Free Staters and assessed their attitudes (see Section 7.7.3.3) towards the ANC in 1990, 1995, 2000, and 2005 telephonically (see Section 7.7.4).

The merit of such a panel design is that it may indicate whether different subgroups exhibit different changes over time.

FOR EHAMPLE A panel design would be able to bring to light whether the attitude of people from the rural areas towards the ANC has become more negative, whereas that of individuals living in urban areas has become more positive or remained constant. Stated statistically, it could investigate whether there was an interaction between subgroups and the passage of time. Other examples, such as an investigation into age-related changes in racial prejudice, may also be studied in this manner.

In a **cross-lagged panel design** two or more variables (see Section 2.3) are measured at **two or more different points in time** (for the same group of individuals). Such a design enables us to investigate whether one variable at one point in time relates to another variable at a later point in time. However, there are statistical problems in analysing the data obtained in such a design (Cook & Campbell, 1979).

5.4.3.2 COHORT DESIGNS

The basic difference between a cohort design and a panel design is that a **cohort design** does not involve a representative sample (see Section 4.3) from some or other population (such as members of a particular group). In a cohort design study, we use an intact group (see Section 5.2), such as the financial accountancy class that completed its studies in 1998 or the soldiers who began their military training at the Parachute Battalion at Tempe, Bloemfontein, in 1998. Such a group is then followed over several years and measured in respect of the same dependent variable(s) (see Section 2.3).

5.4.3.3 TREND DESIGNS

In a **trend design** we measure **different samples** (see Section 4.3) from the same population (such as the voters who were born in a particular year), rather than the same sample (compare panel studies and cohort studies) at different times (see Figure 5.11).

The trend design does not necessarily have to involve people and historical studies (see Sections 2.3.3.1 & 8.2) and it may utilise some or other documentary record as measure of the dependent variable (see Section 2.3).

FOR EXAMPLE:

- The number of registered business owners committing fraud (and trying to cheat the tax collection system) over different years (for example before, during, and after a new law to prevent fraud has been introduced) may serve as basis for a trend design.
- A content analysis (see Section 9.2) of editorials of newspapers may be examined with a view to determining whether any change in the form of evaluating the policies of the ANC has taken place over time, or whether the style of reporting on a certain issue, for example a business leader, or sports star has changed over time.
- Condom sales before, during, and after the public denouncement of AIDS is another example.

NOTE: In the above examples, archival research, longitudinal designs (see Section 5.4.3), and quasi-experimental designs (see Section 5.3) overlap.

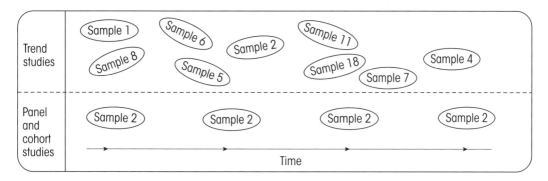

Figure 5.11 *Trend designs as opposed to panel and cohort designs*

ACTIVITY 5.6

Read the following problem statement and answer the question. Compare your answer with the given answer.

PROBLEM STATEMENT

A machine operator thinks that fumes emitted in the workshops play a role in the low efficiency of the operators. The operator would like to prove this to the supervisor through a scientific research study.

QUESTION

Would the study be a cross-sectional or a longitudinal design? Briefly explain your answer.

ANSWER

This is a *longitudinal design* (panel study), because the efficiency of the output of operators at a specific level (production level) is measured against/compared to the quantity/levels of the fumes measured. The measurement of this phenomenon (producing information/data) has to occur more than once to confirm its effect.

5.4.4 Prediction studies

In a **prediction study** we measure the units of analysis (see Section 4.2) in respect of one or more variables (see Section 2.3) at one point in time. These variables are usually called **predictor variables**. These units of analysis (people or organisations) are then measured (usually considerably) later in terms of another variable. The independent variables (see Section 2.3) are biographical, psychological, and other variables that apply to the units of analysis themselves at the initial point in time. A prediction study has a **time dimension** (like a longitudinal study), but different variables are measured at different points in time (usually only two).

NOTE: These variables are also known as **predictor variables** because they are intended to predict eventual behaviour (for example heart attacks or juvenile delinquency respectively) but it may also involve membership of different occupational groups or political parties or something similar. Eventually subjects are thus divided into different criterion groups (those with heart disease and those without it; those who have become delinquent and those who have not; or different occupational groups) (see Section 5.4.2.2). We then compare the groups on various variables which have been seen to be accurate predictors of the measure. For example, in comparing people of different occupation groups we might look at their level of education, social class, and so on.

There are two types of prediction studies, namely retrospective and prospective designs.

5.4.4.1 THE RETROSPECTIVE DESIGN

In a **retrospective design** we know to which criterion groups individuals belong. We therefore wish to determine in terms of which (possible) predictor variables they differed in the past.

The use of this design resulted from the observation that already existing criterion groups may have differed previously in terms of one or more variables which may be used as predictor variables (see Section 5.4.4) of current criterion status.

FOR EXAMPLE It may appear that a great proportion of juvenile delinquents (such as cellular phone thieves) come from broken homes. This observation may lead to the following hypothesis (see Section 2.4): a broken home background will be a contributory cause of juvenile delinquent behaviour.

In true experimental research (see Section 5.2.1), we examine the effect of the independent variable (see Section 2.3) on the dependent variable. Through random assignment we make two or more groups the same in terms of all the variables except for the independent variable (see Section 2.3); we then examine the dependent variable for possible differences.

As the supposed cause in the retrospective prediction design has taken place in the past, we have no control over it and cannot expose some individuals to it and prevent others from being exposed to it. Instead, we begin with the observation that two or more groups differ in terms of the dependent variable – for instance, one group is delinquent but not the other group. Consequently, we obtain samples (see Section 4.3) that represent the levels of the criterion variable and examine them with a view to determining whether they differ in terms of one or more variables in their past which may possibly have contributed to the present difference.

FOR EXAMPLE We may obtain:

- a sample of juvenile delinquents and
- a sample without any delinquent behaviour and determine whether there is a higher incidence of a broken home background in the sample of juvenile delinquents than in the sample without any delinquent behaviour.

The supposed predictor variable (*social status*) is a biographical variable and we may ascertain with a reasonable degree of certainty whether it has preceded delinquency or whether it has accompanied it.

NOTE: The main problem with the retrospective design is the same as for all non-experimental research, that is, the third-variable problem. We will discuss this problem in greater detail in Section 6.2.3.3.

The meaningfulness of the retrospective design and the conclusions that we may reach in terms of it thus depend to a large extent on our knowledge of possible nuisance variables (see Section 5.2.1.3) that are active in a particular field of study and whether they may be controlled by matching (see Section 6.2.8) or not.

EXAMPLE

Suppose social status is the main cause of juvenile delinquency, so that any sample of juvenile delinquents (such as cellular phone thieves) would tend to come from a lower socio-economic group than would a sample of non-delinquents.

If we measure variables such as the motivation to be respected in the eyes of one's friends rather than social status itself, the retrospective design may lead us to draw incorrect conclusions because we have overlooked the most important predictor variable.

Suppose we measure the motivation to earn the respect of one's friends for the two groups (delinquent and non-delinquent groups) and we find a significantly greater level of motivation for the delinquent group. Such a finding may lead us to conclude that a high motivation to earn the respect of one's friends contributes to juvenile delinquency, whereas, in fact, social status leads to both a high motivation to earn the respect of one's friends and juvenile delinquency.

On the other hand, suppose we suspect that social status rather than motivation to earn the respect of one's friends was the main cause of juvenile delinquency and decide to match subjects in terms of motivation to earn the respect of one's friends. For each person with a particular score (high or low) on motivation to earn the respect of one's friends in the group of delinquents we look for someone with the same score in the non-delinquent population for inclusion in the two groups, thus controlling the potential nuisance variable.

However, due to the correlation between social status and motivation to earn the respect of one's friends, we may end up with two groups with more or less the same social status, and thus fail to find a difference in this variable for the two groups.

5.4.4.2 THE PROSPECTIVE DESIGN

In a **prospective design** we initially measure units of analysis (see Section 4.2) in terms of the supposed predictor variables (see Section 5.4.4) and then establish their criterion-group membership **at a later point**. This design is used to investigate the extent to which the future position of research participants on one or more variables, known as the **criterion variables** (see Section 5.4.2.2), may be predicted on the basis of the participants' original score on one or more **predictor variable**(s).

Thus, we measure the scores of individual units of analysis on the presumed predictor variables and, some time later, we measure their scores on the criterion variable.

FOR EXAMPLE Suppose we test the attitudes (see Section 7.7.3.3) of all prisoners towards crime on their release from prison. After two years, we determine whether they have broken the law in the meantime (their criterion status). We could then correlate (see Section 9.4.2.3) their original attitude scores with their criterion status to determine whether the attitude tests satisfactorily predict who will return to criminal behaviour.

ACTIVITY 5.7

Read Case Study E in Appendix D on page 306.

QUESTION

Does the prediction study in Case Study E entail a retrospective or prospective design? Provide a brief reason for your answer.

ANSWER

Case Study E entails a *retrospective design* because it was already known to which criterion groups the small businesses belonged (bankrupt or non-bankrupt) at the start of the research. The researcher now wishes to determine in terms of which predictor variables (bank overdraft usage and cash flow problems) they differed in the past.

5.4.5 Opinion polls

In survey research (see Section 5.4.1) the proportions (or percentages) (see Figure 9.8) of a population falling into particular categories of some variable (see Section 2.3) are estimated on the basis of a sample drawn from the population (see Section 4.2). Typically, this variable relates to individuals' preference for various election candidates or for product brand names (such as Toyota, Volkswagen, and so on), or individuals' opinions, beliefs, and convictions regarding some topic (such as reinstating the death penalty). An **opinion poll** is thus one example of survey research and differs from hypothesis testing surveys (see Section 5.4.1) in that it does not involve testing a hypothesis. It is a record of what people feel about something, or what they believe to be true or false.

FOR EXAMPLE We could conduct a survey to determine the popularity of different political candidates prior to a general election. This may involve merely the estimation of the proportions (or percentages) of supporters of the various candidates.

However, a survey is not restricted to predicting the percentages (frequencies – see Section 9.4.2) of one variable in the various categories. It may also be directed at discovering the relationship between such preferences or opinions, beliefs, and attitudes (see Section 7.7.3.3) on the one hand, and certain biographical variables (for example *gender*, *age*, *race*, *marital status*, *income*, *educational qualification*, and *occupation*) on the other (see Section 9.4.2.3). Questions such as the following may be investigated:

▶ Do the majority of men support candidate *X* whereas the majority of women support candidate *Y*?

▶ Are there differences in the expectations about the future of South Africa between unemployed male and female South African voters?

In Research Example V we describe a survey of the opinions of various population groups about AIDS.

RESEARCH EXAMPLE V   **AN OPINION SURVEY ABOUT AIDS**

Between 13 and 16 May 1991, 54 interviewers conducted telephonic interviews (see Section 7.7.4) on behalf of the HSRC with 2 096 respondents. The samples (see Section 4.3) for whites, Asians, and coloureds were drawn countrywide from both rural and urban areas with the exclusion of the then TBVC states (Transkei, Boputhatswana,

➡

Venda, and Ciskei). The 919 blacks were drawn from the entire Republic of South Africa with the exception of Venda and Bophuthatswana.

At each residential telephone number one person was drawn randomly (see Section 4.3.2) from all persons of 18 years and older at that address. In the white residential areas the telephone numbers were drawn in such a manner that a geographically representative sample (see Section 4.3.2.3) could be obtained in terms of the 1985 census. As far as the other population groups were concerned, the samples were based on the estimated numbers of telephones per area.

Four questions were asked, concerning:
- whom the respondents regarded as responsible for the spreading of AIDS
- whether they regarded AIDS as a personal threat to their safety
- the use of precautionary measures
- the compulsory reporting of the incidence of AIDS to health authorities.

The results were as follows: whites and coloureds considered homosexual persons, blacks, and immoral persons, in this order, to be the most guilty of spreading AIDS; blacks followed by whites and people from the then TBVC blamed immoral persons for this phenomenon; of the Asians, 50% viewed blacks and 25% viewed immoral persons as responsible for this problem; whereas 3% of the blacks blamed their own population group for the spread of AIDS, less than 1% of the whites and the coloureds blamed their own group.

Altogether 51% of the respondents were of the opinion that they would not get AIDS. Among blacks, 70% in the age group 16 to 24 years and 42% of those older than 25 years indicated that they had decided to use precautionary measures against infection by AIDS. Ninety-four per cent of the whites and Asians, 88% of the coloureds, and 75% of the blacks favoured the compulsory reporting of AIDS cases to the health authorities.

5.4.5.1 CENSUS

We should distinguish between a survey and a census. Whereas a survey is conducted on samples (see Section 4.3), in a **census**, each member of the population is supposed to be included and to be classified in terms of certain biographical variables (for example *gender, employment status*).

The objective of a census is to determine the approximate number of people in the various categories of such variables for the entire population. A census focuses on questions that may vary from how many men and women there are in the population to the number of households that has no television set, one, or more than one television set.

We usually conduct a survey on a relatively small sample (see Section 4.3.5) from the total population, and it has certain advantages over a census:

▶ Firstly, it requires less time and financial expenses.

FOR EXAMPLE Even if we were to take only a few minutes per person, a telephonic interview (see Section 7.7.4) conducted on the entire population of voters would require so much time and money that it would simply be impossible.

▶ Secondly, we may obtain data (information) of a higher quality through surveys. Because surveys usually involve fewer participants, fewer interviewers are required and, as a result, they may be trained more efficiently and their effectiveness could be better controlled. Consequently, more accurate information may be collected.

▶ Thirdly, a survey may measure the state of affairs at a specific time so that the opinions of all respondents are comparable. A corresponding census, on the other hand, will typically have to be conducted over a longer period of time.

FOR EXAMPLE Suppose a research organisation wanted to investigate the attitude of South Africans towards reinstating the death penalty. It would be possible, at least theoretically, to complete a telephone survey within a week.

A census, on the other hand, would require at least several months. In the meantime, events such as a series of rape cases may influence opinions so that the information obtained at the final stages of the study may differ from that procured at the beginning. (The information obtained at the end may perhaps no longer reflect attitudes towards reinstating the death penalty only, but also attitudes towards the ensuing rapes.)

▶ Fourthly, a factor that promotes greater accuracy in the information obtained by surveys is the greater co-operation and frankness that may be obtained from people who are willing to respond. This is especially relevant in cases of questions about sensitive issues, such as opinions about other races or sexual practices.

SUMMARY

The design of a study concerns the plan to obtain appropriate data for investigating the research hypothesis and/or questions. Research can be conducted in laboratory and field settings. The category of quantitative research consists of three sub-categories, namely, experimental research, quasi-experimental research, and non-experimental research. In the simplest case, the experimental design, scores on one variable (for example salary – the independent variable) are used to measure and sometimes to predict scores on another variable (for example work productivity – the dependent variable) for one group of individuals (known as the experimental group). The control group does not receive the treatment (for example a rise in salary).

In the case of quasi-experimental research, random sampling is not used. There are two designs in this category – the non-equivalent control group design and the interrupted time-series design. Neither random assignment nor planned intervention occurs in non-experimental research. An example of this type of design is survey research. The correlational design, criterion-groups design, and cross-sectional design are examples of non-experimental research designs involving measurements at a single time.

Longitudinal designs involve measuring the same sample at different time intervals. In predictive studies, such as retrospective and prospective designs, the units of analysis are measured in respect of different variables and different points in time. Opinion polls are used to estimate the proportion of a population falling into certain categories of some variable and involve using a sample drawn from the population.

TEST YOURSELF

Question 1: Multiple-choice questions

Only one of the answers to each question is correct. Identify and mark the correct one. (Answers appear in Appendix A on page 299.)

1.1 Experiments are especially appropriate for research projects involving all of the following except:
   a) small-group interaction
   b) hypothesis testing
   c) descriptive research
   d) explanatory research.

1.2 For a causal relationship to exist, there must be evidence:
   a) of an empirical correlation between the variables
   b) that one variable precedes the other in time
   c) that a third variable did not cause the changes observed in the first two variables
   d) all of the above.

1.3 The 100 km/h speed limit for buses was introduced in South Africa in 1999. Shortly thereafter the number of bus accidents declined. We can conclude that:
   a) the reduced speed limit caused the decline in the number of bus accidents
   b) the reduced speed limit had nothing to do with the decline in bus accidents
   c) the reduced speed limit and the number of bus accidents are causally related
   d) the reduced speed limit may have caused the decline in bus accidents.

1.4 An advantage of field research is:
   a) it enables the researcher to draw conclusions about the population
   b) the researcher can control the variables under study
   c) the phenomenon can be studied in a natural setting
   d) hypotheses can be rigorously tested.

1.5 The 100 km/h speed limit for buses was introduced in South Africa in 1999. If this legislation was a result of years of investigations into the number of traffic fatalities on many of the major highways, it illustrates the use of:
   a) pretest-posttest one group design
   b) the interrupted time-series design
   c) the non-equivalent control group design
   d) the one-shot case study.

1.6 Let the assumption (hypothesis) be that one defective electrical transformer affected a second one which, in turn, affected a third, and so on. This caused a fire to break out. To analyse the data one should use:
   a) factor analysis
   b) time-series analysis
   c) two-way analysis of variance
   d) curvilinear regression analysis.

1.7 When one manipulates one or more independent variables in order to determine their effect in a natural situation, the procedure is called:
   a) naturalistic observation
   b) a field experiment
   c) controlled observation
   d) a structured experiment.

Question 2: True/false questions

Indicate whether the following statements are true (T) or false (F). (Answers appear in Appendix A on page 299.)

2.1 Turning 18 years old is a necessary cause (not sufficient cause) for voting in South Africa.

2.2 Ex post facto hypothesising refers to the development of hypotheses "predicting" relationships that have already been observed in the data.

Question 3: Self-evaluation questions

(Some answers appear in Appendix A on page 299.)

3.1 A researcher sent false application forms of (fictitious) prospective students who differed in terms of gender, race, and ability to 12 randomly assigned groups of 20 universities. (Some "applicants" were male, white, and highly intelligent, other "applicants" were female, white, and highly intelligent, and so on). If an application was accepted with encouragement, it was scored 5; if it was merely accepted, it was scored 4; and so on. Those who were unsuccessful obtained a score of 1.

Identify (a) the type of research and (b) indicate whether it was a laboratory or a field study.

3.2 Suppose a researcher wants to investigate the effectiveness of a programme designed to increase the assertiveness of first-year students. All these students complete an assertiveness test at the beginning of the year. Those who appear to be in the greatest need of this programme are enrolled in it. At the end of the semester their assertiveness is measured again.

Identify (a) the type of research and (b) the design that is used here.

3.3 In 1981 the film *Death of a student* in which a 19-year-old student jumped in front of an oncoming train, was shown on a German television channel. In the two-month period after the film was shown, three times as many young adults committed suicide in this manner than before 1981. In terms of which quasi-experimental design were these data (the number of suicides before 1981 and in the two-month period following the show) collected?

3.4 Which quasi-experimental design would you recommend to investigate whether the lack of illegal immigrant influx control led to an increase in burglaries in urban areas in South Africa?

3.5 Zweigenhaft (1970) studied the relationship between the size of library users' signatures on the lending cards and their status (students and professors). He came to the conclusion that the higher the users rate their status, the bigger their signatures tend to be.

Identify (a) the type of research and (b) the research design involved in this example.

3.6 Explain the difference between a panel design, cohort design, and trend design by describing how you would use these different designs to investigate the attitudes of young white adults towards the attitudinal object "the new South Africa" during 2005.

3.7 Explain the difference between retrospective and prospective designs by describing how you would use these two designs to investigate the role of family conditions during childhood in the development of drug dependency.

3.8 Does the longitudinal study in Research Example IV (see Section 5.4.3, page 96) qualify as a panel design, a cohort design, or a trend design?

Validity of conclusions

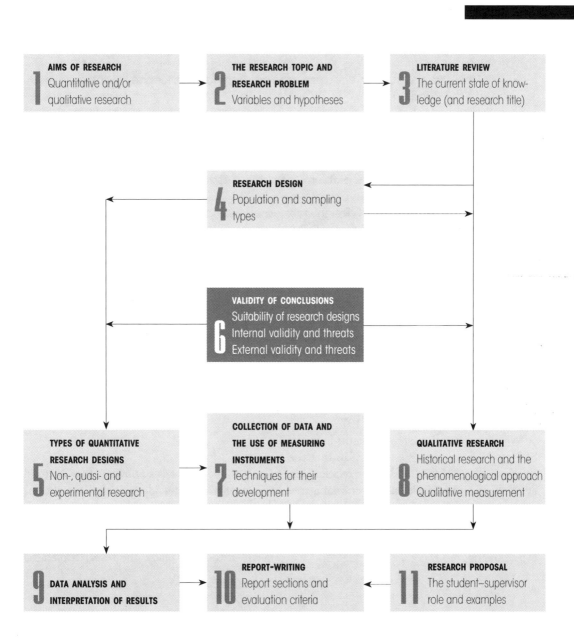

LEARNING OUTCOMES

In this chapter we look at the concept of validity. This concept is crucial to the integrity of a research project and the conclusions that can be drawn from it. We can distinguish between two types of validity, namely internal and external. The presence and influence of third variables play a role with regards to internal validity. Depending on the type of research design that was selected for a specific project, these variables can constitute a potential threat. It is therefore important to consider these issues when deciding on a specific research design.

After studying this chapter, you will be able to:
- illustrate the control of variables
- distinguish independent variables from intervening, moderating, nuisance, and third variables
- identify the third variables in a research project that could influence the internal validity of the conclusions
- evaluate the effect of a sample used in research on the external validity of the study
- identify whether the conclusions of a research study are ecologically valid
- explain how the following factors may threaten the internal validity of a research design and means of preventing it: history, spontaneous change, development and maturation, the third-variable problem, the subject effect, the experimenter effect, pretest sensitisation, selection of groups
- show how true experimental designs take care of the above internal validity problems as well as the threats to external validity.

6.1 Introduction

We test research hypotheses (see Section 2.4) to help us decide whether or not a specific implication inferred from a theory is tenable, or to provide an answer to a research question. To have confidence in these conclusions, they have to meet several requirements. In this chapter, we briefly define these requirements in terms of Cook and Campbell (1979).

We can explain these requirements in terms of Figure 2.3 on page 30; they mean that the conclusion we reached about the relationship symbolised by the dark one-directional arrow at the bottom of the figure should be a true reflection of the relationship represented by the dark one-directional dotted arrow at the top of the figure.

FOR EXAMPLE In Research Example II (see Section 2.3, page 17), a greater number of reactions such as finger pointing, or utterances such as "I will kick you" or "I will punch you", were observed among the group of trainee supervisors who had observed the corresponding behaviour by a supervisor.

The conclusion that iron-fisted role model management style behaviour leads to more iron-fisted management style behaviour among trainee supervisors should be warranted.

A requirement that is so obvious that we tend to accept it as self-evident, is that the chosen design should be able to answer the research question (see Section 2.3) and thus serve the purpose for which the research was undertaken in the first place. The research plan, as represented in the circle at the top right-hand side of Figure 2.1 (see Section 2.2.), must eventually provide feedback in connection with the formulated research hypothesis that is represented by the circle at the top left-hand side. For example, if we wish to investigate whether attitudes have changed over the course of time, a design that selects data at only one point in time would be inappropriate. The concept of validity is of central importance here.

6.2 Internal validity and threats

6.2.1 Defining internal validity

If a relationship between the independent and the dependent variables exists, the question arises as to whether this relationship may be interpreted as being of a **causal nature** (see Section 5.2.2). As we have seen (see Section 5.2), the purpose of experimental research is to identify causal relationships, that is, to determine whether one or more independent variables are responsible for changes in the dependent variable. When we wish to investigate the effect of an independent variable on the dependent variable, there is usually a host of other factors, apart from the independent variable under study, which may bring about changes in the dependent variable and which therefore may adversely affect internal validity. The term **internal validity** describes the degree to which changes in the dependent variable are indeed due to the independent variable rather than to something else. Therefore, the conclusion that changes in Y, the dependent variable as measured, may be attributed to X, the independent variable as operationalised, is internally valid to the extent that Y may unequivocally be attributed to X rather than to Q, R or S.

FOR EXAMPLE In Research Example II (see Section 2.3, page 17), the researcher wished to ascribe the ways in which trainee supervisors managed the subordinate,

Bobo, to the role model's (supervisor) management style that they had observed. However, if another researcher found support for the rival hypothesis (see Section 2.4), namely that the management style in the experimental group (trainee supervisors) was due to something other than exposure to the role model's particular style in managing the subordinate, the internal validity of the original conclusion would be questioned.

Internal validity is therefore of critical importance in the case of experimental research (see Section 5.2). The distinguishing feature of experimental research designs stems from its objective to promote internal validity.

To meet the *ceteris paribus* principle (see Sections 5.2.2 & 5.3) and thus to promote internal validity, it is necessary to eliminate all possible threats to internal validity. If we allow the threats to operate unchecked, we cannot unequivocally interpret observed changes in the dependent variable as the effect of the independent variable, and this will render the internal validity of our conclusions suspect. Should we succeed in controlling these threats and should the groups still differ in respect of the dependent variable, we may attribute this difference with greater confidence to the independent variable than to any other factors.

The minimum requirement for internal validity regarding experimental research designs is some basis of comparison. This may be obtained by using:
- at least two groups that are
- equal in respect of both the dependent variable and all nuisance variables.

There are two ways in which such a basis for comparison can be created, namely:
- by **randomly assigning** participants to two or more groups
- by **matching participants** in respect of the relevant nuisance variables and randomly assigning the members of each matched pair or trio, and so on (see Section 4.3.2) to the groups.

To the extent that such a basis of comparison has been created, we can maintain with greater certainty that differences in the dependent variable may be attributed to the independent variable rather than to any nuisance variables. Internal validity does not depend on whether or not the experimental intervention has indeed had an effect, but on our ability to draw a conclusion as to whether or not the experimental intervention caused the effect. In the absence of a group that was not exposed to the intervention (control group – see Section 5.2), it is usually impossible to make such a conclusion with a reasonable degree of certainty.

NOTE: In terms of Figure 2.3 on page 30, the requirement of internal validity means that the two squares (boxes) at the bottom left-hand side should provide a complete explanation for the two squares (boxes) to the right.

6.2.2 Pre-experimental designs

In terms of the way in which we decide which of the participants should be subjected to which intervention, we may distinguish between:
▶ pre-experimental
▶ true experimental (see Section 5.2)
▶ quasi-experimental (see Section 5.3) research designs.

Pre-experimental designs indeed include an experimental intervention, but do not meet one or more of the requirements mentioned above. There are two types of pre-experimental designs, namely the one-shot case study and the premeasurement and postmeasurement single-group design.

In the **one-shot case study** a single group is subjected to an experimental intervention (see Section 5.2) and is subsequently measured on the dependent variable.

FOR EXAMPLE Suppose Researcher A arranges for a group of trainee supervisors to be exposed to the iron-fisted role model management style reaction towards a subordinate's behaviour (as was done to the experimental group in Research Example II). Using the one-shot case study, the management style of the trainees' reaction towards the same subordinate behaviour will therefore be observed afterwards.

A **premeasurement and postmeasurement single-group design** (see Section 5.2) involves measuring a sample on a specific characteristic, applying an intervention, and then measuring the sample for the same characteristic.

FOR EXAMPLE In conducting a study similar to that of Research Example II, suppose Researcher B firstly obtains one or other measurement of the management style of a group of trainee supervisors, exposes them to the iron-fisted role model management style behaviour towards the subordinate, and then measures their management style again. Here we are dealing with a premeasurement and postmeasurement single-group design (see Section 5.2).

It differs from the one-shot case study in that the dependent variable is measured **both before and after** the experimental intervention. The objective is therefore to ascribe differences between the pre- and postmeasurements to the experimental intervention.

Both these pre-experimental designs are characterised by a single sample (see Section 4.3) of participants who are exposed to some or other treatment or experimental intervention (to which they would not have been subjected in the normal course of events). Although they involve some form of experimental intervention, these designs do not qualify as true experimental designs because they do not provide a sufficient basis of comparison for us to unambiguously ascribe changes in the dependent variable to the independent variable. If such change is observed, we cannot determine whether it would have occurred in any case, that is, without the experimental intervention.

The internal validity of the conclusions reached by means of the two single-group designs may be extremely suspect because it tends to be compromised by factors beyond the researcher's control. These factors (for example history and spontaneous change) will be discussed in the next section.

6.2.3 **Factors beyond the researcher's control**

Factors which are beyond the researcher's control include the following:
- history
- spontaneous change
- other third-variable problems.

History and *spontaneous change* are **third variables**, which the researcher may eliminate statistically in order to have control over them. It may also be more appropriate to say that in experimental research rival explanations take the form of history or spontaneous change.

6.2.3.1 **HISTORY**

The threat of **history** refers to events that take place *concurrently* with the experimental intervention and that may also affect the dependent variable. This threat is particularly relevant to studies that take place over a **long period of time**. Usually participants are not under the direct control or supervision of the researcher for 24 hours per day. Consequently, there is a possibility that participants may be affected by events apart from the independent variable in which the researcher is interested, and which take place at the same time as his or her research. As a result, changes in the dependent variable cannot be attributed convincingly to the independent variable in question alone because the uncontrolled variables could also have played a role.

This type of threat is present in both the one-shot case study and the premeasurement and postmeasurement single-group design and we can illustrate the effect by using the examples from Section 6.2.2 (also compare Research Example II, page 17).

FOR EXAMPLE Suppose there was a general power failure during the hours immediately preceding the researcher's intervention, so that none of the trainee supervisors had anything hot for breakfast that morning, causing them to be frustrated. The iron-fisted management style behaviour of the trainees of both researchers A and B could thus not be attributed exclusively to the researcher's intervention (the screening of the role model's management style on video).

The rival hypothesis may be that the iron-fisted management style behaviour was caused by the interruption in their eating habits which made them irritable, rather than the researcher's intervention. The threat of history therefore compromises the validity of the research conclusions.

NOTE: A **rival hypothesis** refers to a research hypothesis that is different from the research hypothesis under investigation (see Section 2.4) and to a different possible answer to the research problem that will have to be investigated in another study (research project). This means that the rival hypothesis refers to an independent variable different from that of the research hypothesis under investigation.

FOR EXAMPLE If our research hypothesis refers to the influence of a type of cure for AIDS, the rival hypothesis will state that it is something totally different (that may have been regarded as a third variable in the first-mentioned study) that may cure AIDS.

6.2.3.2 **SPONTANEOUS CHANGE (DEVELOPMENT, MATURATION, RECOVERY OR DETERIORATION)**

Spontaneous change refers to factors such as development, deterioration, maturation or recovery and the influence of these aspects on research results can be illustrated in the following examples:

EXAMPLE

If researchers A and B in the above example observed aggressive responses among the trainee supervisors, we cannot ignore the possibility that such responses would have occurred in any case at that stage of **development** (e.g. their personalities could have become more aggressive as a result of stressful situations). Since changes may take place within relatively short periods of time among mine workers who are exposed to hazardous working conditions upon which they must act quickly, the possibility of spontaneous development (specifically, **deterioration** of their control of frustration in this instance) should be borne in mind with the trainee supervisors. As far as **maturation** is concerned, the subjects could also have learned to become more aggressive over time or they could have become older and, as a result of ageing, more aggressive. **Recovery** occurs when subjects in a medical experiment, for example, recover spontaneously and not as a result of any medical intervention.

The likelihood that this threat to internal validity may play a role increases as the duration of the experimental intervention lengthens.

The problem with one-shot case study and premeasurement and postmeasurement single-group designs is that they lack a basis of **comparison**. In other words, if we observe a change in the dependent variable, these designs provide no way for us to know whether it would not have occurred in any case, in other words, without intervention (non-equivalent control group design – see Section 5.3). However, even though we may use a control group to draw a conclusion with a reasonable degree of certainty, our conclusion may still be susceptible because spontaneous change may also occur in the control group as in the experimental group (non-equivalent control group design – see Section 5.3.1).

FOR EXAMPLE Suppose, in a non-equivalent control group design (see Section 5.3.1), full-time students, unlike distance education students, tend to start studying in earnest only after the first test. In such an instance, we could not ascribe a greater increase in the academic performance of the full-time students only to the intervention to which they have been exposed; we would also ascribe it to the spontaneous development that was present in this group only.

6.2.3.3 OTHER THIRD-VARIABLE PROBLEMS

The problems which we discuss in this section all relate to the third variable problem. As these occur in all research designs, it is of major importance that they are recognised.

In Sections 5.2.1.3 and 5.2.2.3 we mentioned the **multivariate nature of human behavioural research**. There are seldom only a few independent variables that we can identify as causal factors (see Sections 2.3.1 & 5.2.2). Instead, there is usually a vast array of independent variables that mutually influence and overlap each other. There is always the possibility that a strong relationship (high correlation – Sections 2.3.1 & 9.3.1) between two variables may be explained by a third variable that relates strongly to the other two (both are highly correlated). We might direct our attention to the relationship between X and Y while, without our knowledge, variable Z is the real source of variation of both X and Y. This possibility is referred to as the **third-variable problem** (see Sections 2.3.1 & 5.2.2).

In **true experimental research** we can **eliminate** the problem of nuisance variables by holding all variables constant except the one whose effect we are examining. However, there are many research problems in the human behavioural sciences that cannot be investigated by means of such experimental research. In non-experimental research it is almost impossible to exercise control over variables in these disciplines as we can in experimental research. The "effect" of the socio-economic status of parents on the academic achievement of their children; the socio-economic "effects" of the repeal of influx control locally; and the "causes" of juvenile delinquency can hardly be investigated in true experiments, to mention but a few examples. To complicate matters, we are unable to keep all irrelevant variables constant (for example, by randomly assigning participants to the levels of the independent variable under study – see Section 5.2) as is possible in experiments.

EXAMPLE

The following research conducted by Gerbner and Gross (1976) illustrates these complexities very clearly. Television viewers observe more murders on television in one week than they or their entire family and circle of friends are likely to witness in their combined lifetimes. With this in mind, Gerbner and Gross (1976) interviewed people about their television-viewing habits with regard to how safe they felt and how likely they thought it would be for them to become victims of violence. They found that individuals who watched television for more than four hours per day were more distrustful than others, and that these individuals rated their chances of becoming involved in some or other kind of violent incident greater than those who watched television for two hours or less per day. On the basis of these findings, Gerbner and Gross came to the conclusion that watching television leads to fear of victimisation.

On the surface this research seems fair. However, there are a few complications:

Firstly, and understandably, **these authors did not perform experimental research**. They did not randomly assign people to groups that were forced to watch television for a specified number of hours with a view to determining whether the more frequent viewers experienced more fear than the less frequent viewers.

Secondly, it was **impossible to equate participants on all variables**, except for the number of hours of television-viewing, with a view to investigating whether the number of hours of television-viewing was a cause of the fear of victimisation. Participants had already watched television for a certain number of hours prior to the start of the research. Consequently, the research findings could not be interpreted as showing unequivocally that frequent television-viewing caused fear of being victimised.

Thirdly, a **third variable** could have influenced the research results. Previous research had suggested an (inverse) relationship between the number of hours of television-viewing and socio-economic status; therefore, people in the lower socio-economic groups tended to watch television more often than did those in the higher levels of this variable. Thus, the variable *socio-economic status* may act as a third variable.

Fourthly, there could be **more than one third variable** in operation and, furthermore, the **third variables could interact**. Evidence suggests that the lower a person's socio-economic status, the more likely it is that he or she will be residing in an area with a high incidence of crime. Thus, the variable *residential area* may also act as a third variable and in combination with the variable *socio-economic status*. These research findings suggest the possibility that the most frequent television viewers have an increased fear of possible victimisation because they reside in high-crime areas. These considerations thus possibly bestow on viewers' *residential area* the status of a third variable in the relationship between *watching television* and *fear of victimisation*.

Further research on this topic was conducted by Doob and MacDonald (1979) in Canada. They identified the 10 police patrol areas (out of 210) in Toronto, Canada, with the highest number of reported assaults and the 14 with the lowest number of such reports. Within each designated area they selected two geographic areas of approximately the same size. They visited altogether 204 households within each of these regions and selected one person from each household to respond to questions on his or her television-viewing habits and his or her perceived chances of becoming a victim of violence.

Similar to Gerbner and Gross, Doob and MacDonald found that the more frequently individuals watched television, the more they tended to fear for their own safety. However, the people in the high-crime areas were also the most frequent television viewers.

Once the effect of the residential area had been controlled (by investigating separately the relationship for the two different socio-economic areas), they found no relationship between the *number of hours of watching television* and *fear of crime*.

Consequently, it could not have been watching television in itself that led to an increased fear of victimisation because, if that were the case, this relationship would have been present in both areas. The area in which individuals resided determined both their television-viewing habits and their fear of victimisation. Those residing in high-crime areas were the most frequent television viewers (because it was safer to watch television than to venture out on the streets) and they were also the most fearful (due to the reality of crime around them).

As a result we can therefore state that the relationship observed between *watching television* and *fear* is an incorrect one because it is explained by these variables' separate relationships with a third variable, namely *socio-economic position of residential area*.

Doob and MacDonald (1979) investigated the relationship between *watching television* and *fear* by holding constant the residential area (the so-called third variable). They did this by examining the relationship between *watching television* and *fear* within the respective levels of the variable *residential area*, separately. In this manner a distinction is made between two rival explanations, namely that watching television promotes fear and that the socio-economic standing of a residential area influences both television-watching behaviour and fear.

6.2.3.4 EXPERIMENTAL RESEARCH, NON-EXPERIMENTAL RESEARCH, AND INTERNAL VALIDITY

In general, the conclusions reached by means of non-experimental research tend to be *less internally valid* than those which are based on experimental and quasi-experimental research. On some occasions it is indeed possible to investigate a problem both experimentally and non-experimentally. More or less the same problem that was researched experimentally in Research Example II (see Section 2.3, page 17) was approached non-experimentally in Research Example III (see Section 5.4, page 93). Instead of exposing one group of trainee supervisors to aggressive behaviour shown by the supervisor (model) but not the other, the level of violence of the prisoners' favourite television programmes was correlated with the prisoners' aggressiveness in Research Example III.

However, as we mentioned earlier, research in the human behavioural sciences is complex and true experimental research is not always possible. Consider the issue of the socio-economic status of parents as the cause of juvenile delinquency (retrospective designs – see Section 5.4.4). It is simply impossible to implement socio-economic status as a treatment factor (which implies that individuals are randomly assigned to the various levels of the independent variable), because participants already belong to some or other socio-economic grouping and cannot be randomly assigned to it.

If we do draw a random sample from each of the populations representing the respective levels of the independent variable, the latter is called a **classification factor** (criterion-groups design – see Section 5.4.2.2). By this we mean that the subjects already belong to the various levels of the independent variable prior to the research.

FOR EXAMPLE Suppose we draw three random samples of adolescents, one each from the population of adolescents whose parents have a high, medium, and low socio-economic status. In this case, *socio-economic status* then qualifies as a classification factor.

As soon as we cannot randomly assign subjects to the levels of the independent variable (and thus equate them in terms of all other variables), they may possibly differ in respect of one or more variables other than the independent variable of interest. In such a case we say the participants are **self-selected** in respect of several other known and unknown variables.

In the present example, such variables may have a greater effect than *socio-economic status* on the incidence of juvenile delinquency (criminal acts committed by adolescents).

Even if we found that there is a bigger proportion of juvenile delinquents in the low socio-economic group than in the other groups, it would be risky to identify socio-economic status as the cause of juvenile delinquency. It may be possible that the adolescents from the lower socio-economic level come predominantly from families in which the father is absent. The fathers' absence is then the principal cause that is related to both the socio-economic status of the parents and the incidence of juvenile delinquency among their children. Thus, it may be that the absent father is the main cause of the incidence of juvenile delinquency.

NOTE: In the above example we could have incorrectly directed the spotlight to the relationship between two variables, while the real "action" was taking place outside

the spotlight. In other words, the *ceteris paribus* principle (see Sections 5.2.2, 5.3 & 6.1) is not met.

Although experimental research may thus be better equipped for isolating causal relationships, properly designed non-experimental studies and judiciously chosen multivariate statistical analyses (see Section 9.4) may go a long way to extending our knowledge about multivariate relationships, both correlational and causal.

However, we require a sound knowledge of the following:

▶ Firstly, which variables are relevant in a particular research area so that we can take these variables into consideration when planning research.

▶ Secondly, the necessary multivariate statistical methodology: Doob and MacDonald's (1979) research is a striking demonstration of the importance of knowledge of variables in a particular field for ruling out rival hypotheses. By eliminating rival hypotheses that state that third or fourth variables explain the relationships between the variables of concern (the independent and dependent variables), confidence in our knowledge of the relationships among variables grows.

ACTIVITY 6.1

Read the following problem statement and answer the questions. Compare your answers with those given.

PROBLEM STATEMENT

The manager of TABOK Company observes that the morale of the employees in the company is low. She thinks that if the working conditions, pay scales, and leave benefits of the employees are improved, their morale will also improve. She doubts, however, that increasing the pay scales is going to raise the morale of all employees. Her guess is that those who have good side incomes (by doing other work in their own time) will not be motivated by higher pay.

QUESTION

List the variables and label the third variable. Give brief reasons for your answers.

ANSWER

The variables are: *working conditions, pay scale, leave benefits,* and *morale.* The third variable is *side incomes,* because this variable interferes with the relationship between *pay* and *morale.* If working conditions, pay scales, and leave benefits are high in a work situation, then the employees' morale is high. However, more pay does not result in higher morale of all employees – only of those who do not have a good side income.

ACTIVITY 6.2

Read Case Studies A, B, C, D, and E in Appendix D on page 306.

QUESTION

Compile a list of the three most important variables in each case study and identify whether it is a so-called dependent, independent or third variable (for Case Studies A, B, C, and E). Provide brief reasons for your answer and explain the relationship(s) between the variables.

ANSWER

case study a

The independent variable is *knowledge of AIDS,* the dependent variable is *attitude towards AIDS,* and the third variable is *attitude towards prostitution.*

This is because, according to the introduction, previous research has suggested that effective education about AIDS (that is, an increased knowledge of AIDS) is sufficient to remove prejudices against AIDS sufferers (that is, to achieve a change in attitude towards AIDS). Further research indicates, however, that an attitude towards certain spreaders of AIDS, such as prostitutes, may also influence the attitude towards AIDS – not just the knowledge of AIDS.

For example: suppose a doctor acquires more knowledge of AIDS (such as how it can be spread from one person to another by blood transfusions). We could expect the doctor's increased knowledge (influence of the independent variable) to make him or her more positive and sympathetic towards AIDS sufferers (as an expression of a more positive attitude towards AIDS – this is the effect or consequence on the dependent variable) when handling or treating such patients. However, because this doctor has an antipathy to prostitution (prostitutes are often spreaders of AIDS, causing the doctor to have a negative attitude towards prostitution), his or her attitude towards AIDS cases in general (whether related to prostitution or not) may be negative (influence of the third variable), and he or she will deal with such patients less sensitively.

case study b

The independent variable is *role induction,* the dependent variable is *attitude towards supervision,* and the third variable is *supervision of time.*

The researchers hope that the attitude of the people in the sample towards supervision will become positive, in other words, that their perception of the supervision procedure will change positively (this is the variable whose change depends on the influence of the independent variable). This would be as a result of the participation of the 20 sample members in the role induction procedure, that is, being informed by means of a videotape about the supervision process (the independent variable that the researcher can manipulate, for example, by allowing the sample members to view the videotape once, twice, or more often, thereby altering the level of the independent variable). But the supervision process itself surely has an influence over time on the attitudes of the 20 sample members towards supervision (that is, the third variable also influences the dependent variable).

case study c

The independent variable is *training course,* the dependent variable is *knowledge of management principles,* and the third variable is *learned negative supervisory behaviour.*

The researcher hopes that the knowledge of management principles of first-line supervisors (in the experimental group) who attended the training course will increase significantly. The increase or decrease in knowledge of management principles is thus dependent on the attendance or non-attendance of the training course. Despite this, it is possible that already learned negative supervisory behaviour may cause those who attend the course to distort or even reject the knowledge that they may acquire during the training.

case study d

The independent variable is *speech preparation time*, the dependent variable is *speech quality*, and the third variable is *speech anxiety*.

case study e

There are, in fact, two independent variables (predictor variables) involved, namely *bank overdraft usage* and *cash flow problems*. The dependent variable is *bankruptcy status*, and the third variable is *management skills*.

Seriously exceeding the bank overdraft limit combined with cash flow problems may have caused small businesses to become bankrupt. But as the reference to Levy (1998) in the introduction suggests, highly developed management skills such as co-ordination of enterprise functions may also influence bankruptcy status. Bankruptcy status is thus dependent on the bank overdraft usage and cash flow problems of the small businesses who participated in the research project.

6.2.4 Factors that influence the researcher's control

In human behavioural research the independent variable (see Section 2.3) is typically a construct (see Section 2.4) instead of a directly observable variable. To investigate the effect of such constructs, they have to be **operationalised** (see Section 2.4.2) in terms of observable variables. To operationalise a variable is to put it in measurable terms.

FOR EXAMPLE If we were to operationalise the variable *firm success*, we would use variables such as *turnover*, *profit*, and *market share*. When we consider ways in which to do this, we must bear the issue of the construct validity of the resulting variable in mind.

The **construct validity** of the operationalisation of an independent variable is the degree to which the procedures intended to produce the independent variable of interest indeed succeed in generating this variable rather than something else.

FOR EXAMPLE Suppose our research hypothesis states that anxiety causes a decrease in memory and we operationalise an anxiety-provoking situation by locking up an experimental group of fire fighters in a room where

smoke seeps in under the door. If the individuals in this group later remember fewer details, such as the colour of the walls and the contents of the paintings, than the control group (in a 'neutral' room), it provides provisional support for both the hypothesis being examined and for the construct validity of our operationalisation of anxiety-provoking conditions. If a measure of anxiety (for example a questionnaire) has a mean that is higher for the experimental group than for the control group, it may also support the construct validity of the operationalisation of the independent variable.

In addition, we require evidence that what we observed was not something other than was intended. It would be desirable to collect data suggesting that in the present example anxiety was provoked and not anger (for example towards the person who was held responsible for the locked door).

In practice we seldom investigate the construct validity in itself. Usually, we clearly describe the way in which such a variable has been operationalised and leave it to the reader to judge whether these operations have succeeded in bringing about the desired independent variable. Similar to the construct validity of the dependent variable (see Section 7.4.1), the eventual results provide feedback on both the tenability of the theory and the construct validity of the independent variable.

Christensen (1985) describes some ways in which the construct validity of the independent variable in itself may be checked. In this section we deal mainly with ways in which we can deal with known threats to construct validity, namely:

❱ the subject effect
❱ the experimenter effect
❱ pretest sensitisation.

6.2.4.1 THE SUBJECT EFFECT

Research in the human behavioural sciences differs radically from research in the natural sciences in that, for example, its object of study does not simply react passively to stimuli, but also **interprets them** and **attaches meaning to them**. Research participants therefore do not approach experimental situations as passive, neutral beings. The mere knowledge that they are guinea pigs in a research project may cause them to react differently than they would have done otherwise.

The reason why individuals participate in a research project may play a role in their subsequent behaviour in the experiment as well. These reasons include, for example, curiosity, the opportunity to earn extra pocket money, or being required to do so as part of a course.

We often use the term **reactivity of research** in this connection. This term refers to the fact that the participants are affected by some or other aspect of the research scenario apart from the treatment the effect of which is being investigated. This may be compared to the reaction of spectators at a rugby match who behave quite differently the moment a television camera is aimed at them. This phenomenon may cause the implemented version of the independent variable to differ from the one the researcher has in mind. It creates the possibility that any effect observed in the dependent variable may be attributed to the independent variable, while it actually reflects a subject or reactivity effect.

In medical research the subject effect is called the **placebo effect**. A placebo is a tablet, capsule or injection that looks exactly like the drug whose effectiveness is to be investigated, but which has no medicinal value. In such investigations it is frequently found that the subjects to whom the placebo is administered also show improvements in the ailment for which the experimental drug is intended.

A term which we can regard as synonymous with the subject effect is the **Hawthorne effect**. An experiment was conducted at the Hawthorne factory of the Western Electric Company to determine which changes in the working environment (adjustments in temperature, working hours, and so on) would increase productivity. Interestingly enough, all these changes led to such an increase. After due consideration, it was decided that it was not the changes themselves that were responsible for this increase, but the workers' awareness that they were participating in an experiment designed to increase their productivity.

Participants' belief in the efficacy of a programme may therefore cause them to show an improvement in the aspect which the programme is supposed to improve.

If the research participants are familiar with the research hypothesis (see Section 2.4), they may consciously or unconsciously act in such a manner that their behaviour facilitates the confirmation of the hypothesis. In this context, we often use the term **demand characteristics** to refer to the real or supposed clues that participants infer from the task that confronts them in an experiment and to which they react so as to portray themselves in a particular light.

FOR EXAMPLE If physically disabled (challenged) workers conclude that the purpose of an experiment is to raise their assertiveness and if this kind of behaviour is viewed favourably, they may act in such a manner that their behaviour will confirm the hypothesis.

Subjects often regard the researcher as an expert and they may tend to provide those responses which they suppose will reflect positively on them (for example regarding their job satisfaction or organisation commitment).

On the other hand, subjects may deliberately try to frustrate the researcher by sabotaging his or her research project. This may occur especially when workers, as part of their training course, are required to participate in a research project.

Just as the Hawthorne effect may arise in the experimental group, so the so-called **John Henry effect** may occur in the control group. The John Henry effect refers to the effect that appears when members of the control group, aware of the fact that their performance will eventually be compared with that of the experimental group, exert an extra effort and consequently perform better than expected. This phenomenon is named after John Henry, a drill driver who, in response to the proposed replacement of human labour by a steel drill in building the railroad in the United States in the nineteenth century, over-exerted himself and beat the machine – but with fatal consequences.

Whether it be the Hawthorne or the John Henry effect, we should see to it that, as far as possible, the demand characteristics are the same for both the experimental and control groups (see Section 5.2). This requires that the following conditions are met:

▶ Firstly, the control group should **match** the definition of such a group perfectly. In other words, the control group should differ from the experimental group only in that they receive a different level of the independent variable. In all other respects the two groups should be treated exactly the same. Suppose, for example, that we wish to investigate the effectiveness of a programme that is intended to improve the self-image of sexually harassed workers. Suppose we subject the experimental group to the programme but we do not pay any attention to the control group. Strictly speaking, the control group does not qualify as a control group, because it differs from the experimental group in

more respects than simply withholding the particular programme.

FOR EXAMPLE If the experimental group meets on a weekly basis to undergo the programme, the control group should also meet every week and be subjected to some control programme. It may very well be that merely attending any old programme, and not just that of the researcher, will have a beneficial effect.

▶ Secondly, an attempt should be made to **prevent** the members of either the experimental or the control groups *from knowing to which group they belong*. As soon as participants realise that they are members of either the experimental or the control group, there is the possibility that the subject effect, either the Hawthorne or the John Henry effect, may influence the results.

In medical studies the creation of a placebo to administer to the control group (while the experimental group receives the experimental treatment) usually does not present serious problems. In such studies it is therefore easy to prevent subjects from knowing whether they are members of the experimental or the control group.

However, in the human behavioural sciences the design of such a control treatment may require a great deal of ingenuity and creativity on the part of the researcher. When it is impossible to come up with such a control treatment, the control group should still not differ from the experimental group in terms of the impression that they are receiving a treatment designed to have a positive effect. The control group should not feel threatened by or consider themselves to be in competition with the experimental group, just as the experimental group should not be given the impression that they are something special.

Christensen (1985) discusses two additional ways in which we may attempt to counter the problem of the subject effect, namely deception and disguised experiments.

In the case of **deception**, all partici-pants are deliberately misled as far as the purpose of the study is concerned.

FOR EXAMPLE In Research Example VI (see below), participants were told that their personal problems as university students in an urban environment were to be discussed. In actual fact, their helping behaviour as a function of the supposed number of co-participants was investigated.

Christensen (1985) is of the opinion that it is apparently preferable to provide subjects with a false yet plausible hypothesis than to say nothing in this respect. If they are kept in the dark, participants may try to satisfy their curiosity by attempting to infer a hypothesis. Different participants may reach different conclusions, which could also create an unnecessary source of variation.

A **disguised experiment** is conducted in such a fashion that neither the experimental nor the control group is aware that they are participating in an experiment.

Research Example VI also qualifies as an example of this approach. The participants were not aware of the fact that they were participating in an experiment in which the experimenter varied the number of co-participants.

The ethical principle (see Section 7.9) that participants should preferably be in a position to refuse participation in an experiment, is naturally disregarded in a disguised experiment.

In view of the important effect that demand characteristics may have on the results of an experiment, and as a result of the difficulty of always anticipating them, it is frequently advisable to interview participants after an experiment. In such an interview, known as a **debriefing interview**, the participants are asked about what they regarded the objectives of the experiment to be and to what degree these have affected their behaviour. If the information gained in this manner suggests that demand characteristics may have affected the results, this should be taken into consideration when the results obtained are interpreted or new research about the particular problem is planned.

RESEARCH EXAMPLE VI A LABORATORY EXPERIMENT ON THE NUMBER OF BYSTANDERS AND HELPING BEHAVIOUR

Latané and Darley (1968) performed a series of laboratory and field experiments to investigate the conditions under which bystanders would help someone in distress.

In an example of a laboratory experiment, each research participant was seated in a cubicle at a table and provided with headphones and a microphone and asked to listen to the instructions.

All participants were led to believe that they were to discuss personal problems in a stressful urban environment. Furthermore, they were seated in the cubicles and would conduct the discussion over the intercom to prevent embarrassment and to maintain anonymity. Some were told that they were one of two such participants, others that they were one of three, and the rest that there were another five such participants.

The subjects were told (individually) that to prevent their being inhibited by the presence of an outsider, the experimenter would not listen in on their discussion but would obtain their reactions later by means of a questionnaire.

In reality there were no other participants, but the impression was created that they were there, by playing tape recordings of people expressing ideas on the topic (personal problems in an urban environment).

The order in which the subjects were given an opportunity to talk was determined mechanically in that their microphones were switched on one after the other for about two minutes to signal their respective turns. The "co-participant" who had his turn first said that he was prone to seizures. During his next turn, the impression was created that he was in need of assistance because he stuttered, indicated that he was in need of help, and then became quiet. The participant was actually listening to a tape recording of a previously simulated emergency. ➡

The dependent variable was the time between the point at which the "co-participant" became silent and the point at which the subject left his cubicle to report the emergency to the experimenter. The most important independent variable was the number of subjects which the (only real) participant was informed were participating in the discussion.

In the situations where the participant and the supposed victim were alone in the "group", 85% of the subjects reacted before the end of the "emergency". The corresponding percentages for the groups of two and five "other participants" were 62% and 31% respectively.

6.2.4.2 THE EXPERIMENTER EFFECT

The **experimenter effect** refers to the effect of the following on the obtained data:

▶ the researcher's **expectations** about the data to be collected
▶ certain of the researcher's **biographical attributes** (gender, culture, age, and so on).

If such effects are present, it means that the participants are not exposed to the independent variable as intended, but to the independent variable as administered by the experimenter.

The fact that subjects who participate in an experiment have particular expectations is true to an even greater extent of researchers. The researchers (experimenters) are not merely neutral, detached observers of the experimental situation because, as designers of the experimental intervention, they have vested interests in the eventual results.

It is not uncommon for researchers to become so involved in their research that their personal dignity is at stake. They are thus no longer concerned merely with the scientific ideal of the expansion of scientific knowledge as set out in Section 1.2.

The researcher's expectations may possibly play a role when:

▶ the independent variable is implemented
▶ the dependent variable is measured.

FOR EXAMPLE A researcher who has developed a programme to improve the self-image of sexually harassed workers would like to believe that it is a successful programme. If the researcher himself or herself adminis-

ters the programme, the thoroughness and enthusiasm with which this is done may possibly result in success, whereas if someone else implements it, it may make no difference.

Or else, the researcher's expectations may be conveyed to the participants in a way which influences the eventual results. The researcher's expectations then become part of the demand characteristics of the experimental situation.

At the end of the programme the subjects may present those responses that they surmise will satisfy the experimenter. In such a case, improvements in self-image would not be due to the effectiveness of the programme exclusively but also to the effect of both the experimenter and the research participant.

When the researcher acts as rater and assesses the dependent variable by means of ratings (see Section 7.7.3.4), he or she may unintentionally rate the experimental group higher than the control group.

Just as subjects ideally should be unaware of the group, that is, experimental or control, to which they belong, so the test administrator or the rater or coder of subjects' behaviour should not be informed about this aspect. In the so-called **double-blind experiment**, neither the subjects nor the researchers (or their assistants) administering the levels of the independent variable or measuring the dependent variable, are aware of the group membership (experimental or control) of any particular individual. It stands to reason that the possible effect of the experimenter's expectations should be recognised in advance and that the researcher's biographical features (such as gender) should be taken into account in an attempt to deal with the threat to construct validity.

6.2.4.3 PRETEST SENSITISATION

In a premeasurement and postmeasurement single-group design a measurement of the dependent variable is obtained before the experimental intervention. There may be other reasons for pretesting apart from investigating whether the experimental and control groups are comparable initially or matching these groups in respect of this variable. Pretesting may also be performed with a view to determining whether a ceiling effect exists.

FOR EXAMPLE If individuals had already obtained pretest scores of 16 to 20 on a test with a maximum possible score of 20, we could hardly demonstrate an improvement in attitude towards the donation of blood. These scores mean that the individuals are already as positive as possible towards donating blood, that is, their attitude has reached the ceiling. If a pretest had been administered, it may have identified such a ceiling effect and would have alerted the researcher to consider another attitudinal measure.

It is possible, however, that if the participants complete a pretest, they may react differently to the experimental intervention than they would have reacted had they not been exposed to the pretest. We refer to this phenomenon as **pretest sensitisation**.

The pretest therefore sensitises the individuals in the experimental group to the subsequent intervention and affects their eventual scores on the dependent variable either negatively or positively. The independent variable as implemented therefore does not correspond with the independent variable as conceptualised because the subjects are not subjected to the independent variable only, but to the pretest as well.

6.2.5 Measurement problems

In this section we describe two additional threats to internal validity that are the result of the very use of pretests (see Section 6.2.3), namely:

▶ measurement reactivity
▶ instrumentation.

Each threat offers another possible explanation for observed changes in the dependent-variable scores.

6.2.5.1 MEASUREMENT REACTIVITY

Participants' awareness that they are completing a test (a measuring instrument such as a questionnaire – see Section 7.7.3.1) may affect their responses to the test or their subsequent completion of the test without the experimental intervention having been related to it at all. We refer to this phenomenon as **measurement reactivity**.

Participants may remember the answers that they gave on one occasion and wittingly or unwittingly change them on subsequent occasions. On the subsequent testing occasion they may thus tend to respond differently from the way they would have if they had not been tested before. The potential effect of measurement reactivity is not something that can be determined by mere speculation but should be investigated empirically. Such an investigation falls outside the scope of this book.

6.2.5.2 INSTRUMENTATION

This threat refers to changes in the measurement of the dependent variable, rather than in the dependent variable itself. **Instrumentation** therefore involves the unreliability of the measuring instruments used in the tests.

FOR EXAMPLE Suppose we modify the method in which a management training course is presented after the first test has been written. We now want to examine the effect of this modification by comparing the scores on the second test with those on the first test (for example in a premeasurement and postmeasurement design).

If these two tests were incomparable due to different levels of difficulty, it would constitute an example of the threat of instrumentation.

If we assess the dependent variable (see Section 2.3) by means of ratings (see Section 7.7.3.4), the raters may be more tired, or more experienced, or more bored when performing the ratings after the intervention than before it. As a result, the findings would not be valid.

If we use official statistics (see Section 7.7.2) as a measure of the dependent variable, the accuracy in reporting the phenomenon may differ after the intervention from before it.

FOR EXAMPLE Suppose a campaign is launched to combat sexual harassment of workers. The number of molestations which are reported to official bodies is taken as a measurement of the extent of this problem. The publicity given to the campaign on radio and television may lead to a heightened awareness among the general public, so that cases which previously would have gone unreported are now brought to the attention of the authorities.

As a result there may be an increase in the number of reported cases of sexual harassment of workers that may conceal any decrease in the actual incidence of this problem.

6.2.6 Group differences

We have already indicated (see Section 5.2) that if only one group (which receives the experimental intervention) is used, we cannot be sure that the considerable changes in the dependent variable would not have occurred without any such intervention. A control group which does not receive the experimental intervention is required. Although the threats of history and spontaneous change (see Section 6.2.3) are controlled by making use of a control group, the internal validity of such a design is subject to threats that involve the composition of the groups used. These threats include:

▶ selection
▶ interaction between selection and spontaneous change.

6.2.6.1 SELECTION

Selection is concerned with initial or preexisting differences between the experimental group and the control group.

Because the experimental group and the control group are not necessarily equal in respect of the dependent variable or all possible nuisance variables, the design could lack an adequate basis of comparison.

If the one group (mentioned in the first example of Section 5.2) of trainee supervisors is more aggressive after exposure to the aggressive role model than the so-called control group, the other group of trainee supervisors, the increase in aggressive behaviour cannot be attributed conclusively to that exposure, because this group possibly may have been more aggressive even before the beginning of the investigation.

Another way in which selection can cause problems is when the sample chosen for the study is not similar to the wider population. In this situation it would be very difficult to generalise the results.

6.2.6.2 INTERACTION BETWEEN SELECTION AND SPONTANEOUS CHANGE

Even if the experimental and control groups were equal in terms of both the dependent variable and all nuisance variables initially, the one group may subsequently show a greater degree of spontaneous development, maturation, recovery or deterioration than the other. In such a case we are dealing with an **interaction** between the threats of selection and spontaneous change.

FOR EXAMPLE Although trainee supervisors in both groups (Research Example II – see Section 2.3, page 17), may have exhibited the same degree of management style initially, the trainee supervisors at one regional company office may react differently to a particular intervention than the trainee supervisors at another regional office. This might happen because the one group is stationed in a particular geographical area where riots have started to take place, for instance.

For the same reason, it would be unwise to use teenage boys and teenage girls as two treatment groups in any research, even if these groups were equated in terms of their pretest scores on any variable that is susceptible to development. At that stage of development males and females tend to develop at different rates so that, without any intervention, these groups may reveal differences in their post-test scores.

6.2.7 Random assignment to groups

The purpose of **random assignment** is to equate the groups in terms of all known and unknown nuisance variables, that is, variables apart from the independent variable in terms of which groups may possibly differ and that may affect the dependent variable. **True experimental research** (such as the different randomised group designs – see Section 5.2.1.2) differs from **pre-experimental research** (see Section 6.2.3) in that all the groups being used have been randomly assigned.

FOR EXAMPLE Suppose the independent variable is *training method* and the dependent variable is *examination marks.* It is generally known that there is a substantial relationship (correlation – see Section 9.4) between intelligence and examination marks. If the group taught by the one method was on average more intelligent than the other, we would not know to what extent an eventual difference in mean examination achievement would be attributable to the different training methods rather than to possible differences in intelligence.

By randomly assigning participants to the two treatment groups, we attempt to have more or less an equal number of highly intelligent participants, and an equal number of moderately intelligent participants, and so on, in each of the two groups.

If the one group still significantly outperforms the other group, we can ascribe this difference more confidently to the greater effectiveness of the method to which they were subjected rather than to possible differences in intelligence. Naturally, we do not necessarily succeed in equating the two groups in terms of all nuisance variables, but if a sufficiently large number of participants are assigned randomly, the chances are high that the resulting groups will meet this requirement.

6.2.8 Matching

We may consider **matching** participants in terms of a nuisance variable in cases where we know that there is a very strong relationship (considerable correlation) between this nuisance variable and the dependent variable.

FOR EXAMPLE We pointed out earlier (see Section 6.2.6) that there is a relatively high correlation between intelligence and examination marks. Intelligence thus operates as a systematic source of variation in this instance in that the more intelligent individuals consistently tend to outperform the less intelligent, irrespective of the training method to which they are subjected.

Of course, this matching technique (**matched groups design**) need not be restricted to two groups. If, for example, there are four training methods, groups of four participants each with more or less the same intelligence quotient (IQ), may be randomly assigned to four groups that are subsequently taught by the four training methods respectively.

However, as the number of groups increases, it may become more difficult to obtain groups of the required size of which all the members are more or less the same in respect of the nuisance variable (on which they should be matched). For example, it would be more difficult to obtain six subjects with an IQ of more or less 140, than to obtain only two with this IQ.

If there is no considerable relationship (correlation – see Section 9.4) between the nuisance variable (see Section 5.2) and the dependent variable (see Section 2.3), it is better to use the regular randomised groups design (see Section 5.2) with the same number of participants, rather than the matched groups design.

There are three methods in which matching can be done: **precision control**, **multiple nuisance variable matching**, and **frequency distribution control**.

6.2.8.1 PRECISION CONTROL

In the case of **precision control** we subdivide the participants into pairs so that the members of each pair are similar in respect of one or other nuisance variable the effect of which we want to eliminate. We then randomly assign the members of each pair to the two levels of the independent variable.

FOR EXAMPLE We may equate groups that are to be subjected to different teaching methods by matching them in terms of the positively identified nuisance variable *intelligence*. We administer an intelligence test to all participants and then rank them in terms of their intelligence-test scores. In other words, the person with the highest score is ranked first, the one with the second highest is placed second, and so on, until the one with the lowest score appears in the bottom position.

Starting with the people in the first two positions, we subdivide participants into pairs so that the members of each pair have more or less the same intelligence-test score. Finally, the two members of each pair are randomly assigned to the two groups. In other words, for each person with an IQ of, say, 106 who is assigned to the one group, someone else with more or less the same IQ is allocated to the other group. The two groups formed in this manner will have more or less the same mean intelligence-test score. If one of these groups then performs better on average in the examination, this difference may be ascribed more readily to the greater effectiveness of the teaching method to which they were subjected rather than to a higher intelligence.

6.2.8.2 MULTIPLE NUISANCE VARIABLE MATCHING

Matching does not have to be limited to a single nuisance variable. If we want to match individuals in respect of both IQ and gender, it means that for each man with an IQ of, say, 106, who is assigned to the one group, a man with a similar IQ should be placed in the other group. For each woman with an IQ of 102 allocated to the one group, another woman with a similar IQ should be placed in the other group as well.

Each of the variables that is matched in this fashion should show a high correlation with the dependent variable, but a low correlation with the other variables in terms of which matching is done. It is necessary to match individuals only in terms of the variables that are highly correlated with the dependent variable. A high correlation between any two nuisance variables indicates that they overlap partially and that matching on both of them may be superfluous.

In practice, it is generally difficult to match individuals on more than two such variables, mainly because it is usually difficult to find two (or more) individuals who are equal in respect of the specific variables. As the number of variables in terms of which groups are to be matched increases, it therefore becomes increasingly difficult to effect matching.

NOTE: We equate groups only in terms of those variables on which they are matched specifically. The problem with matching as the only strategy of equating groups is that there may be several potential nuisance variables which are unknown to the researcher and in terms of which subjects thus cannot be matched. To equate the matched groups in terms of such variables, the individuals in each matched pair or trio, and so on, should still be randomly assigned to the various groups (which are to receive the different levels of the independent variable).

6.2.8.3 FREQUENCY DISTRIBUTION CONTROL

In the case of the **frequency distribution control method**, we should ensure that the mean(s) of the nuisance variable(s) is/are the same for the different treatment groups.

FOR EXAMPLE If *age* is the nuisance variable, the ages of the members of one group may be 15, 17, 19, 21, and 23, whereas those of the other are 17, 18, 19, 20, and 21. Each of these groups has a mean of 19 although there is, for example, no 16-year-old in either of the groups.

This method differs from the precision control method. In terms of the precision control method, matched individuals are placed in groups of two or more each before they are randomly assigned to the respective treatment groups. All the members of such a group are therefore the same in respect of the nuisance variable(s). Using this method, the researcher has to omit individuals for whom nobody with approximately the same status on the nuisance variable(s) can be found. The frequency distribution method, however, does not require a partner with approximately the same status on the nuisance variable(s) for each research participant. The **advantage** of the frequency distribution method is therefore that it results in the elimination of fewer participants. A **disadvantage** of this type of matching becomes evident when there are two or more nuisance variables that have to be taken into account.

FOR EXAMPLE Suppose we need to match two groups in terms of both *gender* and *intelligence* while the number of men and women in the two groups or the mean IQs for the two groups remain the same. The one group may then contain only men with high IQs and women with low IQs, whereas the other group may contain only men with low IQs and women with high IQs.

6.2.9 Unplanned developments within and between groups

Threats to internal validity may become apparent during the course of the research project even if we equate all samples in terms of all possible variables initially. As researchers, we are to a great extent, if not exclusively,

at the mercy of the co-operation of research participants. However, as we are dealing with humans, changes are inevitable and can cause problems from the point of view of validity. In this respect we need to consider the following aspects (compare Section 9.3.1):

▶ communication between treatment groups
▶ differential attrition between participants.

6.2.9.1 COMMUNICATION BETWEEN TREATMENT GROUPS

In order for valid comparisons to be made, control groups should be treated in exactly the same way as experimental groups. The only difference is the level of the independent variable to which the control groups are exposed. This requirement is necessary to enable us to ascribe eventual between-group differences in the dependent variable to the independent variable exclusively.

If the groups are to share their respective experiences in the research project, the control group may be exposed to the same experience as the experimental group indirectly, or they may even compete with the experimental group.

FOR EXAMPLE If the experimental group undergoes a relaxation programme, members of the control group may obtain details of this programme and may implement or simulate some aspects of it. Similarly, access to the programme to which the experimental group is exposed may cause the members of the control group to feel neglected, resentful, and demoralised.

All these contingencies represent threats to the internal validity of the eventual conclusions.

6.2.9.2 DIFFERENTIAL ATTRITION OF PARTICIPANTS

It is not uncommon for participants to "disappear" during the course of a research project. In this connection the term **subject mortality** is often used as an analogy for biological studies in which organisms may literally die.

The fact that subjects disappear is not only problematic from the point of view that less data are obtained ultimately. The most important complication is the fact that the disappearance of subjects might be connected to the level of the independent variable to which they were exposed. As a result, the phenomenon is also referred to as the **differential attrition of subjects**.

FOR EXAMPLE Suppose we want to test the effectiveness of a computer-assisted teaching method compared to a conventional method of lecturing. We then randomly assign students to two groups and subject the experimental group to a computer-assisted course in research methodology. The control group is taught by means of the conventional method of lecturing. The independent variable is *teaching method* and the dependent variable is *achievement in research methodology*. Suppose the students with poorer numerical skills tend to fare poorly in research methodology. The students from this group who are in the experimental group terminate their course in greater numbers than those in the control group. The computer-assisted method of teaching emphasises their weak numerical ability. The disappearance of subjects from the experimental group, therefore, is directly related to the nature of the level of the independent variable (teaching method) to which they have been exposed.

The pretest scores of the individuals who remained in the experimental group have a higher mean on the dependent variable than both the original experimental group and the control group. Although the two groups were initially equal in respect of the dependent variable (*achievement in research methodology*), there was a difference eventually in favour of the experimental group because the students with the weakest numerical skills had dropped out of this group. Because the experimental group eventually fared better on the dependent variable than the control group, we cannot attribute this difference convincingly to the greater effectiveness of the computer-assisted method alone.

6.3 **External validity and threats**

6.3.1 **Introduction**

A theory always holds for a specific population of units of analysis (for example individuals, organisations, and so on) and a universum of conditions. Any implication deduced from such a theory that is subjected to empirical testing, is similarly applicable to such a population and universum. As the population can consist of millions of individuals, we preferably work with a **representative sample** from the population. Such a (random) sample should consist of at least 25 units, but it is not necessary to use a sample of more than 500, for instance (see Section 4.3.5). The degree of population validity achieved thus depends exclusively on how representative the sample is of the population from which it has been obtained (see Section 4.3.5).

6.3.2 **Population validity**

Research hypotheses are concerned with postulated relationships (between variables) in one or more populations. In the human behavioural sciences hypotheses typically involve very large populations and, as a result, researchers have to rely on the data obtained for samples from such populations.

Population validity refers to the degree to which the findings obtained for a sample may be generalised to the total population to which the research hypothesis applies.

FOR EXAMPLE In Research Example II (see Section 2.3, page 17) population validity refers to the degree to which the results obtained for a sample of trainee supervisors may be generalised to the total population of all trainee supervisors. If watching management style role model behaviour were to make the sample of trainee supervisors more inclined to imitate an iron-fisted management style, the researcher would like to conclude that watching such management style behaviour would have the same effect on the total population of trainee supervisors. To make such generalisations, researchers have to draw, as far as possible, a random sample from the population to which they would like their results to apply.

Whereas the *random selection of participants* is required for *population validity*, the *random assignment of participants* promotes *internal validity* (see Section 6.2.7).

Kempthorne (in Bracht & Glass, 1968) makes the following distinction:

▶ The **target population** is the population to which the researcher ideally would like to generalise his or her results.

▶ The **experimentally accessible population** is the population that corresponds to the sampling frame from which a random sample is actually drawn.

FOR EXAMPLE In Research Example II (see Section 2.3, page 17), the target population may have consisted solely of trainee supervisors younger than 30 years, while only those in the specific company constituted the experimentally accessible population.

Strictly speaking, the statistical model only permits generalisation to the experimentally accessible population from which a random sample (see Section 4.3.2) has actually been obtained. The generalisation from the experimentally accessible to the target population can only be made on extrastatistical grounds.

Suppose the researcher can argue convincingly that trainee supervisors younger than 30 years in a specific company are representative of all trainee supervisors younger than 30 years in South Africa as far as susceptibility to an iron-fisted management style is concerned. The results obtained for a random sample from the population of trainee supervisors younger than 30 years in the specific company may then be extrapolated to the population of all trainee supervisors younger than 30 years in South Africa. However, convincing arguments to the contrary would restrict such generalisations.

Although conducting research on subjects from an easily available population (whether it be mine workers, prisoners or hospital patients) is perfectly admissible, we should be careful not to generalise the results obtained to the entire human race. Results should be generalised to the experimentally accessible population only. Knowledge about any population is valid as long as it is presented as knowledge about that specific population. Moreover, populations that are clearly distinguishable in terms of some variables may be expected to show a great degree of similarity in, for example, physiological-psychological investigations. However, when we are dealing with personality and social-psychological research, such similarities should be less readily assumed as fact. Researchers would do well to investigate relationships previously found in populations of white university students, in different populations. Alternatively, the effect of both the independent variable and group differences and the interaction between these two variables may be investigated in randomised block designs (see Section 9.3.2.3).

The use of **volunteers** may similarly affect the population validity of results obtained. To the extent that volunteers differ from the remainder of the relevant population in respect of variables related to the dependent variable, biased results may be obtained.

FOR EXAMPLE Suppose we wish to investigate the effectiveness of a computer-assisted system to teach research methodology to students in the human behavioural sciences. Suppose we obtain a sample of volunteers and randomly assign them to two groups that subsequently undergo the computer-assisted and conventional methods respectively. Students interested in computer-assisted methods and who present themselves as volunteers for this kind of research, are likely to achieve different results from those of students in general. The results we obtain for the sample of volunteers interested in computer-assisted methods will thus be less readily generalised to the population of students.

Finally, we should point out that population validity is regarded as less important in experimental research (apart from programme evaluation) than in survey research. *Internal validity* is of primary importance in *experimental research* where the purpose is to draw conclusions about causal relationships. In *non-experimental research*, especially in attitude surveys, *population validity* is of extreme importance. The assumption, again implicit, is that subjects tend to exhibit great variation in respect of the variables that are usually studied in non-experimental research. Biased results may therefore be obtained if data are obtained for unrepresentative samples. Consequently, we should take great care to obtain representative samples if we conduct non-experimental research.

6.3.3 **Ecological validity**

We may wish to generalise the results obtained in a specific laboratory situation to all real-life situations in which such behaviour is manifested.

FOR EXAMPLE If workers at a mining company, in response to aggressive role model behaviour, acted aggressively in a laboratory, we would like to conclude that they would act similarly in response to comparable behaviour by their supervisors in the work place.

This requirement relates to ecological validity. The **ecological validity** of the obtained results refers to the degree to which they may be *generalised to all circumstances that are implied by the research hypothesis* (see Section 2.4). We may also interpret ecological validity as part of the construct validity of the independent variable on which we focused in Section 6.2.3.

Usually we obtain research data that are relevant to a particular sample of subjects, as well as a particular research setting or set of conditions (experimenter, apparatus, venue, time of the day and year, and so on). Seldom, if ever, do we wish to restrict our findings to a particular group of individuals under a specific research setting.

FOR EXAMPLE Suppose we investigate the effect of television violence on the aggressiveness of mine workers by showing a violent video to a group of mine workers during a regular training session. Ecological validity in this instance refers to the degree to which the obtained results are not restricted to the particular video shown in a training situation, but may be generalised to all (violent) videos, including those shown on television at home as part of scheduled television programmes or rented from video stores.

Here, the ecological validity would have been suspect if mine workers reacted differently to a violent video shown in a training situation than they would to videos that they watch alone at home or in the company of their families.

While population validity refers to the generalisation of the results obtained to the population to which the research hypothesis applies, ecological validity involves the generalisation to situations other than the one in which the experiment has been carried out. In other words, ecological validity refers to the generalisation to a relevant universe of conditions.

Naturally, the presence of subject effects, experimenter effects, and pretest sensitisation (see Section 6.2.4) may restrict the degree to which the results obtained can be generalised and thus adversely affect ecological validity. Typically, we would like to generalise our research findings to situations in which the subject effect, the experimenter effect, and the pretest sensitisation are not of any consequence.

Findings obtained in a laboratory, for example, may be of little value if they do not tell us something of human behaviour in everyday life. According to some critics, the advantage of laboratory experiments as far as the control of nuisance variables (see Section 5.2) is concerned, also represents its greatest drawback. In an attempt to maximise internal validity, a laboratory experiment may be planned in which all possible nuisance variables (environmental noise, fluctuations in temperature, and so on) are eliminated. However, this approach may result in a highly artificial environment that yields trivial results that cannot be generalised to real-life situations, and that have an unsatisfactory ecological validity.

Consequently, research is frequently carried out in a field situation, not because it is impossible to do it in a laboratory but because the field situation is **preferred** on account of the greater degree of **naturalness** it affords. According to many authors (for example Kerlinger, 1986), ecological validity increases in so far as the research situation becomes more realistic, in other words, the more it corresponds to real, everyday situations. According to the proponents of field research, generalisations to "real people in everyday, real life" may be made only on the basis of research conducted in natural surroundings. The advantage of field experiments in comparison to laboratory experiments therefore lies in the greater ecological validity they offer.

Whether or not a laboratory environment as such is an obstacle in achieving ecological validity does not depend on its naturalness. The realism with which the independent variable is operationalised (see Sections 2.4, 6.1 & 6.2.3) is the most important factor, irrespective of the environment in which this is done.

In the final analysis, whether findings obtained in a laboratory experiment can indeed be so generalised cannot be settled by means of speculation or debate, but should be investigated empirically. Thus, if we would like to know whether watching violent behaviour will be followed by aggressive behaviour in a field situation, as is the case in a laboratory situation, we should investigate this phenomenon in a field setting.

ACTIVITY 6.3

Read Case Studies A, B, C, D, E, and F in Appendix D on page 306.

QUESTION

To what extent does the research design used in each case study make provision for threats to internal and external validity? Explain your answer in terms of the aim of each study and discuss the sampling critically.

ANSWER

case study a

Because there are many health professionals in South Africa who are involved with AIDS cases (the population in this case – also called the target population), it is advisable for the researcher to work with a sample instead of the total population. However, this sample should contain members who are representative of the total population concerned (that is, they should be selected randomly with regard to the relevant criteria such as age, population group, and so on) to increase the population validity of the study (as part of external validity). By doing so, the results obtained for the sample could be generalised to the whole population, namely all nursing sisters and doctors who work with AIDS cases in South Africa.

The sample of 74 people who work at a general hospital and serve mainly white and coloured popula-

tion groups was obtained on the basis of convenience. As a result, the threat to external validity (that the results may not be generalised) has therefore not been avoided in this particular case study. If the external validity of the study had been high, we could have said that the knowledge of, and attitude towards AIDS and prostitution of all health professionals in South Africa who work with AIDS cases (the sample framework from which the sample had to be drawn) show a relation that matches that of the sample.

Because the study involved a correlational design (not an experimental design – where internal validity is important), there was no question of the influence of the independent variable on the dependent variable. However, a moral question, such as attitude towards prostitution, could pertain to the relation between *knowledge of AIDS* and *attitudes towards AIDS*, in that it could have an uncontrolled influence on both variables, and so negate the internal validity of the study.

case study b

The threat to the internal validity of this investigation is that a change or lack of change in the apprentices' attitude to the supervision procedure may not be unambiguously attributable to their participation in the role induction procedure, but that other variables such as age also play a role. Because they are all young (19 to 20 years old) it could be, for example, that they are rebellious and negative towards any form of authority and therefore also towards supervision. The socio-economic status of the households from which they come and/or their level of education could also have an influence.

It appears, therefore, that the study could have had a higher internal validity if the sample members were drawn randomly from various strata and subjected to the effect of the role induction procedure.

Regarding the external (population) validity of the study, the same arguments apply as those given above in Case Study A. The sample of apprentices in this investigation is not representative of all the members of the population of goldsmith apprentices. Only the 20 at one large jewellery firm were used. The results of the study can therefore not be generalised to all goldsmith apprentices. The role induction procedure took place during the apprentices' training in their natural, everyday setting. As this setting corresponds to the time when and circumstances under which such a procedure is typically applied, the ecological validity of the study is not threatened.

case study c

In the non-equivalent control group design that was used in the investigation, two existing groups were used respectively as an experimental and a control group. Provision is made, however, for the threat of group differences; these are differences that could have existed between the groups as a result of previous experience, acquired management skills, and so forth. This is done by using the non-equivalent control group design and measuring both parties before the experimental intervention (attendance of the training course) on the dependent variable. This was achieved by measuring both

groups' knowledge of management principles and ensuring that the average was the same for both groups.

If the groups do not differ with regard to their knowledge of management principles before attending the course but indeed with regard to their knowledge after the course, the latter difference can certainly be ascribed to the influence of the training course. As a result of the presence of a control group, provision is therefore made for the threat of the internal validity of the investigation.

The threat of external validity (in terms of population validity) is rejected in that an equal sample of participants from the population of first-line supervisors is drawn, which ensures that the results of the investigation can be generalised to the population.

case study d

The threat to the internal validity of this investigation concerns the fact that *speech quality* is not only influenced by *anxiety* but also by variables such as *gender, socio-economic status of the households from which the students come*, as well as their *personalities* (outgoing or introverted, and so forth). Should a student whose mother tongue is Zulu, for example, have to deliver a speech in Afrikaans, it would take such a student longer to prepare this speech than it would an Afrikaans-speaking student. It therefore appears that the study would have a higher internal validity if the subjects could be drawn equally from various strata (with regard to, for example, their home language, personality, age).

As far as the external (population) validity of the study is concerned, the same argument as in Case Study C applies. The sample of students in public speech-making in this investigation was not representative of all members of the relevant population of students because it was not a stratified random sample. If this had been done, the threat of external validity with regard to the population validity could have been rejected.

case study e

The research design used in this investigation involved using two existing groups. Factors such as *business size* (number of workers employed) and *business sector* (cafés, coffee shops, florists, and so on) could have acted as third variables in the measurement of the dependent variable (bankrupt or not bankrupt). In other words, these third variables could also have acted as predictor variables in predicting whether bankruptcy would occur in the group of bankrupt small businesses as well as the group of non-bankrupt small businesses.

However, provision was made for these differences by ensuring that corresponding business size and comparable business sectors existed between the two groups. This eliminated most of the possible threats to the internal validity of the study. It cannot be assumed, however, that it was mainly the independent variables that predicted the dependent variable to differentiate between the two groups – management skills may also have had an influence.

The threat to external validity (in terms of population validity) is not compensated for by the use of an accidental sample (see Section 4.3.4). Therefore, the businesses involved in this study are not representative of the population of small businesses, and the results of the investigation cannot be generalised to the population of small businesses in South Africa as a whole.

case study f

Various third (nuisance) variables could have an influence on the results of the study on the innovative problem-solving styles and therefore on the results of the study. These variables could covary with the levels of the independent variable (entrepreneurs/managers) and therefore constitute a threat to internal validity. These are as follows:

- Age – the average ages of the two groups differ significantly. (The average age of the entrepreneurs was 28 years while the average age of the managers was 42 years.)
- Gender – proportionately more men were included in the entrepreneurial group (100 males to 12 females) than in the manager group (70 males to 40 females).
- Other variables such as *intelligence* or *motivation* could also have an influence on the level of innovative problem-solving styles of the respondents.

With regard to external validity, in particular population validity, the sample of business people (entrepreneurs and managers of big businesses) was not representative of all members of the relevant target population of entrepreneurs/managers in Gauteng and the Western Cape because an accidental sample, and not a random sample, was used. If random sampling had been done, the threats to the external validity with regard to the population validity of this study could have been overcome.

However, the ecological validity of the study is also under threat because only business people from the Western Cape and Gauteng were included. Depending on the different localities, businesses may differ in terms of their focuses, for example wine-making in the Western Cape, heavy industry in Gauteng, and sugar cane production in KwaZulu-Natal.

SUMMARY

Any study has to be valid in terms of the control of possible third variables. This concerns the internal validity of the study. It means that we have to be able to contribute a change in the dependent variable only to the effect/cause of the independent variable.

Although most scientific studies in business are focused on specific units of analysis and the circumstances of such cases (the ecological validity of the study), the results may benefit the broader community if the results can be generalised to them (the population validity of the study). It is therefore important to ensure that the cases and samples we use are representative of most South African circumstances and of a South African target population. If our studies are not valid, we may come to incorrect conclusions.

Table 6.1 summarises the above-mentioned aspects. (Note that the table makes broad generalisations because the type of validity – be it high or low – depends on the specific research example's definition and empirical characteristics.)

Table 6.1 Types of research and their correspondence to external and internal validity (compare Chapters 5 and 8)

Type of research	Type of validity
Experimental	Internal validity is of primary importance while population validity is less important.
Laboratory experiments	Ecological validity is low.
Field experiments	Ecological validity is high.
Quasi-experimental	Internal and external validity are important.
Non-experimental	Population validity is extremely important while internal validity is less important.
Qualitative	Ecological validity is much more important than other types of validity.

TEST YOURSELF

Question 1: Multiple-choice questions

Only one of the answers to each question is correct. Identify and mark the correct one. (Answers appear in Appendix A on page 299.)

1.1 Internal validity refers to:
  a) generalisability
  b) whether the experimental stimulus (independent variable) really affected the dependent variable
  c) the comparison of the results obtained for the experimental group with those obtained for the control group
  d) the determination of the proper time to do the post-test.

1.2 The 100 km/h speed limit for buses was introduced in South Africa in 1999. Shortly thereafter the number of bus accidents declined. We can conclude that
  a) the reduced speed limit caused the decline in the number of bus accidents
  b) the reduced speed limit had nothing to do with the decline in bus accidents
  c) the reduced speed limit and the number of bus accidents are causally related
  d) the reduced speed limit may have caused the decline in bus accidents.

1.3 If the findings of a research study can be generalised to different populations, circumstances, and conditions not included but represented in the original study, the findings are said to have:
  a) internal validity
  b) ecological validity
  c) transfer validity
  d) external validity.

1.4 Which of the following statements concerning the external validity of a scientifically conducted investigation is true?
  a) Neither laboratory nor field research will provide externally valid results.
  b) Field and laboratory research are equally likely to ensure valid results.
  c) Both field and laboratory research are likely to ensure valid results.
  d) Field research is more likely than laboratory research to ensure externally valid results.

1.5 If the possibility exists that the participants of one's study are exposed to injury, it is essential for the researcher to obtain:
  a) conditional consent
  b) implied consent
  c) informed consent
  d) participation.

Question 2: True/false questions

Indicate whether the following statement is true (T) or false (F). (Answers appear in Appendix A on page 299.)

2.1 The problem of external validity refers to the generalisability of results.

Question 3: Self-evaluation questions

(Some answers appear in Appendix A on page 299.)

3.1 Suppose Researcher A wishes to investigate the effectiveness of a programme designed to increase the assertiveness of disabled workers. All these workers complete an assertiveness test at the beginning of the year. Those who appear to be in the greatest need of this programme are enrolled in it. At the end of the year their assertiveness is measured again.

In terms of this example, explain what is meant by the internal validity of conclusions and evaluate this feature of the design by identifying possible threats to it.

3.2 Suppose Researcher B investigates the same problem as Researcher A in question 3.1. She selects the same group as Researcher A but randomly assigns them to two groups and subjects one group, but not the other to the programme.

Evaluate the internal validity of the conclusions made possible by this design by identifying possible threats to it.

3.3 On the basis of the relationship between the size of the signature of borrowers of library books on the lending cards and their status (students and professors), Zweigenhaft (1970) concluded that the higher borrowers rate their status, the larger their signature tends to be.

Offer another explanation for the observed relationship by referring to a possible third variable.

3.4 Suppose a psychology lecturer develops a programme to modify the lifestyle of individuals with an unhealthy Type A behaviour pattern. All employees of an insurance company who obtain high scores on a Type A personality questionnaire are randomly assigned to either an experimental or a control group. The experimental group meets weekly for an hour to take part in the programme, which is presented by the lecturer's graduate students. At the conclusion of the project, the members of both groups are subjected to artificial situations supposed to elicit Type A behaviour, in a room equipped with facilities to record the participants' behaviour on videotape. Subsequently the researcher and his master's students rate the participants' behaviour in respect of the occurrence of Type A behaviour (from the videotapes) to investigate whether there is a difference (in this type of behaviour) between the two groups.

Comment on the population and/or ecological validity of the results obtained.

3.5 It has been found in laboratory experiments that the sexual prowess of male rats of an age comparable to men in their twenties is adversely affected by drinking too much beer (Te veel bier [Too much beer], 1991). On the basis of this result, the conclusion has been made that drinking comparable amounts of beer in the corresponding period of time will cause temporary impotence in 20-year-old men. Which kind of validity is involved in this conclusion and why?

Data-collecting methods and measuring instruments in quantitative research

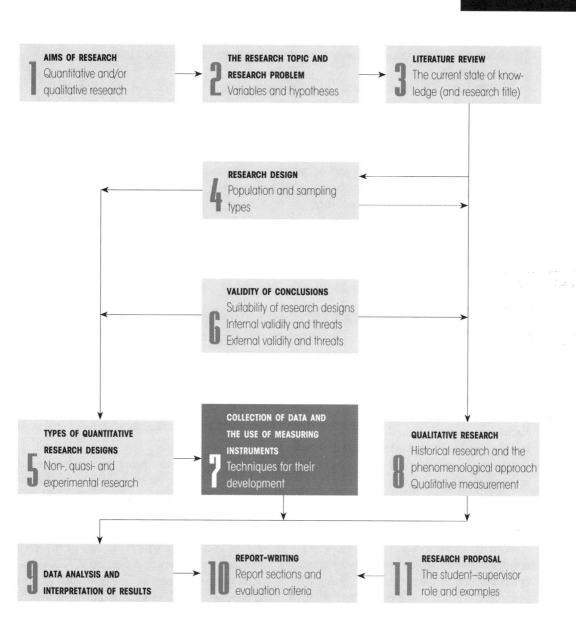

AIMS OF RESEARCH
1 Quantitative and/or qualitative research

THE RESEARCH TOPIC AND RESEARCH PROBLEM
2 Variables and hypotheses

LITERATURE REVIEW
3 The current state of knowledge (and research title)

RESEARCH DESIGN
4 Population and sampling types

VALIDITY OF CONCLUSIONS
6 Suitability of research designs
Internal validity and threats
External validity and threats

TYPES OF QUANTITATIVE RESEARCH DESIGNS
5 Non-, quasi- and experimental research

COLLECTION OF DATA AND THE USE OF MEASURING INSTRUMENTS
7 Techniques for their development

QUALITATIVE RESEARCH
8 Historical research and the phenomenological approach
Qualitative measurement

DATA ANALYSIS AND INTERPRETATION OF RESULTS
9

REPORT-WRITING
10 Report sections and evaluation criteria

RESEARCH PROPOSAL
11 The student–supervisor role and examples

LEARNING OUTCOMES

Once we have decided on a particular research design (see Chapter 5), we have to obtain our research participants (subjects/units of analysis) according to our chosen sampling procedure in order to carry out the research. We then have to consider which data-collecting method is the most appropriate in the light of our research problem and the particular population in question. In this step we put the blueprint which we finalised in the preceding stage (see Chapters 4 & 5) into action.

After studying this chapter, you will be able to:
- illustrate by means of examples how indicators may be used to define and help to measure nontangible things (for example constructs such as values, opinions, expectations, and so on)
- explain briefly the basic requirements for measuring instruments regarding validity and reliability
- distinguish between the validity of a measuring instrument and the validity of the study in which it was used to collect data
- briefly describe different data-collecting methods
- distinguish between measurement and observation
- describe how secondary data (obtained by means of computer simulations) may contribute to the understanding of certain phenomena
- give four examples of secondary information sources and the benefits of using these instead of doing empirical research
- list four steps regarding the follow-up of postal surveys in order to increase the response rate
- describe why and how the semantic differential may be used to collect information
- list six problems with telephone surveys and means to resolve them
- distinguish between different measuring instruments
- classify measuring instruments into four basic strategies for collecting data
- use the guidelines for developing certain types of instruments to measure variables
- explain why it is important to provide clear instructions to respondents on how to complete survey questionnaires
- explain why ethical issues are important in measurement.

7.1 Introduction

Each data-collecting method and measuring instrument has its advantages and drawbacks. Furthermore, what counts as an advantage for one may qualify as a drawback for another, and *vice versa*.

FOR EXAMPLE Employees who cannot read or write cannot complete questionnaires and thus we would have to observe their work behaviour directly. On the other hand, there are certain behaviours (for example which management style, financial practices, and so on

employees support) which we can assess by means of questionnaires and/or interviews only.

In this chapter we focus on measurement theory and various ways in which to use instruments to collect information. This includes situations where we, as researchers, are not in direct contact with the units of analysis (the objects and people we project will be involved with and by our study – Section 7.7.2), situations where we may be involved with groups of people, as well as situations where we are

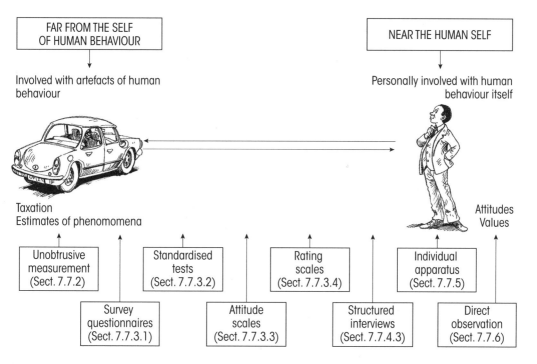

Figure 7.1 *Means of using instruments to collect data*

individually involved with our subjects/units of analysis face-to-face. This range of situations is illustrated in Figure 7.1.

7.2 Systematic observation and quantitative measurement

In the final analysis, all measuring and data-collecting procedures are based on **systematic observation** (see Sections 1.2.2.1 & 2.3.2 and Figure 7.2). By systematic observation we mean that it should be replicable, in other words, that independent observers other than ourselves should also be able to observe and report whatever we, as researchers, observe and report (requirements – see Section 1.2.2.3). This is in contrast to everyday, accidental observation which cannot necessarily be replicated.

7.3 Measurement theory

In this section we will focus on the nature of measurement and the requirements it

should meet from a research perspective. Measurement theory is a highly technical field of study that we will discuss only synoptically and somewhat superficially.

If we wish to investigate the accuracy or "truth" of the research hypothesis (see Section 2.4) of our study, we need to **measure** the dependent variables (see Section 2.3, page 14) appearing in it.

Consider the hypothesis of Research Example II (see Section 2.3): exposure to the iron-fisted role model management style behaviour results in an increase in the iron-fisted management style behaviour of trainee supervisors. To test this hypothesis, the management styles of the trainee supervisors had to be assessed (measured and evaluated).

Measuring variables such as the length or mass of things/people (subjects) does not present many problems. The characteristics that are of interest to the human behavioural sciences, however, are seldom observable variables such as mass, length, and the colour of

Figure 7.2 *Systematic observation: two researchers observing the behaviour of two animals*

someone's eyes. Instead, the variables we wish to measure are constructs. We measure particular characteristics of individuals/things/events (rather than the individuals themselves). Therefore, measuring constructs (see Section 2.5) such as liquidation, paying TV licences, attitude towards affirmative action, entrepreneurship, the regional council, helping behaviour (see Research Example VI, Section 6.2.4.1, page 118), and so on, is more problematic. We usually have to measure these constructs indirectly by means of **indicators**.

We may define any **construct** in the human behavioural sciences in terms of a ***universe of indicators*** *that collectively define that construct.*

FOR EXAMPLE The variable *socio-economic status* is an example of a construct because there is no single indicator that perfectly encapsulates it. To measure someone's socio-economic status we may use, for example, his or her income, occupation, educational level, or the area in which he or she resides as indicators. Each of these variables (**indicators**), therefore, is only a partial and indirect indicator of the construct *socio-economic status*.

Constructs such as *attitude towards affirmative action* or *entrepreneurship* are even less directly

observable than *socio-economic status*. In these examples, the constructs have to be indirectly inferred from supposed indicators of the construct involved. Conceptually it should be possible, for example, to compile a catalogue or inventory of all things/behaviours which may be regarded as indicators of success among small businesses, such as turnover, number of employees, taxable profit, and so on.

7.3.1 The nature of measurement

According to Stevens (1951), **measurement** involves the assignment of numbers, in terms of fixed rules, to individuals (or objects) to reflect differences between them in some or other characteristic or attribute.

FOR EXAMPLE We measure length by determining to which figure on a ruler the object alongside it compares. Certain requirements must be met, such as that the ruler should be straight and not bent.

The rules in terms of which numbers are assigned constitute an **operational definition** (see Section 2.4) of the variable being measured, in this example *length*.

NOMINAL MEASURE EXAMPLE: GENDER			
The unit of analysis (see Section 4.2) in this example is people			
Here are two levels of the variable *gender:*	Male		Female
Coded numerical value:	1		2
NOMINAL MEASURE EXAMPLE: STOCK PREFERENCE			
The unit of analysis in this example is investment sectors on the Johannesburg Stock Exchange (JSE)			
Here are three levels of the variable *stock preference:*	Mining	Industrials	Financials
Numerical values attached:	1	2	3
ORDINAL MEASURE EXAMPLE: ADMINISTRATIVE RANK			
The unit of analysis in this example is administrative ranks			
Here are three levels concerning the variable *administrative rank:*	Assistant officer	Officer	Chief officer
Numbers to be coded:	1	2	3
INTERVAL MEASURE EXAMPLE: TRUST IN A COMPANY'S FUTURE			
The unit of analysis in this example is employees	This company will make a profit till 2020.		
Here are five levels measuring the extent of *trust in a company's future:*	Absolutely ☐☐✗☐☐ Not at all 5 4 3 2 1		
Coded in this case:	3		
RATIO MEASURE EXAMPLE: INCOME PER MONTH			
The unit of analysis in this example is employees			
Here are infinte levels of the variable *income per month* because it is possible that some employees may not receive any income at all per month due to deductions (such as medical aid) from their salary while others may have earned a bonus, and so on:	R0... R1 000... R2 000... R3 000...		
The amount of R2 000 income equals the code:	2 000		

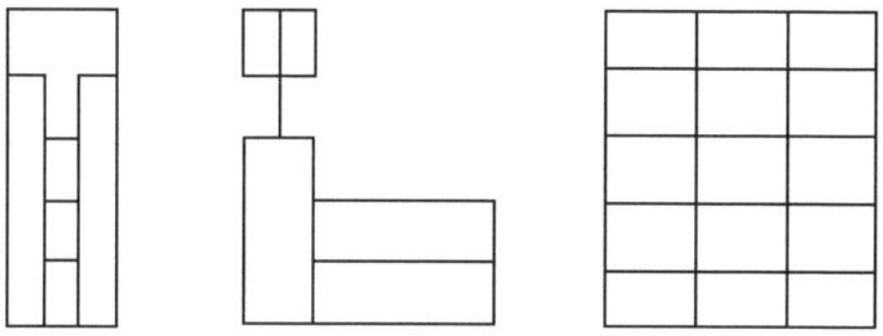

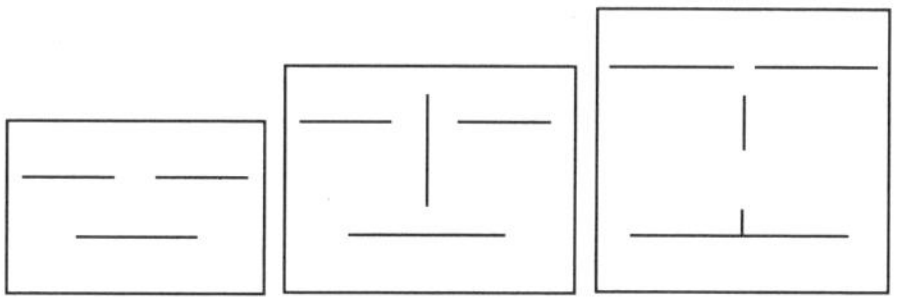

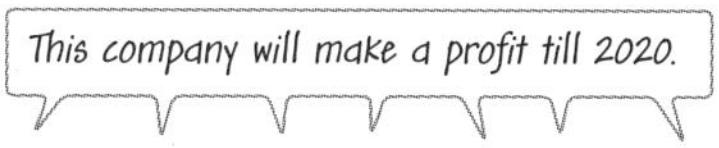

Figure 7.3 *Levels of measurement*

FOR EXAMPLE In Research Example VI (see Section 6.2.4.1, page 118) helping behaviour was operationalised in terms of the time that elapsed from the occurrence of the 'emergency' until the participant left the cubicle to summon assistance. The numbers assigned were the number of seconds the various participants took before summoning assistance.

Naturally, the adequacy of the scores obtained depends on the adequacy of the rules according to which these numbers are assigned.

7.3.2 The levels of measurement

In measurement we distinguish between different **levels of measurement** on the basis of the following four characteristics of numbers assigned in the process:

▶ distinguishability (the number 2 is different from the number 1)
▶ order of rank (2 has a higher rank than 1)
▶ equal intervals between successively higher numbers (0...1...2...3...) and
▶ absolute size (0 – 1 = –1 = 1 – 0 = 1).

These characteristics form a hierarchy in the sense that the fourth characteristic presupposes the third one, the third one presumes that the second one applies, and so on. If the numbers exhibit the feature of equal intervals, there has to be a rank order among them and they have to be distinguishable from each other. Corresponding to each of these four characteristics, a different level of measurement may be distinguished. These levels of measurement are (compare Figure 7.3):

▶ nominal measurement
▶ ordinal measurement
▶ interval measurement
▶ ratio measurement.

7.3.2.1 NOMINAL MEASUREMENT

In the case of **nominal measurement**, the numbers we assign to individuals only serve to distinguish them in terms of the attribute being measured.

FOR EXAMPLE Suppose a sample of subjects must be classified according to the variable *occupation*. In this case you would count how many directors, managers, administrators, and so on there are in the sample.

In this kind of measurement, we place individuals in different, mutually exclusive and exhaustive categories in respect of such a characteristic. By **mutually exclusive** we mean that each person belongs to one of the categories only (a particular behaviour should fall into one category only), while **exhaustive** implies that all individuals can be accommodated in some or other category (together they should provide for all possible forms of behaviour that qualify as indicators of the particular dependent variable).

FOR EXAMPLE We could measure someone's occupation by assigning the number 1 to all attorneys, the number 2 to all real estate agents, the number 3 to all personnel practitioners, and so on. In this example, the numbers only serve to distinguish between the various occupations. For this purpose we could just as well have used the letters A, B, C, and so on, or different colours.

With the number 2 we do not in any way imply a greater magnitude of the variable *occupation* (whatever this means) than with the number 1.

FOR EXAMPLE In terms of the variable *stock preference*, we could measure the classification of stocks on the Johannesburg stock exchange by assigning the number 1 to mining stocks, the number 2 to industrials, 3 to financials, and so on.

In terms of the variable *gender*, we could measure a customer's gender by assigning the number 0 to all males and the number 1 to all females. The category *gender* is therefore mutually exclusive in that each customer belongs to one category only.

The only information that we convey by assigning numbers at the nominal level of measurement is that those to which we assign the same number are the same or similar in respect of the particular variable, and that those to which we assign different numbers, fall into different categories of the variable. Although nominal measurement may be used, very few statistics can be properly applied to data collected in this form.

7.3.2.2 ORDINAL MEASUREMENT

Measures on an **ordinal** (ordered) **scale** have the same amount of information as measures on a nominal scale, since data can be classified in terms of equality and difference. However, ordinal scales permit you to order individual data. In the case of **ordinal measurement**, therefore, the numbers we assign not only reflect differences among individuals (in the variable being measured) but also **rank order**. The assumption is made that those to whom we assign higher numbers exhibit more of the particular attribute than those to whom we assigned lower numbers.

FOR EXAMPLE Suppose the order of rank (in ascending order) for administrative staff in a company is as follows: assistant administrative officer, administrative officer, first administrative officer, and chief administrative officer.

Using ordinal measurement we therefore assign the numbers 1 to 4 as follows:
- 1 to the rank of assistant administrative officer
- 2 to the rank of administrative officer
- 3 to the rank of first administrative officer
- 4 to the rank of chief administrative officer.

Of course, we could also assign the number 1 to the highest rank; 2 to the second highest rank, and so on, in which case the numbers are assigned in inverse order. However, the important point remains that the sizes of the assigned numbers are indicative of rank order only. Since the arithmetic mean cannot be calculated with data recorded in this form, the use of many other statistics is also excluded.

7.3.2.3 INTERVAL MEASUREMENT

An **interval scale** has all the characteristics of both nominal and ordinal scales, but provides additional information regarding the degree of difference between individual data items within a set or group. Thus, if you have an interval scale you can place each data item precisely along the scale and determine exactly where the intervals are. Most measures of human characteristics have interval properties. In **interval measurement**, therefore, we use the property of **equal differences** between consecutively higher numbers.

FOR EXAMPLE The classical example in this instance is the measurement of temperature. The difference between 10 °C and 20 °C is just as big as that between 30 °C and 40 °C, and twice as big as that between 20 °C and 25 °C.

However, note that 20 °C does not indicate a temperature that is as twice as hot as 10 °C. This statement would only make sense if 0 °C meant the complete absence of temperature. However, the zero point on both the Centigrade and Fahrenheit scales has been chosen arbitrarily – a reading of zero on the former corresponds to one of 32 on the latter (see Figure 7.3). Precision in interval scales is therefore limited. Another drawback of the interval scale is that some statistics, such as the geometric mean, are excluded from use with data collected in this form.

Strictly speaking, most measurement instruments in the human behavioural sciences yield measurements at the nominal and ordinal levels. For practical purposes, though, the scores on, for example, standardised tests, attitude scales, and self-constructed questionnaires (see Section 7.8), may probably be regarded as satisfactory approximations of interval measurement (Kerlinger, 1986).

FOR EXAMPLE Although we probably could not maintain with much conviction that the difference in intelligence as expressed by an intelligence quotient (IQ) score between 100 and 105 is just as large as one between 120 and 125, few experts would deny that the difference between, for example, 100 and 110 is greater than that between 110 and 115. Someone who maintains that IQs merely represent ordinal measurement would have to deny the latter statement and insist that no significance should be attached to the size of the differences between successive IQs. (Compare CD-ROM manual.)

7.3.2.4 RATIO MEASUREMENT

Ratio scales represent the highest level of precision. Only in **ratio measurement** is there a fixed and **absolute zero** point. The ratios between numbers assigned at this level of measurement can therefore be interpreted meaningfully. It further corresponds to the property of **equal differences** between consecutively higher numbers as used in interval measurement.

FOR EXAMPLE A reaction time (for example the time it takes to switch on a machine when a light flashes a warning) of 0 seconds implies the complete absence of reaction time. Consequently it makes sense to say that a reaction time of 1,60 seconds is twice as long as one of 0,80 seconds. The same properties apply to the example of the number of cigarettes a person smokes per day (see Figure 7.3).

The advantage of using the ratio scale is that any statistical analysis can be used on data collected in this form.

ACTIVITY 7.1

QUESTIONS

1. Name two variables that would be naturally considered for nominal scales. Set up mutually exclusive and exhaustive categories for each of the variables mentioned above.
2. Develop an ordinal scale (with instructions to the research subjects) for consumer preferences for four different brands of cold drink.
3. Name three variables that could be measured on an interval scale.

ANSWERS

1. Gender and language group.

| Male |
| Female |

and

| English |
| Zulu |
| Sotho |
| Afrikaans |

2. Arrange the following brands of cold drinks according to your preferences. Write 1 in the block next to your favourite brand, 2 in the block of your next favourite brand, and continue until every brand is numbered. Tick (✔) the last block if you do not drink cold drink at all.

  ☐ Coke ☐ Iron Brew
  ☐ Sprite ☐ Ginger Ale
  ☐ Do not drink cold drink

3. Morale, satisfaction, and experience.

ACTIVITY 7.2

Read Case Studies A, B, C, D, E, F, and G in Appendix D on page 306.

QUESTION

What type of measurement level (nominal, ordinal, interval, or ratio measurement) is involved in the dependent and independent variables (consult answers to Activities 2.1 and 6.2)? Explain your answer briefly.

ANSWER

case study a

The dependent variable *attitude towards AIDS* is measured with the aid of a five-point Likert scale. An *interval measurement* is therefore involved: point 5 (agree fully) is more positive than, for example, point 4 (agree) or point 1 (do not agree at all). A feature of an attitude scale such as the Likert scale is the equal differences between progressively higher numbers, which is characteristic of an interval measurement. (We discuss the Likert scale in Section 7.7.3.3.)

case study b

The dependent variable *attitude towards supervision* is measured with the aid of a semantic differential (a seven-point scale), and it therefore involves an *interval measurement:* point 7 represents a specific attitude towards supervision (for example positive), and point 1 represents the opposite attitude (negative). The feature of equal differences between progressively higher numbers (characteristic of an interval measurement) is involved in an attitude scale such as a semantic differential. (We discuss the semantic differential in Section 7.7.3.3.)

case study c

The dependent variable *knowledge of management principles* is measured with the help of a one-hour written test. A *ratio measurement* is therefore involved – the first-line supervisor who, for example, scored 80% in the test, has twice as much knowledge (it is generally believed) as one who scored 40%. There is, furthermore, an absolute zero mark involved seen in terms of the learning objectives of the training course.

case study d

Although time (measured in seconds, minutes, and so forth) can be classified as a ratio measurement, it can be argued that total preparation time involves an *interval measurement.* This is because speech preparation includes various aspects and it therefore cannot be proven that the student who took 30 minutes to prepare was twice as well prepared as someone who took 15 minutes.

The two other variables also involve interval measurement because the characteristics that are measured involve equal differences between consecutively higher

amounts as is typically the case with judgement scales (five- or four-point scales).

case study e

The independent variables *bank overdraft usage* and *cash flow problems* are measured in terms of the average amount exceeding the bank overdraft limit per month and by means of a four-point scale respectively.

Thus, the variable *bank overdraft usage* concerns *ratio measurement* because a small business that exceeded the bank overdraft limit by, for example, R20 000,00 per month used twice the amount of one that exceeded the limit by R10 000,00. There is also an absolute zero involved for businesses that did not exceed their bank overdraft limits.

The other variable, *cash flow problems*, involves *interval measurement* because the characteristics that are measured involve equal differences between consecutively higher degrees of experiencing cash flow problems than is typically the case with rating scales (four-point scales). No absolute zero is involved because any business at some time could have cash flow problems.

case study f

In the case of the dependent variable *innovative problem-solving style, ordinal* (or at most interval) *measurement* is involved. This is because, according to the KAI scale, there are five levels of the style (the KAI scale consists of 32 five-point items: $5 \times 32 = 160$) and there are equal differences between consecutively higher numbers.

The independent variable *business people* has two levels (entrepreneurs and managers) with no successive rank between them; *nominal measurement* is therefore involved. (In other words, we could have mentioned the managers first and then the entrepreneurs, or *vice versa.*)

case study g

The dependent variable *attitudes towards HIV/AIDS patients* is measured by means of unstructured in-depth interviews (see Section 8.4.3) and therefore involves *nominal measurement.* The measurement in this case has only two levels (answering the open-ended questions of the interviewer or no answers at all). Here only two levels can be coded namely one (1) or zero (0) because the answers can only be classified in these two mutually exclusive and exhaustive categories.

7.4 Validity (construct validity of the dependent variable)

As you will know from Chapter 6, validity is the extent to which the research findings accurately represent what is really happening in the situation. An effect or test is valid if it demonstrates or measures what the researcher thinks or claims it does (Coolican, 1992, p. 35). Research errors, such as faulty research procedures, poor samples, and inaccurate or misleading measurement, can undermine validity.

FOR EXAMPLE We may be interested in whether employees understand their company's occupational pension scheme. We therefore ask them to calculate their pension entitlements. The question is, do their answers reflect their understanding of the scheme, or whether they have read the scheme, or how good they are at remembering the details of the scheme, or even their ability to make calculations?

Any given measuring instrument measures three components, namely:
▶ the construct (see Sections 2.2.1 & 7.4) intended
▶ irrelevant constructs
▶ random measurement error (reliability – see Section 7.5).

The first two components represent **systematic sources** of variation because they remain constant for any given individual. The last component refers to **accidental factors** that may vary from one measuring occasion to the next, and from one individual to the next in a completely haphazard fashion. It is therefore an unsystematic source of variation (reliability – see Section 7.5).

FOR EXAMPLE A paper-and-pencil measurement/test of mechanical aptitude may possibly measure the following aspects:
• mechanical aptitude (the construct intended)
• the ability to read and comprehend the instructions of the measurement/test (an irrelevant construct, because

it is impossible to measure his or her mechanical aptitude) if the person cannot read or write
• measurement error (the third component – see Sections 7.5 & 9.3.1).

There are various types of validity that relate to the independent variable. In this section we will discuss two kinds of validity, namely:
▶ construct validity
▶ criterion-related validity.

Other forms of validity such as content and face validity are not addressed in this book.

7.4.1 Construct validity

When we measure something with an instrument, the instrument we use to measure the variable must measure that which it is supposed to measure. We refer to this requirement as the **construct validity** of the scores obtained on a measuring instrument. The construct validity of a measuring instrument refers to the degree to which it measures the intended construct rather than irrelevant constructs or measurement error.

FOR EXAMPLE If the general level of communication skills of the trainee supervisors had been measured in Research Example II (see Section 2.3, page 17) instead of their management style, it would have led to incorrect conclusions being drawn.

Note that construct validity is of special importance to research.

We pointed out (see Section 2.3.1) that there may be more than one operational definition or measuring instrument of the same construct and that these various indicators may overlap and differ to some extent.

FOR EXAMPLE The importance of designated group (black, coloured, Indians, and so on), academic qualifications, and relevant work experience may overlap in their importance to the operational definition of affirmative action in different company policies.

Furthermore, none of these individual measures or indicators completely succeeds in representing the construct because they also reflect other, irrelevant constructs. In fact, if any of these indicators did manage to represent the construct perfectly, we would no longer be dealing with a construct, but with a directly observable variable.

As any given measure of a construct also reflects irrelevant constructs, it is advisable to use more than one measure of the same construct. If this is not done, it is impossible to examine to what extent any given measuring instrument measures anything else but itself.

FOR EXAMPLE There are various indicators of the construct *socio-economic status*, for example, the person's income, occupation, educational level, or the area in which he or she resides,. Each of these indicators only partially represents it, and also partially overlaps with other indicators. However, collectively such indicators offer a more complete representation of the construct.

Some authors compare this approach (that is, using more than one measure of the same construct) with **triangulation** in navigation. This is a procedure to determine the correct position of a ship or plane by comparing its position with those of two known navigation points.

The more that two measures measure the same construct, the more they overlap and the higher the relationship (correlation – see Section 9.4) between them tends to be. The construct validity of an instrument is not only supported by high relationships (correlation – see Section 9.4) with other measures of the same construct (**convergent validity**), but also by low correlations with measures of different constructs (**discriminant validity**).

An important threat to the construct validity of questionnaire measurements of personality, interests, and attitudes lies in **measurement reactivity** (see Section 6.2.5.1). The response sets of faking and social desirability and the response style of acquiescence imply that individuals' responses are not true reflections of their personalities, interests, and attitudes.

Faking means that participants deliberately distort their responses in order to create a desired impression and is the most dangerous response set.

FOR EXAMPLE To the question, *Do you easily lose your temper?*, a job applicant may answer negatively because he wishes to create a good impression; whereas a murderer may answer positively in an attempt to appear mentally disturbed.

In the case of **socially desirable responses** subjects deliberately or inadvertently provide the responses (answers or actions) that they believe to be socially acceptable.

FOR EXAMPLE To the question, *Do you like everybody you know?*, individuals may answer positively because they believe that it would be socially unacceptable not to like some people.

Acquiescence refers to the phenomenon where research participants tend to consistently answer "yes" (to yes/no items) or "true" (rather than false), irrespective of the content of the question.

FOR EXAMPLE An interviewee may reply "yes" to both of the following statements:

I prefer to spend a night out on the town with friends instead of staying at home reading a book.

and

I prefer spending a quiet night at home reading a book instead of partying with friends.

Answering "yes" to both questions is contradictory because on the one hand it appears that the subject likes to go out, while on the other hand the subject likes to stay at home.

In personality questionnaires (see Section 7.7.3.2) we utilise various strategies to make provision for the possible effect of these response sets and response styles. Paper-and-pencil questionnaires of personality, interests, and attitudes are susceptible to problems of distortion, social desirability, and acquiescence. However, most of these instruments have built-in precautionary measures to provide for these problems. Some personality questionnaires, for example, have lie or social desirability scales which identify individuals who provide such invalid responses. Using more than one measure can also counter these problems; for example, if we have to measure extroversion (that is, the tendency to be sociable, warm, and active), it may be advisable to use questionnaires (see Section 7.7.3.1) as well as, for instance, ratings (see Section 7.7.3.4) on this construct.

7.4.2 Criterion-related validity

Criterion-related validity is another kind of validity that is essential to applied business and administrative practice. Criterion-related validity refers to the degree to which diagnostic and selection measurement/tests correctly predict the relevant criterion. The **relevant criterion** refers to the variable that is to be diagnosed or on which success is to be predicted respectively.

Depending on whether the criterion is present at the time of testing, or whether it will only become available some time after the test is completed, we distinguish between **concurrent validity** and **predictive validity**.

We may investigate the **concurrent validity** of a group intelligence measurement/test by correlating it with scores on an individual intelligence measurement/test (the criterion) that may be available at about the same time. Individual measurement/tests typically require more administration time and it might be preferable to substitute them for the more economical group measurements/tests. Both the group measurement/test and the individual measurement/test are administered to a large sample of individuals who are representative of the population (see Section 4.3) for which

the intelligence measurement/test is intended, and the two sets of scores obtained are correlated (see Section 9.4).

When we investigate the **predictive validity** of a selection measurement/test, all applicants from a large, representative sample from the population for which the measurement/test is intended must complete the measurement/test and be admitted to the course or job (or for whatever purpose selection is required). When the scores on an eventual or intermediate criterion (signifying success in the work or course respectively) become available, these are correlated with the measurement/test scores obtained originally.

FOR EXAMPLE If a measurement/test is considered for selecting junior managers, the intention is to predict which candidates will eventually become successful senior managers (the eventual criterion), or which of them will successfully complete the management training course (an intermediate criterion).

The predictive validity of a selection measurement/test for junior managers may be investigated by correlating scores on the measurement/test (see Section 9.4) with the success criteria (for example obtaining an MBA-degree or a number of management certificates) of all the original applicants obtained four or more years later.

NOTE: It is important to note that if this correlation is obtained only for those who have exceeded a particular cutoff score on the measurement/test, it will typically underestimate the actual measurement/test-criterion correlation (Huysamen, 1989b, Section 8.3).

A typical problem in criterion-related validation is trying to locate a measure of the criterion that has a sufficient reliability (see Section 7.5) and construct validity (see Section 7.4).

FOR EXAMPLE Management success/achievement (as measured by means of a paper-and-pencil examination) in a management training course is not necessarily a construct valid indicator of successful managerial characteristics.

For an instrument to be construct valid (for example the paper-and-pencil management examination mentioned in the previous example), it would have to involve items that form a representative sample (see Section 4.3) of all management success indicators. This actually entails the definition of content validity mentioned in Section 7.4.

Sometimes ratings (see Section 7.7.3.4) of the criterion variable are used, but the reliability (see Section 7.5) of such ratings may be just as suspect as that of the measurements whose criterion-related validity is to be examined.

7.5 Reliability

Reliability is concerned with the findings of the research and relates to the credibility of the findings. In determining whether our findings are reliable, we need to ask the following question: *will the evidence and conclusions stand up to the closest scrutiny?* (Raimond, 1993, p. 55). It stands to reason that if we measure a construct (for example small business or management success) (see Sections 2.4 & 7.4) by means of a particular instrument (for example taxable profit calculation formula or a management training course examination paper), comparable measurements should be obtained for the same individuals/objects irrespective of, for example, when the instrument is administered, which particular version of it is used, and who is applying (administering and scoring) it.

FOR EXAMPLE If the rank (first, second, third, and so on) of Bongani's score on a measurement/test of a stable construct depends on whether the measurement/test is administered on Monday or Tuesday so that, for example, he would earn more marks than Ann on Monday but do less well on Tuesday, the reliability of such a measurement/test is suspect.

In Research Example I (see Section 1.2.1.5, page 4) it would have been undesirable if the relative positions of the participants (trainees) depended on the particular sample of addition problems they had to solve.

In Research Example II (see Section 2.3, page 17) it would similarly have been unacceptable if the number of iron-fisted management style reactions recorded for any trainee was determined by the rater (researcher) who was recording the incidence of these reactions.

The requirement of **generalisation** relates to the reliability of the scores obtained. By generalisation we mean the consistency of the ranking (of the scores) that we assign to the individuals or objects, irrespective of when the measuring instrument was applied, which form of it was used, and by whom it was administered or scored. Reliability therefore refers to the extent to which the obtained scores may be **generalised** to different measuring occasions, measurement/tests forms, and measurement/test administrators. Scores that are assigned to individuals should therefore be consistent irrespective of the time of measurement, the test used, and the person administering the test.

NOTE: An unreliable measurement cannot adequately measure what it is supposed to measure; in other words, it cannot be construct valid (see Section 7.4). Reliability is also important for statistical purposes (see Chapter 9).

7.5.1 Estimating reliability

If a research finding can be repeated, it is reliable. In other words, if anyone else were to repeat the research, they should be able to obtain the same results as those obtained originally. For example, if we found that a group of workers who had attended a training course doubled their previous productivity levels, and another researcher obtained very similar results, the measurements are reliable. Repeating a research study in order to establish reliability is known as **replication**.

We can distinguish between (at least) three irrelevant sources of systematic variation in measurement (see Section 7.2), namely:

- measurement occasion
- measurement form
- measurement user.

Each of these sources relates to different types of unsystematic sources of variation. Because reliability is affected by such **unsystematic sources of variation**, we may distinguish a different kind of reliability for each of the above systematic sources of variation, namely:

▶ test-retest reliability
▶ parallel-forms reliability
▶ internal consistency
▶ split-halves reliability
▶ interrater/intercoder/tester/test or measurement-scorer reliability.

7.5.1.1 TEST-RETEST RELIABILITY

To determine the **test-retest reliability** of a measuring instrument, we must administer it on at least two occasions to the same large, representative sample (see Section 4.3) from the population for which the instrument is intended. We then correlate (see Section 9.4) the two sets of scores obtained in this way and calculate a correlation coefficient for the two sets of data. This coefficient is an **index of reliability**. **Test-retest reliability** refers to the degree to which a measurement/test is immune, so to speak, to the particular measurement/test occasion on which it is administered. Scores obtained on one occasion may be generalised to those that could potentially have been obtained on other comparable occasions.

FOR EXAMPLE We have all had the experience of being, without any explanation (such as poor preparation), more measurement/test-ready on some measurement/test occasions than on others. On one day we may feel on top of the world and the very next day we feel miserable. Test-retest (or simply, retest) reliability pertains to such unsystematic sources of variation relating to measurement/test occasions.

The time interval between the two administrations should not be too long to prevent real and permanent changes from taking place in the attribute being measured. At the same time, it should not be too short so that participants may remember the responses given on the first administration (Huysamen, 1989b, Section 2.2).

A disadvantage of this method is that it is often difficult to persuade respondents to answer questions a second time. Furthermore, if they do answer the questions a second time, they may think more deeply about the questions on the second occasion and provide different answers. Also, since ambiguous items and unclear instructions may cause subjects to interpret them differently on different occasions, such items and instructions may adversely affect reliability. The measurement/test compiler should therefore write unambiguous items and clear instructions.

7.5.1.2 PARALLEL-FORMS RELIABILITY

Parallel-forms reliability of a measurement/test is determined by using interchangeable versions of a measurement/test that have been compiled to measure the same construct equally well but by means of different content. The different versions are administered to the same representative sample and the obtained scores are correlated.

FOR EXAMPLE Standardised tests (see Section 7.7.3.2), such as parallel spelling tests, for example, are composed of different words (which are to be spelled), but are equally difficult.

Another example may be found in estimating the taxable value of individual citizens of South Africa. Two or more different formulae/equations/calculations of measuring the amount of money payable to the receiver of revenue may be used to determine the reliability of an existing form of taxation.

Thus, if there is reason to believe that the amount of money someone must pay to the receiver of revenue, as estimated by the existing form of taxation, provides an unrepresentative picture of his or her taxable value, a parallel measurement/formula/ equation/calculation may be administered subsequently to his or her financial position.

Just as retest reliability pertains to the degree to which the scores obtained on one occasion may be generalised to those that may be obtained on other measurement/test occasions, parallel-forms reliability deals with the generalisability over parallel measurement/test forms.

Concerning the measurement of human abilities (such as the ability to recognise depth or three-dimensional pictures), parallel measurement/test forms contain different items. In this way the potential benefits of memory (remembering the items from the previous test) are negated.

Just as individuals' measurement/test preparedness may be higher on one measurement/test occasion than on another, they may be more familiar with specific items in one measurement/test than in a parallel form by mere accident.

FOR EXAMPLE A primary school pupil may remember that London is the capital of the United Kingdom because some of her relatives happened to visit this city.

7.5.1.3 INTERNAL CONSISTENCY

A high **internal consistency** implies a high degree of generalisability across the items within the measurement/test. In other words, if someone performs well on a few items in such a measurement/test, the chances are good that he or she will fare equally well on the remaining items in the measurement/test (compare Section 7.7.3.3(a) – last example). Every item is correlated with every other item across the entire sample and the average inter-item correlation is taken as the index of reliability.

To determine the reliability of a measuring instrument by using the internal consistency method (Huysamen, 1989b), we administer the measurement/test only once to a large, representative sample. Cronbach's (1951) **coefficient alpha** is a measure of the internal consistency of a measurement/test. This index shows the degree to which all the items in a measurement/test measure the same attribute.

To compute coefficient alpha, both the variance (see Section 9.4) on the (total) measurement/test scores and the variances of the individual items are required. The reliability coefficient obtained may be interpreted as an estimation of the parallel-forms reliability of the measurement/test.

It is important to note that the longer a measurement/test is, in other words, the more appropriate content it covers, the higher its internal consistency should be.

However, internal consistency will be improved only if the measurement/test is lengthened by items that are similar to those in the original measurement/test.

Formulae (for example Spearman-Brown) are available to estimate the number of such items by which a measurement/test with a given reliability should be lengthened to achieve a required degree of internal consistency (Huysamen, 1990b).

7.5.1.4 SPLIT-HALVES RELIABILITY

Split-halves reliability is calculated by correlating the scores on one half of the test with the scores for the other half of the test. The test is therefore divided into two equal halves which are then correlated in terms of the scores for each half. There are various ways of splitting a test, for example the responses to the odd-numbered questions can be separated from the responses to the even-numbered questions. Alternatively, the responses to the first half of the questions can be separated from the answers to the remainder. The correlation coefficient for the two halves is then calculated and indicates the reliability for the test.

7.5.1.5 INTERRATER/INTERCODER/TESTER/TEST OR MEASUREMENT-SCORER RELIABILITY

This type of reliability refers to accidental, inconsistent behaviour on the part of the individuals administering or scoring the measurement/test.

FOR EXAMPLE It is frequently found that a particular tester consistently marks too strictly or too leniently. This will result in scores that are unreliable.

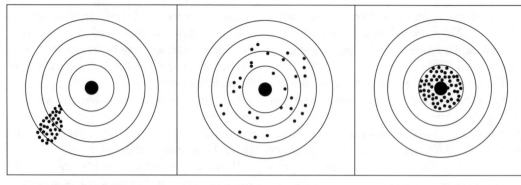

Reliable but not valid   Valid but not reliable   Valid *and* reliable

Figure 7.4 *An analogy to validity and reliability (measuring the large dot-research question, with small tries-method and measuring instruments) (Source: Babbie & Mouton, 2001, p. 124. Used with permission.)*

Especially in the case of ratings (see Section 7.7.3.4), it is advisable to investigate **inter-rater reliability**. This is done by having more than one rater rate the same individuals (on the relevant attribute) and correlating (see Section 9.4) the ratings obtained.

7.6 Pilot studies in the development of an instrument

When a new measurement instrument is developed, it is useful to "test it out" before administering it to the actual sample. This process of "testing out" is done by means of a **pilot study**, which entails administering the instrument to a limited number of subjects from the same population (see Section 4.3) as that for which the eventual project is intended. The pilot study is therefore a "dress rehearsal" for the actual research investigation.

The purpose of a pilot study can be summarised as follows:

▶ **To detect possible flaws in the measurement procedures** (such as ambiguous instructions, inadequate time limits, and so on) as well as in the operationalisation of the independent variable(s) (in experimental research).

▶ **To identify unclear or ambiguously formulated items**. In such a pilot study the actual questions are put to the "partici-

pants", and they are then asked to indicate how they have interpreted the formulated questions.

▶ **An opportunity for researchers and assistants to notice non-verbal behaviour** (on the part of the participants) that may possibly signify discomfort or embarrassment about the content or wording of the questions.

A pilot study is particularly useful if the researcher has compiled the measuring instrument specifically for the purposes of the research project. In such a situation it may even be necessary to investigate the validity (see Section 7.4) and reliability (see Section 7.5) of the instrument in an independent project (instead of in a pilot study). (Compare Figure 7.4.)

NOTE:

• It is virtually mandatory to test survey questionnaires (see Section 7.7.3.1) on a small group of individuals who are representative of the populations for which they are intended. If the instrument is extensively revised in reaction to the results of the pilot study, the revised instrument should be subjected to a new round of testing.

• If a self-developed instrument is not tested in a pilot study, it is advisable to at least ask an experienced researcher/expert in the field to check the instrument with a view to spotting glaring flaws (determining, *inter alia*, its face validity).

- The development of a valid and reliable measuring instrument is such a comprehensive project that it should be avoided as far as possible as part of a typical dissertation or thesis.

7.7 Measuring instruments

7.7.1 Introduction

Because the constructs in the human behavioural sciences often involve human attributes, actions, and artefacts, it may appear to lay people that these can be appropriately measured by merely asking research participants directly about them. Thus, in the case of the construct *dominance*, lay people might argue that participants should simply be asked whether or not they are dominant by nature. However, the reliability and validity of the measurements obtained in this fashion would be highly suspect.

On the one hand, participants may have insufficient knowledge about themselves, or they may be unable to verbalise their innermost feelings. On the other hand, participants may deliberately provide incorrect answers with a view to putting themselves in a positive or negative light. Moreover, the reliability of a measure (of a construct such as dominance) that consists of a single question, would tend to be highly unsatisfactory.

We can distinguish between secondary and primary data sources (see Section 3.3.2). **Secondary data** are information collected by individuals or agencies and institutions other than the researcher him- or herself. **Primary data** are original data collected by the researcher for the purposes of his or her own study at hand.

In this section we deal with various types of measuring instruments and provide guidelines for constructing some of them. These instruments include:

- **Survey questionnaires** (see Section 7.7.3.1), **standardised measuring instruments** (see Section 7.7.3.2), and **attitude scales** (see Section 7.7.3.3). These do not involve direct observations of the behaviour of subjects but, instead, individuals' reports of their behaviour. These measuring instruments are therefore susceptible to measurement reactivity (see Section 6.2.5.1), the consequences of which may vary from the withholding of co-operation to deliberate deception.
- **Rating scales** (see Section 7.7.3.4), which require raters to assess the behaviour of participants. Bias on the part of the raters can invalidate such information.
- **Indicators** such as the inflation rate, consumer price index, retail sales, building plans passed, registered unemployed, and so on. These are compiled and calculated by people such as actuaries in government offices, including Statistics South Africa (Stats SA), the Board on Tariffs & Trade (BTT), university bureaux, chambers of commerce, portfolio managers, and so on. These people collect information regarding the size and market share of different enterprises and companies, as well as their imports and exports.

This information (figures) is published, *inter alia*, in reports, state budgets, manuals, and academic journals and includes the following:

- Corporate profit growth addressing ratios such as wages as a percentage of production and its relation to an index such as the Gross Domestic Product (GDP).
- Foreign Direct Investment (FDI) as a result of privatisation.
- Cuts in tariff rates according to the World Trade Organisation (WTO).
- Statistics from the South African Revenue Service (SARS).

- Performance tables of different unit trusts in the Unit Trusts Quarterly Survey.
- Databases by private companies such as EDS Small Business Database.

Some of this information is also available on the Internet. (See list of web sites on page 302.)

7.7.2 Unobtrusive measurement

In this section we deal with approaches in which the participant, and sometimes also the researcher, is unaware that measurement is taking place for research purposes. The simplest form of unobtrusive measurement occurs when a subject's behaviour is observed through one-way mirrors or recorded by concealed video cameras. There are various other ingenious ways in which researchers can behave like detectives to collect information that people routinely and even unwittingly generate for purposes other than research. Consequently, the problem of measurement reactivity (see Section 6.2.5.1) is completely eliminated. These procedures may often be used together with other measurement methods to check whether comparable results are obtained. However, because the researcher has to rely on the residue of past events, it may sometimes be difficult to rule out alternative explanations for the obtained results (as may be in the case of investigating a crime). The following methods can be used in unobtrusive measurement:

▶ physical traces
▶ personal documents and mass media material
▶ official statistics and archival sources.

7.7.2.1 PHYSICAL TRACES

These measures are based on physical changes that take place over time. In this category we can distinguish between measures of **erosion**, which involve the wear and tear of materials, and measures of **accretion**, which are based on the formation of deposits on materials.

FOR EXAMPLE Suppose we want to identify the most popular exhibits at a museum. If we conduct interviews with visitors to the museum, or request them to complete questionnaires, we may eventually have measurements that are susceptible to unconscious or deliberate faking (see Section 7.4.1). The presence of observers in a museum, again, may affect visitors' spontaneous inspection of the exhibits. But, by examining the wear and tear on the carpets (a measure of erosion) in front of the different exhibits, an unobtrusive measure of their relative popularity may be obtained. This measure is unaffected by the response styles of either the participants or the observers.

However, the problem of ruling out alternative explanations is evident from this example. Suppose all visitors to the museum are obliged to use the same route through the museum. They also tend to spend more time at the initial stages of their visit but become more hurried as their time runs out. The greater degree of wear on the carpets in front of the exhibits at the beginning of the route than on the tiles at the end (exit) would then not be attributable to the greater popularity of the former, but to their favourable position along the route through the museum.

In the United States the popularity of television programmes has been gauged by monitoring the decrease in water levels during the screening of commercials. The assumption was that people are glued to their television sets during popular programmes and limit their visits to the toilet to commercial breaks.

Examining garbage dumps may be used as a technique of measures of accretion. The eating and drinking habits of present-day people can be studied by inspecting garbage bags.

7.7.2.2 PERSONAL DOCUMENTS AND MASS MEDIA MATERIAL

This measuring method entails investigating the means of communication of:

▶ the mass media (for example newspapers, magazines, films)
▶ organisations and associations (for example minutes of their meetings)
▶ those of a more personal nature (for example paintings, diaries, personal letters, and so on).

Content analysis is used to investigate these (see Section 9.2.2).

7.7.2.3 OFFICIAL STATISTICS AND ARCHIVAL SOURCES

These data are originally typically collected for purposes other than their use in human behavioural research. In the following examples mass media material and official statistics were used together.

FOR EXAMPLE:

- Statistics South Africa publishes information about birth registrations, deaths, marriages, divorces, unemployment, and road accidents on a quarterly basis. It also conducts a census every five years, although this period may be changed due to circumstances. (For example, the one scheduled for 1990 was conducted a year later and the next one took place during 1996. The last census took place in 2001.)
- Official statistics and archival data may be used in an interrupted time-series design (see Section 5.3.2), for example. In the investigation into the effect of the crackdown on speeding in the American state of Connecticut during the fifties and sixties, archival records were consulted to obtain the road fatalities over a number of years.
- Locally, Naude (1990) used official statistics to compare the application of the death penalty in South Africa with that in the United States. He compared the sentencing in terms of the race of the offender and the race and gender of the victim, and he compared commuting of the sentence in terms of the race of the offender.

- To investigate the relationship between fertility rates as idealised in magazine stories and actual fertility, Middleton (in Webb, Campbell, Schwartz & Sechrest, 1966) recorded the size of families in stories in eight American magazines at three points in time (1916, 1936, and 1956), and official statistics on family size at the same dates. It appeared that the shift in the size of fictitious families in the stories was closely related to the corresponding shift in the actual levels of fertility. Carlsmith and Anderson (1979) correlated newspaper reports of the incidence of urban riots and daily temperature reports in the United States and found that the probability of such riots increased with higher temperatures. However, Tyson and Turnbull (1990) failed to duplicate these results locally.

Apart from the non-reactivity associated with the unobtrusive nature of official statistics and archival sources, their greatest advantages are the **ease** and **low costs** involved in obtaining them. They are especially useful in large-scale investigations on macro level (as in the above example of road fatalities over time) that cannot be researched in other ways. In addition, these sources may provide information about human reactions to events such as earthquakes, riots, and so on, which researchers cannot create for practical and ethical reasons (see Section 7.9).

Because this information is often collected at regular intervals (for example census information), it makes **trend analyses** (see Section 5.4.3.3) possible. Although official statistics do not involve excessive time and costs to collect, the screening process and the search for evidence to rule out alternative explanations may indeed require a considerable effort. Often it requires ingenuity to transform the available information into indicators of the appropriate constructs. Consequently, the construct validity of the data obtained may be occasionally suspect. As the researcher is not in a position to ensure that the original collection of data took place systematically, there is also the possibility that the available sources may be incomplete.

Consequently, there may be doubts about how representative the obtained data are of the relevant universe.

FOR EXAMPLE We could not compare the number of deaths at birth for different population groups if, firstly, a greater percentage of births in one group took place at home instead of in hospitals and clinics, and, secondly, if such deaths at home often went unreported.

7.7.3 Group contacts

Collecting data from groups of people have many advantages which can be set out as follows:

▶ Captive audiences such as students or prisoners, the elderly in a home for the aged, and workers at a wine cellar or other factory are available to work with. This procedure then corresponds to the administration of a group measurement/test.

▶ Since a single person (with possibly a few assistants) is required to provide the instructions in one room or hall, the cost per questionnaire (in the case of surveys) is much lower than that of personal interviews.

▶ The researcher is in full control of the completion of the questionnaires. The session is arranged with the permission of the appropriate authorities (for example school, university, and so on) so that no respondent has an excuse for not completing the questionnaire. Consequently, a response rate (the percentage of questionnaires handed back/returned/posted back) of close to 100% is the general rule.

▶ Since the researcher and his or her assistants are present, queries about the completion of survey questionnaires may be answered immediately. (In the case of standardised group tests (see Section 7.7.3.2), the instructions are fixed and no deviations are actually allowed.)

▶ The group contact way of administering questionnaires corresponds to the personal interview (see Section 7.7.4) as far as the presence of the interviewer is concerned, but it allows for the same degree of anonymity as the typical postal survey (see Section 7.7.3.1). The personal interview does not allow this.

The only disadvantage of this method is that it is limited to a few populations. Associated with this disadvantage is the fact that such groups typically represent accidental samples (see Section 4.3.4.1), so that the population validity (see Section 6.3.2) of the obtained results becomes highly suspect. We will discuss the following categories of group contacts:

▶ survey questionnaires and postal dispatch
▶ standardised tests
▶ attitude scales
▶ rating scales and situational tests.

We will also briefly consider the problem of response styles.

7.7.3.1 SURVEY QUESTIONNAIRES AND POSTAL DISPATCH

We may use **survey questionnaires** to obtain the following types of information from the respondents:

▶ biographical details (age, educational qualifications, income, and so on)
▶ typical behaviour (which brand of toothpaste they use or which television programmes they favour, and so on)
▶ opinions, beliefs, and convictions (about any topic or issue, for example the present state of the economy)
▶ attitudes (for example towards affirmative action).

FOR EXAMPLE The following is a typical question found in survey questionnaires:

Mark your choice in one of the boxes.
The leadership in my organisation at the present time is:

Hard-working | 1 | 2 | 3 | 4 | 5 | *Lazy*

Attitudes should preferably be assessed by means of attitude scales (see Section 7.7.3.3) rather than survey questionnaires. Whereas attitude scales (see Section 7.7.3.3) are completed by the respondents (typically under the supervision of research staff), we can obtain information about biographical particulars, typical behaviour, opinions, and beliefs in person, by telephone (see Section 7.7.4), mail, or email.

When compiling the questionnaire, we should take the eyesight and the literacy level (see Section 7.8) of the intended respondents into consideration. Not only should the intended respondents be able to read and write, but they should also be able to follow the instructions.

Ignorant respondents may find complicated **filter questions** (see Section 7.8), which involve different routes for different responses, confusing. The purpose of filter questions is to determine whether respondents should answer all subsequent questions, or whether they can omit some of them (see Section 7.8). Unlike personal interviews or telephonic interviews (see Section 7.7.4), the respondents cannot fall back on anybody else but themselves since the interviewer is not available to direct them around irrelevant questions.

Conducting a typical postal or mail survey involves the following two stages:

▷ we first assemble the questions (asking for information about biographical particulars, typical behaviour, opinions and beliefs) that we want to put to the respondents in a structured questionnaire
▷ then we post the questionnaires to respondents with the request that they be completed and returned by mail or fax.

The advantages of postal surveys are as follows:

▷ **Cost and ease of application**. A postal survey is the least expensive of all survey methods. Irrespective of how far and wide respondents are scattered across the country, they can all be reached by means of relatively low postal costs.

▷ **Anonymity**. Of all survey methods the postal survey provides the greatest possibility of anonymity, that is, no name or identification is given. As a matter of fact, in most cases the questionnaire may be returned without any indication of who has completed it. As a result, the chances are better that such questionnaires are completed honestly, even though socially acceptable responses may be given at times.

The disadvantages of postal surveys are as follows:

▷ **Control over responding**. The researcher has the least control over the conditions under which postal questionnaires are completed. The respondent's family may show little consideration when, for example, their mother or father sits down to complete a questionnaire in silence and privacy. The chances are great that some questions may be omitted or not be responded to in the order presented, or even that someone else may complete or censor some of the questions. (When a respondent leaves a single question unanswered, it may mean that the remainder of his or her responses cannot be used for purposes of analysis.)

Of course, this lack of control could also hold a potential advantage in the sense that respondents are allowed to complete the questionnaires at their own convenience. For example, they are under no obligation to complete the questionnaire in a single session.

▷ **Response rate**. The researcher's lack of control over the completion of the questionnaires may result not only in poorly completed questionnaires, but also a poor response rate (the percentage of questionnaires handed back/returned/posted back). Postal surveys accordingly tend to have the lowest response rate of all survey methods. This rate frequently falls below 50% of the target population if the population involves the general public. Bluen and Goodman (1984) report response rates of 36% in South African postal surveys conducted on registered personnel practitioners.

As we can infer (see Section 6.3.2), a low response rate restricts the usefulness of a survey because we do not know to what extent a biased and consequently unrepresentative sample has been obtained. If those who have failed to respond systematically differ from those who have indeed responded, and the group who responded represents a minority (that is, a response rate of less than 50%), an entirely incorrect picture of the population may be obtained.

FOR EXAMPLE Suppose we conduct a postal survey to assess the attitudes of nurses towards their working conditions. If only those who are highly dissatisfied were to react (possibly in the hope that something would be done about their situation), and if this group consti- tuted a minority, a totally incorrect impression would be obtained of the opinion of the population of nurses.

If the majority of the target population fails to respond, it may be advisable to conduct per- sonal interviews (see Sections 7.7.4.1, 7.7.4.2 & 8.4.3) with a random sample (see Section 4.3.5) of the non-respondents. The purpose of this exercise would be to check whether their reason for failing to respond also distinguished them in terms of the relevant variable (for example attitude towards attitudinal object) from those who did indeed respond.

Respondents do not necessarily keep back questionnaires because they refuse to respond. Questionnaires may get lost or the respond- ents may have moved or have been out of town for an extended period of time.

In general, more satisfactory response rates are usually obtained from special target pop- ulations (purposive samples – see Section 4.3.4.3), especially when they have some loyalty towards the organisation undertaking the survey, such as the alumni of a university who are also donors of the university.

FOR EXAMPLE Strümpfer (1989) managed to realise a response rate of about 65% in a survey among busi- ness and industrial managers in Johannesburg and part- time MBA students of the University of Johannesburg.

Of course, a high response rate in itself is not of much value if the population (for which the response rate has been obtained) is not rep- resentative of the intended target population (see Section 6.3.2).

In order to improve the response rate of postal surveys, the questionnaires may be:
- delivered in person to the respondents' addresses with a request that they be posted back on completion
- posted and collected personally
- both delivered and collected personally.

Of course, as the region in which the survey is conducted **increases in size**, the economic advantages of postal surveys may disappear if questionnaires are to be delivered and/or col- lected in person.

Questionnaires can also be followed up by letters or postcards reminding the respond- ents to complete and return the question- naires. Although such additional dispatches raise the costs, this still should not place the total expenses of the postal survey in the same category as that of personal interviews.

Bailey (1987) provides an extensive discus- sion on the role of the following factors on the obtained response rate of postal surveys: sponsorship; format, length, and colour of the questionnaire; covering letter; ease of completing and returning the questionnaire; inducements to respond; nature of the respond- ents; type of dispatch (for example airmail or regular mail); day, week or month of dispatch; and reminders.

Dillman (1978) provides useful guidelines for the execution of postal surveys. Although data collection by mail is associated with surveys (see Section 5.4.1), it is not restricted to this kind of non-experimental research (see Section 5.4).

ACTIVITY 7.3

Read the following questions on achievement motivation and develop an interval scale (that includes a graphical scale) to measure these questions. You may re-phrase the questions without changing their meaning if you wish.

These questions were developed so that the answers from respondents would be indicative of their level of achievement motivation (those low on achievement motivation would perhaps choose the more routine jobs and/or not seek any feedback from any fellow worker at any time).

QUESTIONS

1. To what extent would you prefer a job that is difficult but challenging to one that is easy and routine?
2. To what extent would it frustrate you if people did not give you feedback on how you were progressing in your job?

ANSWERS

1. Would you prefer a difficult, challenging job to an easy, routine job?
   - ☐ Not at all
   - ☐ Perhaps
   - ☐ To some extent
   - ☐ Definitely
   - ☐ Most definitely.

2. Would it frustrate you if people did not give you feedback on how you were progressing in your job?
   - ☐ Not at all
   - ☐ Perhaps
   - ☐ To some extent
   - ☐ Definitely
   - ☐ Most definitely.

7.7.3.2 STANDARDISED TESTS

A **standardised test** is a collection of tasks in which:

▶ the content
▶ the administration (giving the instructions and so on)
▶ the scoring of the obtained responses are the same, irrespective of who is administering it, to whom it is administered, and by whom it is scored.

Standardised tests can take on a variety of forms. **Individual tests** may only be administered individually, in other words, a test administrator can administer it to only one testee at a time (see Section 7.7.5). On the other hand, **group tests** may be administered to more than one individual simultaneously in one session. Standardised tests can furthermore be divided into paper-and-pencil measurements/tests and apparatus measurements. In the case of **apparatus measurements/tests** (see Section 7.7.5), testees have to manipulate an object manually to make the end result meet certain requirements. Because a certain degree of expertise is required to administer and interpret standardised tests, they are made available to suitably qualified persons only.

At present, the Human Sciences Research Council (HSRC) is the most important local publisher of standardised tests. Primarily these tests are intended for educational, counselling, and clinical use and not necessarily for research. However, there are also other publishers and distributors of psychological assessment instruments.

In South Africa, the release and distribution of tests is controlled by the Health Professions Council of South Africa (HPCSA) in terms of specific legislation. For this purpose, standardised tests are divided into three categories. Of these categories:

▶ tests in Category C may be administered by registered psychologists only (or intern psychologists, registered psychometrists, and intern psychometrists under supervision of a registered psychologist), whereas

▶ tests in Category A may be administered by psychotechnicians as well, but under supervision of a registered psychologist.

In terms of the characteristics (attributes) measured by standardised tests, we can distinguish between the following types of tests: aptitude tests (which include intelligence tests), academic achievement tests, personality tests, and interest tests.

Whereas aptitude tests are aimed at the capacity of individuals to acquire skills in particular areas with the necessary training, achievement tests are focused on the knowledge and skills individuals have already learnt in a particular course.

7.7.3.3 ATTITUDE SCALES

An **attitude** is a disposition towards a particular issue, the so-called attitudinal object. The **attitudinal object** may refer to:

▶ a political, economical, or social issue (for example abortion, tax on wealth creation, the death penalty)
▶ a custom (for example greeting by kissing on the mouth or the slaughtering of animals at a wedding feast)
▶ a group (for example COSATU)
▶ a single person.

Attitudes may be influenced by individuals and events and are less permanent than personality traits. There is an example of an attitude scale in the Example Box below.

EXAMPLE (COMPARE THE CD-ROM MANUAL): AN ATTITUDE SCALE TO TEST THE EFFICIENCY OF A LOCAL BUS SERVICE

The typical service user (passenger) is asked to indicate his or her choice of answer to the question/item by marking the preferred box.

	Strongly agree	Agree	Agree in some cases	Do not agree	Strongly disagree
Buses are on time	1	2	3	4	5
Drivers are reckless	1	2	3	4	5
Fares are too high	1	2	3	4	5
Service is regular	1	2	3	4	5

As there are only a few attitude scales available commercially, researchers as a rule have to compile their own attitude scales to measure the attitudes relevant to their research. (See list of web sites on page 302.)

There are four different types of attitude scales, all of which comprise sets of items that measure different degrees of attitudes towards the attitudinal object, namely:

▶ the summated or Likert scale
▶ semantic differential
▶ the Guttman scale
▶ the Thurstone scale.

These attitude scales are based on different assumptions about the relationship between individuals, their attitudes, and their responses to the items. We will address the first two types of scales.

(a) The summated or Likert scale

The **summated** or **Likert scale**, introduced by Likert (1903–1981), is at present the most popular type of scale in the social sciences (Kidder & Judd, 1986). Its popularity stems from the fact that it is easier to compile than any of the other attitude scales (more particularly, those of Guttman and Thurstone which we do not discuss here). The Likert scale, unlike other scales, may be used for multidimensional attitudes.

A summated attitude scale consists of a collection of statements about the attitudinal object. In respect of each statement, subjects have to indicate the degree to which they agree or disagree with its content on, for instance, a five-point scale (for example strongly differ, differ, undecided, agree, strongly agree). Some statements represent a positive attitude, whereas others reflect a negative attitude (towards the attitudinal object).

FOR EXAMPLE A negatively formulated item on a scale to measure attitude towards taxation, for example, in a study to determine preference for indirect taxation (VAT) rather then direct taxation (on one's salary – PAYE) could read:

Taxation on bread is nothing else but murder.
An example of a positively formulated item might be:
Taxation on bread is essential for government income.
Respondents have to indicate the degree to which they agree with such a statement by encircling, for example, the number 1 if they totally disagree with it, and 5 (on a five-point scale) if they totally agree with it.

An attitude scale should contain approximately the same number of positively and negatively formulated items to counteract the acquiescent response style (see Section 7.4).

We regard all positive items as being equal in attitudinal intensity, and the same applies to all negative items. In other words, a score of 5 on one positive item is interpreted as being just as positive as a score of 5 on any other (positive) item.

We can explain this as follows:

▶ If there are 20 such statements and the respondent encircles a 5 on each item, a total score of $20 \times 5 = 100$ would be obtained, which would indicate a highly positive attitude towards the specific attitudinal object.

▶ A score of $20 \times 1 = 20$, by contrast, would signify a highly negative attitude.

▶ A score of 60, for example, could be obtained in different ways, and they would all be supposed to reflect the same attitudinal intensity.

FOR EXAMPLE Suppose one person obtains a score of 60 by encircling a 5 on the first ten items and (plus) a 1 on the remaining ten items; while another obtains the same score by encircling a score of 1 on the first ten items and (plus) a 5 on the remaining items.

Such a result could indicate that all the items in the scale do not measure attitude towards the same object; put differently, that the scale is multidimensional rather than unidimensional. Unless all the items measure attitude towards exactly the same object, and to the same extent, two such scores of 60 will not reflect the same attitudinal intensity.

If attitude towards some object is multidimensional, it is advisable to compile a separate subscale for each of the dimensions (compare Section 7.5.1.3).

(b) The semantic differential

The **semantic differential**, which was developed by Osgood and his colleagues (Osgood, Suci & Tannenbaum, 1957) follows a rather different approach from that of the Likert scale. Each item in a semantic differential scale consists mostly of a seven-point scale, of which the two end points are two opposite adjectives (words that describe the attributes/characteristics of an object such as "a strong leader").

FOR EXAMPLE If we want to measure attitude towards taxation on bread, we could use bipolar adjectives such as the following:
Good ☐☐☐☐☐☐☐ Bad
Moral ☐☐☐☐☐☐☐ Immoral

The seven scale points may be left open as in the above example, or the numbers 1 to 7 may appear in the corresponding sections, as follows:
Good ☐☐☐☐☐☐☐ Bad
　　7 6 5 4 3 2 1

Moral ☐☐☐☐☐☐☐ Immoral
     7 6 5 4 3 2 1

Respondents have to indicate their attitude towards the particular attitudinal object by making a cross somewhere along the continuum (between the two endpoints) for each item.

FOR EXAMPLE A respondent who thinks that taxation on bread is very bad, would make a cross in the section closest to "Bad", like this:
Good ☐☐☐☐☐☐☒ Bad
      7 6 5 4 3 2 1

A respondent who regards taxation on bread as neutral in terms of this continuum, would indicate this by means of a cross in the middle section (the fourth one), like this:
Good ☐☐☐☒☐☐☐ Bad
      7 6 5 4 3 2 1

A respondent who thinks that taxation on bread is very good, would make a cross in the section closest to "Good", like this:
Good ☒☐☐☐☐☐☐ Bad
      7 6 5 4 3 2 1

Actually, each pair (item) of bipolar adjectives represents a scale on its own. A respondent's total score on the scale is the sum of the chosen scale values of all the individual items (number of items necessary for reliable measurement – see Section 7.5.1.3).

NOTE: Osgood *et al.* (1957) published 50 such pairs of bipolar adjectives of which the factor structure (the dimensions represented by them) is known. Although this list may possibly be sufficient for most purposes, it does not include all possible pairs and nothing prevents researchers from including new pairs that they consider to be more relevant to their particular studies. It is important, though, that these pairs elicit different ratings from different individuals, in other words, that they show variance (see Section 9.3.1). It is also recommended that researchers investigate the factor structure (see Section 9.2.1) of such new items.

ACTIVITY 7.4
Read Case Studies A and B in Appendix D on page 306.

QUESTION
1. Is the type of scale used to measure the attitudes of the subjects in each article the most suitable? Give a brief reason for your answer.
2. Develop graphic examples (items) of any two attitude questions used in the questionnaire in each article.

ANSWER
case study a
1. Yes, the type of scale used is the most suitable, because the other attitude scales (Guttman, Thurstone, and semantic differential) cannot be used like the Likert scale to measure multidimensional attitudes (such as moral judgements on AIDS or the rights of prostitutes). The attitudes (towards AIDS and prostitution) were measured by way of 24 questions in random order.

2.

	Agree fully	Agree	Uncertain	Do not agree	Do not agree at all
AIDS is a punishment for immoral activities	5	4	3	2	1
Prostitutes must have job opportunities	5	4	3	2	1

case study b

1. Yes, the type of scale used (semantic differential) is the most suitable, because the attitude of the sample members towards supervision had to be measured on three occasions. By adding the scores of each sample member for the six items, a total score for each member could easily be obtained for each occasion – something that is not as easy to do with the other scales (Likert, Guttman, and Thurstone).

The instrument's reliability could also be determined easily and compared with the test-retest correlation of 0,85 that Osgood calculated for the semantic differential. It was assumed that all the apprentices could read and write so as to complete the attitude scale.

2. Supervision is GOOD ☐☐☐☐☐☐ BAD
                  1 2 3 4 5 6 7
   PUNCTUAL ☐☐☐☐☐☐ LATE
               1 2 3 4 5 6 7

7.7.3.4 RATING SCALES AND SITUATIONAL TESTS

In the measuring instruments that we have covered thus far, the research participants reported on their own behaviour by answering questions about it.

In **rating scales** a rater assesses the behaviour of the participants. In some cases the raters are familiar with the behaviour of the participants and therefore base their ratings on their memory about such behaviour. In **situational tests** the participants have to respond to questions or execute certain commands in the presence of the raters. Participants are then rated on the basis of their execution of these tasks. Alternatively, we may make video recordings of the participants' performance, in which case the rater need not be present at the original execution of the tasks but may use these recordings for rating purposes.

FOR EXAMPLE A workshop manager may be requested to rate each worker on a five-point scale in terms of the degree of compliance that he or she normally displays in terms of workplace safety measures.

Rating scales can be presented in different ways, but basically consist of:
- a collection of items, each of which
- involves a continuum of between three and nine rank-ordered scale points (for example from "very good" at one end to "very poor" at the other).

The rater's task is to place each subject in terms of each of these items so that this placement reflects the subject's position in terms of the item involved. The different scale points could be labelled by one or more words or even brief descriptions.

FOR EXAMPLE How compliant (adhering to the rules) is the worker in terms of workplace safety?
- ☐ Not at all compliant
- ☐ Only slightly compliant
- ☐ Moderately compliant
- ☐ Very compliant
- ☐ Extremely compliant.

In the case of a **numerical rating scale**, the description that appears at each point is replaced by a number (1, 2, 3, and so on) and a description such as "good" or "poor" is affixed to the two end points only.

FOR EXAMPLE How compliant (adhere to the rules) is the worker in terms of workplace safety?

POOR | 1 | 2 | 3 | 4 | 5 | GOOD

In the case of a **graphical rating scale**, each item is represented by a horizontal line and the various scale points are indicated at equal intervals by short, vertical lines. The two end points are accompanied by descriptions so that the rater may know which one is the positive end point and which one the negative end point.

FOR EXAMPLE How does the worker get along with the other workers?

WELL |—|—|—|—|—| BADLY

The rater's task is to indicate the subject's position in respect of the item by means of a cross somewhere along the horizontal line.

FOR EXAMPLE How does the worker get along with the other workers?

WELL |—|✗|—|—|—| BADLY

We may increase the interrater reliability (see Section 7.5) of rating scales by identifying as clearly as possible the behaviour that is to be rated by each item. With this in mind, each of the scale points in a **behaviourally anchored rating scale** is illustrated with concrete examples of behaviour.

FOR EXAMPLE

We can break down a construct such as *aggression* into different, clearly described components, such as:
- physical aggression and
- verbal aggression.

In addition, we can provide concrete examples of behaviour which qualifies as:
- "physically very aggressive"
- "physically moderately aggressive", and so on.

To pinch someone may count as an example of moderately aggressive behaviour, whereas to give somebody a well-aimed blow with the fist may qualify as one of extreme aggressiveness.

We assign a score to each scale point (for example a score of 1 for "not aggressive at all", and a score of 5 for "extremely aggressive").

We obtain the total score for an individual by adding the scores of the scale points he or she has chosen over all items relating to the same attribute. Both the retest reliability and the interrater reliability (see Section 7.5) of such total scores depend on the number of scale points per item and the number of items that are summed: the greater the number of scale points, or the greater the number of items, the more reliable the total measurement/test scores tend to be.

Naturally we will find that there is a limit to the number of scale points which could be used, for example 10 scale points are likely to require discriminations from the raters which are too difficult.

Apparently, most researchers agree that five scale points per item constitute the optimal minimum.

7.7.3.5 RESPONSE STYLES AND HOW TO PREVENT THEM

We cannot separate rating scales from the people (the raters) who are implementing them. The validity (see Section 7.4) of rating scales is usually negatively affected by the presence of certain **response styles** on the part of the raters. These response styles include:

▶ the halo effect
▶ the severity or stringency error and the leniency error
▶ the error of central tendency
▶ the logical error
▶ the proximity error
▶ the contrast error.

(a) The halo effect

The **halo effect** occurs when the rater, because of the general impression created by either a favourable or an unfavourable attribute of an individual, tends to rate the latter favourably or unfavourably in terms of all other attributes – even those that are unrelated to the attribute being rated.

FOR EXAMPLE

- A training course member with an attractive handwriting may obtain high marks on variables such as *knowledge about the subject studied,* which may have little to do with handwriting.
- An individual who is verbally fluent may be rated highly on anything ranging from good interpersonal skills to general intelligence.

In an attempt to **prevent the halo effect** from occurring, we can do the following:

▶ Rate all participants in respect of one attribute (to permit a mutual comparison between them).
▶ Rate participants separately in respect of each of the other attributes (instead of rating each person on all attributes simultaneously and then doing the same with the next person).
▶ Use behaviourally anchored rating scales.

(b) The severity or stringency error

The **severity or stringency error** means that a rater tends to rate all individuals rather too strictly, while the **leniency error** means that the rater tends to rate all individuals rather positively. To counteract the biases of the severity or stringency error and the leniency error, the raters may be asked to place the subjects in a rank order in terms of the attribute in question.

(c) The error of central tendency

Raters who are hesitant to assign extreme ratings and consequently tend to place most individuals in the centre of the scale, commit the **error of central tendency**. To prevent distortion by the error of central tendency, we should, at the compilation stage, avoid statements that reflect extreme positions.

FOR EXAMPLE We could replace *I am completely satisfied with my work* with *In general, I am satisfied with my work.*

(d) The logical error

The **logical error** is the tendency to rate individuals similarly on attributes that are incorrectly considered to be logically related. To prevent the logical error from occurring, maximally different names with clear descriptions may be used for the various attributes.

(e) The proximity error

The **proximity error** refers to the tendency to rate those attributes that appear close to each other on the rating scale similarly. This can be prevented by simply having different raters evaluate the attributes in a different order.

(f) The contrast error

The **contrast error** occurs when raters exaggerate the difference between themselves and the ratees in respect of the attribute in question.

FOR EXAMPLE A rater who highly regards the correct use of language, may tend to rate incompetent language users more strictly than is necessary.

Research on ways and means to assess rating errors such as the contrast error, and to correct them, includes that done by Saal, Downey and Lahey (1980) and Murphy and Balzer (1989).

(g) Increasing the reliability of rating scales

We mentioned earlier (see Section 7.5.1.3) that the reliability of measurements/tests can be increased by adding similar items to lengthen them. Similarly, the reliability of rating scales (where each individual's score is equal to the sum of all raters' ratings) increases as the number of comparable raters increases.

Other methods of increasing the reliability include the following:

▶ Raters should first be trained properly.
▶ Their ratings should preferably:
  • first be compared with one another, and
  • then discussed in a trial run in order to
  • eliminate misunderstandings in the conceptualisation of the attribute being rated and differences in stringency or leniency.
▶ In addition (see Section 6.2.4), audio or audiovisual recordings may be used to eliminate the possible effect of the researcher's expectations on the obtained results.
  • Instead of just one observer, rater or coder, more than one who are not aware of the treatment groups to which the different subjects belong, may rate their behaviour from the audio or audiovisual tape recordings.
  • The greater the number of raters or coders that are used, the smaller the possibility that they will all commit the same errors.
  • Differences in the obtained ratings could be discussed and be ironed out individually by the raters.

However, video recordings frequently require rooms that are especially equipped for this purpose, which raises the question of the ecological validity (see Section 6.3.3) of the conclusions obtained. If participants behave differently in such a specially-equipped venue than they would behave otherwise, the ecological validity of the results may therefore be adversely affected.

ACTIVITY 7.5
Read Case Studies D and E in Appendix D on page 306.

QUESTION
1. Is the type of scale used to measure the speech quality of the subjects in Case Study D and the type of scale used to measure the cash flow problems of the businesses in Case Study E the most suitable? Provide a brief reason for your answer.

2. Develop one numerical example (item/question) that might have been used in the speech quality rating scale in Case Study D.
3. Develop one graphical evaluation scale (items/question) that might have been used in Case Study D, and one that might have been used in the cash flow problems in Case Study E.

ANSWER

case study d

1. Yes, because the rating scale can be used to measure each of the eight elements as indicated on the video tape. By adding together each subject's score for the eight items, a total mark for each subject could easily be acquired, irrespective of which rater did the rating.

2. Eye contact of the student is

Not good — — — — — Exceptionally
at all   1   2   3   4   5   good

3.

	Almost never	Sometimes	Often	Almost always
I get out of breath before I have to give a speech				

case study e

1. Maybe not, because the owners of the businesses in the study may be very subjective on the rating scale reporting experiences of cash flow problems. It may have been more suitable to ask them to report directly the amount in rands that they needed per month to pay the expenses, cover their costs, and so on.

3. My business experienced more cash flow problems than most other businesses

F	f	t	T

With each of the scales, there would naturally have been instructions on how to complete the questionnaires, for example, *Indicate your preference by making a cross over your choice.*

7.7.4 Personal visits and communication by telephone

7.7.4.1 PERSONAL VISITS

When we collect data by means of **personal interviews**, interviewers visit the respondents at home or at their work place. In the case of **opinion polls** (see Section 5.4.5) they may also approach people at public venues where there is an influx of people, such as shopping centres, post offices, and so on.

As a data-collecting method, the **interview** may vary from methods that are completely unstructured (see Section 8.4.3) on the one hand, to those that are completely standardised and structured, such as those used in survey research (see Section 5.4.1), on the other hand. In all these cases the interview functions as a data-collecting method, and as

such should be distinguished from therapeutic or counselling interviews in which the objective is to help clients.

The advantages and disadvantages of personal interviews are as follows:

▶ **Cost and ease of application**. While we regard flexibility and adaptability as the great advantages of a personal interview, its high costs as far as its preparation and application are concerned, are regarded as its greatest drawback. Apart from the time required to conduct interviews, there are the costs associated with the proper training of interviewers. In addition, interviewers have to be paid for conducting the interviews and have to be reimbursed for their travelling costs. Interviewers are usually paid more for interviews conducted at respondents' homes or work-places than for telephonic interviews. In the case of vast geographic regions, the travelling costs of the interviewers may also amount to considerable expenses.

▶ **Time**. Personal interviews may be time-consuming. This includes not only the time taken by the interview itself, but also that used to arrange suitable appointments. It may even happen that interviewers have to return to a respondent's address several times before the interview can take place.

▶ **Control over responding**. Probably the biggest advantage of personal interviews is that the interviewers are in complete control of the interview situation. If respondents are evasive, interviewers can attempt to gain their confidence. Moreover, they can ensure that the respondent's first response as well as any changes to it are recorded, that all questions are answered, and that someone else does not provide the responses on the respondent's behalf. The interviewer is in a position to notice and to clear up any misunderstanding (in the case of semi-structured interviews) on the part of the respondent, to explain any questions that may be unclear, and to follow up on incomplete and vague responses. The responses obtained are thus of a high quality.

▶ **Anonymity**. Naturally, interviewers cannot always conduct personal interviews anonymously. When they approach strangers in public places, anonymity can still be maintained. However, when they locate respondents by means of their names and addresses, anonymity is impossible. As a result, there is the possibility that in responding to questions on opinions and attitudes, respondents may provide those responses that they think the interviewer expects of them rather than those that are accurate. Interviewers should be properly trained not to reveal information that may be construed as a hint about what is regarded as a desired response.

▶ **Response rate**. Since the interviewer physically confronts the respondent, there is less chance of the respondent eluding the interview. Respondents who may be unwilling to complete a questionnaire may be entirely prepared to talk to the interviewer. Consequently, personal interviews tend to have a higher response rate than telephonic interviews and postal surveys (see Section 7.7.3.1).

7.7.4.2 TELEPHONIC INTERVIEWS

In the case of **telephonic interviews**, the interviewer asks questions from the interview schedule over the telephone and records the respondent's responses. When an interviewer poses the questions contained in structured questionnaires to the respondent, whether in a personal interview or over the telephone, such a previously compiled questionnaire is known as an **interview schedule**.

Telephonic interviews are used mainly in survey research (see Section 5.4.1). Naturally, standardised tests (see Section 7.7.3.2) and attitude scales (see Section 7.7.3.3) cannot be administered telephonically. Because the respondents do not have the questions in front of them, telephonic interviews are less suited to complicated questions. Even the number of alternatives in multiple-choice questions may present problems in telephonic interviews. Respondents may find it difficult to remember all the alternatives with a view to comparing them and finding the most appropriate one.

Naturally, telephonic interviews will be shorter than personal interviews, with 10 to 15 minutes being the norm. Where computers are used to dial the respondents, the interviewer simply reads the questions as they appear on the screen or monitor and immediately keys in the respondent's responses. An advantage of such computer-assisted telephonic interviews is that, where appropriate, the questions may be put in different orders for different respondents with a view to preventing any sequence effects from occurring. Computer-assisted telephone interviewing such as the CATI system or call-centres can be used.

NOTE: Dillman (1978) provides useful guidelines for the execution of telephonic interviews.

We noted the danger of unrepresentative samples arising from using the telephone for data-collecting purposes earlier (see Section 4.3). If an appreciable percentage of the population on which a survey is to be conducted does not have access to a telephone, the list of names in the telephone directory may differ in important ways from the population in which we are actually interested.

The advantages and disadvantages of telephonic interviews are as follows:

▶ **Cost and ease of application**. One of the most important advantages of telephonic interviews is the speed with which they may be completed. Especially when respondents over a vast geographical area have to be contacted, telephonic interviews may be conducted much faster than personal interviews as the interview is conducted from one central location and travelling is not required.

  • The factor of speed is of special importance when respondents' reaction to something like a bomb explosion or a television programme, or an event of which the actuality may tend to dissipate quickly, is to be investigated.

  • Associated with the speed with which telephonic interviews may be carried out, is the lower cost. Even if long-distance calls have to be made, their costs still tend to be considerably lower than the travelling expenses required for personal interviews.

▶ **Control over responding**. Interviewers have less control over the interview situation than in (personal) interviews where they are physically present with the respondents. A potential drawback of telephonic interviews is that respondents may

be suspicious of the interviewer's intentions. For example, they may suspect that the interviewer wants to sell something or may even be playing the fool with them. Although it is possible to overcome such reservations, it remains more difficult to get the whole-hearted co-operation of the respondent over the telephone than in a personal interview. Naturally, it is difficult to cover anything but rather simple, superficial questions in telephonic interviews. It also is easier for the respondent to summarily terminate a telephonic interview than a personal one.

▶ **Anonymity**. The respondent has a greater impression of anonymity in telephonic interviews than in personal interviews and this may result in greater honesty and fewer false responses. Usually the quality of the obtained responses compares favourably with that of personal interviews (Kidder & Judd, 1986).

7.7.4.3 INTERVIEWS

In research we use three types of interviews: structured, semi-structured, and unstructured interviews.

(a) Structured interviews

In a **structured interview** the interviewer puts a collection of questions from a previously compiled questionnaire, known as an **interview schedule** (telephonic interviews – see Section 7.7.4.2), to a respondent face-to-face and records the latter's responses. The interviewer is restricted to the questions, their wording, and their order as they appear on the schedule, with relatively little freedom to deviate from it.

Each question is read and the response is recorded on a standardised schedule, usually with pre-coded answers. While there is social interaction between the researcher and the respondent such as explanations that must be provided, the questions should be read in the same tone of voice so that bias is not indicated.

Interviewers should be trained properly. They should be thoroughly familiar with the questions in the questionnaire so that they may read them fluently or even ask them from memory without deviating from the questions as they are formulated. Interviews demand real interaction between the researcher and the respondent. To be able to run the interview efficiently and without any disturbances, the researcher needs to know the respondent, his background, values, and expectations. Interviewers should, furthermore, know how to respond in specific situations.

FOR EXAMPLE If the respondent appears to be surprised or upset about a question, the interviewer may repeat the question, but without paraphrasing it. (If this precaution is not taken, the responses that different interviewers obtain from different interviewees may not be comparable.)

Semi-structured and unstructured interviews, however, are non-standardised.

(b) Unstructured interviews

Unstructured interviews are informal and are used to explore a general area of interest in depth. Such interviews are referred to as **in-depth interviews** in this book. There is no predetermined list of questions to work through in this situation, although the researcher needs to have a clear idea about the aspect or aspects that he or she wants to explore. The interviewee is given the opportunity to talk freely about events, behaviour, and beliefs in relation to the topic, so that this type of interaction is sometimes called **non-directive**. It has been labelled as an **informant interview** since it is the interviewee's perceptions that guide the conduct of the interview. In comparison, a **respondent interview** is one where the interviewer directs the interview and the interviewee responds to the questions of the researcher.

We usually employ unstructured interviews in **qualitative** or **explorative** research to identify important variables in a particular area, to formulate penetrating questions about them, and to generate hypotheses for further investigation. Due to the unfamiliarity of the area being entered, it is usually impossible to compile a schedule for interviews in such instances. Furthermore, in in-depth interviews we can ask questions about sensitive and highly emotional issues that we cannot do in telephonic interviews and postal surveys. (As a matter of fact, the terms in-depth telephonic interview and in-depth postal interview are self-contradictory.) We will return to this kind of interview in detail in Section 8.4.3.

(c) Semi-structured interviews

Between the completely structured interview on the one hand and the completely unstructured interview on the other hand, various degrees of structuredness are possible. Interviews between these two extremes are usually called semi-structured interviews (see Figure 7.5).

In **semi-structured interviews** the researcher has a list of themes and questions to be covered, although these may vary from one interview to the next. Instead of an interview schedule (telephonic interviews – see Section 7.7.4.2), **interview guides** are used in semi-structured interviews.

An interview guide involves a list of topics and aspects of these topics (note, not specific questions) that have a bearing on the given theme and that the interviewer should raise during the course of the interview (that is, if the interviewee does not do so him- or herself). This means that some questions may be used in particular interviews, given the specific organisational context that is encountered in relation to the research topic. The order of questions may also be varied depending on the way in which the interview develops. On the other hand, additional questions may be required to explore the research question and objectives given the nature of events within particular organisations. Although all the respondents are asked the same questions, the interviewer may adapt the formulation, including the terminology, to fit the background and educational level of the respondents.

Semi-structured interviews offer a versatile way of collecting data. We can use them with all age groups (for example with young workers participating in ABET who are still unable to read, as well as with elderly people with poor eyesight). This method may often be used when no other one is available or appropriate.

FOR EXAMPLE It would be highly insensitive to shove a questionnaire into the hands of victims immediately after an earthquake, or of the survivors of a sea disaster immediately after they had landed on dry soil, with a request to complete it. In such a case a semi-structured interview would be more appropriate.

Unlike completely structured interviews (see Section 7.7.4.3), unstructured and semi-structured interviews (see Section 7.7.4.4) allow the interviewer to use probes with a view to clearing up vague responses, or to ask for elaboration of incomplete answers.

Such probes may vary from "Why?" to "Could you elaborate on this?" Even by remaining silent with the pencil poised to continue writing, the respondent may be given the necessary encouragement to proceed. The nature of the questions and the ensuing discussion mean that data will be recorded by note-taking, or perhaps by tape-recording the conversation.

We may consider semi-structured interviews when:
- the topics are of a very **sensitive nature**
- the respondents come from **divergent backgrounds** and

- **experienced** and **expert** interviewers are available for conducting the interviews.

NOTE: Kahn and Cannell (1957) is a source that is several decades old, but still contains valuable advice on interviewing. (A more recent reference is Cannell & Kahn, 1986.)

7.7.4.4 CONDUCTING STRUCTURED AND SEMI-STRUCTURED INTERVIEWS

There are four stages involved in conducting structured and semi-structured interviews.

(a) Preparing for an interview

The first steps in preparing for an interview involve the following:
- analyse the research problem
- understand what information must be obtained from an interviewee
- identify those who would be able to provide the information.

The next step involves drafting an interview guide or interview questions. These questions should be compared with the research problem several times, partly to test consistency between the two and partly to determine whether these questions are thorough and correct enough to elicit the required information.

This draft questionnaire has to be pre-tested as a pilot study (see Section 7.6). The advantages of a pilot study are as follows:
- the understanding of the interviewee regarding the research problem and interview questions can be determined
- first-hand insight into what might be called 'cultural endowment' of the informants can be gained

Figure 7.5 *The structuredness of different types of interviews*

▶ additional information with regards to improving the final draft of the questionnaire can be obtained and

▶ it can determine the amount of time needed for the questions.

Once all aspects of the interview have been considered and an **interview guide** has been prepared, the interviewee(s) have to be approached. This can be done by means of a letter or telephone call. It is important to explain the **purpose of the study** by providing a short problem statement and describing the type of information the researcher is interested in collecting. In this letter the researcher may also mention that he or she will be calling to request an **appointment** for an interview. The **amount of time needed** for the interview should also be mentioned as well as specific times or days (if applicable). The interviewee also needs to be made aware how the information will be recorded, that is, using tape or video recorders.

(b) Pre-interview

Various factors may cause respondents to provide biased or even false information. Here are some general rules and recommendations:

▶ Interviewers should schedule their time properly. This is important if more than one interview is conducted per day. Enough travelling time should also be allowed.

▶ They should dress in more or less the same way as the respondents. Social convention should be adhered to.

▶ They should at all costs avoid any indications of affiliation with some or other group or organisation, for example, a Blue Bulls rugby tie or a Cosatu emblem.

▶ Although interviewers may be dressed discreetly, factors over which they have no control, such as their gender, race, physical appearance, and background, may affect the respondents' responses. Consequently, interviewers should be careful not to engender resistance (among the respondents) against them.

▶ There is often the danger that the respondents may view the interviewer as an intruder. Especially in the South African context, white interviewers should be mindful of the possibility that black respondents may regard them as intruders, and *vice versa*.

▶ The equipment that will be used in the interview, such as the tape or video recorder, must be checked to ensure that it works properly.

▶ Finally, interviewing is a skill that should be rehearsed or practised with regard to understanding, time taken, the questions, and so on.

NOTE: Bailey (1987) offers useful hints regarding the training of interviewers and conducting of interviews.

(c) The interview

The first important issue here is to introduce the study and its purpose and to orient the respondents as to what the research questions are. It is important to realise that the respondent is asking the questions and the interviewer has to provide satisfactory answers.

The language used in these early minutes and in the subsequent interaction is of great importance. The interviewer should use simple and understandable language, while being particularly careful when using certain terminology or concepts from a particular discipline, such as finance or management. The interviewer, irrespective of questioning technique, must leave it entirely to the informant to provide answers to questions. In other words, the questions should not be asked in a leading or directed manner, as this pressures the respondent to answer in one particular way or even to provide the answer that he or she thinks the interviewer wants to hear.

The interviewer also needs to manage time. The interviewee has to be given reasonable time for each question and should not be interrupted every now and then. However, some respondents often like to discuss their experiences and expertise at length and should therefore be controlled, but with care. Sensitive topics should be addressed with great care. Often these questions can be phrased or asked in a way which makes it less uncomfortable to discuss. The researcher must, furthermore, ensure that he or she obtains answers to all the questions within the specified time.

(d) Post-interview

The researcher should take care to write down the important points from the interview as well as notes on the practical details. This can include whether he or she was able to obtain all answers or how much time it took, some opinions about the respondent, such as very open or reserved person, as well as his or her perception of the interaction and relationship with the interviewee. This information can be of great value at a later stage. In case the interview was not recorded, the researcher should go through the notes and write a complete descriptive report of the interview immediately (or as soon as possible) after the interview. In that way important aspects will not be forgotten and confusion will be minimised.

The researcher should also write a 'Thank you' letter to the respondent. Further information about the research project should also be made available to the respondent.

Reporting or transcribing an interview is an important and tedious job. As mentioned earlier, interviews which are not recorded should be written as a narrative story as soon as possible. For structured interviews, the researcher should check the forms to see if they have been completed correctly. Interviews which are recorded should be supplemented by some support material to help the researcher remember important aspects of the interview. It is often best to first write down all the information on the tape in the same order, and to develop a descriptive report of the relevant interview later. In the second

stage the researcher can then discard all irrelevant information.

7.7.5 Individual apparatus (measurements/tests)

In **individual apparatus measurements/tests** the measurement/test administrator presents the subject with tasks (contained in a measurement/test) that should be executed (for example to complete a puzzle). The administrator assigns marks in terms of the manner in which the subject completes the task (for example by using a stop-watch to determine how long the subject takes to complete the puzzle – see Figure 7.6).

Complete this flat figure by drawing five lines in order to make it a three-dimensional figure (giving it depth)

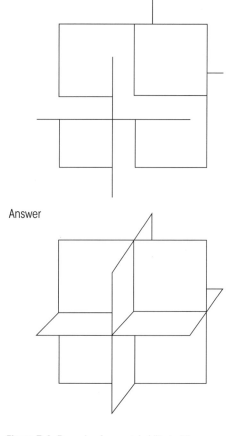

Figure 7.6 *Example of a mental ability test item*

169

The instructions given to the subject, as well as the way in which marks should be assigned, are fixed and measurement/test administrators are not permitted to deviate from them.

7.7.6 Direct observation (checklists)

Whereas the use of rating scales (see Section 7.7.3.4) involves rating participants in terms of the raters' recollection of the participants' behaviour, in **direct observation** the participants are observed directly (by the observer). In the final analysis, the observer is the measuring instrument in direct, systematic observation. Sometimes mechanical aids (for example audio- or videotape recordings) are used to record the relevant behaviour, but the recording obtained in this manner ultimately has to be observed and coded or evaluated. The reliability and validity of the measurements (see Sections 7.4 & 7.5) thus obtained depend on the experience and skills of the observer(s). (See time and event sampling, p. 171.)

The results of observation can be recorded and analysed qualitatively or quantitatively. Observation can be done with the naked eye or with the help of sophisticated equipment. Time-lapse photography can be used to photograph an area automatically at set periods, aerial photography can be used to gain a panoramic view of a whole work site, and video recording can also be used.

(a) Contexts

There are a number of contexts where observation is an appropriate or necessary part of management research:

▶ **Use of work sites**. Observation can provide useful information about the workplace, including how space is used, the level of use of particular areas, traffic flows, and the movement of material and people. In many cases the only way managers can obtain information on these processes is by observation.

▶ **Workplace behaviour**. Observation allows a range of workplace behaviours to be examined, although observing behaviour over a long period can be expensive when compared to alternative research methods. It is possible to observe an individual's physical actions, non-verbal behaviours (such as tone and body language), and the time taken to perform tasks, as well as physical distances between people and work. Other forms of observation can provide insights into workplace behaviour. The amount of work completed may be implied from parts used over a period of time in a car assembly process or the volume of turnings found under the lathe. Patterns of usage can be determined by wear on carpets, the amount of toner and paper used by the photocopier, and so on.

▶ **Consumer testing**. Consumer testing is another potentially fruitful but under-exploited use of observation. While interviews constitute one way of obtaining information on the quality of the experience offered by a shopping centre, an additional way involves assuming the role of *incognito* user/customer/observer. Such an observer would be required to make use of facilities or services armed with a checklist of features to observe, such as cleanliness, information availability and clarity, product availability, and staff performance. A report is then compiled after using the facility. Again, ethical and employee relations issues may arise in such a study because the element of deception involved in playing the part of the customer.

▶ **Complementary research**. Observation can be a necessary complement to interview surveys in order to correct for variation in sampling rates. For instance, five interviewers working at a typical railway station may be able to interview virtually all users in the off-peak periods, but only manage to interview a small proportion of the users during the busy morning and afternoon period. The final sample therefore, in this case, over-represents off-peak users and under-represents peak hour users. If these two groups were to have different characteristics, it would have a biasing effect on the information obtained, such as the balance of views expressed by the users. Additional information such as counts of the hourly levels of use can provide data which add an appropriate weight to the peak hour users.

▶ **Social behaviour**. Observation has been used in sociological research to develop ideas and theories about social behaviour. Researchers use an interactive and inductive process to build explanations of social behaviour from what they observe. Observation may be used when seeking to understand an industrial dispute between management and employees in a waterfront setting, for instance, or to provide court evidence. Very often, a key feature of such studies is the way in which the researchers seek to confirm what they have observed with what has apparently been observed by others, particularly those with influence or authority. This includes people such as safety inspectors, insurance assessors, supervisors, union officials, senior management, police, the media, and so on. Observational research can challenge existing stereotypical interpretations of events.

(b) Main elements of observational research

Observation is essentially a simple research method. However, precision, painstaking attention to detail, and patience are required from the researcher. The main steps in planning and conducting an observational project are as follows:

1. Choose site.
2. Choose observation point.
3. Choose study time period.
4. Decide on continuous observation or sampling.
5. Decide on number and length of sampling periods.
6. Decide on what to observe.
7. Divide into zones.
8. Design a recording sheet.
9. Conduct study.
10. Analyse data.

(c) Sampling

In **continuous observation** the observer records by means of a tally (see Section 9.3) each occurrence of an example of the selected behaviour. Alternatively, only samples (see Section 4.3) of the behaviour may be recorded.

▶ In **point time sampling**, the observer checks only at specific points in time (say, every ten seconds or every second minute) whether or not the subject exhibits the selected behaviour.

▶ In **interval time sampling**, the observer notices whether or not such behaviour occurs in a particular interval (say, any time within every 60 seconds or every two minutes).

These time sampling methods are especially appropriate when a large number of behaviours has to be recorded.

▶ **Event sampling** can be considered in the case of behaviour that does not occur as a matter of routine (for example temper tantrums, riots, bank robberies) and that may therefore be missed by time samples. In this type of sampling, the researcher should be ready to observe such an event if it does occur, and to make the necessary recording.

It is also important that the researcher knows exactly which behaviour must be selected and recorded. In direct observation the observers are not expected to record all the behaviour (of the subjects) that they observe, but only those behaviours that are regarded as indicators (see

Section 7.2) of the dependent variable (see Section 2.3) in question. Sometimes a checklist is compiled that provides explicit descriptions of all the different concrete behaviours that should be regarded as indicators of the dependent variable.

FOR EXAMPLE In Research Example II (see Section 2.3, page 17), the dependent variable (*management style*) was divided into subcategories, namely:
- non-verbal rude behaviour
- verbal rude behaviour.

Concrete examples of behaviours in each of these categories were listed, for example:
- To point a finger was listed as an example of non-verbal rude behaviour.
- To utter phrases such as "I will kick you and punch you", represented verbal rude behaviour.

Behaviours that did not fall into these clearly described categories were ignored.

The researcher should also make a decision concerning the recording or coding of the selected behaviours. The observer may make a tally opposite a category when he or she observes behaviour that falls into that category. In this manner, the observer determines the number of times he or she observes behaviour that is considered to be indicative of the dependent variable.

FOR EXAMPLE In Research Example II, if aggressive reactions (say, of trainee supervisors who have observed an iron-fisted management style role model, namely, their supervisor) are to be studied, the number of times any of the trainees exhibits any of the iron-fisted management style behaviours listed (for example pointing a finger at a subordinate) is established.

(d) Advantages and disadvantages of observation

The advantages and disadvantages of direct observation are as follows:
- The behaviour which is to be studied is recorded **first-hand**, as compared to interviews and questionnaires in which

information is presented as second-hand. Consequently, researchers do not have to depend on the participants' possibly misleading reports (either in interviews or on questionnaires) about the relevant behaviour, but, instead, observe it directly.
- However, this potential advantage also has two drawbacks:
  - Firstly, the **presence of the observer**, usually a stranger to the respondent, may influence the behaviour to be observed, resulting in reactive measurement (see Section 6.2.5.1).

    FOR EXAMPLE Suppose, after workers have experienced a violent clash in negotiations, a stranger (researcher) who intends recording evidence of aggressive behaviour, observes them on the shop floor. The workers may fool around to draw attention and thus exhibit behaviour that the researcher may interpret as being aggressive.

    In some cases it is possible to eliminate the possibly undesirable side-effects of the observer's presence by means of one-way mirrors or concealed video-camera recordings.

    For example in Research Example II (see Section 2.3, page 17) the behaviour of the trainee supervisors was watched through a one-way mirror from an adjacent room.

  - Secondly, the observers' prejudices may affect their observation and consequently the validity (see Section 7.4) of their ratings. (We indicated ways in which to deal with this in Section 7.7.3.4.)

(e) Issues of reliability and validity

Irrespective of how explicitly the checklist has been defined, observers act as raters of behaviour, because to a greater or lesser extent they have to decide whether or not a particular behaviour falls within a particular category.

Interrater reliability (estimation of reliability – see Section 7.5) may be improved in such instances by the following:
- carefully defining the dependent variable as explained above

▶ training observers properly in advance about the specific, concrete behaviours that should be regarded as indicators of the dependent variable
▶ warning observers about the danger of letting fatigue or over-confidence negatively influence the quality of their ratings
▶ letting any of the response styles that may be present in rating scales (see Section 7.7.3.5) have an effect on their ratings.

The less the observer is expected to evaluate or interpret whether or not a particular behaviour is indicative of the dependent variable, the better the chances of obtaining a satisfactory interrater reliability (see Section 7.5). At the same time, there is the danger that such a precaution may negatively affect measurement validity because behaviours not listed (on the checklist) have to be ignored.

However, behaviour that does not appear on the previously compiled checklist, but that may possibly be appropriate (as indicators of the dependent variable), may be noted with a view to discussing its relevancy later. Preferably, however, all specific, concrete behaviours that qualify for inclusion should have been identified in a pilot study (see Section 7.6).

Of course, if the behaviour that is to be rated is available on videotape, different raters may rate the same behaviour, and their **interrater reliability** may be examined. The examination of the interrater reliability may be done by computing the percentage of agreement between assignments (to the different categories) of two or more independent observers.

Retest reliability (see Section 7.5) may also be investigated by having the same observers rate a video recording of the subjects' behaviour, say, two weeks apart.

Validity (see Section 7.4) may be investigated by comparing the rating results with the results obtained by other measuring instruments for the same construct.

Subject error may cause the data to be unreliable. Suppose a researcher wants to observe the output of sales administrators as measured by the amount of orders they process in a day. Subject error may be evident if he or she chose administrators in a section that was short-staffed owing to illness. This may mean that they had to spend more time answering telephone calls, and less time processing orders, as there were fewer people available to handle telephone calls. The message here is clear: choose subjects who in as many respects as possible are "normal" examples of the population under study.

Closely related to the issue of subject error is that of **time error**. It is essential that the time at which the observation is conducted does not provide data that are untypical of the total time period in which the researcher was interested. Therefore, the output of the sales administrators may be less in the immediate hour before lunch as their energy levels are lower. If we were interested in the number of customers using a retail store, we would have to conduct observations at different times of the day and week to provide a valid picture of total customer flow.

One of the most powerful threats to the validity and reliability of data collected through observation is that of the **observer effect**. The process of the observer's study of behaviour changes the nature of the behaviour owing to the fact that the subject is conscious of being observed. The simplest way to overcome this effect is for the observation to take place in secret. However, this is often not possible, even if it were ethically sound to do so. Robson (2002) notes two strategies for overcoming the observer effect. The first, **minimal interaction**, means that the observer tries as much as possible to 'melt into the background', having as little interaction as possible with the subjects of the observation. This may involve sitting in an unobtrusive position in the room and avoiding eye contact with those observed. The second strategy is **habituation**, where the subjects observed become familiar with the process of observation so that they take it for granted. If we were to use a tape recorder to record discussions, we may notice that the respondent is very wary of the machine initially; however, after a short period this apprehension wears off and the machine is not noticed.

7.8 Developing and constructing questionnaires, interview schedules, and attitude items

When an interviewer poses the questions contained in a structured questionnaire to a respondent in a personal or a telephonic interview, such a previously compiled questionnaire is also known as an **interview schedule**.

NOTE: Schuman and Presser (1981) conducted valuable research on the formulation of questions in questionnaires and interview schedules.

The decision to conduct a questionnaire survey should itself be the culmination of a careful process of thought and discussion, involving consideration of all possible techniques. The concepts and variables involved and the relationships being investigated – possibly in the form of hypotheses, theories, models or evaluative frameworks – should be clear and should guide the questionnaire design process. It is not advisable to begin with a list of questions to be included in the questionnaire. The starting point should be an examination of the management, planning, policy or theoretical question to be addressed, followed by the drawing up of a list of information required to address the problem. Questions should only be included in the questionnaire if they relate to the research questions.

When designing a questionnaire, the researcher should seek out as much previous research on the topic or related topics as possible. More specifically, if it is decided that the study should have points of comparison with other studies, then data will need to be collected in a similar fashion. Questionnaires from previous studies then become part of the input into the questionnaire design process.

In this section we briefly discuss several considerations that should be borne in mind when formulating questions for such instruments. Some of these considerations are more important when opinions and beliefs are assessed than when information about biographical details and typical behaviour is to be collected. In the case of biographical details and typical behaviour, other considerations may be important. Minor adaptations may be required at times in the formulation of questions in view of the nature of personal visits and telephonic communication (see Section 7.7.4) or postal surveys (see Section 7.7.3.1) respectively.

FOR EXAMPLE It is desirable to ask specific questions. Instead of asking:
Which brand of toothpaste do you usually use?
We should rather ask:
Which brand of toothpaste is in your bathroom right now? Do you normally use that brand?

CONSIDERATION 1: CHOOSE JUDICIOUSLY BETWEEN OPEN-ENDED AND CLOSED-ENDED (MULTIPLE-CHOICE VARIETY) QUESTIONS

We can make the questions in questionnaires or interview schedules open-ended so that respondents have to formulate their responses themselves. Alternatively, we can also present them as multiple-choice questions in which respondents have to select the response that best applies to them from among two or more alternative responses.

An **open-ended question** is one in which the interviewer asks a question without any prompting with regards to the range of answers expected. The respondent's reply is noted *verbatim*. In a self-completed questionnaire a line or space is left for the respondent to write his or her own answer and there is no prior list of answers.

FOR EXAMPLE An open-ended question about smoking behaviour may read as follows:

> *Approximately how many cigarettes do you smoke per day? Answer …*

The advantage of open-ended question is that the respondent's answer is not influenced unduly by the interviewer or the questionnaire and the *verbatim* replies from respondents can provide a rich source of varied material which might have been untapped by categories on a pre-coded list.

A **closed or pre-coded question** is one which offers the respondent a range of answers to choose from, either verbally or from a show card. In the case of a self-completed questionnaire, a range of answers is set out in the questionnaire and the respondent is asked to tick the appropriate boxes.

FOR EXAMPLE The corresponding multiple-choice item for the question in the previous example may list alternatives such as the following, from which the relevant response should be selected:

☐ one per day
☐ between two and five per day
☐ between six and 10 per day
☐ more than 10 per day.

The categories reflected in the alternatives should be mutually exclusive and exhaustive (levels of measurement – see Section 7.3.2) in order to make provision for each and every possible response (alternative), although not simultaneously so in more than one category.

When it is difficult to anticipate all possible responses, or when there are too many possible responses to list, we may include the category "other" or use open-ended questions.

FOR EXAMPLE If we ask the residents of a city what they regard as the most important problem in their city, there may be many possible responses. In such a case the category "other" or open-ended questions may be useful.

In fact, we can use open-ended questions in unstructured interviews (see Section 7.7.4.4) in pilot studies (see Section 7.6) with a view to determining which answers should be included (in a multiple-choice format) in later studies.

Multiple-choice items in which only two alternatives such as "agree" and "disagree" appear, should be used with great caution. If such questions are indeed used, questions that suggest a positive and a negative attitude respectively towards the particular issue, should be alternated to counteract the possible effect of acquiescence (see Section 7.4).

In addition, a question to which the respondent has to choose between "agree" and "disagree" should preferably be reformulated to be more specific.

FOR EXAMPLE The question, *Ethnic differences are a greater cause of violence in South Africa than the police* should preferably be reformulated to read:

> Which, in your opinion, is the greater cause of violence in South Africa?
> A   ethnic differences
> B   the police.

What may count as an advantage of open-ended questions, may represent a drawback of multiple-choice items, and *vice versa*:

▶ Some respondents may feel irritated because multiple-choice items restrict them to particular responses that may not provide for their unique situation. As a result, they may prefer the freedom to express themselves in a way that is allowed by open-ended questions.

▶ At the same time, this advantage of open-ended questions may be a drawback in that they require:
  • a better ability to express oneself and
  • usually a higher level of education on the part of respondents than with multiple-choice items.

- Moreover, respondents who meet these requirements may be unwilling to exert the special effort required by open-ended items.
- Multiple-choice items:
  - do not rely on the ability of respondents to express themselves verbally, but, on the other hand,
  - tend to be superficial.
- The greater freedom afforded by open-ended questions results in the following:
  - the responses obtained are more difficult to score
  - more time is needed for scoring than with multiple-choice items.
- Furthermore, it is more difficult to compare different respondents' responses to open-ended questions than is the case with multiple-choice questions.
- The possibility of obtaining inappropriate responses is also greater in the case of open-ended questions than with multiple-choice questions.

  FOR EXAMPLE In response to the question on the approximate number of cigarettes smoked daily, someone may reply:

  More than is good for my health.

  In this specific example, we could attempt to avoid an inappropriate response by formulating the open-ended question as follows:

  What is the approximate number of cigarettes that you smoke every day?

- However, inappropriate responses may also be obtained on multiple-choice items when respondents who:
  - are unfamiliar with the answers or
  - do not have an opinion, respond to the question in a lackadaisical manner. (In fact, it is not uncommon to find that when alternatives containing incorrect or even fictitious information are deliberately included, there are indeed individuals who select such alternatives.)
- Nothing prevents the researcher from using both open-ended and multiple-choice items in the same schedule.

- Multiple-choice items may be compiled in connection with biographical details (gender, age, marital status, and so on).
- Open-ended questions may be formulated on opinions that cannot be reduced to multiple alternatives.

Even if a questionnaire consists exclusively of multiple-choice items, it may be a good idea to conclude it with an open-ended question with a view to determining whether anything of importance to the respondent has been omitted.

CONSIDERATION 2: TAKE THE RESPONDENTS' LITERACY LEVEL INTO CONSIDERATION

When we formulate the questions, we should use words and concepts with which we can expect the respondents to be familiar. The command of language of the group that is investigated should therefore be taken into account. Since we want to obtain accurate information from the respondents, it stands to reason that they should know exactly what is being asked of them. With this in mind, technical terms should be avoided.

EXAMPLE   USING UNFAMILIAR TERMINOLOGY

Bachrach (1981, p. 166) relates the following example of a question formulated by a state department for small businessmen as follows:

How many employees do you have, broken down by sex?

The term "broken down" is standard jargon that means "divided in terms of". However, one business-man who was unfamiliar with this terminology replied:

None, our big problem is alcohol.

CONSIDERATION 3: BE CAREFUL NOT TO OFFEND

We should not only avoid technical terms, but also terms that might offend the respondents.

FOR EXAMPLE The interviewer should refrain from asking for example:

Is your boss an idiot?

Rather ask:

Do you think your boss is an intelligent line manager?

Similarly, the use of gang language in an attempt to gain the co-operation of gang members may be counterproductive because the gang members may tend to regard their language as their own and may resent it if out-siders (including the interviewers) use it too.

CONSIDERATION 4: BE BRIEF AND FOCUSED

We should give preference to questions that are concise (brief and to the point) without being ambiguous (having more than one meaning). The longer a question, the longer it takes to read and the greater the possibility that it may create resistance in the respondents. If the

abstractness and/or complexity of the topic make(s) it difficult to cover in a single ques-tion, it should rather be dealt with in several simple, consecutive questions.

If we formulate a question ambiguously, individual respondents may interpret it dif-ferently. They will then, in effect, respond to different questions. This consideration is especially important for questionnaires used in postal surveys (see Section 7.7.3.1), where the respondents, by definition, are left to their own resources to complete the questions. This consideration is also important in a structured interview situation (see Section 7.7.4.3). If interviewers have to explain the questions, various interviewers may do it differently and, as a result, the obtained responses may no longer be comparable.

There are various aspects to consider when eliminating ambiguity from questions:

▶ The following may give rise to ambiguity:
  • questions that are not formulated clearly
  • questions that are stated incompletely.

FOR EXAMPLE To the question:

Do you approve of taxation on food?

a respondent may reply:

It depends on the type of food you are talking about.

▶ Double-barrelled questions that actu-ally contain more than one question but require a single response also lead to ambiguity.

FOR EXAMPLE Read the following question:

Do you disapprove of taxation on food and do you think people who are guilty of evading such tax should be fined?

A respondent may prefer to respond posi-tively to the first part of the question but negatively to the second part.

The occurrence of words such as "and" (as in the present example) or "or" often, but not always, betrays the presence of a double-barrelled question.

Even when such words do no not occur in the question, it can still be double-barrelled.

FOR EXAMPLE Suppose respondents are asked about their attitude towards the fringe benefits regarding their remuneration. A respondent may have a positive attitude towards the company's contribution to his or her medical aid fund, but a negative one towards the company's housing subsidy policy. A single response may therefore not be sufficient.

Obviously, the solution is to reformulate such questions as two (or even more) separate questions.

▶ To prevent ambiguity, words such as "always", "regularly", "very often", "frequently", "seldom", and "never" should preferably be replaced with specific frequencies (numbers) such as in the example of the number of cigarettes being smoked.

FOR EXAMPLE A question about smoking behaviour may read as follows:

Approximately how many cigarettes do you smoke per day? Answer: ...

Otherwise, alternatives such as the following may be listed, from among which the relevant response should be selected:

☐ one per day
☐ between two and five per day
☐ between six and 10 per day
☐ more than 10 per day.

▶ We should bear in mind that in a multicultural society such as South Africa, the same question could be interpreted differently in different cultures. Such questions should be avoided or be reformulated to prevent them from yielding confusing information. (Also, compare Preston-Whyte's (1982) evaluation of the applicability of the interview schedule in studies on poverty among rural blacks.)

CONSIDERATION 5: MAINTAIN NEUTRALITY
We should not formulate questions in such a way that we encourage respondents to answer in a particular way. Consider the following recommendations in this regard:

▶ Avoid leading questions. A **leading question** is one which is formulated in such a way that it suggests certain responses rather than others. It usually begins with: Do you agree that ...? or Are you satisfied that ...?

FOR EXAMPLE *Do you agree that affirmative action is necessary?*

▶ Avoid loaded questions. A **loaded question** is a leading question in which social acceptability or unacceptability may likewise influence the respondent to reply in a particular manner.

FOR EXAMPLE *Is your opinion concerning affirmative action that people should be compensated for injustices that have been committed towards them in the past?*

Irrespective of their opinion towards affirmative action, there would not be many people who would be against rectifying past injustices.

▶ Facilitate responses that may be regarded as indicative of socially unacceptable attitudes or habits.

FOR EXAMPLE A questionnaire to be completed by visitors to a clinic for venereal diseases should ask:
How many sex partners have you had during the past three months?
rather than:
Have you had more than one sex partner during the past three months?

▶ Do not suggest the range of acceptable responses.

FOR EXAMPLE Respondents may give different responses (that do not include frequencies in order to prevent ambiguity) depending on whether the question reads:
Do you often tend to feel negative?
rather than:
Do you sometimes tend to feel negative?
This is because "often" is nearer to "always" in the range of response categories (and it is not socially acceptable to feel negative always), while "sometimes" is nearer to "never" (a socially more acceptable feeling).

Even asking:
How long?
rather than:
How short?
the negative phases (a socially unacceptable feeling) tend to last, may have an effect on the responses obtained.

- Carefully consider questions about sensitive issues.
  FOR EXAMPLE Instead of asking respondents:
  Have you completed your high school training?
  rather ask:
  Indicate the highest school grade that you have passed.
  Similarly, rather ask respondents for their dates of birth instead of their ages.
  Questions about income should preferably not require an exact amount but rather provide broad categories (in a multiple-choice format). This may look like the following:
  ☐ No income
  ☐ R00,00 to R499,00 per month
  ☐ R500,00 to R1 000,00 per month
  ☐ More than R1 000,00 per month.

CONSIDERATION 6: USE A JUSTIFIED SEQUENCE

We should carefully consider the order in which we put items because earlier items may affect responses to subsequent items. To put the respondent at ease, it is recommended that the questionnaire should begin with a few easy and non-threatening items (for example multiple-choice questions with only a few alternatives) that are clearly related to the stated purpose.

More in-depth questions may follow later. (Should the respondent offer resistance by that time, only the questions towards the end of the questionnaire will be affected.) Of course, what qualifies as a sensitive issue varies from time to time and from one context to the next, but may range from questions about:

- illegal behaviour (for example tax evasion, illegal drugs, and so on)
- personal customs and practices (for example of a sexual nature)

- attitudes (for example towards other races), to questions about
- age
- income
- political affiliation.

In the final analysis we will find that the rapport (a trusting relationship) which the interviewer has established with the respondent is of crucial importance in answering questions about sensitive issues. Consequently, telephone surveys (see Section 7.7.4) and postal surveys (see Section 7.7.3.1) are usually less suited for asking such questions.

We should preferably group questions that are related to the same aspect together so that respondents do not repeatedly have to switch their focus. The transition from one topic to the next should be clearly identified and should still be connected with the stated aim of the project.

FOR EXAMPLE A survey of attitudes towards the new war on terrorism, could be introduced by saying:
Until now we have talked about the continued maintenance of western standards. Now we get to the position of Islam.

The following two aspects must also be kept in mind:

- **Sensitive topics** should also be announced and their relationship with the overall topic should be clear. (The respondent should not get the impression that the other questions served merely as a cloak for the sensitive questions.)
- Within a particular topic, the so-called **funnel order** may be used. This means that we commence with a general question that is followed by increasingly specific questions. Not only is this practice in agreement with the preceding recommendation, but it is usually also easier to relate the general question rather than specific ones to the stated aim of the project.

Since preceding questions may have an effect on the answers given to subsequent items, the order in which questions are set should be identical for all respondents. An exception to this rule is the use of filter questions. As mentioned earlier, the purpose of filter questions is to determine whether all subsequent questions should be asked or whether some of them may be skipped.

CONSIDERATION 7: BE SURE THE QUESTION IS APPRECIABLE TO ALL RESPONDENTS

Questions to single respondents asking how long they have been married, or to unemployed persons about how long they have worked on their current jobs, are typical examples.

Sometimes the questions are applicable to all respondents, but not the options in a structured item.

FOR EXAMPLE Consider the question in Figure 7.7. People working full-time from home might well object to this question. Sometimes people will respond to one of the options simply to oblige the questioner or to avoid embarrassment. This often occurs when they are asked their opinion on some topic they have not previously considered and on which they really have no opinion.

How would you describe your current employment status?

A Unemployed

B Part-time employed (less than 40 hours per week)

C Full-time employed (40 or more hours per week)

Figure 7.7 *A question with an incomplete set of options*

The necessary pretesting and planning for surveys using branching is worthwhile, as it makes it unnecessary to develop several sets of instruments for different types of respondents, and the identification of the respondent sub-samples that may be impossible prior to the administration or mailing of a survey.

One of the strengths of computer-administered surveys is that such branching is done automatically, as the respondents see only those questions that are relevant to them based on their prior answers. (Q 1 YES   NO; if "yes", go to question 19.)

FOR EXAMPLE If someone replied (for example in section A) in the negative to the question whether he or she is presently married, he or she does not have to respond to following questions about the age and occupation of his or her spouse (in section B) and may go directly (by skipping section B) to subsequent questions about attitudes towards affirmative action (in section C).

Similarly: in an opinion questionnaire about affirmative action, for example, it may be advisable to first ask whether respondents know what is meant by this concept and even to ask that it be defined to determine whether all subsequent questions should be asked or whether some of them may be skipped.

CONSIDERATION 8: THE LAYOUT

A questionnaire must be laid out and printed in such a way that the person who needs to read it, whether the interviewer or the respondent, is able to follow all the instructions easily and answer all the questions that he or she is meant to answer. Layout becomes particularly important when a questionnaire contains filters, for instance.

In the case of respondent-completion questionnaires, extra care must be taken because it can be very difficult to rectify 'faults in the field'. Clarity of layout and the overall impression given by the questionnaire are important in obtaining valid information.

Mail surveys in which the researcher does not have direct contact with the respondent, are the most demanding to prepare. A professionally laid out, typeset, and printed questionnaire will pay dividends in terms of level, accuracy, and completeness of responses. In so far as the length of a questionnaire can affect the response rate in a postal survey, a typeset format can reduce the number of pages considerably.

The use of coloured paper can make a mail questionnaire stand out from other paper on a busy person's desk. There is some evidence to suggest that the use of warm colours such as yellow or peach will achieve a higher response rate than cold colours such as blue or green. Avoid dark colours that will make the questionnaire hard to read.

When interviewers use questionnaires in the field, a compact design can make the papers easier to deal with. In this situation a double column format, which is relatively easily achieved with modern word processing packages, is worth exploring.

7.9 **Ethical considerations**

Ethical behaviour is important in research, as in any other field of human activity. Certain ethical considerations, concerned with such matters as plagiarism and honesty in reporting of results, arise in all research, but additional issues arise when the research involves human subjects, in both the biological and social sciences. The principles underlying 'research ethics' are universal and concern issues such as honesty and respect for the rights of individuals.

Professional groups such as market researchers have established explicit codes of ethics to which members are obliged to adhere. Most universities now have codes of ethics enforced by 'ethics committees', which must approve all research projects involving humans or animals. These codes of ethics have intrinsic value in protecting the rights of humans and animals who may become involved in research, but they also serve a professional and organisational function. Researchers may be subject to litigation and could lose professional indemnity if they are not seen to have adhered to the appropriate code of ethics. A related consideration is the question of public relations and the public standing within the community of organisations responsible for the research. Some practices might be ethical, but they may still give offence, so the value of the data collected using such practices must be weighted against the ill will that could be generated.

Ethical considerations come into play at three stages of a research project, namely:

▶ when participants are recruited
▶ during the intervention and/or the measurement procedure to which they are subjected (see Section 6.2.4.1)
▶ in the release of the results obtained.

The general principles usually invoked in codes of research ethics are, firstly, that no harm should befall the research subjects, and secondly, that subjects should take part freely, based on informed consent. Field experiments, field studies (see Section 5.2.3) and participant-observational studies (see Section 8.4.2), especially, often require that research participants be involved in a research project without their consent or knowledge. Consider, for instance, Research Example VII in which the effect of the number of bystanders on helping behaviour in an emergency situation is investigated.

RESEARCH EXAMPLE VII   **A FIELD EXPERIMENT ON THE NUMBER OF BYSTANDERS AND HELPING BEHAVIOUR**

In a field experiment by Piliavin, Rodin and Piliavin (1969), two male and two female student assistants boarded a New York subway train before it ran non-stop for about seven minutes. After 70 seconds one of the men, both of whom were standing, staggered forward and slumped to the floor. On some occasions the man who collapsed would be a white man, whereas on other occasions it would be a black man; in some trials he smelled of liquor and carried a liquor bottle wrapped in a paper bag, whereas in others he carried a black walking stick (pretending to be ill).

▬▶

The two female students sat in the section next to the area where this "emergency" occurred and, as unobtrusively as possible, made notes about the gender, race, and location of the passengers and how many of them were in the area where the "emergency" took place. They also made a note of the gender, race, and location of each helper and how long it took before they rendered assistance.

If the "victim" was not assisted, the other male student helped him to his feet either about 70 seconds or about 150 seconds after the former had collapsed.

All students disembarked at the next station and then proceeded to another platform to board a train in the opposite direction for the next trial.

The major findings were that an apparently ill person was more likely to be assisted than one who appeared to be intoxicated; that the race of the victim had little effect on the race of the helper except when the former appeared to be drunk (in which case help was more likely to come from someone of the same race as the victim); that the longer the "emergency situation" continued without assistance being offered, the greater the probability was that someone would leave the emergency area; and that as the size of the group of passengers increased, the speed at which assistance was given, decreased.

If the passengers were first approached and requested to participate in a project in which they would be confronted by someone in distress, it would have made no sense to continue with the project. Obtaining their permission would have destroyed the internal and external validity of the results obtained, because individuals were likely to have reacted differently had they been aware of the nature of the study.

As a matter of fact, research suggests that if subjects are fully informed about the reasons for research, even if there is no possibility of physical pain of discomfort, they lose interest and highly unreliable results are obtained.

On the other hand, it is common practice to subject students, without their knowledge, to research procedures that require no deviation from their daily routine.

FOR EXAMPLE To expose training course members to one training method rather than another, does not imply any change from their daily routine because they would have been exposed to some or other method in any case.

The same consideration applies when the effect of encouraging comments on subsequent academic achievement is investigated by writing such comments on the test papers of some training course members but not on those of other, comparable trainees.

The only ethical objections that we might level against the above practices relate to the withholding of a potentially beneficial treatment from some participants.

Other important ethical issues include the following:

▶ **Competence**. A researcher should not embark on research involving the use of skills in which they have not been adequately trained. To do so may risk causing harm to subjects, abusing a subject's goodwill, damaging the reputation of the research organisation, and may involve wasting time and other resources.

▶ **Literature review**. Any research should be preceded by a thorough review of the literature to ensure, as far as possible, that the proposed research has not already been done elsewhere.

▶ **Plagiarism**. The use of others' data or ideas without due acknowledgement and permission where appropriate, is unethical.

▶ **Falsification of results**. The falsification of research results or the misleading reporting of results is clearly unethical.

ACTIVITY 7.6

Read Case Studies C and F in Appendix D on page 306.

QUESTION

Briefly discuss possible shortcomings concerning the validity and reliability of the measuring instrument used in these case studies.

ANSWER

case study c

Validity: The measuring instrument must measure what it is supposed to measure, namely knowledge of management principles and not something else, in order to avoid a shortcoming with regard to construct validity. In this respect, the validity of a written test to measure the knowledge could be questioned – would it not perhaps be more valid if the managers and subordinates of the first-line supervisors were asked to judge the knowledge of the course attendants in the workplace?

If the questions (items) of the measuring instrument (the three-hour-long written test) were not representative of the total spectrum of management principles that were offered during the training course, there would naturally be a shortcoming regarding the content validity thereof.

Reliability: If the marks of the course attendants remained the same irrespective of when they wrote the test, whether it was shorter or longer than an hour-long test (form/version differs), and who might mark it, there would not be a threat with regard to the reliability of the measuring instrument.

The above-mentioned answers are, however, speculative because the researcher does not mention anything about the validity and reliability of the measuring instrument in the case study or whether its characteristics were ever investigated.

case study f

Validity: The KAI scale may not be a valid instrument for measuring innovative problem-solving styles because it is a printed questionnaire, while a large number of problems in real life have to be solved immediately without first being printed as questions. Also, if the 32 questions of the KAI scale are not a representative sample of typical problems to be solved, the scale cannot fully measure innovative problem-solving styles. There may also be other shortcomings because it is a self-reporting instrument – the managers and entrepreneurs may fake their answers and/or obtain the help of others while completing the questionnaire.

Reliability: The instrument may not be reliable if it measures different scores on different occasions.

SUMMARY

In order to determine whether the independent variable is related to the dependent variable or caused a change in its levels, some form of measurement must be involved. The measurements of variables involve methods and techniques to obtain appropriate data for investigating the research hypothesis and/or question(s). By means of these methods and techniques, numbers are assigned to the characteristics of the units of analysis in order to reflect differences between them in the dependent variable.

Four levels of measurement can be distinguished, namely nominal, ordinal, interval, and ratio. As far as the dependent variable is concerned, a distinction can be made between construct and criterion validity. The former involves measurement reactivity. The reliability of a measure refers to the extent to which the obtained results can be generalised. There are various types of reliability, including test-retest, parallel-forms, internal consistency, split-halves, and interrater reliability.

Pilot studies play a very important role in the development of measurement instruments. Unobtrusive forms of measurement include physical traces, personal documents and mass media material, and official statistics and archival resources. Using groups as a source of information has many advantages and includes four categories: survey questionnaires, standardised tests, attitude scales, and rating scales and situational tests. Response styles such as the halo effect, stringency error, leniency error, error of central tendency, logical error, proximity error, and contrast error offer a serious threat to the reliability and validity of information obtained in rating scales. Interviews, whether structured, unstructured, or semi-structured, allow researchers with valuable data-collecting opportunities, and so do observation methods. The construction of questionnaires is not an easy process and requires a great amount of consideration with regards to the types of questions to use, and so on.

Whatever data-collecting method is used, ethical considerations are of extreme importance and must always receive the necessary attention.

TEST YOURSELF

Question 1: Multiple-choice questions

Only one of the answers at each question is correct. Identify and mark the correct one. (Answers appear in Appendix A on page 299.)

1.1 Classifying an electrical stove as working or not working treats its functioning as:
   a) a nominal variable
   b) an ordinal variable
   c) an interval variable
   d) a ratio variable.

1.2 When the variable source of electrical power is classified as hydro, nuclear, and coal-fire station, this variable has the important quality of being:
   a) mutually exclusive
   b) exhaustive
   c) ratio scale
   d) ordinal scale.

1.3 Which of the following dependent variables is most likely to represent a ratio scale of measurement?
   a) ratings of intimacy of eye contact of a prospective customer with a promotional item
   b) rank ordering of amount of eye contact of a prospective customer with a promotional item
   c) duration of eye contact of a prospective customer with a promotional item
   d) occurrence of eye contact of a prospective customer with a promotional item.

1.4 The lowest level of measurement that applies to physical as well as psychological measurement involves:
   a) ordinal scale
   b) ratio scale
   c) interval scale
   d) nominal scale.

1.5 The degree to which nine independent observers are in agreement is referred to as:
   a) cross-observer reliability
   b) replicated-observer reliability
   c) paired-observer reliability
   d) interrater reliability.

1.6 Which of the following is not illustrative of unobtrusive observations?
   a) examining the floor tiles at a museum to determine which exhibits are the most popular
   b) examining the number of beer cans in the garbage collections of a company's social club to determine beer consumption patterns amongst the workers

c) examining the wear on the tyres of security vehicles to determine the extent of security patrols

d) examining the communication effectiveness of workers by walking around the shop floor and making notes of their behaviour.

1.7 In contrast to interviews, self-administered questionnaires have the advantage(s) in survey research of:
a) being more effective in dealing with complicated issues
b) producing fewer incomplete questions
c) dealing with the context of work life
d) dealing with sensitive issues more effectively if the surveys are anonymous.

1.8 Assume that the following would be reasonable conversational questions based on an interviewee's previous statement. Which is the weakest probe/question?
a) "In what way is that a better job?"
b) "How is that a better job?"
c) "How do you mean that's a better job?"
d) "So you say X is a better job than Y?"

1.9 The best way to order items in an interview is to:
a) begin with the most interesting question
b) begin with the most threatening question
c) begin with demographic questions
d) randomise the questions.

1.10 The reliability of a measuring instrument is indicated by its:
a) coherence
b) precision
c) testability
d) consistency.

Question 2: True/false questions

Indicate whether the following statements are true (T) or false (F). (Answers appear in Appendix A on page 299.)

2.1 There is only one way to measure a variable.

2.2 A particular variable can usually be measured in several ways using different sources of information and various observation techniques.

2.3 When the research purpose is not clear, it is advisable to choose the highest level of measurement.

2.4 Validity refers to the link between the operational and conceptual definitions.

2.5 Predictive validity is another term for criterion-related validity.

2.6 If a measurement is reliable, it must also be valid.

2.7 Unobtrusive measures reduce the impact of the data collection on the phenomena being studied.

2.8 For a scale or index to be considered unidimensional, its component items should be indicators of only one dimension.

2.9 In survey research the interviewer should be a neutral medium through which questions and answers are transmitted.

Question 3: Self-evaluation questions

(Some answers are provided in Appendix A on page 299.)

3.1 Identify the level of measurement in each of the following:
a) the score on an attitude scale
b) military rank (for example corporal, sergeant, captain, and so on)
c) blood group of a person
d) marital status of a subject.

3.2 Suppose a finger dexterity test consists of round circles (on an answer sheet) that testees have to encircle as quickly as possible with a pencil. The test score is the number of circles that are encircled in this way within a given time limit.

Briefly describe how the retest reliability of such a dexterity test for trainees is to be investigated.

3.3 Suppose a researcher wants to investigate the attitudes of the same group of individuals towards three constitutional models simultaneously. According to which method could the researcher's attitude scale be compiled?

3.4 Explain the differences between the Likert and semantic differential approaches by using examples of possible items to measure the attitudes of white managers towards the concept of a new South Africa.

3.5 List the possible advantages and drawbacks of the various unobtrusive measurement procedures.

3.6 Which data-collecting method was used in Research Example VII (see Section 7.9, page 181)?

3.7 Compare personal interviews, telephonic interviews, and postal questionnaires in terms of the following:
a) cost and ease of application
b) response rate
c) quality of obtained responses.
Assume that a researcher who wishes to conduct a survey of respondents' opinions about affirmative action has to select one of these data-collecting methods.

3.8 Suppose a researcher in a postal survey attempts to maintain the impression of anonymity as well as determine from whom a completed questionnaire has been returned (for example to study the attitudes of the same person over time). Consequently, she affixes identification numbers in invisible ink to the questionnaires. Discuss the ethical implications of this strategy.

3.9 Suppose a psychology lecturer developed a programme to modify the lifestyle of individuals with an unhealthy Type A behaviour pattern. All employees of an insurance company who obtained high scores on a Type A personality questionnaire are assigned randomly to an experimental group and a control group. The experimental group meets weekly for an hour to take part in the programme that is presented by the lecturer's graduate students. At the conclusion of the project, the members of both groups are subjected to artificial situations supposed to elicit Type A behaviour in a room equipped with facilities to record the participants' behaviour on videotape. Subsequently, the researcher and his master's students rate the participants' behaviour in respect of the occurrence of Type A behaviour (from the videotapes) to investigate whether there is a difference in this type of behaviour between the two groups. Comment on the construct validity of the measure of the dependent variable.

Qualitative research designs

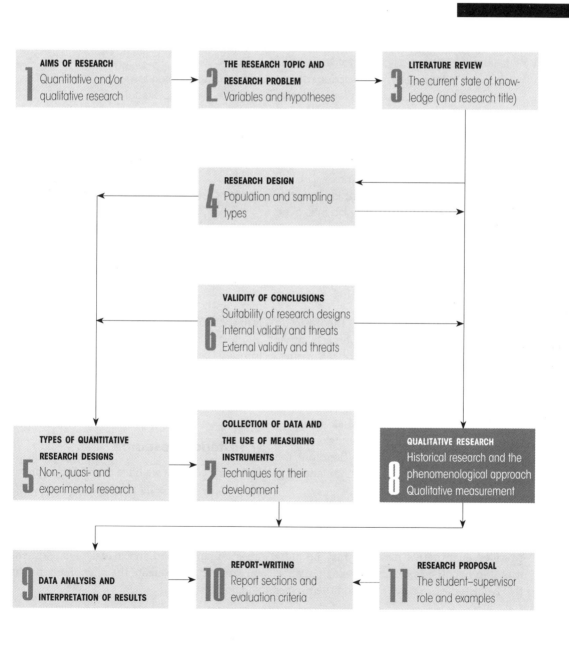

1 AIMS OF RESEARCH
Quantitative and/or
qualitative research

**2 THE RESEARCH TOPIC AND
RESEARCH PROBLEM**
Variables and hypotheses

3 LITERATURE REVIEW
The current state of knowledge (and research title)

4 RESEARCH DESIGN
Population and sampling
types

6 VALIDITY OF CONCLUSIONS
Suitability of research designs
Internal validity and threats
External validity and threats

**5 TYPES OF QUANTITATIVE
RESEARCH DESIGNS**
Non-, quasi- and
experimental research

**7 COLLECTION OF DATA AND
THE USE OF MEASURING
INSTRUMENTS**
Techniques for their
development

8 QUALITATIVE RESEARCH
Historical research and the
phenomenological approach
Qualitative measurement

**9 DATA ANALYSIS AND
INTERPRETATION OF RESULTS**

10 REPORT-WRITING
Report sections and
evaluation criteria

11 RESEARCH PROPOSAL
The student–supervisor
role and examples

LEARNING OUTCOMES

In this chapter we focus on qualitative research methods. These methods are used in situations where the quantitative approach of hypothesis-testing cannot or should not be used. Although the emphasis of qualitative research differs vastly from that of quantitative research, valuable information can be obtained by using these methods.

After studying this chapter, you will be able to:

- distinguish and/or compare historical research from and/or with the unobtrusive design described in Chapter 7
- discuss the role of historic research in the presiding judgement used in corporate law and auditing
- explain why case study research approaches can be described as qualitative research and not as quantitative research
- describe briefly participant observation and unstructured interviews as data-collecting methods and analysing techniques of the case study approach
- describe how focus groups are used to obtain information
- list the circumstances under which open-ended instead of closed-ended questions are to be used to collect information to explore a phenomenon
- defend the use of qualitative methods instead of quantitative methods to study a new specific research problem
- describe by means of examples how the reliability (see Section 7.5) of qualitative measuring instruments may be improved
- keep records of the phenomena being studied by means of qualitative methods
- identify 20 types of units of analysis (see Section 4.2) that cannot in their natural state be researched by means of qualitative methods.

8.1 Introduction

Qualitative research can, theoretically speaking, be described as an approach rather than a particular design or set of techniques. According to Van Maanen (1979, p. 520), it is an "umbrella" phrase "covering an array of interpretive techniques which seek to describe, decode, translate, and otherwise come to terms with the meaning of naturally occurring phenomena in the social world." Therefore, the qualitative approach is also fundamentally a **descriptive form of research**.

Qualitative field studies can be used successfully in the description of groups, (small) communities, and organisations. Whereas the so-called quantitative methods may be more useful in hypothesis-testing research, qualitative field studies, in turn, may lend themselves more aptly to studying cases that do not fit into particular theories.

NOTE: Visit the following web site for journal articles on qualitative and quantitative research: conjunctions and divergences:
http://qualitative-research.net/fqs/fqs-eng.htm.

8.2 Historical research

In the approaches we have dealt with in previous chapters, present phenomena are directly observed, manipulated, and measured. Researchers have to generate the data themselves (for example by administering tests or questionnaires) and, in the case of experimental research, even create the phenomenon that should be studied.

Historical researchers, by contrast, have to locate existing sources. Such sources may consist of documents (for example newspaper reports, law reports, correspondence), official statistics (see Section 7.7), and relics in which information about the past has been preserved. The researcher in no way interferes or intervenes with the events and typically does not observe them directly; instead, the researcher describes, analyses, and interprets those events that have already taken place.

In the human behavioural sciences, historical research is especially applicable to sociology, criminology, law, auditing, and education. If we knew the origin of the present educational, social, economic, and political conventions and problems, we would have a better understanding of these conventions and problems.

8.2.1 The principles of historical research

8.2.1.1 PRIMARY VERSUS SECONDARY SOURCES

The first basic principle of historical research is that, wherever possible, we should give **preference to primary** rather than secondary information sources (see Section 3.3.2). The reason is that with each transfer of information from one source to another, the information may be inadvertently or deliberately distorted.

FOR EXAMPLE Zietsman (1990, p. 14) points out a literary-historical example of the dangers resulting from using secondary sources.

During the Anglo-Boer War, Milner's Director of Education wrote a letter in English. This letter was subsequently translated into Dutch before being translated back to English. In the original letter, the sentence reads:

Our military police has gathered the greater part of the child population into these camps … and I feel that the opportunity during the next year of getting them all to speak English is golden.

The third-hand version reads as follows:

Our military operations have resulted in the greater part of the boys now remaining in the camps and I am convinced that we have no better opportunity than now to make them all English-speaking next year.

If eyewitnesses to the event or practice being studied are available, we can collect their verbal evidence as primary sources. We can procure these people *by means of purposive or snowball sampling* (see Section 4.3.4) and then conduct unstructured, rather than structured, interviews with them.

8.2.1.2 STRINGENT CRITICISM

Secondly, we should subject the information, irrespective of whether it is obtained by means of primary or secondary sources, to **stringent criticism**. In this context, a distinction is made between external and internal criticism. Whereas **external criticism** is directed at the authenticity of a source, **internal criticism** deals with the accuracy or credibility of the contents of the source. The question to be answered by external criticism, for example, is whether the supposed author of a document is really its author. Internal criticism, however, is concerned with the absence of bias in the evidence yielded by a source. It is not uncommon that under traumatic circumstances eyewitnesses tend to remember only certain aspects of an event. The eyewitness reports of people who have a vested interest in an event may also be coloured or distorted by such interest.

We should also establish the developmental or educational level of the eyewitnesses. Documents that have been accepted as satisfactory as far as external criticism is concerned (that is, in terms of the authenticity of their author), may still fail the test of internal criticism (for example if bias is suspected on the part of the author). The credibility of information may be enhanced if it can be corroborated by different, independent eyewitnesses and other sources.

According to Gottschalk (1969), internal and external criticism require researchers to be historically-minded, by which we mean that they should have an intimate knowledge of the milieu (individuals, conventions, practices, and so on) of the period in which the event being studied took place. If we are equipped with such knowledge, we may suspect inconsistencies and question the authenticity or the validity of sources.

8.2.1.3 CAUSAL EXPLANATIONS

Thirdly, we must synthesise and interpret the information (so-called facts) that has stood the test of internal and external criticism, in an attempt to propose **causal explanations** (see Section 5.2.2). Such explanations involve interpreting the evaluated information by means of **inductive logic** (see Section 2.5). These explanations usually proceed from a particular point of view or frame of reference.

FOR EXAMPLE Tyack (1976) and Rhoodie (1986) explained respectively the origin of compulsory education in the United States and revolutionary activities locally in terms of such frames of reference.

It is not uncommon for studies operating from different points of view to present apparently contradictory explanations for the same historical event. Consider the contradictory explanations that people operating from different political frames of reference may put forward for the rise and demise of apartheid.

As far as the causal explanations are concerned, there are three aspects to which attention must be paid: replicability, internal validity, and sampling.

(a) Replicability

In historical research the scientific requirement of replicability (see Section 1.2.2.3) does not refer to repeating the events or phenomena, but to the ability to **duplicate** the procedures, analyses, and conclusions. This means that another researcher should be able to come to a comparable conclusion after locating, evaluating, synthesising, and interpreting the sources.

(b) Internal validity

In historical research, internal validity (see Section 6.2) is obtained to the extent that the available sources make it possible to **rule out alternative explanations**. External validity (see Section 6.3) which, in view of the uniqueness of historical events, does not enjoy a high priority in historical research, refers to the effectiveness with which such research enables us to predict the course of events in other times and places.

(c) Sampling

Historical research is typically based on **accidental sampling** (see Section 4.3.4.1) insofar as it depends on the accidental survival of documents. (The documents themselves are the products of unobtrusive measurement (see Section 7.7.2).)

As a result of accidental sampling, one of the most important drawbacks of historical research is that sufficient information to reach scientifically justified conclusions may often be lacking.

The disadvantages of historical sampling are as follows:

- typical flaws of historical research include:
  - an excessive dependence on secondary information sources
  - succumbing to personal biases and favourite convictions. One researcher may convincingly argue the case for one explanation for a historical event, whereas someone else may equally convincingly put forward one with exactly the opposite drift.
- the inability to refute explanations of events that have taken place in the past, or even worse, the deliberate concealment of such explanations
- the four key problems of which historical researchers should be mindful, as singled out by Kaestle (1988), namely:
  - inferring causality on the basis of correlational relationships
  - the vague definition of key concepts and the assumption that terms have had their present meanings in the past

- the failure to distinguish between documented, official or professional prescriptions on the one hand, and whether such prescriptions were indeed heeded by society on the other hand
- the tendency to deduce the intentions of historical figures from the consequences of their actions as if they could have foreseen such consequences as we can now observe them by hindsight.

8.3 The phenomenological approach

We can describe the different approaches of the positivist and the anti-positivist (see Section 1.3) proponents in terms of different themes. To illustrate these differences, we will contrast the most extreme positions of these approaches with each other. We will refer to some ways (methods) in which the phenomenological approach may be applied.

8.3.1 The role of the researcher

While the positivists claim to study a psychological or sociological reality independent of an individual's experience of it, the phenomenologists *question the possibility of studying such a reality with so-called objectivity.*

According to the phenomenologists, what the researcher observes is not the reality as such, but an interpreted reality. We cannot detach ourselves from the presuppositions of our cultural inheritance, especially concerning the philosophical dualism (between the observable body and the intangible mind) and our glorification of technological achievements. As a result, the positivists and the anti-positivists interpret the researcher's role differently.

While natural scientists have nothing in common with their research objects (plants, gases, minerals, and so on), human behavioural scientists are in reality members of the group being studied. This enables direct understanding; this implies that the researchers can understand the circumstances of the object of study because they can picture themselves in the latter's shoes – something that is naturally impossible with natural-scientific research.

While a positivist researcher withdraws as far as possible from the research situation to avoid being biased, the anti-positivist researcher becomes absorbed in the research situation. The anti-positivist approach is most clearly evident in participant observation (see Section 8.4.2) in which the researcher, by taking part in the activities of the group, strives to become part of the group.

8.3.2 The importance of the context of the study

Valle, King and Halling (1989, p. 7) express the unity between humans and their world as follows:

In the truest sense, the person is viewed as having no existence apart from the world and the world as having no existence apart from persons. Each individual and his or her world are said to co-constitute one another.

Thus, a person derives his or her true meaning from his or her life world, and by existing he or she gives meaning to his or her world. By **life-world**, a term which is peculiar to the phenomenologists, we mean the world as lived by a person and not some entity separate from or independent of him or her. The person is dependent on his or her world for his or her existence and *vice versa*. The philosopher Heidegger talks of *"being-in-the-world"*. Because of the unity between the researcher and what is being researched, the phenomenologist believes that human behaviour cannot be understood without appreciating the context in which it takes place. Although the meaning of human existence is not equated with its context, it cannot be separated from it. Contrary to this, the positivists are searching for universal, context-free generalisations.

Figure 8.1 *Symbolic experience of affirmative action*

8.3.3 The aims of research

While the positivists aim at uncovering general laws of relationships and/or causality (see Section 5.2.2) that apply to all people at all times, the phenomenologists are concerned with understanding social and psychological phenomena from the perspectives of the people involved. Phenomenologists therefore attempt to experience these phenomena as the individuals involved must have experienced them personally.

As a result, phenomenologists are not concerned with the description of phenomena, because these exist independently of the participants' experience of them; instead, they are concerned with the **participants' experience of these phenomena**.

8.3.4 Research design and methods

Whereas the positivists require a research design to be decided on before data are collected, the anti-positivists usually favour **emer-gent designs**. This means that researchers may adapt their data-collecting procedures during the study to benefit from data of which they have only become aware during the research process itself.

FOR EXAMPLE If a research participant (employee of an organisation) is described as being negative about the organisation's affirmative action policy and the researcher is aware of this, the phenomenologist will attempt to understand how the participant experiences this feeling and attaches meaning to it. (See Figure 8.1.)

Whereas phenomenological researchers aim at letting the phenomenon speak for itself, the danger exists that positivist researchers, by using interview schedules (see Sections 7.7.4 & 7.8), checklists (see Section 7.7.6) for systematic observation, commercially available questionnaires (see Section 7.7.3.1), and so on, may force a possibly inappropriate structure on the phenomena being studied. However, the possible inappropriate structure may be prevented to some extent by conducting appropriate pilot studies – See Section 7.6.)

8.4 **Qualitative research methods**

The approaches that we will discuss originated from the **ethnographic methods** applied by cultural and social anthropologists in their field studies of social groups and communities. These approaches have been taken over and adapted by sociologists, psychologists, and education-ists, among others, and are often referred to as **qualitative research approaches**.

Ethnography can be described as an essen-tially *descriptive design* which is used in investi-gations amongst individuals or groups within a given community, group, or organisation. It is focused on the behavioural regularities of everyday situations, for example relation-ships between individuals or within groups, attitudes, rituals, and so on. These regularities are usually expressed as patterns, roles, and language, and are meant to provide the infer-ential keys to the group of people under study, such as a business community.

The primary task of ethnographic research (collecting field notes) is to uncover and expli-cate the ways in which people in particular settings come to understand, account for, take action, and manage their situations as well as the problems and difficulties they encounter. The processes of uncovering and explicating are typically based on successive observations and interviews. These are then evaluated ana-lytically to guide the researcher to the next stage in the investigation process.

According to Smith (1992), the terms eth-nography, case study (see Section 8.4.1), and participant observation (see Section 8.4.2) can be regarded as practically the same type of research approaches.

8.4.1 **Case study research**

The term **case study** pertains to the fact that a limited number of units of analysis (often only one) (see Section 4.2) is studied intensively. The units of analysis include individuals, groups, and institutions. The term *case study* does not refer to a specific technique that is applied.

In hypothesis-testing research we deal with the general and the regular deduction. In case studies, on the other hand, we are directed towards understanding the uniqueness and the idiosyncrasy of a particular case in all its complexity (see Section 2.2.4.2.).

FOR EXAMPLE Usually the objective of a case study is to investigate the dynamics of some single bounded system, typically of a social nature, for example an organi-sation, a family, a group, a community, or participants in a project, a practice (for example employing an accountant as personnel manager in rural financial bank branches) or an institution.

In this regard, the units of analysis can be either typical or atypical:
- On the one hand, if a single individual is studied in a case study, he or she should be highly representative of a particular popu-lation (see Section 4.2).
- On the other hand, such an individual should be extremely atypical of the phe-nomena being studied.

A case study cannot be both typical and atypi-cal. Furthermore, the unit of analysis (see Section 4.2) does not necessarily have to be human (for example an individual, family, community, and so on), but may also involve personal documents (for example diaries or letters) and records (indexes, ratios, and calcu-lation formulae).

Although a case study may involve a single individual, we must distinguish it from one-shot case studies (see Section 6.2.3) because its purpose is not to examine the effect of some or other intervention.

When we investigate a group or institution, we often make use of **fieldwork**, conducting the investigation on the spot under the natural circumstances of the specific case.

FOR EXAMPLE Page (1976) investigated the reactions of the entire community of Tulbagh to the earthquake in 1969. In this study Page and his research team, equipped with notebooks and tape recorders, had to stay for some time in the area a few days after the earthquake occurred.

As far as the research procedure itself is concerned, **participant observation** (see Section 8.4.2) and **unstructured interviews** (see Section 8.4.3) are usually used to study the chosen case, but in some instances even descriptive statistics may be appropriate.

FOR EXAMPLE An example of where descriptive statistics may be appropriate is a university principal's annual report (Stake, 1988) that describes the student community in terms of the numbers of students in the different faculties, and so on.

Whereas the extent of mass media material (papers, journals, and so on) permits the application of content analysis (see Section 9.2), the small number of personal documents available for case studies may necessitate an analysis similar to that performed on the data obtained by means of participant observation (see Section 8.4.2).

Three aspects deserve special mention as far as conducting case studies is concerned:

▶ Firstly, the case should be **defined** or **demarcated**, in other words, its boundaries should be determined. In some instances (for example if a single individual is involved) this decision is obvious. In other examples the researcher may, during the course of the study, find it necessary to adjust the boundaries that in any case have initially been determined arbitrarily.

FOR EXAMPLE The study done by Page (1976) was at first supposed to be limited to only the white farmers and the coloured community in the vicinity of the Steinthal Mission. It was extended later to also include some of the coloured workers of the white farmers as well as residents of Newtown, a coloured township.

▶ Secondly, whichever technique is used to collect data, the concern is not merely to describe what is being observed, but to **search**, in an inductive fashion, **for recurring patterns and consistent regularities**.

FOR EXAMPLE Page (1976) encountered people who attributed the earthquake to a divine purpose as a recurring theme.

▶ Thirdly, **triangulation** (see Section 7.4.1) is frequently used to discern these patterns. Because the number of cases is limited, the very purpose of case studies is to intensively examine those cases that are indeed available. In view of the consideration that the researcher himself or herself is the research instrument, an attempt is usually made to corroborate findings according to at least three different approaches.

FOR EXAMPLE Page (1976) used tape recordings of conversations, semi-structured interviews, and newspaper reports to investigate the reactions of the entire community of Tulbagh to the earthquake.

8.4.2 Participant observation

Participant observation requires the researcher, for an extensive period of time, to take part in, and report on, the daily experiences of the members of a group, community or organisation, or the people involved in a process or event (or whatever is being studied).

In participant observation, we do not observe the experiences of the individuals involved as detached outsiders, but experience them first-hand as insiders. The participant observer thus becomes a member of the inner circle of the group or event that is being studied.

FOR EXAMPLE To study the phenomenon of homeless people by means of this approach would, strictly speaking, require us to live for a few days, weeks or longer with homeless people and to participate in their day-to-day activities.

As may be evident from this description, participant observation is mostly applied to study groups (for example People Against Gangsterism and Drugs (PAGAD), youth gangs), organisations (for example a police department, Anglo American's executive management), or communities (for example the Jewish community in South Africa) in fields such as anthropology, sociology, and criminology.

Participant observers have to assume the roles of the group members in order to personally:

- experience what the group members experience
- understand their life-world
- see things from their perspective
- unravel the meaning and significance that they attach to their life-world, including their own behaviour.

Instead of discussing their activities with group members, complete participant observers strive to experience them internally. As indicated by their name, participant observers deliberately intend to distinguish themselves from detached observers.

The participant observer approaches the research situation with a minimum of preconceived ideas. Similarly, the flexibility of the participant-observation process allows room to follow up a host of clues that the researcher supposedly noticed.

8.4.2.1 DEGREES OF PARTICIPATION

The extent to which researchers participate in the activities of a group may vary from the situation in which the researcher, similar to systematic observation (see Section 7.2), maintains a distance from the phenomenon being studied, to that in which the researcher becomes a member of the inner circle of the group and becomes fully absorbed in all group activities. However, it remains the task of the researcher to watch the activities and experiences of the group closely with a view to writing them down.

Researchers therefore have to perform a dual role: one of experiencing the activities of the group and the other of observing and recording his or her experiences. As researchers move away from the position of the detached observer and increasingly surrender themselves to the activities of the group, it may become increasingly difficult to report the events naturally. A possible conflict between the roles of participant and observer cannot be ruled out.

The possibility that participant observers may become so engrossed in group activities that they abandon their role as observers in the process, represents a real danger in participant observation. Participant observers must decide which degree of participation may endanger their role as observer – a role that is indispensable from a research point of view.

8.4.2.2 THE PROCESS/COURSE OF PARTICIPANT OBSERVATION

In order to conduct participant observation, procedures should be followed, even though the research situation is less structured than in qualitative research. These procedures are as follows:

- Once a researcher has decided to investigate a specific group, organisation or process by means of participant observation, he or she has to obtain the **permission** of the group members or of their representatives. Such permission, of course, is unnecessary if the research is to be carried out in public venues – open spaces such as parks and beaches or closed spaces such as bars and public restrooms.
- The researcher should also **disclose the objectives** of his or her research to the group members. Although honesty is required in this connection, internal validity (see Section 6.2) is likely to be promoted by revealing too little rather than too much. It is especially important that the information divulged does not cause group members to react differently from their normal behaviour. On the other hand, it

may harm the researcher's position of trust if group members should later discover that they had been misled.

▸ There should in any case be no doubt among the group members that their **anonymity** (that is, not disclosing their identity/name) would be ensured in future. It is usually preferable to gain access to participants by means of a mediator who has the confidence of both the participants and the researcher (see Research Example VIII).

▸ The researcher should build up a position of **trust** with the group members. This is often easier said than done. For instance, if the group follows practices and conventions with which the researcher is unfamiliar, he or she may unknowingly violate these practices and conventions, and thereby sabotage the potential success of the study.

▸ As a result of the extensive periods of time that participant observers live together with the groups they study, they often develop firm friendships with the group members. On the one hand, such friendships have the advantage of allowing the participant observer to understand group members better. On the other hand, it poses the danger that the observer may become so **involved** with them that he or she fails to notice some developments that could have been detected immediately by outsiders.

▸ The participant observer is the actual **research instrument**. The observer has to rely on his or her experience, expertise, and intuition and, as such, runs the risk of arriving at highly idiosyncratic conclusions over which there may be no control.

▸ The researcher must write a **report**. Regardless of how comprehensive or how true to life the researcher's observations may be, the written report constitutes the final account thereof. When writing a report, the researcher should be careful not to simply summarise what is happening, because such summaries may involve premature interpretations. The researcher should rather describe in detail who has done what to whom, and how, where, and when this was done, in respect of each event. The report should include the verbal as well as non-verbal (facial expressions, gestures, and tone of voice) expressions of group members' observations of their environment and experiences.

▸ These **observation notes** should preferably be made while the group activities are taking place. This is, of course, impossible when the research is carried out in secret, or if note-taking is likely to interfere with the spontaneity of the group activities. If notes cannot be taken during the events, they should be written immediately thereafter (in secret, if necessary), so that as much of the observations are preserved as possible.

▸ The researcher may also consider taking along an audiotape recorder and to **record** his or her commentary on the activities while these are in progress. This can then be transcribed later. Naturally, such recordings will also be impossible if the research is carried out in secret, or will be undesirable if they interfere with the group activities.

▸ As the group activities continue, the researcher makes inferences from, or **interprets**, what is taking place. The researcher should be on the lookout for themes or repeated patterns of behaviour that appear in the group activities, as well as for deviations from these themes or patterns. The notes of these inferences and interpretations are referred to as **analytical notes**, and should be made and kept separately from the observation notes.

▸ Finally, researchers can make **methodological notes** for their exclusive use. These notes serve to remind them of things to look out for during future occasions or to caution them against potential pitfalls. They may make notes of their own feelings and emotions so that they can establish at a later time whether these have affected their observations.

RESEARCH EXAMPLE VIII   THE EXPERIENCE OF HAVING FIRE BOMBS THROWN AT ONE'S HOUSE

Cleaver (1988) conducted a study to gain an understanding of the experiences of individuals who had been victim-ised by having fire bombs thrown at their houses during the unrest situation in South Africa in 1988. With the help of an intermediary who was familiar to both the researcher and the participants, Cleaver came into contact with black adults whose houses in informal settlements in the former Transvaal had been burnt down in this manner.

Cleaver used unstructured interviews because she thought that a questionnaire would "[force] a subject into a particular mode and secondly, [that] such a questionnaire [could] only be produced after the researcher has par-ticularized the structure of the experience of the subject" (p. 77). To gain the confidence of the participants, Cleaver (being a white researcher from an Afrikaans-medium university) first talked with the participants for about an hour before recording the actual interviews on audiotape. Participants were told that the information they provided would be used for the analysis of their experiences and that their identities would not be revealed. They were also told that their experiences, rather than their political beliefs, were of importance.

The actual interview commenced with the following instruction: "I would like you to tell me about the experience of having your house damaged. Tell me what happened, how it affected you, and what you felt during and after the incident. Take your time. You can start wherever you like."

During the interview, Cleaver used phrases like: "Could you tell me more about that?" or "Could you explain that to me?" It was left to the participants to determine how long the interviews would be.

According to Cleaver, the interviews provided rich descriptions of individuals' experiences of having their houses burnt down. She provides direct quotations from the way in which participants described their experience of the attacks before, during and after they took place. Here are a few examples:

Luke: "This happened to other people. I thought no man will ever think of committing such a crime to me."

John: "I only realised later that I could not build it up again. I just sat down and stared."

Paul: "I must go all over again for what I had. I felt I was half-way along the new road; now I am at the beginning and the road is too steep."

Next, Cleaver interpreted the participants' experiences in terms of the recommendations of previous authors. She suggests that the intentions of the victimisers were to intimidate the victims to change their socio-political views, but that they did not succeeded in achieving this. The attacks were seldom reported to the police because, among other reasons, the police were mistrusted and many blacks felt that they were not protected by the judicial system. Apart from the loss of material possessions, feelings of vulnerability and helplessness were experienced as an integral part of victimisation.

8.4.3   **Unstructured in-depth interviews**

Just as observation may vary from detached observation on the one hand to complete participation on the other hand, interviews may vary from completely structured to unstructured. **Unstructured interviews** are usually employed in explorative research (see Section 2.3) for specific purposes:

▷ to identify important variables in a par-ticular area

▷ to formulate penetrating questions on them and

▷ to generate hypotheses for further investigation.

To preclude questions that do not allow any room for revealing the feelings and beliefs of individuals, unstructured interviews purpose-fully do not use an interview schedule, as used in structured interviews.

In our discussion of structured interviews (see Section 7.7.4.3) we stressed that in this kind of interview the interviewer should keep as much as possible to the previously formulat-ed questions contained in the interview sched-ule to prevent different interviewers from collecting information that is not comparable. Because the area being researched in qualitative studies is so unfamiliar, it is usually impossible to compile a schedule for interviews in such instances (see Sections 7.7.4 & 7.8). We also indicated (see Section 8.4.2) that participant observers purposefully deviate from the ideal of detached observation in order to experience the life-world of the group members in terms of the latter's perspective. A similar approach is followed in unstructured interviews.

8.4.3.1 NATURE

According to Fontana and Frey (1994), unstructured interviews provide a greater wealth of information than other forms of data-collecting methods because of their qualitative nature. Some authors differentiate between in-depth (ethnographic) interviewing and participant observation (see Section 8.4.2). Lofland (1971), however, alleged that these methods are interrelated as data was collected from informal interviewing in the field in a great amount of research that was done by means of participant observation.

Unstructured interviews differ from structured interviews in many ways (see Section 7.7.4.3). In unstructured interviews the interviewer simply suggests the general theme of discussion and poses further questions as these come up in the spontaneous development of the interaction between interviewer and research participant.

FOR EXAMPLE Cleaver (1988) used unstructured interviews to better understand the experience of the owners of houses that have been burnt down (during political violence) and to explore the theme of intimidation (see Research Example VIII, page 197). Furthermore, the interviewer interacts with the individual with whom the interview is conducted and does not assume the role of detached interviewer.

In unstructured interviews an attempt is made to understand how individuals experience their life-world and how they make sense of what is happening to them. The interviewer's question should thus be directed at the participant's experiences, feelings, beliefs, and convictions about the theme in question. Interviewers should be extremely careful not to suggest certain responses in the way in which they phrase their questions such as, for example, by asking leading questions (except when the researcher looks for underlying or hidden attitudes (see Sections 7.8 & 8.4.4.3)). In this regard, compare the instructions that were given in Research Example VIII (see Section 8.4.2.2) to the research participants.

In an unstructured interview, the interviewer focuses on the participants' first-hand experience of their life-world rather than on their interpretation or speculative explanations of it. Previously compiled questions such as those that suggest a particular theoretical point of view, should be restricted to a minimum if not avoided altogether. However, the interviewer should remain in control of the interview situation by, for example, encouraging the individual kindly yet firmly to continue if he or she is getting bogged down and to revert to the theme if he or she is straying from it.

The important advantage of unstructured interviews is that, unlike in telephonic interviews (see Section 7.7.4) and postal surveys (see Section 7.7.3.1), questions about sensitive and highly emotional issues may be asked in in-depth interviews. As a matter of fact, the term in-depth telephone interview and in-depth postal interview are self-contradictory terms.

8.4.3.2 PROCESS/COURSE OF THE INTERVIEW(S)

At the beginning, the interviewer explains the **purpose** of the study to the prospective participants and seeks their co-operation. Among other things, the researcher should provide an indication of how long the interview or series of interviews is expected to take.

There are several guidelines to keep in mind when conducting an unstructured interview.

(a) Compiling of field notes

Although qualitative interviewing may sound simple (just a question of open conversation), it is not necessarily the case. Qualitative researchers should be trained to be careful and systematic in the ways in which they:

▶ make observations
▶ record observations
▶ plan their participation
▶ ask questions.

Field notes can be described as detailed notes and observations that are made by the interviewer/researcher. Notes should be made of everything that is said during the interview. For this purpose a tape recorder can be particularly useful. The researcher should also take note of any non-verbal behaviour of the respondent(s). Double brackets can be used in the report to report non-verbal behaviour such as pauses in conversation, sitting arrangements, and body gestures.

FOR EXAMPLE "I feel angry ((pause)). My supervisor always shouts at me ((makes a fist)). He never praises me for delivering quality work! ((Heaves a sigh))"

(b) The setting

Researchers should consider the practical issue of gaining access to the setting. This strategy varies from group to group and depends on the type of research (Fontana & Frey, 1994).

FOR EXAMPLE One may have to wear appropriate clothing in order to go down a mineshaft to interview a group of mineworkers at a gold mine in Johannesburg. One may have to be imprisoned for a week to befriend and study the behaviour of gangs amongst prisoners.

(c) Presenting oneself

Another decision concerns the way in which researchers should present themselves to the respondents. This is especially pertinent in South Africa: do researchers represent a specific culture or do they represent the rainbow nation in South Africa? Another issue which the researcher has to consider concerns wearing the appropriate clothing. These decisions are important as first impressions can have a profound impact on the interview.

(d) Trust

It is important for the interviewer in unstructured interviews to gain the trust of the respondents. This is closely related to the nature of the interview topic.

FOR EXAMPLE If the interview is focused on a relatively innocuous topic such as the crime rate in South Africa, it will not be too difficult to gain the trust of the respondents. However, when discussing sensitive topics such as the frequency of sexual intercourse in an investigation to establish the increase of AIDS-contamination in the mining industry, establishing trust is not only more difficult, but also more important.

As in participant observation, **frankness** and **honesty** are required from the interviewer to establish a position of trust with the prospective participants. The prospective participants should not feel that they are among several who are going to be subjected to questioning, but rather that the interviewer is interested in them as **individuals** and that he or she respects their uniqueness. Not only should the participants be assured of complete **anonymity**, but they should also feel completely free to **express their true feelings and opinions** without fear of disapproval (or condemnation) from the interviewer.

Only when there is a relationship of mutual confidence and respect between the two parties, are the chances good that the participant will feel free to reveal his or her innermost feelings and beliefs to the interviewer. This is especially true when these feelings and beliefs are in conflict with the generally accepted norms of a community. Questions dealing with contentious issues should therefore be withheld until the middle or latter phases of the interview or series of interviews.

(e) Rapport

Rapport correlates highly with understanding in unstructured interviews. According to Fontana and Frey (1994, p. 367):

He or she must be able to put him- or herself in the role of the respondents and attempt to see the situation from their perspective, rather than impose the world of academica and pre-conceptions upon them.

Establishing good rapport with the respondents opens many doors for the researcher and will lead to the collection of valuable information. However, it can also create problems because the researcher can become too involved in the problems of the respondents. The researcher must therefore take care to remain objective.

FOR EXAMPLE If a researcher wants to establish rapport by taking part in a illegal strike by mineworkers, he could end up in jail with them!

The interviewer should neither approve nor disapprove of the participants' actions, but be understanding. Even if a participant were to act (verbally) aggressively towards the interviewer or display signs of resistance, the interviewer should show understanding (instead of becoming aggressive or showing resistance).

Although this emphatic living through of experiences by the interviewer corresponds with the aim of the typical therapeutic interview, the purpose at present is to **facilitate the revelation of information** and not to provide therapy.

(f) Language and culture differences
These aspects are very important in the South African context. Often the researcher will be in a position where he or she has to conduct cross-cultural interviews.

FOR EXAMPLE The researcher might be English-speaking and the respondents Zulu-speaking.

Although respondents may be fluent in the language of the interviewer, various expressions have different meanings in the different languages. Often in certain cultures certain topics should not be discussed at all. The language and cultural values of the respondents must therefore be taken into consideration. Researchers often experience difficulties when they have to rely on interpreters in cross-cultural interviews. This can lead to misunderstandings and biases which can have serious detrimental implications for data-collecting (Fontana & Frey, 1994).

(g) Sexual differences
Apart from taking language and cultural differences into account during unstructured interviewing, the researcher should also be aware of sexual differences. Male researchers or interviewers should be careful not to act in a paternalistic way towards female respondents, for instance.

Oakley (1981) suggests that the interviewer(s) as well as the respondent(s) should be regarded as "faceless" and "invisible" and that the discussion of the topic should be value-free. The respondents should not be allowed to propagate their religious or political or sexual affiliations, for example.

Fontana and Frey (1994), however, allege that the gender of the interviewer will have a profound influence on the interview because each interview always takes place within the specific cultural boundaries of a community where masculine identities usually differ from feminine identities. The authors also stress that unstructured interviews already take place in a hierarchical environment with the respondent in a subordinate position. Therefore, in the cases where the respondent is a female, the problem is much more accentuated. Female interviewers also have the added burden of experiencing sexual overtures or harassment from the male respondents during interviews. Nowadays it can sometimes also happen the other way around! In the case of homosexual interviewers and respondents the situation becomes even more complicated.

In conclusion it can be said that in the process of developing a close relationship between the interviewer(s) and the respondent(s), differences in sexual status should be minimised and any hierarchical situation between the sexes should be eliminated as far as possible.

8.4.3.3 ETHICAL CONSIDERATIONS

There are four ethical considerations to which the researcher should pay attention:

- **Informed consent**. The researcher should obtain the necessary permission from the respondents after they were thoroughly and truthfully informed about the purpose of the interview and the investigation.
- The respondents should be assured of their *right of their privacy*. For instance, they should be informed that the identity of the respondent will remain anonymous.
- *Protection from harm*. The respondents should be given the assurance that they will be indemnified against any physical and emotional harm.
- *Involvement of the researcher*. Researchers should guard against manipulating respondents or treating them as objects or numbers rather than individual human beings. They should not use unethical tactics and techniques of interviewing (Fontana & Frey, 1994).

FOR EXAMPLE Unethical behaviour in unstructured interviewing occurred in 1970 when a researcher named Humphreys was unable to find homosexual men in public restrooms who were willing to be interviewed during the Tearoom Trade Research (Fontana & Frey, 1994). He then secretly recorded their licence number plates and used these to trace the men to their residences. He even went so far as changing his appearance to be able to interview the men at their residences without being recognised!

8.4.3.4 ADVANTAGES AND DISADVANTAGES OF UNSTRUCTURED INTERVIEWS

The advantages and disadvantages of unstructured interviews can be summarised briefly as follows:

- Unstructured interviews are very useful in cases where the researcher wants to launch an **explorative investigation** as well as pre-testing a questionnaire.
  They help to clarify concepts and problems and allow the establishment of a list of possible answers and solutions which, in turn, facilitates the construction of multi-choice questions, the elimination of superfluous questions, and the reformulation of ambiguous ones (Bless & Higson-Smith, 1995, p. 110).
- The disadvantage of unstructured interviews is that the researchers or interviewers are directly involved and in control of the respondents. The researchers may therefore **display bias** in the interview situation.
- Unstructured interviews can be **time-consuming** as some interview sessions can last for up to three or four days. Consequently it can also be very expensive as the researcher should make provision for travelling expenses, meals, and even accommodation expenses of the respondents.

8.4.4 Focus groups

Focus groups are also described as **group in-depth interviews**. These groups consist of a small number of individuals or interviewees that are drawn together for the purpose of expressing their opinions on a specific set of open questions. According to Fontana and Frey (1994), the purpose of group interviews is based on the collection of qualitative data. According to these authors, the term *focus group* was coined by Merton, Fiske and Kendall (in Fontana & Frey, 1994).

Group interviews are essentially a *qualitative technique* for collecting information. The researcher directs the interaction and inquiry either in a very structured or unstructured manner, depending on the aim of the investigation. The aim of using such group interviews is not to replace individual interviewing but to gather information that can perhaps not be collected easily by means of individual interviews.

FOR EXAMPLE The researcher might be interested in the discussion of opinions by members of an organisation and use focus groups to try to establish how they react to each other's arguments.

Focus groups can also serve to **elicit responses** between the members of the groups. Blumer (in Fontana & Frey, 1994, p. 365) notes that "[a] small number of such individuals brought together as a discussion and resource group, is more valuable many times over than any representative group."

The explorative purpose of a focus group can be elaborated to pre-test the wording and questions of a quantitative questionnaire (Fontana & Frey, 1994).

8.4.4.1 COMPILATION OF FOCUS GROUPS

The researcher should use an appropriate sample (usually purposive or snowball) (see Sections 4.3.4 & 8.4.4.5) consisting of not more than 12 and not fewer than six participants. These respondents should be *knowledgeable* or *experienced* with regards to the topic of the investigation that will be discussed.

Stewart and Shamdasani (1990) highlight the following potential problems regarding the compilation of focus groups which should be taken into account:

 - The members of a focus group should be selected carefully to prevent any problems regarding the quality of information. Therefore, the researcher must not select friends or family members as they will have a negative influence on the anonymity of answers given by respondents.
 - The participation of so-called "experts" on the subject under discussion should also be controlled or limited because they can intimidate or inhibit responses from others.
 - Hostile respondents should also be controlled or not selected.
 FOR EXAMPLE If some of the participants have a specific interest in the topic under discussion, it may happen that they try to prevent other participants from expressing their opinions by means of hostile behaviour.

8.4.4.2 PHASES IN CONDUCTING FOCUS GROUPS

The phases in conducting focus groups are as follows:

 - The researcher introduces the topic to the focus group.
 - The researcher sets rules indicating, for example, that only one person should speak at a time.
 - Each participant (in turn) makes an opening statement regarding their experience of the topic.
 - The researcher guides the open group discussion by asking questions such as "Most people here mentioned Z, but how does that fit in with A?"
 - The session ends with each person (in turn) giving a final statement that may not be challenged.

8.4.4.3 THE QUESTIONS

The researcher usually makes use of an unstructured interview schedule (see also Section 7.7.4) to guide the interview. In general, the interview starts with a general question based on the aim or main topic of the investigation. The purpose is to elicit the first responses from the respondents. Next, the researcher moves to more structured questions in order to obtain specific information. Ideally, the researcher should not ask more than 10 to 12 questions during the focus group interview.

The following types of questions could be used (Stewart & Shamdasani, 1990, based on Wheatley & Flexner, 1988):

 - **Main questions** should define the purpose of the investigation.
 FOR EXAMPLE If the purpose of an investigation is to establish the attitudes of a group of nurses towards HIV/AIDS patients, the researcher should start the group session by asking the respondents what they think of the HIV/AIDS patients in their care.
 - **Leading questions** should be used to look for underlying or hidden attitudes only.
 FOR EXAMPLE "Do you really think that AIDS can be contracted by using the same cutlery as AIDS patients?"

The purpose of **testing questions** is to rephrase the answers of the respondents to activate the group to react or to challenge the questions.

FOR EXAMPLE "So, in your opinion, the salaries that you earn are not satisfactory compensation for the hours that you have to work?"

Steering questions are used to guide the group back to the main theme under discussion.

FOR EXAMPLE "Apart from your low salaries, tell me more about your feelings when you have to care for an HIV/AIDS patient that is seriously ill."

Indirect questions allow the respondents to discuss difficult aspects by answering the questions in terms of the behaviour, reactions, or feelings of other people.

FOR EXAMPLE By showing the respondents a sketch, photograph, or video clip of the negative behaviour of a nurse towards a HIV/AIDS patient, the researcher can ask the respondents about their opinions on the behaviour, reactions, or feelings of the nurse in the sketch, photograph, or video.

Factual questions allow respondents to discuss controversial aspects and can be used when the discussion becomes too emotional.

FOR EXAMPLE "Seeing that we have different opinions on a realistic payment for what you are doing, can anybody tell me what the actual salary is of someone in the private sector who has the same qualifications that you have?"

The purpose of **emotional questions** is to elicit the expression of personal feelings amongst the respondents. The researcher should be mindful not to hurt any one's feelings.

FOR EXAMPLE "Do you really have enough sympathy with the family of a patient in your care when he or she is dying?"

Anonym questions usually start with the researcher asking the respondents to describe their first thoughts about a specific topic. The researcher then waits in silence for any responses without disrupting the silence.

8.4.4 ADVANTAGES AND DISADVANTAGES OF FOCUS GROUPS

The advantages and disadvantages can be summarised as follows:

Focus groups provide sources of information that can be obtained rapidly and at a low cost. It can be conducted within a wide range of settings and a vast range of respondents can be selected (Stewart & Shamdasani, 1990).

Since the researcher communicates directly with the respondents, he or she can easily clarify some aspects of the questions put to the respondents. The researcher can also ask the respondents to elaborate on their answers (Stewart & Shamdasani, 1990).

Focus groups enable the participants in the group to discuss their opinions and experiences in such a way that a consensus of opinion regarding research problems can be reached. According to Bless and Higson-Smith (1995), this aspect of focus groups is very useful during participatory (see Section 8.4.5) and action research (see Section 8.4.5.1) when members of communities are equal participants in the planning and implementation of research. It is useful to allow participants to share their opinions because it may lead to new ideas amongst the different respondents allowing them to reconsider their initial responses.

Interviews can be conducted with respondents who are not be able to complete self-reporting questionnaires (such as in the case of quantitative research methods). For instance, in the case of small children or individuals with a low level of education (Stewart & Shamdasani, 1990).

Focus groups can also be used by means of teleconferencing (see Section 7.7.4.2). Respondents from different places can be drawn together for an interview without being physically together at a specific place (Stewart & Shamdasani, 1990).

▶ The disadvantage of a focus group in comparison to an individual in-depth interview is that it often inhibits the responses of participants. Some respondents are not able to express their feelings freely because they are intimidated by the presence of other respondents in the group.

8.4.4.5 SAMPLING RESPONDENTS FOR UNSTRUCTURED INTERVIEWS AND FOCUS GROUPS

Whereas quantitative research aims to use *random* samples that are representative of a population, qualitative samples tend to be *purposive* rather than random (Miles & Huberman, 1994). The reason for this is that qualitative researchers work with limited universes and that "social processes have a logic and coherence that random sampling can reduce to uninterpretable sawdust" (Miles & Huberman, 1994, p. 27). Since populations in qualitative designs usually consist of a small number of cases, bias may occur when using random sampling.

Therefore, the qualitative researcher usually obtains individuals with whom to conduct unstructured interviews or focus groups by means of *purposive* or *snowball sampling* (see Section 4.3.4). Often, preference is given to key informants who, on account of their position or experience, have more information than regular group members and/or are better able to articulate this information.

FOR EXAMPLE The leaders of gangs in prisons may be used as key informants when such gangs are studied by means of unstructured interviews.

In the above-mentioned example we may refer to focus groups where more than one individual is interviewed at a time. By doing so, the interviewees stimulate each other and share their ideas and thoughts.

8.4.4.6 ANALYSIS OF INFORMATION OBTAINED FROM UNSTRUCTURED INTERVIEWS AND FOCUS GROUPS

Similar to participant observation, the eventual analysis of the information obtained from unstructured interviews and focus groups is based on the interviewer's records. The interviewer may take notes of the participants' responses with a view to writing a more complete report afterwards. As an alternative, a tape recording may be made with a view to transcribing it later. In both cases the interviewer should still take notes of the participant's presumed non-verbal communication. Neither taking notes, nor recording on tape should, however, inhibit the participant's spontaneous behaviour. See section 9.2 for a detailed description of qualitative data analysis.

8.4.4.7 COMPILING A QUALITATIVE RESEARCH REPORT

The interviewer should compile a complete report as soon as possible after the conclusion of the interview(s). Wolcott (1990) stressed that the researcher should start *as soon as possible* in writing a **qualitative research report**, even writing the first draft before starting field work. At the same time, the interviewer should jot down **reflective notes** similar to the analytical and methodological notes in participant observation, with a view to using them in further interviews or in analysing the information obtained. On the basis of the descriptions of the individuals' experiences, the researcher must attempt to capture the essence of the contents and of the recurring themes that bind them together accurately.

According to Miles and Huberman (1994), all qualitative reports, in the first instance, could use the same format that is applied in quantitative report-writing, namely: statement of the problem and conceptual framework; research questions; methodology; data analysis; conclusions and discussions (see Chapter 10).

However, there are also *differences* between quantitative and qualitative report-writing that should be taken into consideration. These occur due to a "circular" linkage that exists between the writing of a research question, methods, data collection, and interim analysis. This circular linkage is based on the fact that each new analysis can open new leads in reporting the data. Some qualitative researchers therefore do not start with the conceptual framework but, rather, discuss it at the end in the discussions of the results (Miles & Huberman, 1994).

According to Zeller (in Miles & Huberman, 1994), qualitative researchers don't report "out" as in the case of quantitative report-writing; instead, they report "scenes", that is, they report the periodical contacts with the respondent(s) within their surroundings. Atkinson (1991, p. 164) described the dynamic characteristics of qualitative report-writing in the following way:

> *The analytical induction of categories, themes and relationships: the explication of meaning; and the understanding of action may all proceed via the writing itself … The 'writing up' of the qualitative study is not merely a major and lengthy task; it is intrinsic to the 'analysis', the 'theory' and the 'findings'.*

8.4.5 Participatory research

Participatory research involves the integration of elements such as the following:

- social investigation
- educational work
- action in an interrelated process.

Action research (see Section 2.3.3.3) is a form of participatory research in which action and research complement each other.

We can distinguish between participatory research and other conventional types of research on the basis of the roles of the researcher and participants as follows:

- The participants are actively involved in the planning and implementation of the research outcomes and are thus empowered.
- In bringing about social change, the researcher is dependent on the participation of the affected community members, state functionaries, and political parties.

We mainly use **unstructured (in-depth) interviews** (see Section 8.4.3) and **focus groups** (see Section 8.4.4) to collect data in participatory research.

8.4.5.1 ACTION RESEARCH

Action research is not a singular approach and different people who profess to use this research may emphasise different aspects of it. The following concise summary captures the most important common factors of these aspects.

(a) Versatile design

A distinguishing feature of action research is that it uses a versatile design that may continually be changed and **adapted** in reaction to information and results obtained during the research project.

In action research we do not finalise the research design in advance and consistently follow it up to the end of the research project – it evolves as the project progresses. A cyclical progression through phases of tentative planning, acting, observation, reflection on, and evaluation of the preliminary results, may be distinguished. The evaluation of the preliminary results, in turn, provides feedback for the first phase of a following cycle.

In a certain sense, the empirical cycle of Figure 2.1 (see Section 2.2) is repeatedly executed in an informal manner in action research.

(b) Participant involvement

Action research places a high premium on **involving all participants** in each of the phases (tentative planning, acting, observation, reflection on, and evaluation of the preliminary results).

FOR EXAMPLE In an organisational training context, the trainers and course members will not be regarded as subjects who are going to be subjected to some treatment devised by an outsider. All interested parties, among others the administrators, employers, stakeholders, trainers, and course members, will be jointly involved in the project.

This emphasis on the participation and the perspectives of the interested parties ties in with the qualitative researcher's preference for participant observation (see Section 8.4.2), for example. Insofar as these groups accept responsibility for the execution of the research and the implementation of its results, action research may be characterised as democratic.

The contribution of action research to social change is therefore met with approval in certain sociopolitical circles. In its purest form, action research is undertaken from within an organisation, for example by the employees of an organisation, instead of by someone approaching from the outside and retaining the role of an outsider. It "allow(s) participants to influence, if not determine, the conditions of their own lives and work, and collaboratively to develop critiques of social conditions which

sustain dependence, inequality, or exploitation in any research enterprise in particular, or in social life in general" (Kemmis, 1985, p. 36).

(c) External validity

Finally, we can conclude that external validity (see Section 6.3) does not enjoy a high priority in action research. The programme of action that is developed and found successful in action research in one specific situation, is not necessarily held up as a solution for any other similar situation.

FOR EXAMPLE A programme that was developed through action research to provide school training in Soweto for black youths who had become alienated from the prevailing educational system, need not necessarily be equally successful for similar black youths in the Cape Peninsula.

ACTIVITY 8.1

Read Case Study F in Appendix D on page 306.

QUESTION

What type of research design and measuring instruments, other than the KAI scale, could the researchers possibly have used for the aim of this investigation? Explain your answer briefly.

ANSWER

The researchers could also have used a qualitative design instead of a quantitative design by making use of the following types of research and measuring techniques:

- In historical research the business documents and financial statements of businesses that are run by managers and entrepreneurs can be analysed. By comparing these indicators, the researchers could conclude the extent to which entrepreneurs are able to solve their problems more innovatively than managers (or *vice versa*).

- The researchers could also make use of the case study method and participant observation, thereby studying the innovative problem-solving styles of two or more typical managers and entrepreneurs in the course of their day-to-day business activities. By conducting unstructured (in-depth) interviews and focus groups, the researchers could determine the styles of the business people.

ACTIVITY 8.2

Read Case Study G in Appendix D on page 306.

QUESTIONS

1. What type of *research design* (approach) is involved in Case Study G? Explain your answer specifically.
2. Which type of *data collection method* has been used to measure the attitudes of the nurses towards HIV/AIDS patients? Explain your answer in detail.

ANSWERS

1. The qualitative *case study design* was used as the objective of this investigation was to investigate the attitudes of a limited number of units of analysis (20 nurses). A qualitative case study differs from hypothesis-testing research because its purpose is not to examine the effect of some or other intervention, but to understand the uniqueness and idiosyncrasy of a particular case (such as the attitudes of nurses towards HIV/AIDS patients at a specific hospital) (see Section 8.4.1).

2. *Unstructured in-depth interviews* were used to identify important themes (variables) regarding the attitudes of nurses towards HIV/AIDS patients. Unstructured interviews are also used to formulate penetrating questions and to generate hypotheses for further investigation (see Section 8.4.3).

SUMMARY

Qualitative research is not concerned with the methods and techniques to obtain appropriate data for investigating the research hypothesis, as in the case of quantitative research. Qualitative data are based on meanings expressed through words and other symbols or metaphors. Qualitative studies can be used successfully in the description of groups, (small) communities, and organisations by studying cases that do not fit into particular theories. These studies are particularly useful in the case of historical research.

According to the phenomenological approach, the researcher attempts to understand the participant's life-world and focuses on the participant's experience of specific phenomena. In order to achieve this, emergent designs are used. The designs that are used most often include case study research, participant observation, unstructured in-depth interviews, focus groups, and participatory research.

TEST YOURSELF

Question 1: Multiple-choice questions

Only one of the answers to each question is correct. Identify and mark the correct one. (Answers appear in Appendix A on page 299.)

1.1 Eight focus groups were audiotaped to examine citizens' attitudes toward the building of an electric power station in their region. The advantage of using this approach to focus groups is:
   a) interviewers need little skill
   b) interviewers can easily control the focus group's discussion
   c) the tapes are easily analysed
   d) high face validity.

1.2 An advantage of field research is that:
   a) it enables the researcher to draw conclusions about the population
   b) the researcher can control the variables being studied
   c) the phenomenon can be studied in a natural setting
   d) hypotheses can be rigorously tested.

1.3 In field research the unstructured interview is used to:
   a) minimise interviewer bias
   b) gain in-depth understanding of respondents' views
   c) obtain responses to close-ended questions
   d) control factors that may affect the respondents' answers.

1.4 The basic tool of field research is:
   a) a notebook and pencil
   b) a tape recorder
   c) a camera
   d) a telephone.
1.5 Participants in unstructured interviews and focus groups are usually sampled by means of:
   a) a stratified random sample
   b) accidental and quota samples
   c) purposive and snowball samples
   d) no sample at all.
1.6 One of the purposes of explorative research is to:
   a) generate hypotheses
   b) collect information
   c) make objective observations
   d) gain the trust of the participants.
1.7 A focus group should ideally consist of:
   a) one participant
   b) 20 participants
   c) 13 participants
   d) eight participants.
1.8 One advantage of a focus group is that it can be used:
   a) in teleconferencing
   b) to protect the privacy of a participant
   c) to involve all the members of a population
   d) to inhibit the responses of some participants.

Question 2: True/false questions

Indicate whether the following statements are true (T) or false (F). (Answers appear in Appendix A on page 299.)

2.1 An evaluation of the industrial revolution can best be done by means of unstructured interviews and focus groups.

2.2 We describe the behaviour of a trade union in qualitative research by means of ethnographic studies.

2.3 In case study research we can only investigate single individuals.

2.4 There is only one way to measure a variable.

2.5 The use of several different research methods to test the same finding is called triangulation.

2.6 A particular variable can usually be measured in several ways; using different sources of information and various observation techniques.

2.7 Field research differs from other forms of observation in that it is both a data-collecting and a theory-generating activity.

Question 3: Self-evaluation questions

(Some answers appear in Appendix A on page 299.)

3.1 Use one of the non-probability samples that are usually used in unstructured (in-depth) interviews and obtain a sample of 10 individuals.

3.2 Conduct unstructured interviews on a one-to-one basis with the 10 individuals in the sample selected in Question 3.1 about their opinion on any chosen topic. Record your questions and the interviewees' answers on paper because you will have to analyse it later (see Chapter 9).

Data analysis and interpretation of results

9

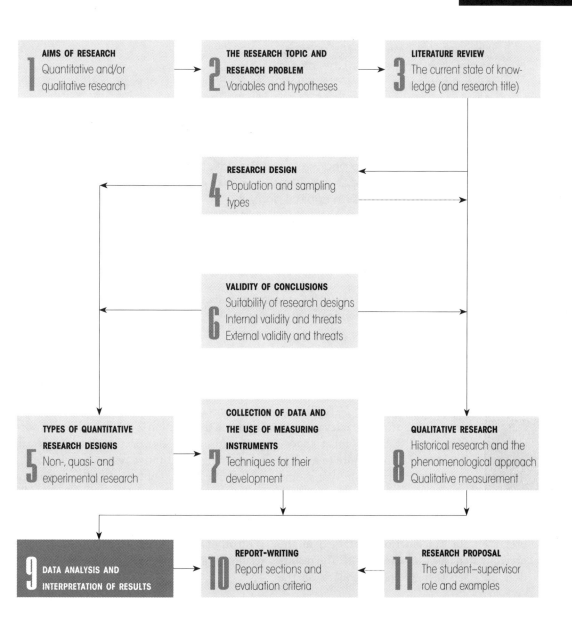

AIMS OF RESEARCH
1 Quantitative and/or qualitative research

THE RESEARCH TOPIC AND
RESEARCH PROBLEM
2 Variables and hypotheses

LITERATURE REVIEW
3 The current state of knowledge (and research title)

RESEARCH DESIGN
4 Population and sampling types

VALIDITY OF CONCLUSIONS
6 Suitability of research designs
Internal validity and threats
External validity and threats

TYPES OF QUANTITATIVE
RESEARCH DESIGNS
5 Non-, quasi- and experimental research

COLLECTION OF DATA AND
THE USE OF MEASURING
INSTRUMENTS
7 Techniques for their development

QUALITATIVE RESEARCH
8 Historical research and the phenomenological approach
Qualitative measurement

9 **DATA ANALYSIS AND INTERPRETATION OF RESULTS**

REPORT-WRITING
10 Report sections and evaluation criteria

RESEARCH PROPOSAL
11 The student–supervisor role and examples

LEARNING OUTCOMES

Until now we have discussed issues regarding the research topic, literature review, selection of research design, and collection of data by means of measuring instruments. The most important stages of the research process, however, involve the analysis and interpretation of data as well as the publication of these results. The analysis and interpretation of the data ultimately reveal to what extent the research hypothesis was proven or disproven. This information is extremely valuable to the research community. The process of analysis and interpretation applies to qualitative as well as quantitative data, although the specific techniques vary.

After studying this chapter, you will be able to:
- use the technique of qualitative data analysis to identify the most important themes that highlight your interviewees' answers
- code the data (answers from the interviewees)
- compile a coding list, a table of the frequencies, and a matrix of importance attributed to each of your themes
- select the appropriate statistical graphical techniques to present your results per theme in qualitative analyses
- use matrices and networks to display qualitative data
- use quantitative methods to analyse qualitative data by means of content analysis
- know how sampling influences the internal validity of a content analysis
- describe the coding process in content analysis
- explain the difference between descriptive and inferential statistics
- list some of the assumptions underlying inferential statistics
- group a collection of scores in tables and give a graphic representation of the scores
- provide advice on selecting a statistical technique in helping to analyse the results of a research study
- explain the importance of knowing the levels of measurement (see Section 7.3.2) in order to choose an appropriate statistical technique to analyse the data of a research project.

9.1 Introduction

Once we have decided on an appropriate research design (see Chapters 5 & 8) and suitable means of measuring the relevant variables (see Chapters 7 & 8), we must choose an appropriate statistical procedure to analyse the data we will eventually obtain. We should make this choice even before we begin to collect the data.

Therefore, in this step we analyse and interpret the data (information) obtained in the previous step (see Chapters 7 & 8). The results thus obtained then provide feedback on the tenability or untenability of the originally formulated research hypothesis (see Section 2.4) and, consequently, on the theory if deduced from one (see Section 2.3.1.3): either it is supported (provisionally), or it is refuted (especially regarding quantitative research methods).

If the results we obtained are in agreement with the hypothesis, we have not proven finally and irrefutably that the theory is correct; it is only provisionally supported insofar as there is no other known theory that may explain the results obtained.

FOR EXAMPLE Because the research in Research Example II (see Section 2.3, page 17) supported the specific implication being investigated, it withstood an attempt to falsify (see Section 2.5) the learning theory and, as a result, our confidence in this theory was strengthened.

In this approach (where the theory is not finally and irrefutably proven to be correct, but is only provisionally supported), the data obtained will finally determine whether or not the theory receives support rather than, for example, the authority of the person (see Section 1.2.1.1) who has come up with the theory in question.

Data analysis by means of (mainly) statistical techniques helps us to investigate variables (see Section 2.3) as well as their effect, relationship, and patterns of involvement within our world.

In this chapter, we will first address the data analysis of recurring themes in **qualitative research** (see Chapter 8). Two methods of measurement are dealt with, namely the analysis of **in-depth unstructured individual interviews** (see Section 8.4.3) and **group interviews (focus groups)** (see Section 8.4.4). These methods are used in approaches such as ethnographic and case study research as well as in participant observation. Secondly, **content analysis** of historical and personal documents, mass media, open-ended questions, as well as unstructured interviews will be discussed. Following this, we will address **data analysis of quantitative research** (see Chapters 5 & 7), and describe **complex experimental research designs**. Finally we will provide a brief reference to the **reporting of results** (see Section 9.5).

9.2 Qualitative data analysis

9.2.1 Analysis of unstructured in-depth individual interviews and group interviews (focus groups)

9.2.1.1 PREPARING FIELD NOTES AND TRANSCRIPTS

As we indicated in Chapter 8, field notes can be described as detailed notes made by hand, tape recordings, and observations, and are compiled during qualitative interviewing (see Sections 8.4.3 & 8.4.4). In order to analyse the raw field notes, these have to be processed. This entails **converting the notes into write-ups** which should be intelligible products that can be read, edited for accuracy, commented on, and analysed.

Since raw field notes, when reviewed, stimulate the fieldworker to remember things said at that time that were not included in the original notes, write-ups can be used to replace some of the missing content. Tape recordings and dictation should be transcribed to text before it can be subjected to the same processing as handwritten notes. It is important that the "uhs", "ers", pauses, word emphases, mispronunciations, and incomplete sentences are taken into consideration in the write-ups.

9.2.1.2 THEME IDENTIFICATION METHODS

According to Ryan and Bernard (n.d.) **theme identification** is one of the most fundamental tasks in qualitative research. Themes can be described as "umbrella" constructs which are usually identified by the researcher before, after, and during the data collection. Themes can also be identified by reviewing the original field notes. According to Ryan and Bernard (no date) the following techniques are usually used in identifying themes:

- Word analyses (word repetitions, keywords in context, and indigenous terms)
- Reading of larger units (for example comparing and contrasting material and searching for missing information)
- Intentional analysis of linguistic features (metaphors, transitions, and connectors)
- The physical manipulation of texts (unmarked texts, pawing, and cut and sort procedures)
- Secondary data analysis.

(a) Counting words and repetitions of words

This quantitative method consists of **counting keywords** in the field notes that may occur more frequently than others.

FOR EXAMPLE While conducting an in-depth interview with Thabo about his work satisfaction at Goldsmiths, he repeatedly referred to his feelings or attitudes towards his work, the bad relations with his supervisors, the fact that he is unsure about his interests, and so on. The researcher simply read the text and noted words or sentences that the respondent used frequently.

(b) Indigenous categories and keywords in context

This method consists of identifying the **indigenous characteristics** of the language of a group of people, for instance focus groups (see Section 8.4.4). The researcher should try to identify the important words and the meanings that a specific group attaches to these. The researcher should let them explain the meanings of these words.

FOR EXAMPLE A group of students at a South African university may use words such as *cool, swot, spot, varsity,* and so on.

Keywords in context are closely associated with indigenous categories (Ryan & Bernard, n.d.). These keywords have a different meaning within the context of the interview than their usual meaning outside the context of the inter-

view. The researcher uses **simple observation** to see in which context the words were used in order to understand the specific concept in the text. The researcher should make sure that he or she knows the correct meaning, else it can be misinterpreted. This method is particularly useful during the early stages of theme identification.

(c) Comparisons and contrast

This method is used in focus groups and entails comparing the answers given by members of different groups within the focus groups. The researcher **compares** sections of the text and tries to identify the reasons why chunks of texts differ from each other.

FOR EXAMPLE The researcher may find that male respondents provide different answers than females, or that younger respondents' answers may differ from those of older respondents.

This approach corresponds with the ethnographic interview style (see Section 8.4).

(d) Searching for missing information

If researchers should note that specific information was **deliberately left out** by the respondent(s) during the interview, they should go back to the field to determine why certain information was not disclosed by the respondent(s). This information could have an important impact on the findings. Much can be learned from a text by what is not mentioned and silence is often an indication of important information that the respondent(s) do not want to disclose or discuss.

(e) Metaphors and analogies

Respondents often make use of **metaphors** and **analogies** in the interview to express their thoughts, behaviour, and experiences in a "poetic form". If any of these aspects are used during an interview, the interviewer should not interpret it literally but, instead, ask the respondent to explain the specific metaphor or analogy.

FOR EXAMPLE Suppose Thabo said that his supervisor is just as immovable in his opinions as the Rock of Gibraltar. In this case he actually referred to the supervisor's dictatorial point of view.

Cultural schemes used in the interview should also be explained by the respondent(s).

(f) Transitions and connectors

Linguists who worked with recorded texts in Native American languages noticed the recurrence of elements like *now*, *then*, *now then*, and *now again*. These elements are indications of thematical changes (Ryan & Bernard, n.d., p. 6) and are called **transitions**.

Connectors refer to words that connect different sentences in a causal way. Words such as *because*, *since*, and *as a result of* are examples of connectors (Ryan & Bernard, n.d., p. 6). Researchers should look out for both transitions and connectors in order to identify the logical development of the course of the interview.

(g) Unmarked text

New themes can be identified by examining texts in the field notes that have not been associated with a theme previously. Usually the text is read a few times in order to identify these themes. The salient themes are generally marked first so that the more unobtrusive themes can be identified during the second reading.

(h) Pawing, cutting, and sorting

Other methods of dealing in a more quantitative way with data involve pawing, cutting, and sorting. Although they are not regarded as particularly scientific methods, they are valuable. As far as **pawing** is concerned, it is usually suggested that a researcher uses an "ocular scan method" to read through the text in order to familiarise himself or herself with it. The researcher then simultaneously marks different aspects by using different coloured pencils to underline key phrases (Ryan & Bernard, n.d., p. 7).

Cutting and sorting is a more formal method than pawing and it is especially useful to identify themes. The technique involves identifying the most important remarks in the text first. Each quote is then cut out and pasted onto an index card. The researcher then writes the name of the person who said it and where in the text it could be found on the back of the index card. Then all the index cards are sorted into different piles of similar quotes. Each pile is named afterwards according to the theme it represents.

(i) Secondary data analysis

The researcher should consult other reports or information (**secondary data**) on the same topic that is being analysed. The field notes (**primary data**) can then be questioned and reviewed in the light of any new information found.

9.2.1.3 CODING THE DATA

After the researcher has compiled and processed all information, the challenge is to reduce the huge amount of data to manageable and understandable texts. A chronic problem of qualitative research is that it is done chiefly with *words* and not with *numbers* as in quantitative research (Miles & Huberman, 1994). According to these authors, words are "fatter" than numbers and usually have multiple meanings. This complicates analyses and research considerably. Although one can perhaps regard words as more unwieldy than numbers, these words render more meanings than a set of numbers and should be used throughout the entire data analysis. In qualitative research the solution is therefore to convert words to numbers or symbols but to retain the words and use these together with the numbers/symbols throughout the analysis.

(a) Coding

The purpose of **coding** is to analyse and make sense of the data that have been collected. **Codes** are tags or labels that attach meaning to the raw data or notes collected during field work. These tags or labels are used to retrieve and organise chunks of text in order to *categorise it according to particular themes* (see Section 9.2.1.2). The purpose of coding is therefore to understand material that is unclear by putting names to events, incidents, behaviours, attitudes, and so on. We can use the following types of coding:

▶ **Descriptive codes**. These codes need little interpretation and involve attributing a theme category to a segment of the text.

FOR EXAMPLE Thabo: "Last year I had to do a course in computer technology and I hated it!"

In this example the code *attitude to work* can be applied to the text.

▶ **Interpretative codes**. These codes relate to the reasons, explanations, and motives behind the factual information and are identified when the researchers are more familiar with the text.

FOR EXAMPLE The fact that Thabo rejoined Goldsmiths can be attributed to his personal attributes of stubbornness and the fact that he does not like to quit easily.

▶ **Pattern codes**. These codes connect different sections of the text and help the researcher create a more meaningful whole.

FOR EXAMPLE In an in-depth interview about his work satisfaction at Goldsmiths, Thabo repeatedly referred to the role conflict he experienced at work and his bad relations with the supervisors.

▶ **Reflective remarks**. These remarks consist of aspects such as pauses or respondents' non-verbal behaviour (see the example of the excerpt of the interview with Thabo on page 216) that the interviewer notices during the interview. Reflective remarks are usually placed between *double brackets*. These remarks can also be added when the researcher converts the original raw data into a write-up. In this case, typical reflective remarks include the researcher's afterthoughts about the meaning of what the respondent(s) "really" said during a discussion or about some of the respondents' answers during the interview.

FOR EXAMPLE Thabo: We unofficially evaluate the capabilities of our supervisor and I think it was quite an effective measurement. ((*This sounds pretty vague to me!*))

▶ **Marginal remarks**. These remarks consist of the researcher's ideas about and reactions to what is being discussed and are written to the right of the text while he or she is coding the material. The marginal remarks point to important issues that may not be captured by a given code in the text and suggest a revision in the coding scheme. Researchers could ask colleagues to review their write-ups and make marginal remarks.

FOR EXAMPLE Thabo: I was asked by my supervisor to check the other clerks who underwent training in the hall. I could not believe what I saw. Some have already stepped out of the hall and others were chatting with each other without listening to the speaker! ((*Discipline important*))

In this example the remark "discipline important" was added to the coding.

▶ **Revising codes**. These codes involve changing the codes as the data analysis continues. The researcher will become aware that some codes do perhaps not work or others decay or become inappropriate.

The coding process can be regarded as *completed* when all incidents, behaviours, attitudes, perceptions, and so on have been classified sufficiently and all categories are "saturated". Codes are usually put to the left of the text (see Table 9.1). They should be represented by letters or symbols that are clear and close to the concept it is describing. The codes should also be checked for *validity* and *reliability*. The best way to do this is to review the codes with other researchers.

(b) Creating codes

Codes can be created in the following ways:

▶ Codes can firstly be created by using the conceptual framework of the research question(s) **prior to the unstructured interviews**. The list of codes can then be revised upon closer examination of the field notes.

▶ Secondly, the researcher can first collect the data and then **divide the field notes into different segments afterwards**. This is especially useful in the case of a focus group when the subgroups (for example males and females) have different opinions on a topic (see Section 9.2.1.2 (c)).

  Categories or labels are then applied to the appropriate paragraphs or segments of the material. The material can also be sorted into piles (see cutting and sorting in Section 9.2.1.2 (h)) so that the researcher can determine the frequencies of each category.

▶ Thirdly, the researcher can create codes for **conditions** in the field notes (words like *because* or *since*), consequences (words like *as a result of* or *because of*) (see Section 9.2.1.2(f)), interaction amongst the participants, strategies, and tactics used during the interview as well as phrases that are used repeatedly (see Section 9.2.1.2 (a)).

While creating codes, the researcher should look out for the following aspects within the text (field notes):

▶ **Definitions of the interview situation**, that is, the way in which the respondent(s) understand, give meaning to, and define the topic under scrutiny.
  FOR EXAMPLE Thabo defined his job satisfaction in terms of rather negative attitudes towards his work, his roles in the work situation, his interests, and so on (see Table 9.1).

▶ **Process**, that is, the sequence of events and changes over time described by the respondent(s). This includes aspects such as transitions, turning points, and changes over time in the life history of the respondent(s) (see Section 9.2.1.4(a)).

▶ **Events**, that is, specific activities that are described in the interviews. Infrequent events often have great impact.
  FOR EXAMPLE Thabo's decision to join Goldsmiths after matriculating (see Section 9.2.1.4 (a)).

▶ **Relationships and social structures**, that is, the relation of the respondent(s) to other people, for example friendships, enemies, employer–employee relations, and so on (see Table 9.1).

Bearing the above-mentioned scheme in mind, the researcher can then categorise the different codes. The researcher must compile a coding list which contains the symbol for each code, its name, as well as a definition of the code. Table 9.1 illustrates how such a coding list should be compiled by the researcher.

EXAMPLE   **CODING AN INTERVIEW**

This example is based on an interview conducted with a young employer named Thabo at a gold mine company (Goldsmiths). The topic or research problem that was investigated concerned Thabo's experience of job satisfaction. The case study design was used (see Section 8.4.1). The coding list is shown in Table 9.1 and illustrates which codes were used to categorise sections of the original raw data or field notes according *to particular themes* (for example attitudes, roles, and so on).

Table 9.1 Coding list of unstructured interview with Thabo on his job satisfaction

Code	Themes	Definition
A	Attitudes (feelings)	
AN	Negative attitudes or feelings	Negative attitudes or feelings towards work
AP	Positive attitudes or feelings	Positive attitudes or feelings towards work
RO	Roles in work situation	
ROC	Role conflict	Simultaneous existence of two or more role expectations
ROO	Role overload	Too many responsibilities or duties in a particular role
ROA	Role ambiguity	Feelings of uncertainty with regards to aspects of work
RE	Relationships with colleagues and superiors	
RESN	Negative relationships with superiors	Bad relations (communication/perceptions) with superiors
I	Interests	
IU	Unsure of interests	Unsure/no clear definition of interest
PA	Personal attributes	Characteristic qualities that Thabo ascribed to himself

The following table contains an excerpt of the interview with Thabo. The reader can clearly see how codes were attached to the descriptive information of the field notes. The codes were placed to the left of the text and are close to the concept they are describing.

Table 9.2 Excerpt of the coded interview

Researcher (interviewer):		Can you tell me more about your work at the company?
Thabo:		Uhm … ((pause)) … Yes, I'm in my third year at Goldsmiths now. Last year I had to do a course in
	AN	computer technology ((frown)) and I hated it! I took a long holiday in December, but this year I
	ROO	don't think I will have the time … ((frown)) too much work ((pause)). I can't cope. Therefore I don't
	AN	enjoy my work; I am still not sure what I am supposed to be doing … not very much interested in
	IU	what I'm doing at the moment. At the moment they expect of me to accept responsibility for a
	ROC	project in another division. And … ((pause)) the supervisor has the audacity to criticise me if I work
	RESN	overtime to complete my own job!
Researcher (interviewer):		Why are you staying on at this job at Goldsmiths?
Thabo:	PA	I guess I'm stubborn ((laugh)). I don't like quitting because I was not brought up like that. This is
		perhaps why I rejoined Goldsmiths in 2001. But on the other hand I think it is not a good thing
	ROA, RESN	staying on here although one is always unsure about your supervisor's demands.

Researcher (interviewer):	Do you still believe in the things that motivated you in the first place to work at Goldsmiths?

Thabo: AP
         PA
    RESN
	I still think that Goldsmiths is a dynamic and competitive company. And I think this is a positive side of the company. I think that I have the right type of personality to be dynamic you know … outgoing and competitive. But … ((pause)) on the other hand I feel that my superiors are too autocratic and arrogant and it is not nice to talk to them because they are insensitive.

After the coding list has been compiled, the researcher should also construct a frequency table of the themes that have been identified to illustrate the results. See the example of the frequencies of the five themes that have been identified in the interview with Thabo in Table 9.2.

Table 9.3 Frequencies of themes

Theme	Code	Frequency
Attitudes (feelings)	A	8
Roles in work situation	RO	7
Relationships with colleagues and superiors	RE	12
Interests	I	4
Personal attributes	PA	3

Next, the frequencies are divided into class intervals in order to relate the information to a five-point scale (see Table 9.4). The scale indicates the importance that the respondent (Thabo) placed on each theme as indicated by the number of responses.

Table 9.4 Matrix of importance attributed to each theme as indicated by frequency

Themes	Importance of themes				
	None	Some	Average	Very	Extremely
Attitudes (feelings)				✗	
Roles in work situation				✗	
Relationships with colleagues and superiors					✗
Interests		✗			
Personal attributes		✗			

Presenting the results (see Sections 9.3.1.3(a) & 9.3.1.5)

The dependent variable *job satisfaction of Thabo* was measured by means of unstructured in-depth interviews (see Section 8.4.3) and therefore involves *nominal measurement*. Nominal measurement has only two levels that can be coded: answering the questions (1) or not answering the questions (0). The answers can be categorised into two mutually exclusive and exhaustive categories (see Section 7.3.2.1). The most appropriate *graphical representations* that can be used to illustrate the frequency of themes in Table 9.4, are a *bar diagram* and *pie chart*.

Discussion of the results (see Section 10.3.8)

Thabo's profile is summarised in Tables 9.3 and 9.4 and Figures 9.1 and 9.2. These indicate that Thabo places little value on his interests and personal attributes in his evaluation of his work satisfaction while attitudes, roles, and relationships are extremely important. It seems that in Thabo's case, relationships, work attitudes, and roles play the most important role in his experience of work satisfaction.

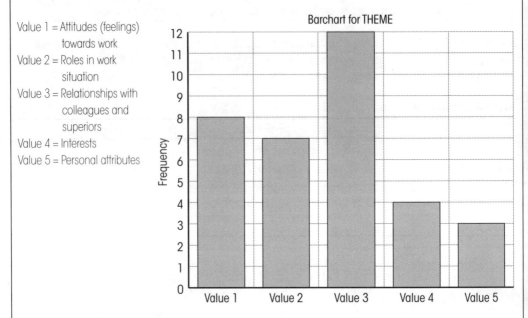

Value 1 = Attitudes (feelings) towards work
Value 2 = Roles in work situation
Value 3 = Relationships with colleagues and superiors
Value 4 = Interests
Value 5 = Personal attributes

Figure 9.1 *Frequencies of the themes represented in a bar chart*

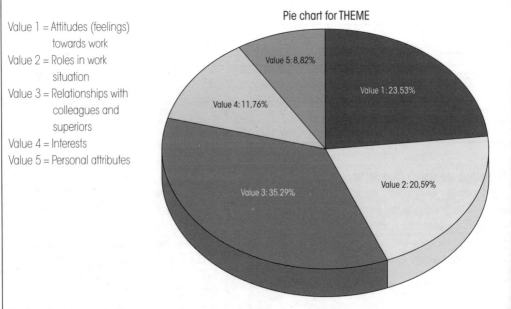

Value 1 = Attitudes (feelings) towards work
Value 2 = Roles in work situation
Value 3 = Relationships with colleagues and superiors
Value 4 = Interests
Value 5 = Personal attributes

Figure 9.2 *Frequencies of the themes represented in a pie chart*

9.2.1.4 DISPLAYING THE DATA

A **data display** is a systematic, visual representation of information which enables the user to draw conclusions about qualitative material collected through unstructured interviews, and to take the necessary action. Data displays are methods or tools of qualitative analysis and aim to provide a **descriptive explanatory framework** of the investigation. According to Miles and Huberman (1994), extended qualitative texts form a weak and cumbersome display of the material. In such a display that stretches over many pages, it is very difficult to analyse the material and to see it as a whole. This sequential, rather than simultaneous, display makes it difficult to look at several variables at once. However, data displays enable the researcher to obtain a complete view of the full data set and are arranged systematically in order to answer each question of the interview. Data display formats are always driven by explorative research questions or the development of concepts which are often in the form of codes (see Section 9.2.1.3). Formats can be built directly from a conceptual framework although true clarity is achieved much later in the investigation when the researcher begins to understand the structure and the empirical data begin to take shape.

There are several types of data display formats, but these generally fall into two major categories: **matrices** with defined rows and columns and **networks** with a series of nodes with links between them (Miles & Huberman, 1994). The display selected depends on the object of the investigation which can include a general situation, detailed chronologies, the attitudes, decisions or behaviour of people, different roles of people, or the interplay between conceptual variables.

(a) Matrix displays

Matrix displays enable the researcher to understand the flow of events and the connection between these events. **Time-ordered matrix displays** are usually used to describe the flow of events by listing them chronologically. The series of concrete events are arranged into several categories according to chronological time periods. In the time-ordered matrix the columns are arranged by sequential time periods (see Table 9.5.), so that it is easy to see when particular phenomena occurred. No explanation is given in this type of display.

EXAMPLE **MATRIX DISPLAY**

The event listing in Table 9.5 is an example of a descriptive time-ordered display (see Section 9.2.1.4(a)). This matrix focuses on the understanding of the chronological events that occurred in the employment history of Thabo (the respondent). According to the matrix, Thabo matriculated in 1994 with two distinctions; he was ambitious, unsure about his future goals and interests, and was searching for a dynamic and competitive job. He regarded himself as a stubborn person and as somebody who did not like quitting. He worked at Goldsmiths from 1995 to 1998 as an administrative officer, experiencing a large workload and pressure from his superiors, yet remained unsure of his goals and interests. Thabo resigned from Goldsmiths in 1999. He was unemployed during 1999 and 2000, and was reappointed at Goldsmiths in 2001, again as administrative officer. Since then he has been experiencing role ambiguity, role conflict, role overload, negative attitudes towards his work, bad relationships with his superiors, and still feels unclear about his goals and interests.

Table 9.5 Matrix diagram: events listing

High school education (matric)	Employment at Goldsmiths	Resign from Goldsmiths	Return to Goldsmiths
1994	1995–1998	1999–2000	2001>
– Two distinctions – Ambitious – Unsure about goals and interests – Look for dynamic and competitive career – Does not like quitting – Stubborn	– Administrative officer – High workload – Pressure from superiors – Unsure about goals and interests	– Resign from Goldsmiths: 1999 – Unemployed: 2000	– Administrative officer – Role ambiguity – Role conflict – Role overload – Negative relations with superiors – Bad attitudes towards work – Unclear about goals and interests

(b) Network displays

It is often difficult to explain something satisfactorily before a complete understanding of all the underlying factors has been achieved. In order to understand a phenomenon, researchers start with a descriptive approach (for example life history of Thabo). In the process a "map" is created which contains information about the specific events which took place, when these took place, and where (see Table 9.5). Building a more thorough model explaining how variables are connected and how they influence each other is then a natural progression. The aim is to construct a "deeper story" and to integrate this "deeper structure" in an explanatory framework which explains the sequence of the events. Such a framework is a *network display*.

A **network display** shows the most important independent and dependent variables as well as the relationship between these by means of arrows (see Figure 9.3). The relationship between the independent variables and dependent variables should be regarded as causal and not correlational (see Chapter 5). As a result, we can assume that the independent variables exert a direct influence on the dependent variables.

EXAMPLE   **NETWORK DISPLAY**

In this example we use a causal network display to explain the reasons why Thabo (the respondent) joined Goldsmiths after he matriculated. From the diagram we can clearly see that, in order to experience *work satisfaction* (dependent variable), he wanted a job which offered *competitiveness* and *dynamism* (independent variables). As a result, Thabo chose to work at Goldsmiths.

Using this display, we can also explain why he *decided to return to Goldsmiths* (dependent variable) after he resigned: this decision can be attributed to his personal attribute of *stubbornness* (independent variable) as well as the fact that he *does not like to quit* (independent variable). These are also the very reasons why he continues to work at Goldsmiths despite experiencing low *job satisfaction* (dependent variable) and negative *attitudes towards his job* (dependent variable) as a result of *role conflict, role ambiguity,* and the *relations with his superiors* (all independent variables).

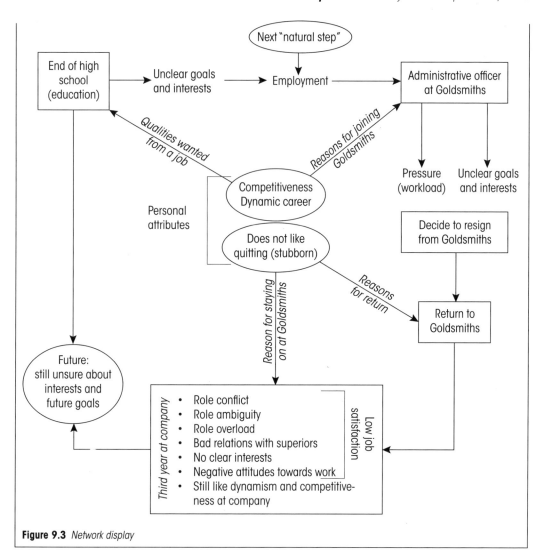

Figure 9.3 *Network display*

9.2.2 **Content analysis**

Content analysis can be described as a *quantitative* analysis of *qualitative data*. The basic technique involves counting the **frequencies and sequencing** of particular words, phrases or concepts in order to identify keywords or themes (see Section 9.2.1.2(a)). Carley (1990), however, proved that specific concepts or variables in qualitative texts cannot necessarily be studied in a quantitative way only because these concepts or variables may have quite different meanings when relationships between the concepts are taken into account.

Network analyses are therefore necessary (see Section 9.2.1.4(b)).

A special application of systematic observation occurs in the *content analysis of personal documents and mass media material* (see Section 7.7.2.2).

Apart from using content analysis to analyse personal documents and mass media material, a content analysis of open-ended questions as well as the contents of unstructured interviews (see Sections 8.4.3 & 8.4.4) may also be conducted. In this way the results can be reported in a quantitative way (see for example

Table 9.2 and Figures 9.1 & 9.2). This can be done in addition to a qualitative analysis of the contents of the interview. Such a qualitative analysis involves examining the contents of these sources systematically to record the relative incidence (frequencies) of themes as well as the ways in which these themes are portrayed (see Section 9.2.1.2).

In Research Example IX we describe how Saling, Abrams and Chester (1983) performed a content analysis of the photographic depiction of women cradling babies in South Africa. The purpose of the analysis was to determine whether there was any preference in terms of the side of the body (left or right) on which the babies were held.

RESEARCH EXAMPLE IX A CONTENT ANALYSIS OF PHOTOS IN RESPECT OF THE LATERAL PREFERENCE IN CRADLING BABIES

Saling, Abrams and Chester (1983) performed a content analysis of magazine photos of black and white women who were cradling babies to investigate the lateral cradling preference of women in this behaviour.

An unspecified number of (unidentified) black- and white-oriented magazines published between 1977 and 1982 were scanned for photos of women who were holding babies on one side of the body (in the arm, over the shoulder, or on the hip).

They classified the 196 photos thus obtained in terms of the race of the woman and the laterality of the position (left or right) in which she held the baby.

For each group the chi-square test (see Section 9.4.3.1) was statistically significant at the 1% level, which suggests a preference for the left side among both racial groups.

According to the authors, this finding was in agreement with previous observational studies and supported a biogenetic model of lateral preference in cradling babies.

9.2.2.1 STEPS IN PERFORMING A CONTENT ANALYSIS

The steps in performing a content analysis correspond to those of direct, systematic observation of behaviour (see Sections 7.2 & 7.7.6).

▶ Firstly, we should clearly **define the phenomenon** to be analysed. In Research Example IX this phenomenon was the lateral cradling preference of women. Of course, this decision is closely connected to the hypothesis or problem that is to be investigated.

▶ Secondly, we should define the **universe of appropriate media** and choose the **sampling methods** (see Sections 4.1, 8.2 & 8.4) in terms of which the editions of the chosen media should be sampled. If we want to analyse the data of a case study by means of content analysis, the universe of respondents or interviewees should be defined. As in all research, the emphasis

should be on the typical or the representative rather than on that which is likely to confirm the researcher's biases.

FOR EXAMPLE Suppose we want to compare the editorials of pro-government and pro-opposition newspapers during the eighties in respect of the democratic values that they emphasised. For practical reasons, it may be impossible to include the entire universe of editorials of all government and opposition newspapers that appeared during that period.

Consequently, we have to decide on which papers we should select – something that is not easy to do, since a daily provincial paper would naturally have a greater influence than a weekly regional paper.

In terms of the above example, after we have made a selection of the newspapers, we have to decide whether to select all editorials over a couple of months or at different times of the year over a few years.

FOR EXAMPLE In Research Example IX an unknown number of editions of (unidentified) magazines published between 1977 and 1982 were systematically studied in search of photos of women cradling babies.

▶ Thirdly, we should provide a description of the way in which the **units of analysis** (see Section 4.2; photos in Research Example IX) should be coded (see also Section 9.2.1.3). This coding process may require recording the number of times (frequencies) that visible content (words or sentences in the notes or transcribed tape recording of the interview or open-ended question answers) considered as indicative of some construct or theme (see Section 9.2.1.2 (a)) occurs.

On other occasions, the latent meaning or intention reflected in units of analysis (for example newspapers) or the responses of individuals should be coded.

FOR EXAMPLE The coder must infer whether a particular television commercial uses sex, humour, utility value, and so on to catch the viewer's attention.

The use of visible content may result in a high intercoder reliability (estimation of reliability – see Section 7.5.1.5), but construct validity (see Section 7.4.1) may suffer as such content may not be the only indicator relevant to the construct.

FOR EXAMPLE The democratic flavour of newspaper editorials may not be gauged properly by the number of times words such as "democracy", "general franchise", and so on are used.

▶ Fourthly, we must **train the coders** (raters) properly. This is especially important if ratings are required not only at a nominal (levels of measurement – see Section 7.3.2) but also at an ordinal level, for example if the degree of preference or disapproval of what is depicted should also be rated – something looks extremely, to some extent, or not at all acceptable. The objective of such training is to ensure high interrater reliability (estimation of reliability, see Sections 7.5.1 & 7.5.1.5), a property that naturally has to be examined.

Figure 9.4 *Selling products*

Typically, the statistical analysis of the obtained data consists of determining the frequencies or percentages of occurrences of the chosen content.

FOR EXAMPLE The word "democracy" in the above example may have occurred 300 times, or there may have been an 87% occurrence of black women holding babies on their left side in Research Example IX.

The frequencies may be illustrated in a figure (such as a bar diagram, histogram or pie chart – see Section 9.4.2.1 as well as Figures 9.1 & 9.2).

NOTE: The phenomena of judicial behaviour and similar applications in the political and administrative sciences can be studied by means of the so-called *q-methodology* and *q-technique*. This technique relies on factor analysis and helps interpret individuals' self-concepts (Brown, 1980).

Weitzman and Miles (1995) describe computer programs that can be used in qualitative research. For computer-aided qualitative data analysis, the software Atlasti and NUD-1st can be used. Zelger (1991) describes GABEK (Ganzheitliche Bewaltigung Sprachlich Erfasster Komplexität), a computer-aided methodology that can be used for the analysis of unstructured textual qualitative data analysis from open-ended instructions. Manual qualitative data analysis can be done with the help of N-Vivo, a tool for qualitative research data analysis.

9.3 Quantitative data analysis

If we postpone the decision on which statistical analysis method(s) to use until after the data have been collected, we may discover, much to our dissatisfaction, that there is either no appropriate statistical method available for analysing the data, or that another method would have been more appropriate if the data had been collected in terms of another design.

A satisfactory research design (see Chapters 4 & 5) therefore suggests the methods in terms of which we should statistically analyse the obtained data.

9.3.1 Statistical validity

If we indeed find a relationship between the variables appearing in a research hypothesis (see Section 2.4), we expect our research hypothesis and our statistical methods to bring this relationship to light; in other words, we wish to make statistically valid conclusions.

If we want to investigate a research hypothesis by means of inferential-statistical methods, we must first transform it into a statistical hypothesis. Such a **statistical hypothesis** consists of two complementary statements, known as:

▶ a null hypothesis (H_0)
▶ a complementary, alternative hypothesis (H_1) (Hays, 1988; Huysamen, 1989a).

Typically, the alternative hypothesis reflects the research hypothesis, and the null hypothesis plays the role of devil's advocate.

Consequently, the research hypothesis will be supported by the rejection of the null hypothesis. In this manner the **falsification principle** (see Section 2.5) is implemented by statistical hypothesis testing. This means that an implication inferred from a theory and represented by a research hypothesis is strengthened by falsifying a counter-hypothesis cast in the form of a null hypothesis.

In experimental research (see Section 5.2) the **null hypothesis** usually implies that there is no difference between the levels of an independent variable. Usually, the research hypothesis and the implication of the theory from which it is deduced are reflected by the **alternative hypothesis**. As a result, such an implication is thus partially supported or strengthened by the rejection of the null hypothesis.

FOR EXAMPLE In Case Study D (see Appendix D on page 306) the research hypothesis (see Section 2.4) (which we can call the alternative hypothesis) was as follows:

There is a significantly high positive relation/correlation between the speech quality and the total preparation time of a group of speech-making technikon students.

The null hypothesis in this case would be:

There is no relation/correlation between the speech quality and the total preparation time of a group of speech-making technikon students.

For Case Study E the research/alternative hypothesis was as follows:

Bankrupt small businesses have exceeded their bank overdraft limits with significantly greater amounts per month and experienced cash flow problems to a greater extent than non-bankrupt small businesses during the past two years.

The null hypothesis would be:

There will be no differences concerning the amount of exceeded bank overdraft limits per month and the extent of cash flow problems experienced by bankrupt and non-bankrupt small businesses during the past two years.

A *t*- or *F*-test statistic (see Section 9.4.3.2) is often used to test such a null hypothesis. This basically consists of the following ratio:

$$\frac{\text{Between-group variation (numerator)}}{\text{Within-group variation (denominator)}}$$

The numerator (between-group variation) of this ratio reflects variance (in the dependent variable), which is due to the independent variable in question. The denominator (within-group variation) represents **error variance**, which is caused by other variables.

Part of the denominator source of **variation** is **systematic** in the sense that it affects the scores of all subjects in a predictable manner.

FOR EXAMPLE If the dependent variable is *academic achievement* (as measured by way of a paper-and-pencil examination), *intelligence* would act as a systematic source of variation because the more intelligent managers always tend to obtain higher academic achievement scores than those who are less intelligent.

Unsystematic sources of variation, by contrast, affect individuals' scores in an entirely accidental and unpredictable manner.

FOR EXAMPLE The points of some managers' pencils may break purely by chance so that their academic performance is affected. In the long run such events should affect all individuals' scores (irrespective of the level of the independent variable to which they belong – more or less intelligent) to the same extent.

Measurement error is one of the sources of within-group variation (denominator). To the extent that the dependent variable (academic achievement) is unreliably measured (pencil points break), some portion of individuals' scores on the dependent variable will consist of measurement error.

The measurement error will increase the denominator (within-group variation) of the test statistic (a *t*- or *F*-test statistic – see Section 9.4.3.2) which, in turn, will decrease the value of the test statistic itself. The smaller the value of the test statistic, the smaller the probability that it will exceed the critical value signifying a statistically significant result (Huysamen, 1989a).

It is possible that two variables (such as *academic achievement* and *intelligence*) are indeed correlated in a particular population (such as managers) but that the denominator (within-group variation – within the less and more intelligent group of managers) of the test statistic is increased. As a result, the value of the test statistic (a *t*-test or *F*-test statistic – see Section 9.4.3.2) (reflected by the ratio) is decreased to such an extent on account of unreliable measurement (of these variables – for example, the pencil points broke) that statistical significance is not achieved.

The higher the ratio (in other words, between-group variation is greater than within-group variation), the greater the power of the statistical test, that is, the probability that the null hypothesis will be rejected.

FOR EXAMPLE The academic achievement (scores in the examination) of the different intelligence groups of managers (those who are less or more intelligent) will not be the same.

Therefore, the null hypothesis will be rejected and the alternative hypothesis will be accepted.

As in the case of any ratio, this ratio will be increased by (compare Section 6.2.9):

- anything which increases the numerator (between-group variance)
- anything which decreases the denominator (within-group variance).

To the extent that the two groups of managers (low and highly intelligent) differ increasingly in respect of the dependent variable (academic achievement), the between-group variance increases in relation to the within-group variance. Thus, the ratio itself increases so that the probability to reject the null hypotheses increases.

Usually the objective is to optimally increase the between-group variance so that the resulting ratio will lead to the rejection of the null hypothesis. By the same token, the within-group variance should preferably be reduced maximally because such a reduction leads to a maximal increase in the ratio.

There are two types of errors which can occur while working with the null and alternative hypotheses. Statisticians refer to these as Type I and Type II errors. A **Type I error** occurs when a decision is made that something is true when in reality it is not. Type I errors might involve concluding that two variables are related when they are not, or incorrectly concluding that a sample statistic exceeds the value that would be expected by chance alone. **Type II errors** occur when the researcher concludes that two variables are not related when they are, or that a sample statistic does not exceed the value that would be expected by chance alone. A Type II error is the inverse of a Type I error. Researchers usually consider Type I errors more serious

and prefer to take a small chance of saying something is true when it is not. It is therefore generally more important to minimise Type I than Type II errors.

9.3.2 **The sensitivity of a research design**

The **sensitivity** of a design (see Chapters 5 & 8) refers to the degree to which the design reduces the within-group variance, thereby optimally increasing the ratio between the numerator (between-group variance) and the denominator (within-group variance), and consequently also the probability that the null hypothesis will be rejected (which is the researcher's aim).

Some research designs, for example most non-experimental designs, are not too sensitive. In these designs the conclusions reached to reject the null hypothesis may be invalid, whereas in others it may be less so. For instance, consider the example of the correlation between the number of churches in cities and towns and the incidence of crime (see Section 5.2.2.1).

9.3.2.1 ELIMINATING RIVAL HYPOTHESES

Rival hypotheses refer to the influence of third variables. There are statistical procedures by means of which rival hypotheses can be eliminated under certain conditions. These procedures can thus enhance the internal validity (see Section 6.2) of conclusions in non-experimental research. One such statistical technique is **partial correlation** (see Section 9.4.2.3). By using this technique, we can determine the correlation between two variables by holding the effect of a third variable constant. Additional methods which can be used include multiple regression, path analysis, and structural equation modelling (Pedhazur, 1982). These methods are typically applied to more complicated situations than the one depicted in Figure 1.2 on page 5.

9.3.2.2 ELIMINATING THE VARIANCE

Matching is one method that can be used to **eliminate the variance** in the dependent variable which is attributable to nuisance variables (see Section 6.2.8). In this way, the denominator (within-group variance) of the test statistic (a *t*- or *F*-test statistic – see Section 9.4.3.2) is reduced and a more sensitive design and a more powerful statistical test are thus obtained.

However, if there is not a considerable correlation (of at least 0,50 in absolute value) between the nuisance variable (see Section 5.2.1.3) and the dependent variable (see Section 2.3), the matched-groups design provides a less powerful statistical test than a regular randomised groups design (see Section 5.2.1.2) with the same number of participants.

In other words, if all other factors remain the same, we need more subjects in the matched design than in the independent-groups design to obtain statistical significance. Thus, unless there is a rather high correlation between the nuisance variable and the dependent variable, it may not pay to match individuals in terms of the nuisance variable.

9.3.2.3 COMPLEX EXPERIMENTAL RESEARCH DESIGNS

There are two reasons why we may consider including two or more independent variables in the same design:

▶ Firstly, we may wish to study the effects of more than one such a variable simultaneously. In other words, our research hypotheses may dictate that a more complex design than a single-factor design be used (as addressed in the preceding chapters).

In the more complex designs, one of the independent variables is usually a **treatment factor** and the other one may either be a treatment factor or a **classification factor** (third variable problem – see Section 5.2.2). A classification factor may be included as another independent variable, either because we are interested in investigating its effect in its own right, or because we are aware that it is a nuisance variable and we want to eliminate its effect.

▶ The second reason why more complicated designs are often used, is to **increase the sensitivity** of our research designs. In the preceding paragraphs it was explained that some test statistics are made up of a ratio that increases in value if its denominator, which is based on the within-group variance, decreases.

By building a nuisance variable into a design as an additional variable, we eliminate that portion of the within-group variance which is due to this variable. As a result, the test statistic increases in value and there is a greater chance of obtaining a statistically significant result.

This approach represents the fourth way in which nuisance variables may be controlled. (The other three were mentioned in Section 5.2.1.3, page 81).

The following are examples of complex experimental research designs:

▶ the completely-crossed two-factor design (Solomon four-group design)
▶ the nested design
▶ the randomised-block design (see Section 5.2.1.2)
▶ the repeated measures design (between-subjects design or intergroup design, within-subjects design or intragroup design, split-plot design)
▶ the multi-factor design.

9.4 Statistical techniques (and coding)

Once we have collected data, we have to make sense of it. In order to do this, we must organise and code it so that we can analyse it (this does not apply to data obtained from psychological tests – see Section 7.7.3.2).

Coding means that we have to identify the variable that we want to analyse statistically and decide on the different code values such a variable level presents.

EXAMPLE   CODING

If we interview 100 registered voters concerning their opinions on the re-introduction of the death penalty, we would at least be interested to know if there are differences between males and females and between different age groups regarding the issue. Differences in their residential area may also be significant in this regard. We could therefore use the codes in Table 9.6 to indicate the different values of certain variables.

Note that the variable *age* will need three spaces in the computer file because if someone is 102 years old, it would occupy three digits. If a respondent's age is nine years, then we will have to code it as 009.

Table 9.6 Coding the values of different variables

Width of computer column (in memory)	Variable	Code name	Code values	Levels
One space	Gender	Gender	1	Male
			2	Female
Three spaces	Age	Age	18+	18 yrs to eldest voter
One space	Residential area	Resarea	1	Rural
			2	Urban
			3	Metropolitan

Once we have coded all the data, it can be captured on a computer in order to proceed with the analysis. We must now do one or more of the following:

- **count**, for example, the number of employees that "strongly disagree" on a seven-point questionnaire item concerning the right of management to make unilateral decisions
- **describe**, for example, the inner experience of prisoners who were assaulted by gang members inside prison
- **compare**, for example, the responses of taxpayers in different income-groups to the government's new proposed taxation system
- **categorise**, for example, identified patterns of themes through the use of statistics (such as the preference averages towards different residential areas).

We also have to determine the level of measurement (see Section 7.3.2) pertaining to our study. This is necessary in order to determine the statistics available for different types of data and to select an appropriate statistical test (Huysamen, 1981; 1989a). (See Figure 7.3 on p. 137.)

- The distinction between discrete and continuous variables refers to the nature of the numerical values that these variables can assume potentially. A **discrete variable** may be defined as a variable that can potentially assume only certain values. For the purposes of the topics discussed in this book it would be sufficient to know that a variable that can assume only whole-number values is an example of a discrete variable. The number of books in a library is an example of a discrete variable because it does not make sense to refer to, for instance, 743,92 books. The number of books in a library can assume only certain numerical values – more precisely, integer values and not fractions.

A **continuous variable** may be defined as a variable that can potentially assume any value, including fractional values, within a certain range. This means that a continuous variable can theoretically assume an infinite number of different values between any two points. An example of a continuous variable is *height*, because there exists an unlimited number of fractional values between 181,54 cm and 181,55 cm. The nearest fraction of a centimetre to which length can be measured is limited only by the capacity of the measuring equipment and not by the nature of the variable itself.

It should be noted that, although some of the variables dealt with in social and behavioural research are continuous, the values obtained by measuring them are invariably discrete. For example, although *IQ* may be regarded conceptually as a continuous variable, IQ test scores can usually assume whole numbers only and thus constitute a discrete variable. Even for a variable such as *time*, which conceptually is a continuous variable, the measurements obtained are in practice discrete. Regardless of these practical restrictions in obtaining continuous measurements, the concept of a continuous variable is useful, as will become clearer later. Usually, variables that conceptually qualify as continuous are treated as such even though their measurement yields scores that are not strictly continuous.

9.4.1 Levels of measurement

(a) Nominal measurement

Turn to Section 7.3.2.1 for an explanation of nominal measurement.

The following statistics can be used for nominal data types (compare the CD-ROM):

▶ **The mode**: The score achieved by the greatest number of units of analysis
▶ **Frequencies** (bar diagram or pie chart): To determine if the distribution is even across all categories
▶ **Correlation coefficients**: A statistic to measure the degree of association between two variables

If both variables are nominal (as in the case of a dichotomous variable such as *gender* (male/female) and *cell phone ownership* (own a cell phone/do not own a cell phone)), the **phi coefficient** should be used. If one variable is nominal and the other ordinal/interval/ratio, the **point-biserial correlation** should be used.

▶ **Chi-squares (χ^2)**: To determine if the difference between statistically expected and actual scores are caused by chance/accident or if they are statistically significant – not caused by chance.

If one group is involved, the **chi-square of independence** must be used. If two groups are involved and they are dependent on each other (related in terms of matching by the researcher (see Section 6.2.8) or because of an already existing relationship or because of measuring the same group twice), the **chi-square of Mcnemar** must be used. If two independent groups are involved (if they are not related as mentioned), the **chi-square of homogeneity** must be used.

▶ **Chaid-analysis and correspondence analysis**: To determine in terms of which predictor variables criterion groups differed in the past – see Section 5.4.4.1.

(b) Ordinal measurement

Turn to Section 7.3.2.2 for an explanation of ordinal measurement.

The following statistics can be used for ordinal data types (compare the CD-ROM):

▶ The **median**: The score in the middle of the list of ranked scores.
▶ **Frequencies** (bar diagram or pie chart): To determine if the distribution is even across categories or if they cluster around one or two categories.
▶ **Correlation coefficient**: A statistic to measure if the scores of one variable correlate with the rank order positions for another variable.

If both variables are ordinal, the **Spearman rank-order correlation** (also called Spearman's rho) should be used.

If one variable is not ordinal but on an interval/ratio scale, the data should first be converted into ranks in order to compute Spearman's rho.

▶ **Chi-squares (χ^2)**: To determine if the frequencies on a nominal variable (for example *gender*) are statistically significantly related to an ordinal variable – that they are not caused by chance.

If one group is involved, the **chi-square of independence** should be used. If two groups are involved and they are dependent of each other (related in terms of matching by the researcher (see Section 6.2.8) or because of an already existing relationship or because of measuring the same group twice), the **chi-square of Mcnemar** should be used. If two independent groups are involved (if they are not related as mentioned), the **chi-square of homogeneity** should be used.

▶ **Tests of difference between distributions** (statistics to measure any statistically significant difference between samples – the null hypothesis (see Section 9.3.1) tested by these tests is that the distributions of the concerned populations are identical).

If the two samples involved are dependent (related in terms of matching by the researcher (see Section 6.2.8) or because of an already existing relationship or because of measuring the same group twice), the **Wilcoxon matched pairs signed rank test** should be used. This can be regarded as the nonparametric alternative to the *t*-test for related groups – see Interval measurement. (Parametric assumptions hold that populations are normally distributed (see Figure 9.5), or that their variances are the same.) If the two samples are independent (in terms of the conditions mentioned), the **Mann-Whitney u test** (which is the nonparametric counterpart of the *t*-test for independent groups – see Interval measurement) should be used. For three or more independent samples,

the **Kruskal-Wallis test** (which can be regarded as the nonparametric alternative to the regular one-factor analysis of variance) should be used.

▶ **Discriminant analysis**: To determine in terms of which predictor variables the criterion groups differed in the past – see Section 5.4.4.1.

▶ **Chaid-analysis and correspondence analysis**: To determine in terms of which predictor variables the criterion groups differed in the past – see Section 5.4.4.1.

(c) Interval measurement

Turn to Section 7.3.2.3 for an explanation of interval measurement.

The following statistics can be used for interval data types (compare the CD-ROM):

▶ **The mean**: The average score for a group (also called the arithmetic mean) and which is equal to the total of individual scores divided by the number of scores.

▶ **Frequencies** (histogram or box plot): To determine if the distribution is even across the intervals or whether they cluster around one or two intervals. Are the responses skewed towards one end of the scale, for example if respondents feel strongly about an issue?

▶ **Standard deviation**: To determine if the scores on a parametric test are evenly distributed and cluster closely around the mean (parametric assumptions hold that populations are normally distributed, or that their variances are the same).

▶ **z-scores** (standard scores): A statistic used to convert scores from different scales (for example one seven-point scale and the other a five-point scale) with different means and standard deviations, to a common scale in order to compare them fairly.

▶ **Pearson's product moment correlation**: A statistic to measure the degree of association between two interval or ratio variables. (A scatter diagram may also be used.)

▶ **Chi-squares (χ^2)**: To determine if the discrete classes into which an interval or ratio variable are grouped, are statistically significantly related to another variable, and that the relationship is not caused by chance.

If one group is involved, the **chi-square of independence** should be used. If two groups are involved and they are dependent on each other (related in terms of matching by the researcher – see Section 6.2.8) or because of an already existing relationship or because of measuring the same group twice), the **chi-square of Mcnemar** should be used. If two independent groups are involved (if they are not related as mentioned), the **chi-square of homogeneity** should be used.

▶ **Tests of difference between distributions**: **t-test statistics** and **analysis of variance** to measure any statistical significant difference between the means and distributions of samples. The null hypothesis (see Section 9.3.1) tested by these tests is that the means and distributions of the concerned populations are identical. If parametric assumptions hold (that populations are normally distributed (see Figure 9.5), or that their variances are the same) and the two samples involved are dependent (related in terms of matching by the researcher (see Section 6.2.8) or because of an already existing relationship or because of measuring the same group twice), the **t-test for related groups** should be used. If the two samples are independent (in terms of the conditions mentioned), the **t-test for independent groups** should be used. For three or more independent samples, the **F-test** (also called the overall F-test of analysis of variance) should be used.

▶ **Discriminant analysis**: To determine in terms of which predictor variables criterion groups differed in the past – see Section 5.4.4.1.

(d) Ratio measurement

Turn to Section 7.3.2.4 for an explanation of ratio measurement.

The same statistics can be used for ratio data types (compare the CD-ROM) as those for interval data types mentioned in the previous section.

Statistical techniques cannot select themselves, or interpret the results that they have obtained, or make conclusions on behalf of the person applying them. The choice of the appropriate statistical techniques and the interpretation of the results obtained remain the exclusive responsibility of the researcher using them. In this regard, we cannot emphasise strongly enough that statistical techniques merely serve as aids in assisting the researcher to come to a justifiable decision on the question of whether or not the data obtained support the hypothesis originally formulated. Consequently, those techniques that would be most helpful in making this conclusion should be favoured.

We can broadly divide statistical techniques into descriptive and inferential categories. If the scores of the units of analysis (see Section 4.2) of an entire population are available, the use of descriptive statistics would suffice. However, sometimes population numbers may be very large and therefore samples (see Section 4.3) must be used to make inferences about the corresponding population properties. In such cases, inferential statistics may be used.

9.4.2 Descriptive statistics

Descriptive statistics are concerned with the description and/or summary of the data obtained for a group of individual units of analysis. If one variable (see Section 2.3) is involved in our study, we call it **univariate analysis**; if two variables are involved, it is called **bivariate analysis** and if more than two variables are involved, it is called **multivariate analysis**.

In this section we will address the grouping of the data and presenting it in the form of tables and graphical distributions. We will also describe means (averages), variance, as well as correlations.

FOR EXAMPLE An example of where descriptive statistics may be appropriate is a university principal's annual report (Stake, 1988) that describes the student community in terms of numbers in the different faculties, and so on.

9.4.2.1 HISTOGRAMS, BAR DIAGRAMS, AND PIE CHARTS

A **histogram**, **bar diagram**, and **pie chart** are diagrams in which columns (in the case of bar diagrams and histograms) or sections (in the case of pie charts) represent frequencies of the various ranges of scores or values of a quantity. This provides an overall image of the description of the units of analysis as a whole group. Histograms are used for interval data, and bar diagrams and pie charts are used for nominal data (biographical variables).

ACTIVITY 9.1
Read Case Studies A, B, C, D, and F in Appendix D on page 306.

QUESTION
Construct suitable graphical representations of a characteristic of the unit of analysis (see Section 4.2) in each case study.

ANSWER

case study a

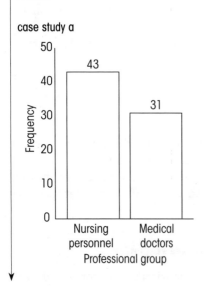

case study b

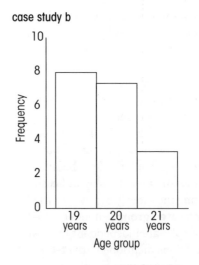

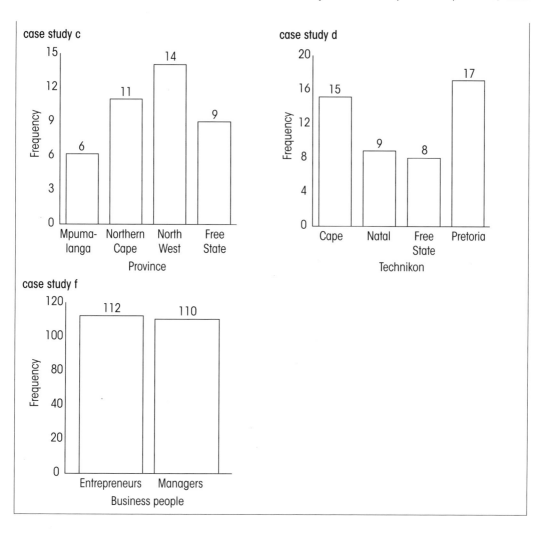

9.4.2.2 MEAN/AVERAGE AND VARIABILITY

The **mean** is the arithmetical average of a set of scores and is denoted by $\overline{X}$. The mean is computed by adding a list of scores and then dividing the total by the number of scores.

Variability refers to the range of the distribution of scores around the mean and we refer to it as the **standard deviation** (denoted by s).

The **standard deviation** is a measure of the spread of scores about the mean. The larger the spread, the further the scores are spread from the mean. Approximately 68% of scores that are normally distributed fall between one standard deviation to both sides of the mean.

A **normal distribution** is a distribution which:
▶ is perfectly symmetrical about its mean
▶ has a bell shape (see Figure 9.5).

In analysing and interpreting the results of surveys (see Section 7.7.3.1), comparisons of basic descriptive data are usually conducted and are necessary to make the results meaningful and to initiate appropriate policy changes.

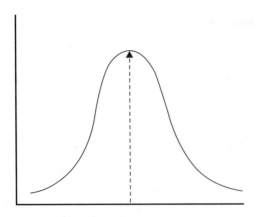

Figure 9.5 *A normal distribution ($\overline{X}$ = average score)*

At least four types of comparative data are possible, namely:

a) comparisons of **different** departments, locations, occupational groups, and so on, **within an organisation**

b) comparisons with **similar** groups in **other organisations**

c) comparisons of the responses of **similar groups across time**

d) comparisons of the **same group** to **different aspects** of some content area, such as a training programme or a work situation.

Without such comparative data, the survey is of little or no use.

When the responses of people in different divisions in an organisation are compared, one question that presents itself is whether the mean differences and percentile differences are meaningful. **Statistical tests of significance** can address the question of whether large differences could be attributable to chance; however, equally important (especially when N's are very large) is the practical significance of the difference. This is a more difficult determination to make and it probably always involves a **value judgement**. In such a case, it may be a judgement as to whether, for example, the relatively low job satisfaction in manufacturing and maintenance is a significant problem for an organisation. Are these

groups characterised by abnormally high rates of turnover, product sabotage, absenteeism, or grievances? If so, then the organisation would want to further explore the reasons for low job satisfaction. Or perhaps there is no evidence that this low job satisfaction is being translated into unproductive behaviour, but the organisation is interested in positive work relations among its employees.

These questions of practicality can be better answered when **other types** of comparative data are also available, for example comparative data for the research and development and manufacturing units in similar organisations. The figures from the research and development unit in organisation A may not look very good in comparison with figures from the manufacturing area that do not appear to be very negative. Both groups may appear relatively average compared to similar groups in organisations B, C, and D.

9.4.2.3 CORRELATIONS AND CROSS-TABULATION

We use **correlations** to describe relationships between variables (see Figure 9.6) such as *income*, *age*, and so on. For example, the relationship between the size of a city and its crime rate may be described with correlational analyses (see Figure 5.5).

Correlations estimate the extent to which the changes in one variable are associated with changes in the other variable. Essentially, a correlation coefficient is a number that summarises what we can observe from a scatterplot (see Figure 9.7). A positive correlation reflects a direct relationship – one in which an increase in one variable corresponds to an increase in the other variable. Two variables that are indirectly or inversely related would produce a negative correlation – indicating that an increase in one variable is associated with a decrease in the other.

Therefore, a coefficient *r* of –1,00 represents a **perfect, inverse relationship**. A coefficient of +1,00 indicates a **perfect, direct relationship**. A coefficient close to zero indicates **no relationship** at all.

A. The uneducated are more prejudiced than the educated.

B. There is no apparent relationship between education and prejudice.

Figure 9.6 *The relationship between two variables or possibilities (Source: Babbie & Mouton, 2001, p. 32. Used with permission.)*

We cannot consider correlational relationships to be causal. This means that we are usually not able to infer that one event is caused by another.

EXAMPLE **CORRELATIONS**

Suppose we take two people as our sample test (see Section 4.3), that is, one male and one female, and we ask them to complete a questionnaire (see Section 7.7.3.1) consisting of 10 items (questions) about road signs. The respondents can score full marks (10 out of 10) for each item (question) if they answer the question correctly.

We can tabulate their scores on the questionnaire as in Table 9.7 (called a spreadsheet).

Table 9.7 Questions and the scores obtained

Question	1	2	3	4	5	6	7	8	9	10
Male	6	3	0	9	0	3	0	4	0	2
Female	6	3	0	9	0	3	0	4	0	2

We can see that there was a 100% comparison. This means that the variable *gender* (male or female) corresponds completely in terms of its relationship with the variable *road sign knowledge*. In other words, there is a perfect relationship (a correlation coefficient of 1,00) between the variables (see Section 2.3) *gender* and *road sign knowledge*.

Suppose a researcher investigated the extent of correlation between a measurement of subjects' attitude towards AIDS and the following two variables *knowledge of AIDS* and *attitude towards prostitution*.

The results could be as follows:

- The correlation coefficient for the correlation between *attitude towards AIDS* and *knowledge of AIDS* is 0,22.
- The correlation coefficient for the correlation between *attitude towards AIDS* and *attitude towards prostitution* is 0,60.
- The correlation coefficient for the correlation between *knowledge of AIDS* and *attitude towards prostitution* is 0,03.

These correlations could be tabled as in Table 9.8 and illustrated in Figure 9.7.

Table 9.8 Correlative findings

	Attitude towards AIDS	Attitude towards prostitution
Knowledge of AIDS	0,22	0,03
Attitude towards AIDS		0,60

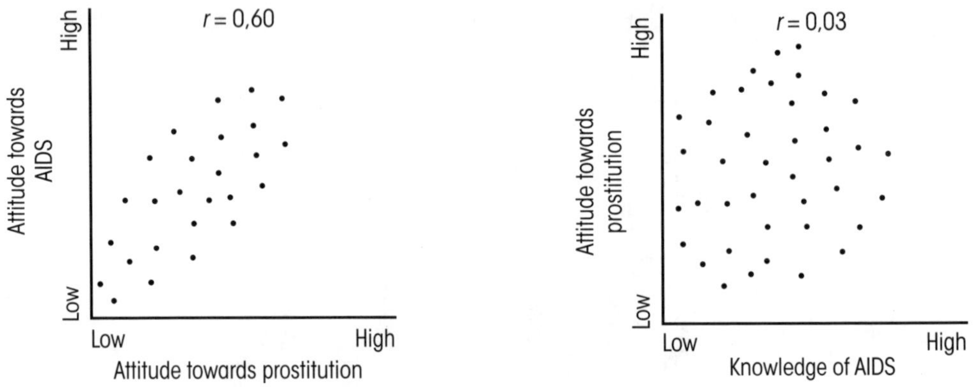

Figure 9.7 *Scatterplots depicting different correlation coefficients (r) between two variables ranging from r = 1,00 to r = 0,00*

Cross-tabulation, or a **contingency table**, requires a table of rows (horizontal from left to right) and columns (vertical from top to bottom), each representing a variable and its level (see Figure 4.8G). It is customary to represent the scores of the dependent variable (see Section 2.3) in the rows (compare the CD-ROM).

9.4.3 Inferential statistics

Broadly speaking, **inferential statistics** are concerned with inferences that we can make about population indices on the basis of the corresponding indices obtained from samples drawn randomly from the populations.

In this section, we will refer briefly to the use of the Chi-square test, and the t- and F-test statistics. We will not deal with more complex statistical analysis techniques in this book.

9.4.3.1 CHI-SQUARE (χ^2) ANALYSIS

We generally use a **Chi-square analysis** to make inferences when the data can be divided into different categories. A Chi-square analysis involves measuring participants in terms of categories such as male–female, voter–non-voter, and so on. By using the Chi-square test, we can determine if, for example, consumers (males versus females) have a preference for a particular product (compare the CD-ROM at the back of this book).

9.4.3.2 *t*-TESTS

The **t-tests** and **analysis of variance** enable us to determine whether two groups have equivalent or different mean scores. Descriptive research involves comparing the mean of one group with the mean of another. In such research *t*-tests (for two groups) and analysis of variance (for more than two groups) are the appropriate statistics to use (compare the CD-ROM).

A **t-test** determines whether an observed difference in the means of two groups is sufficiently large to be attributed to a change in some variable or if it could have occurred by chance. The principle underlying *t*-tests and analysis of variance is the assumption that both groups represent samples from a normal distribution (see Figure 9.5).

9.4.4 Using computers in statistical analysis (use the CD-ROM)

The greater availability of computers has simplified the execution of some statistical procedures considerably. Not only can we use the computer to perform time-consuming and complicated computations, but also to compile tables and to draw graphs and figures, to mention just a few functions. Moreover, computers accurately execute these highly complicated and time-consuming manipulations in a matter of seconds at a relatively low cost.

The notion that computers are able to make sense of any nonsense fed into them is a delusion. In the final instance, the computer executes any command on any data submitted to it. Among computer staff there is the saying "Garbage-in, garbage-out".

When we use a computer, we should do the following:

▶ preferably keep the research hypotheses in mind
▶ limit our statistical analyses:
   • firstly, to those that are required for investigating these hypotheses
   • secondly, to those with which the researcher is familiar.

It is preferable to use commercially available statistical analysis programs rather than to compile or have someone else compile a program specifically for a particular research project. Among these, the *Statistical Package for the Social Sciences* (SPSS), *Biomedical Data Processing System* (BMDP), and the *Statistical Analysis System* (SAS) are the best known (compare MoonStats on the CD-ROM).

Usually the computer centres at universities and technikons have consultants who may assist researchers in processing their data. Such consultants serve as a link between the researcher and the computer. Even if their services are used, it remains the responsibility of the researcher to design the research, select the statistical technique, convey the latter to the consultant, and interpret and write up the results obtained.

9.5 Presenting the results

In view of the principle of public scrutiny (see Section 1.2.2.3) there is no sense in conducting research if we do not release the results obtained to the scientific community. How else could these results be evaluated critically yet objectively and, if they survive such criticism, become part of the discipline's body of knowledge? This is why we should commit to paper the way in which we conducted the research and interpreted the results we obtained, and present them at a scientific conference or submit them to a professional journal for possible publication. Chapter 10 is devoted to the writing of research reports. (See Section 10.3.7.1).

We can present the results in the following ways:

▶ as tables (for example cross-tabulations)
▶ as graphs (for example histograms, bar diagrams, pie charts and scatter diagrams)
▶ as statistical summaries (for example means, standard deviations, correlation coefficient, and so on)
▶ as selected quotations (for example writing representative powerful statements from responses obtained from an interview).

PRESENTING RESULTS

The academic performance results of students in public speech-making may be presented as follows: the number of students involved (710), the mean (39,34), the standard deviation (13,40) and a frequency distribution (histogram) of the marks (see Figure 9.8).

We can present the results (in the form of correlation coefficients) obtained from the study on public speech-making in the form of a table (see Table 9.9), and we can give the distribution of the sample of participants in terms of the technikon from which they were drawn in a pie chart or bar diagram (see Figure 9.9).

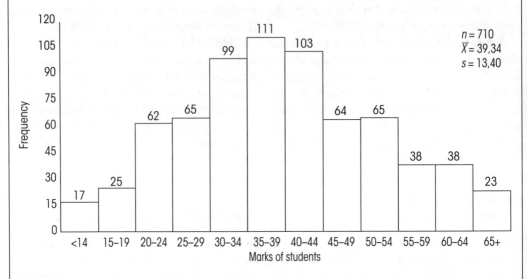

$n = 710$
$\overline{X} = 39,34$
$s = 13,40$

Figure 9.8 *Histogram of academic performance of 710 students in public speech-making*

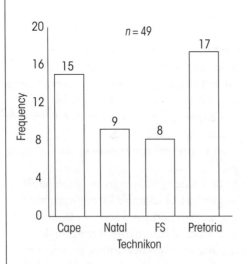

Figure 9.9 *Bar diagram of number of students of technikons who participated in an experiment about brain transplants*

Table 9.9 Correlations between speech quality and other variables

	Speech quality
Speech preparation time	0,75
Speech anxiety	0,03

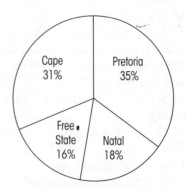

Pie chart numbers in rounded-off percentages

ACTIVITY 9.2

Read Case Study G in Appendix D on page 306.

QUESTION

1. Name the *measurement level* according to which the data in Case Study G were captured (nominal, ordinal, interval or ratio).
2. Choose an appropriate *graphical technique* (see Section 9.4) to represent the results in Case Study G according to *theme*, *age group* and *theme by age* (that is, either bar diagrams, pie charts or histograms). You should use the spreadsheet in Table G1 in Appendix D on page 317 for this purpose.
3. *Present your results* according to your *chosen technique* in (b) graphically by means of a hand-drawn diagram or by means of the CD-ROM's printout procedure.

ANSWERS

1. *Nominal* (see Activity 7.2)
2. *Bar diagrams or pie charts* (because of nominal measurement – see Section 9.4.2.1).
3. Examples of bar diagrams and pie charts of the results (themes and age groups):

Value 1 = Fear of contracting
   HIV/AIDS
Value 2 = Discriminatory
   behaviour towards
   patients
Value 3 = Experience of stress
   when nursing patients
Value 4 = Experiencing mixed
   feelings (doubt, fear,
   sympathy, empathy,
   uncertainty)

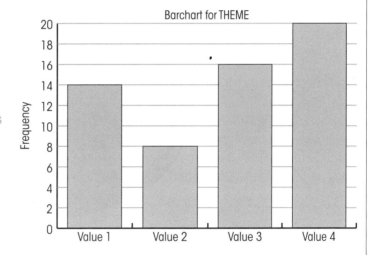

Value 1 = Fear of contracting
   HIV/AIDS
Value 2 = Discriminatory
   behaviour towards
   patients
Value 3 = Experience of stress
   when nursing patients
Value 4 = Experiencing mixed
   feelings (doubt, fear,
   sympathy, empathy,
   uncertainty)

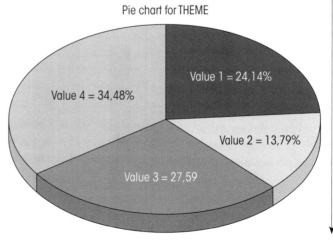

Value 1 = 20–30 years old
Value 2 = 30–50 years old

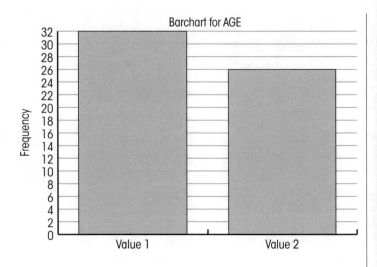

Value 1 = 20–30 years old
Value 2 = 30–50 years old

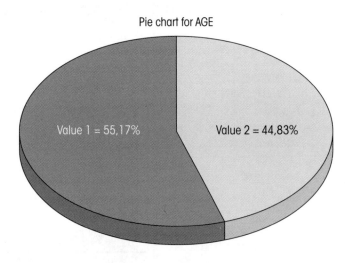

Theme 1 = Fear of contracting
HIV/AIDS
Theme 2 = Discriminatory
behaviour towards
patients
Theme 3 = Experience of stress
when nursing
patients
Theme 4 = Experiencing mixed
feelings (doubt,
fear, sympathy,
empathy,
uncertainty)

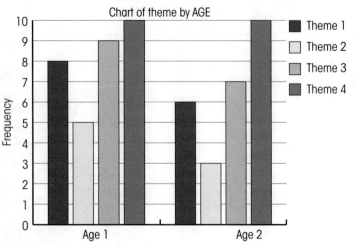

Age 1 = 20–30 years old
Age 2 = 30–50 years old

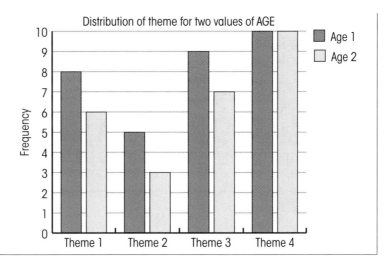

Distribution of theme for two values of AGE

ACTIVITY 9.3
Read Case Study F in Appendix D on page 306.

QUESTION
Briefly explain why the mean was used instead of the correlation in the statistical calculations for interpreting the results of the study.

ANSWER
The mean (arithmetical average) as a descriptive device provides the scores obtained by the whole sample of managers and the whole sample of entrepreneurs for their innovative problem-solving styles. Therefore, by using this statistic (the mean), the value of the scores of the two groups can be compared with one another. A statistic such as the correlation coefficient, on the other hand, indicates the extent to which the individual scores of the managers change in relation to those of the entrepreneurs.

SUMMARY
After research has been conducted according to its planned design, the obtained results must be interpreted. Therefore, the design of a study also concerns the statistical analysis and interpretation of the appropriate data obtained for investigating the research hypothesis by measurement of variables.

A large data file can be reduced to useful information, which can facilitate the interpretation of data as well as the drawing of conclusions by means of descriptive and inferential statistics.

If the scores of the entire population under investigation were available, the use of descriptive statistics would be sufficient. If, however, the population of interest is so large that the data about the population cannot be calculated by hand in a reasonable time, one has to rely on the results obtained from samples of these populations and then use inferential statistics.

Qualitative data analysis often involves analysing interviews and doing content analysis. An analysis of an interview is done by identifying important themes in the interview, coding the data, and then creating frequency distributions for these themes. Data can be displayed in matrix displays or network displays. Content analysis involves counting the frequencies and sequences of words, phrases, and concepts in order to identify keywords or themes.

Quantitative data analysis involves a statistical analysis of the obtained data. Depending on the level of measurement used for the variables of the research study, specific statistical procedures are applied. These procedures include the mode, median, mean, frequencies, correlation coefficients, chi-squares, chaid-analysis, correspondence analysis, discriminant analysis, standard deviation, z-scores, t-tests, and F-tests.

Descriptive statistics involve the description and summary of data, while inferential statistics involve the inferences that are drawn from the results. Ultimately the results of statistical investigations can be represented graphically by means of bar charts and pie charts.

TEST YOURSELF

Question 1: Multiple-choice questions

Only one of the answers to each question is correct. Identify and mark the correct one. (Answers appear in Appendix A on page 299.)

1.1 Themes in qualitative research are identified by means of
   a) t-tests
   b) determining the level of measurement
   c) nominal measurement
   d) counting repetitions of words.

1.2 Network displays are used to
   a) describe a null hypothesis
   b) eliminate a rival hypothesis
   c) describe qualitative relationships between concepts
   d) analyse the content of personal documents and mass media.

1.3 The results of unstructured (in-depth) interviews and focus groups can be graphically presented by means of
   a) coding
   b) a scatterplot
   c) a histogram
   d) a bar diagram.

1.4 The process of analysing qualitative data in a quantitative way is called
   a) filing
   b) classifying
   c) coding
   d) chunking.

1.5 The main purpose of sampling is to be able to select:
   a) a sample whose statistics will accurately portray a known population parameter
   b) a sample whose statistics will accurately portray an unknown population parameter
   c) a sample whose unknown statistics will accurately portray a known parameter
   d) simple random samples.

1.6 Statistical computations assume that you have done:
   a) simple random sampling
   b) systematic sampling
   c) cluster sampling
   d) stratified sampling.

1.7 Which of the following measures of central tendency can be used at any level of measurement?
a) mean
b) mode
c) median
d) standard deviation.

1.8 If the standard deviation equals 0, we may conclude that:
a) there is no dispersion in the data
b) the mean is a good measure of the average
c) the data are homogeneous
d) all of the above are correct.

1.9 Given the following age distribution {4, 7, 15, 32}, the mean is:
a) 4
b) 7
c) 14,5
d) 32

1.10 If, from the same sample of people, events, or objects, two variables are measured and they seem to vary together, then these two measurements are:
a) contingent
b) redundant
c) dependent
d) correlated.

1.11 The absolute size of a correlation coefficient indicates the following about a relationship:
a) complexity
b) strength
c) direction
d) refusion.

1.12 If the points on a scatterplot stretch from the upper left to the lower right along a line, then the correlation between the two variables is:
a) zero
b) negative
c) positive
d) diminutive.

Question 2: True/false questions

Indicate whether the following statements are true (T) or false (F). (Answers appear in Appendix A on page 299.)

2.1 Unstructured interviews can be used to analyse newspaper articles on the Second World War.

2.2 Video recordings of an unstructured interview should be converted to write-ups before it can be analysed.

2.3 A nominal variable is a discrete variable.

2.4 Coding refers to the assignment of a number to the attributes of a variable.

2.5 When the research purpose is not clear, it is advisable to choose the highest level of measurement.

2.6 Secondary analysis refers to the analysis of data collected earlier by another researcher for some purpose other than the topic of the current study.

2.7 Descriptive statistics include both the summary of univariate distributions and the summary of associations between two or more variables.

2.8 Pearson's product moment correlation indicates how much of the variance in the dependent variable has been explained.

Question 3: Self-evaluation questions

(Some answers appear in Appendix A on page 299.)

3.1 Refer to the last self-evaluation question at the end of Chapter 8. Use the technique of qualitative data analysis (see Section 9.2) to:
- identify the five most important themes (see Section 9.2.1.2) that highlight your interviewees' answers
- code the data (answers from the interviewees) according to the specifications of Section 9.2.1.3 and the example in Table 9.2
- compile a coding list of the five themes that you have identified (see Table 9.1)
- compile a table of the frequencies of the five themes (see Table 9.3) and
- compile a matrix which indicates the importance attributed to each of the themes (see Table 9.4).

3.2 At which measurement level (nominal, ordinal, interval or ratio) was the data (i.e. the answers to open-ended questions of the unstructured interviews) captured?

3.3 Select an appropriate statistical graphical technique (see Section 9.4) to represent the results according to theme.

3.4 Present your results according to the technique selected in Question 3.3 graphically (compare Figures 9.1, 9.2 & 9.8) by means of a hand-drawn diagram or by means of the CD-ROM's printout procedure.

Report-writing

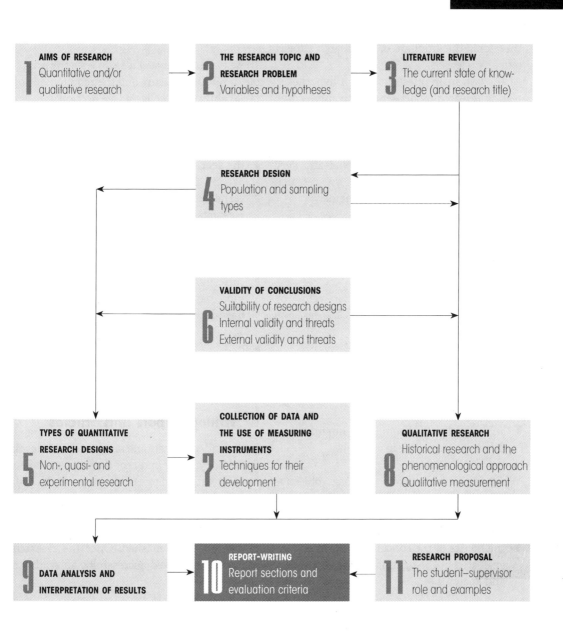

1 AIMS OF RESEARCH
Quantitative and/or
qualitative research

2 THE RESEARCH TOPIC AND
RESEARCH PROBLEM
Variables and hypotheses

3 LITERATURE REVIEW
The current state of knowledge (and research title)

4 RESEARCH DESIGN
Population and sampling
types

6 VALIDITY OF CONCLUSIONS
Suitability of research designs
Internal validity and threats
External validity and threats

5 TYPES OF QUANTITATIVE
RESEARCH DESIGNS
Non-, quasi- and
experimental research

7 COLLECTION OF DATA AND
THE USE OF MEASURING
INSTRUMENTS
Techniques for their
development

8 QUALITATIVE RESEARCH
Historical research and the
phenomenological approach
Qualitative measurement

9 DATA ANALYSIS AND
INTERPRETATION OF RESULTS

10 REPORT-WRITING
Report sections and
evaluation criteria

11 RESEARCH PROPOSAL
The student–supervisor
role and examples

LEARNING OUTCOMES

If we have taken the trouble to carry out a research project, then it deserves to be reported. Writing the research report rounds off the research project and makes the results available to other researchers.

After studying this chapter, you will be able to:
- write a report on your own research project.

10.1 Introduction

The real purpose of research is to expand scientific knowledge. In order to serve this purpose, therefore, the findings of a research project must be released.

The two main questions that a hypothesis-testing research report sets out to answer, are:

- What was the **research problem**?
- How was the **problem investigated**?

However, there are two additional and very important questions to which the research report should provide answers, namely:

- What has been found?
- What are the implications and the meaning of the findings for the original problem?

Research reports add particular value by answering these two questions. The research report may take the form of:

- a **thesis** or **dissertation** (or essay or report) that is submitted for degree purposes (see Table 10.1)
- an **article** that is intended for publication in a professional journal
- an integral part of someone's **normal duties** at a research institution.

Whatever form it takes, the main objective remains the same, namely to provide a *written account of the execution of the project* and of the results obtained so that:

- the merits of the conclusions may be evaluated in the light of the data collection and analyses

- sufficient information is available for the possible replication of the study or for a re-analysis of the data obtained.

These two considerations tie in with the principle of **public scrutiny** and the requirement of **replicability** respectively (see Section 1.2).

In this chapter we will focus on general guidelines regarding the writing of reports on hypothesis-testing research, namely:

- the **sections** of a research report (see Section 10.2)
- certain **conventions** to follow in writing a research report (see Section 10.3; the reference system – see Sections 3.4 & 10.2.9)
- its **editorial revision** in respect of grammar and style (see Section 10.3)
- the criteria in terms of which such reports, more particularly journal articles, are **evaluated** (see Section 10.4 and Table 10.1).

NOTE: Consult Wolcott (1990) on how to write a report on qualitative research (see Chapter 8).

10.2 Writing papers and articles

At the undergraduate and taught master's level, students typically find that their time is taken up fully with studies and research. At M.Phil. and Ph.D. level, at the very least, a student should have written and presented a number of papers at conferences and possibly had one or two articles published. Once the research has been completed successfully, all students should consider presenting conference papers and writing articles. This will improve their academic reputation, enhance their careers, and may even be financially rewarding. One very important factor to remember is that a researcher cannot publish a research report or thesis as it stands. A research report is written for a particular audience, and conference papers and articles have different audiences. Therefore, before an article can be published, a researcher needs to establish what the requirements of these new audiences are.

10.2.1 Conferences

We can distinguish between two types of conferences: commercial and academic conferences. **Commercial conferences** are advertised widely and business people are often required to pay to attend a day's conference. Usually there are a number of speakers who are regarded as experts in their respective fields. Generally the audience is not interested in the research design, literature review, or methodology, but in the actual research results and what it means to them and their counterparts.

Academic conferences are less lavish affairs and can range from small regional conferences to large international conferences. Despite differences in size and location, both audiences are interested in and critical of any research. Several months before the conference there is usually a call for papers. Researchers are generally expected to submit a paper of approximately 5 000 words, together with an abstract for consideration. If the conference organisers consider the paper worthy, they allocate a certain period of time for the presentation of the results. With some conferences this can be as short as 20 minutes, while with others the researcher may be allocated an hour. Researchers are expected to devise a presentation based on the paper, bearing in mind the available time, and allowing time at the end for questions. Academics focus their attention on the research design, methodology, and results.

Students interested in an academic career should present papers at academic conferences. They may find that this leads to a publication, as some organisers publish a collection of selected papers presented at the conference. Once students/researchers attended one or two conferences, they usually find a network of other researchers.

10.2.2 Articles

There are three main types of publications which may be interested in receiving an article about research, each with its own style and word length.

Popular publications include the local and national press, as well as weekly magazines and some of the more popular monthly magazines. With these types of publications, it is likely that the editor will require highly topical articles. Therefore, a study of the hardships suffered by textile workers in the nineteenth century is unlikely to be accepted. However, if a researcher can use his or her research to illuminate and explain current events, he or she may find an outlet for it. The local press is often interested in research that is not topical but focuses on local industry and events.

The associations and societies of professional people, such as accountants, lawyers, engineers, and so on, produce their own **professional journals**, usually on a monthly basis. These concentrate not so much on topical issues, but on items which are relevant to their members. Thus, a wide range of stories may be relevant, although they may only be of historic importance. Researchers might find that their research can be adapted to fit this type of audience. It is often best for researchers to send a synopsis of the article to the editor before it is written, to determine if a journal is interested. They often ask researchers to write from a specific point of view.

Refereed journals are known as such because two or three copies of an article together with an abstract are submitted to the journal. If the editor regards the topic in principle as suitable for the journal, the article is then sent to other academics who act as referees. The author's name is not revealed to them and they may not even know the name of the other referee. This is called a blind review. Thus, the referees decide whether the article is worthy of publication as it is, needs amendments, or should be rejected. Authors of articles that are published in a refereed journal do not receive any payment and may even have to pay a fee when the article is submitted. However, because publication in a refereed journal is hard to achieve, it is the most prestigious form of publication. It is essential for students and researchers to strive

for this type of publication if they wish to have an academic career.

Before submitting an article, it is essential that researchers read the guide to authors which is normally given in each journal. It is also important that they go through copies of the journal of the past five years to find articles in the same general area so that these can be quoted or referred to. The number of rejections by journals is high and for an inexperienced author there is considerable merit in writing an article jointly with someone with greater experience. In this regard, the supervisors of PhD students generally co-author articles.

Lastly it should be noted that, in general, professional journal articles are more condensed than dissertations and theses. Table 10.1 contains the main differences between dissertations and theses on the one hand and journal articles on the other.

Table 10.1 The differences between reports written for dissertations and theses and those for professional journal articles

Dissertations and theses	Professional journal articles
Students may be expected to state things explicitly.	Due to the journal's considerable publication costs, the various aspects are dealt with in a succinct manner.
Students will devote at least a separate chapter to each of the sections indicated.	These sections are separated by headings in capital letters which may be centred on the page. As a result of this and the above-mentioned cost factor, journal articles are much more condensed than dissertations and theses.

10.3 The sections of a research report

The extensiveness of a research report depends largely on the nature of the research project. A research report usually contains a separate section or sections focusing on each of the following aspects:

- an introduction (the research problem)
- theoretical background and the research hypotheses arising from it
- the procedures and methods followed to investigate the research problem
- the results obtained
- an interpretation and discussion of the results.

We may view any research project as an extensive exercise in logical reasoning. This logical train of thought should cover all the stages of research from the formulation of the research problem to the interpretation of the obtained data. When writing the research report, we should be careful not to get lost in details that disrupt the logical train of thought. Rather, the focus should be maintained throughout.

10.3.1 The title

The title of the research report should concisely yet unambiguously reflect the exact **topic** of the project. It should include the **important variable(s)** and, preferably, the **population** (see Chapters 2 & 4).

FOR EXAMPLE The title of the journal article on which Research Example II (see Section 2.3, page 17) is based, reads:

> *Transmission of management style through imitation of iron-fisted supervisory models.*

That for Research Example III (see Section 5.4, page 92) is entitled:

> *Relationship of television viewing habits and aggressive behaviour in children.*

10.3.2 The abstract (executive summary)

The **abstract** is a very brief summary of a journal article usually consisting of no more than 200 words, although the required number of words may vary from one publication to another. It generally appears immediately after the title (of the article) and the name(s) of the author(s).

In an abstract we should preferably answer each of the following questions:

▶ What was the research problem?
▶ How was the problem investigated?
▶ What has been found?
▶ What are the implications and the meaning of the findings for the original problem?

An abstract can therefore only be compiled properly once the research has been completed. In some respects, the abstract is the most important section of the report. There are two reasons for this:

▶ It is the section, apart from the title, which future researchers will scan with a view to determining whether they should study the entire report.

▶ Only the title and the abstract are stored for information retrieval purposes and published in journals (such as *Psychological Abstracts*).

Since it is so extremely condensed, the abstract may require several revisions in an attempt to capture the essence of the report in the required number of words.

NOTE: Exercises concerning writing an abstract follow at the end of Section 10.3.8.

10.3.3 The introduction

The research report begins with a section that stands/acts as an **introduction**. Although this section is known as the introduction, it usually does not have this title in a journal article. The purpose of this chapter is to describe the objective of the particular research project as well as its importance (see Sections 2.1, 2.3 & 2.3.2).

Irrespective of its scope, the introduction (in the case of a journal article) or introductory chapter(s) (in the case of dissertations or theses) begins with a wide, general description of the problem area and progresses to a formulation of the **specific problems** and/or **hypotheses investigated** (problem statement and hypotheses – see Section 10.3.5).

In this respect, Bem (1986) likens the introduction to an hourglass.

It begins with a **general statement**. Subsequently, the description becomes **increasingly specific** (for example in the description of a specific model) up to the point where the **research hypotheses** are formulated.

249

10.3.4 The literature review (see Section 3.3)

The **literature review** is usually presented in a research report (for dissertations or theses) in one or more chapters following the introductory chapter. In a journal article, the introductory comments and the literature review (here condensed into a literature survey) are usually combined in the first section. The literature review highlights the most pertinent findings as discussed by other researchers.

10.3.5 Problem statement and hypotheses

The section on the literature review culminates in the formulation of the **research hypothesis(es)** or **research question(s)** in a journal article and may even occupy a separate chapter in dissertations and theses entitled *Statement of problem*. In dissertations and theses it is especially important to provide the rationale for each research hypothesis.

10.3.6 Methods and procedures

The purpose of this section relates to the requirements of **controllability** and **replicability** which are part and parcel of the scientific method (see Section 1.2). In this section (and the one on the results), the picture of the hourglass reaches its centre. This usually occu-

pies a separate subsection in the report (conventions – see Section 10.4). Few, if any, literature references are allowed in this section, but we should remember to provide enough information on the execution of the project so that readers may be able to evaluate the appropriateness of the methods (in terms of the research objectives) and the results obtained eventually.

In addition, such a careful description of the research procedures makes it possible for anyone who may care to do so, to replicate the study (see Section 1.2). Consequently, it is important to provide sufficient information about each of the topics.

Although the presentation of this section is adapted according to the specifics of a given project and therefore may differ from project to project, it usually contains information on the following:

- units of analysis (humans, groups, organisations or institutions, human products or outputs, or events (see Section 4.2))
- research design, experimental and/or data-collection procedures (see Chapters 4, 5 & 7)
- apparatus and/or measuring instruments (see Chapter 7).

Concerning the units of analysis, we should clearly describe:

- the way in which the units of analysis/subjects (see Section 4.2) were **obtained** (for example by random sampling, and so on)
- from which experimentally accessible **population** (see Sections 4.2 & 6.3.2) they were drawn (for example from factory workers between 20 and 40 years of age)
- how many were involved in the research.

We should describe the final sample in terms of relevant biographical, demographic, socio-economical or other particulars such as:

- gender (how many of each), age, and educational level (mean, median, standard deviation, and range – see Section 9.4.1) in the case of human subjects
- type of industrial sector (how many in manufacturing, distribution, retail, finance, and so on) in the case of organisations; and similar information for any of the other characteristic units of analysis.

NOTE: In describing the ages and educational levels or the types of industrial sectors, we could consider using a frequency table.

Next, we should describe the **design** and experimental and/or **data-collection procedures**. Among other things, we should clearly indicate (in the case of experimental research – see Section 5.2) how the subjects were assigned to the respective treatment groups (see Section 6.2.7). The procedure by means of which the independent variable was operationalised (for example how the treatments, if any, were administered – see Sections 2.3, 2.4, 6.1 & 6.2.3) and the way in which the measurements on the dependent variable were collected (see Section 2.4.3), should be set out clearly. The exact instructions given to subjects (except those for standardised tests) should also be provided in this subsection.

In the case of an extensive programme of instructions, we could consider providing only an abridged version here and including the complete version as an appendix.

If a **nuisance variable** has been controlled experimentally, it should be pointed out (see Section 5.2). Any unforeseen events that have to be taken into consideration in interpreting the ultimate results should be reported. By the same token, indications of the success or failure with which the independent variable was operationalised and the response rates (see Section 7.7.3.1) achieved in postal surveys should be cited.

In dissertations and theses, the statistical procedures (see Section 9.4) by means of which the obtained data were analysed and, if appropriate, the significance level adopted, are also often mentioned in the procedures section.

NOTE: Some supervisors and promoters require their students to provide the reason for using a particular statistical method. In journal articles this is usually required in the case of relatively unknown methods of analysis, or unusual adaptations of regular methods only (especially if there may be doubts about whether their assumptions have been proven). Likewise, only certain supervisors and promoters require that the mathematical-statistical derivation of statistical methods is given. By the same token, whereas dissertation or thesis students are often required

to explicitly state the **statistical hypotheses** (see Section 9.3.1) inferred from their operationally defined research hypotheses, in journal articles these are usually taken to be implied in the statistical tests used.

FOR EXAMPLE If the *t*-test for independent groups has been used, the null hypothesis $\mu_1 - \mu_2 = 0$ is implied (μ_1 being a population's average score).

Instead of explicitly stating the null hypothesis and the alternative hypothesis, some supervisors and promoters of post-graduate students prefer the expected statistical findings to be provided.

FOR EXAMPLE The mean/average decision-making score of the management learning group exposed to the high-level emergency situation will be statistically significantly higher than that of the group exposed to the low-level emergency situation.

A statement like the one above is more concise than the null and alternative hypotheses, and has the added advantage of reflecting the research hypothesis (see Section 2.4).

It should be emphasised that such a statement (in respect of whether or not the expected results will be significant) refers to the values of the sample statistics and not to the population parameters (see Section 9.4).

In journal articles the statistical analysis procedures are usually identified in the next subsection *Results*. A possible exception to this rule occurs when the research project is devoted in its entirety to the development of a measuring instrument and the analyses occupy a central position in the project.

Lastly, if commercially available apparatus or other measuring instruments were used, it is sufficient only to provide their names and references dealing with their development, reliability, and validity. If the researcher has developed his or her own apparatus or measuring instrument, its development, reliability, and validity should be described completely.

Questionnaires or paper-and-pencil tests that were compiled in this manner should be placed in an **appendix** to the dissertation, thesis, or research report. Preferably, a few items from such an instrument should be provided in the *Procedures* section so that the reader may form an idea of its general nature without having to consult the appendix.

10.3.7 The results

In this section we simply present the **results of the statistical tests** performed on the data without discussing or interpreting them. In some cases, it may indeed be more appropriate and permissible to combine the results and their discussion in the same section. If data that were collected in a pilot study (see Section 7.6) and that affected the course of the subsequent main study are presented, they should be identified as such. Normally, this section should not contain any references to other publications.

Tables and **graphs** may be used as concise and well-organised summaries of results.

FOR EXAMPLE If an analysis of variance (see Section 9.4.2.2) was performed, a table with the sample means and the summary table would provide a sufficient description of the results. However, if the results may be conveyed adequately in a sentence or two, it is preferable to report them in this manner rather than in a table.

We should not present tables or graphs if we do not refer to them in the text of the report. On the other hand, we should not describe the tables and figures in such detail in the text that it amounts to duplication. Similarly, tables and graphs should not duplicate each other. Furthermore, we should not refer to tables and graphs in an incidental manner (for example by placing their numbers between brackets/parentheses) and then expect the reader to figure out the necessary information and relevance.

FOR EXAMPLE Provide the specific value in a table to which reference is made and, if necessary, the row and column in which it appears.

A separate series of Arabic numerals (for example 1, 2, 3 and so on) is generally used to number the tables and figures respectively. (Compare the practice in this book.) References to tables and figures are made in terms of their numbers. In other words, one should refer to "Table 3" or "Figure 2" rather than to "the following table".

If reference is made to a figure or table and there is not sufficient space (on the page) immediately following the reference for the figure or table, the remainder of that page does not have to be left blank. Instead, we could continue with the text on that page even if the table or figure appears on the next page. Each table and figure should have a concise yet clear title so that its contents may be understood without having to refer to the table or figure itself. The title of a table usually appears at its top; the title of a figure usually appears below it.

If tests of **statistical significance** (see Section 9.4) were performed, the following should be indicated:

- the calculated values of the test statistics
- their degrees of freedom (between parentheses)
- the levels of significance
- whether one-tailed or two-tailed tests (where appropriate) were involved.

10.3.7.1 PRESENTING THE RESULTS (SEE SECTION 9.5)

(a) Letter symbols

Write letters used as symbols for statistical concepts such as t or F in italics (or underline them in typewritten manuscripts). A sentence should never begin with an abbreviation, symbol, or a number.

(b) Numbers

Write out numbers smaller than 10 as words unless they represent percentages, decimal numbers, sample sizes, ages, and the numbers of tables, graphs, and groups. In these cases figures should be used, irrespective of the size of the number. The same applies to fractions, except common ones such as "half", "quarter", "one-third", and so on, which are written out in full. If a comparison between numbers smaller than 10 and numbers larger than 10 appears in the same sentence, it is recommended that you express both in figures (for example, the ages varied between 9 and 11 years). On the other hand, clarity may often be enhanced if numbers are alternately expressed in figures and words (for example there were 6 five-minute intervals).

If a sentence has to begin with a number, write it out as a word rather than as a numeral. If it is a long number, consider rewriting the sentence so that the number no longer appears at the beginning of the sentence. Leave a space between a number and the measurement unit to which it refers (for example 3 kg and 4 m), except in the case of percentages and the degrees of angles (for example 21% and 14°).

(c) Capital letters

It is customary to refer to:

▶ Table 1, Figure 3, Variable 5, Factor 6, Group B, but to both tables, figures, variables, factors, groups
▶ the Verbal and Non-verbal factors in a factor analysis
▶ the Gender × Ethnicity factor in an analysis of variance where the × refers to a situation where one variable (*gender*) is investigated in relation to another (*ethnicity*).

10.3.8 The discussions and conclusions

In this section, the hourglass-shaped format of the research report begins to **widen** again.

This section contains an interpretation of the statistical results presented in the preceding section in terms of the research problem introduced at the beginning of the report (see Section 10.2). The results are not merely repeated; instead, their meaning and implication are explained in the light of the purpose of the research.

For the sake of perspective, one can begin this section of a report with a summary of the main findings (see Section 10.3.7). In the case of dissertations and theses, each statistical hypothesis should preferably be repeated with an indication of whether it was rejected or retained as well as the implications of these decisions for the respective research hypotheses.

NOTE: If the purpose of the project was:
- to test a hypothesis derived from some theory, we should point out the implications of the results for the tenability or untenability of that theory.
- to fill a gap in our knowledge left by previous studies, we should point out to what degree the obtained results succeeded in achieving this.

In the same manner, we should discuss whether we agree or disagree with the findings of previous research projects. We should consider alternative interpretations of the results obtained and evaluate them objectively.

We should point out possible **practical implications** of the results. This aspect is of special importance if the research involved the implementation of some programme or if the research was funded by an agency or research institution.

We need not dwell unnecessarily on results that have turned out to be statistically non-significant. (Statistically non-significant differences and correlations should, in any case, never be interpreted as the absence of such relationships.) Negative results do not necessarily mean that a study was useless. For instance, if we found that the relationship between two variables (such as *gender* and *ethnicity*) is non-significant, such a finding represents an extension of our knowledge about this relationship. In addition, such a finding may prevent future researchers from wasting their time and resources on this topic.

We should not draw conclusions that we cannot justify by means of the study. Similarly, we should mention any **restriction on the population and internal validity** (see Sections 6.2 & 6.2.3) of the results due to:

▶ shortcomings in the sampling procedure (see Section 4.3)
▶ the assignment to samples (see Section 6.2.7)
▶ the inadequate control of nuisance variables (see Section 5.2)
▶ anything that possibly may have influenced the results.

Of course, such a *post hoc* listing of flaws does not compensate for not having carefully prevented them in the first place. However, it may serve a purpose in that it may recommend alternative ways of addressing the problem in future studies.

Usually we will find that the findings of one research project suggest problems or hypotheses that we may pursue in further research projects. It is not uncommon to discover that the findings of one study raise more questions and problems than they originally set out to answer. Consequently, we usually conclude the report with some suggestions for **further research** that could be carried out profitably.

ACTIVITY 10.1

Read Case Studies A, B, C, D, E, F, and G in Appendix D on page 306.

QUESTION

Complete each case study by writing the last section, namely *Discussions and conclusions*. Pay particular attention to the possibility of causal aspects in the study. Measured against the objectives of the research study, do the results answer the research questions of the investigation? Furthermore, do they support or reject the research hypothesis (see Section 2.4)?

ANSWER

case study a

Discussion: As is evident from Table A (page 307), there is only one significant correlation, namely that between *attitude towards prostitution* and *attitude towards AIDS*.

Attitude towards AIDS correlates quite strongly with *attitude towards prostitution* ($r = 0,60$). It seems that these two variables are intrinsically connected. The stigma of prostitution is possibly aggravated by the association of prostitutes with AIDS through their identification as a high-risk group. The weak correlation between *knowledge of AIDS* and *attitude towards AIDS* ($r = 0,22$) could indicate that the attitudes of the group of health professionals at the hospital concerned are determined by negative associations rather than by factual information.

Conclusion: The research hypothesis cannot be accepted in its entirety, owing to the absence of a relationship between *knowledge of AIDS* and *attitude*

towards AIDS. Although the correlational findings cannot be interpreted as an indication that attitudes towards AIDS are determined by attitudes towards prostitution, the findings do indicate a tendency towards a connection between negative attitudes in the one area and negative attitudes in other areas. In the case of this group of health professionals, the findings indicate that existing attitudes towards the perceived high-risk group (prostitutes) and their sexual practices probably influence their attitudes towards AIDS more strongly than objective knowledge.

It would appear that educational programmes in South Africa should focus on prostitution as well, and particularly on the sexual practices of prostitutes, if more enlightened and objective attitudes towards AIDS are to be brought about. In so doing, educational programmes will have to investigate and counter prejudice against high-risk groups and their sexual behaviour, as well as provide factual information.

case study b

Discussion: The results in Table B (page 309) indicate that the apprentices' judgement of supervision became increasingly negative, as reflected in the evaluation factor of the semantic differential (SD). The evidence of changes before role induction corresponds with predictions made at the beginning of the study, namely that the apprentices' uncertainty and lack of knowledge of the supervision process would lead to negative changes in time.

It appears from the change in the SD between the second and the third evaluations that the role induction procedure did not have the predicted effect of causing the apprentices to evaluate supervision more favourably. Results show that no significant changes occurred as a result of the role induction initiative (a positive change in the mean from 3,24 to only 3,19).

Conclusion: It is notable that no significant changes are found in the SD after the role induction procedure. Since the SD evaluates attitudinal changes, one possible interpretation of the findings is that the role induction strategy used in this study was an intervention focusing on a change in thinking and in the processing of information instead of on attitudinal change. Since the questionnaires were given to the apprentices only one week after the role induction procedure, and there was therefore little intervening supervision, the changes that occurred may well have entailed a reinterpretation of their previous experience of supervision. It could be that the time that elapsed between the second and third tests was inadequate to bring about a change in attitude.

Finally, any conclusions drawn from this investigation must be qualified by an acknowledgement of the limitations inherent in the design of the study. These limitations include the use of self-description instruments to evaluate changes, and the relatively small sample sizes. With a larger sample it would be possible to investigate the effect of role induction in training at different points in time, so as to determine whether there is an optimal period during which the procedure is the most effective.

case study c

Discussion: Table C (page 310) indicates that there was no significant difference between the results of the two groups before the start of the course. The average/mean mark of the experimental group was 57% and that of the control group 58%. The subjects (first-line supervisors) therefore performed equally with regard to their knowledge of management principles before the training intervention.

Table C also indicates that after the experimental group received their training, their knowledge test scores improved significantly – from 57% to 78%. This is an improvement of 21%, while the knowledge test scores of the control group (who did not attend the training course) remained more or less the same (58%–56%).

Conclusion: According to the results in Table C, the hypothesis is thus accepted. It can be accepted with certainty that the significant difference in the pre- and postmeasurement of the experimental group, but not of the control group, is the result of the training intervention. The application of the independent variable (*training course*) indeed had an influence on the dependent variable (*knowledge of management principles*) and caused a significant change.

We can therefore accept that the course did indeed comply with its objectives in the short term with regard to the improvement in knowledge, and it is recommended that the remaining first-line supervisors of the population of 60 attend the training course.
For future research it is recommended that the influence of the training course be evaluated over a longer period of time and be investigated in different types of agricultural organisations.

case study d

Discussion: The results of this study provide a temporary quantitative answer that confirms the personal experience of coaches and the previous perceived relationship between *speech preparation time* and *speech quality*. Although no significant correlation ($r = 0,03$) could be found between *speech quality* and *speech anxiety*, Table D (page 312) shows that there is a high correlation between *speech quality* and *speech preparation time* ($r = 0,75$). The results thus support the first hypothesis that there is a high positive relationship between the speech quality and the total preparation time of a group of public speech-making technikon students and reject the second hypothesis of a high negative correlation between *speech quality* and *speech anxiety*.

Conclusion: It appears that the students who spend more time preparing achieve higher marks for their speeches. This does not, however, mean that manipulating the one variable (*speech preparation time*) will cause a change in the other variable (*speech quality*). As the results of the previous research indicate, more preparation time contributes to greater self-confidence and this, in turn, may lead to a better speech.

From the results it is not clear, however, whether the preparation time of various students differs in quality. Such investigation is recommended for further research. Although two students spent an equal amount of time searching for information and thus preparing for their speech, one student could, for example, have sat in the library and paged through magazines while another student searched methodically for specific information on the topic. Future research will therefore not only have to use better methods of measuring the quality of preparation time, but also make use of a more representative sample in order to increase the population validity of such a study.

case study e

Discussion: From the results of the study it seems that the bankrupt small businesses in comparison to non-bankrupt businesses tend to exceed their bank overdraft limits to significantly greater amounts and experience cash flow problems to a significantly greater extent. However, no significantly high correlation ($r = 0,45$) could be found between cash flow problems and bankruptcy status. This means that businesses that experienced serious cash flow problems do not necessarily go bankrupt, and *vice versa*.

Table E (page 313) shows that there is a significantly high correlation between cash flow problems and bank overdraft usage ($r = 0,83$), and in particular between bank overdraft usage and bankruptcy status ($r = 0,94$). This means that businesses that depend heavily on exceeding bank overdraft limits tend to go bankrupt and tend to have more cash flow problems. The results of this study indicate that cash flow problems combined with bank overdraft usage may, in turn, predict bankruptcy.

This implies that cash flow problems do not in themselves promote bankruptcy but do so in combination with seriously exceeded bank overdraft limits.

Conclusion: The results support the hypothesis that, during the past two years, bankrupt small businesses exceeded their bank overdraft limits with significantly greater amounts per month and experienced more cash flow problems than non-bankrupt small businesses.

This does not, however, mean that manipulating the one variable (*bank overdraft usage* or *cash flow problems*) will cause a change in the other variable (*bankruptcy status*). The results of the previous research indicate that management skills also contribute to bankruptcy.

If we consider the relatively small size of the samples used, the significant results become more noteworthy. However, as the research was limited to small businesses in a specific geographic region (Tshwane, formerly Pretoria) for practical reasons, the sample could have been biased. Replication of these findings is nonetheless necessary and future research will have to use a more representative sample in order to increase the population validity of such a study.

case study f

Discussion: The results indicate that the mean score obtained by the entrepreneurs was 113,9 and the mean score of the managers 96,0. By comparing these mean scores with the highest possible score of 160, it is evident that the entrepreneurs obtained a significantly higher mean than the managers. This difference indicates that the entrepreneurs are definitely more innovative than the managers of big businesses.

The sample of business people in this investigation was not representative of all members of the relevant population of South African entrepreneurs/managers because an accidental sample was used. Therefore, one cannot confidently generalise the results of this study to other business people in South Africa.

Conclusions: The results support the notion of the research hypothesis that entrepreneurs will be significantly more innovative in their problem-solving style than managers of big businesses.

However, nuisance (third) variables such as *age, gender, intelligence,* and so on could still have an influence on the research results. Future research should also take these variables into consideration by using a stratified random sample to ensure the representativeness of the different strata in the study and to enhance the population validity of the study.

case study g (qualitative reporting)

Discussion: As appears from Table G2 (page 317), the four themes that were identified by means of qualitative analysis are: fear of contracting HIV/AIDS, discriminatory behaviour towards HIV/AIDS patients, experiencing stress when nursing HIV/AIDS patients, and experiencing mixed feelings or emotions (that is, doubt, fear, sympathy, empathy, and uncertainty).

As far as fear of contracting HIV/AIDS is concerned, the risk of becoming infected through accidental exposure was of great concern to the respondents. The theme of fear appeared consistently in responses (70% of all the respondents). Although younger nurses were better educated to deal with HIV/AIDS patients, the fear of infection was still higher amongst them in comparison to older nurses (40% versus 30%). Nurses were more protected when approaching these patients although it seems that older nurses reacted with limited interpersonal reaction when nursing HIV/AIDS patients.

It appears from the interviews that discriminatory behaviour towards patients prevailed in both groups (25% of the young nurses and 15% of the older ones). It seems that younger nurses were more discriminatory in their behaviour than older ones. In accordance with Devine (1995) it was found that the discriminatory behaviour amongst the nurses consists of categorising HIV/AIDS patients as the outgroup and as a high-risk, dangerous group that should be nursed in isolation. By labelling HIV/AIDS patients as the outgroup, these nurses reported that they felt safer.

Eighty per cent (80%) of the respondents experienced stress when nursing HIV/AIDS patients. This led to neglect of duties amongst nurses, a tendency to withdraw from HIV/AIDS patients, and loss of interest and commitment to their work. A larger number of younger nurses experienced stress (45% of them) than older nurses (35%).

All the respondents reported mixed feelings when nursing HIV/AIDS patients. These conflicting feelings contribute to the stress of working with HIV/AIDS patients. Although the level of concern for personal risk of infection was perceived as high, strong ethical obligations to treat patients and responsibility towards these patients were expressed.

Conclusion: Nurses, irrespective of age, projected a negative attitude towards nursing HIV/AIDS patients. However, older nurses were less negative than younger nurses. It was expected that older nurses would display a more negative attitude towards HIV/AIDS patients than younger nurses, as younger nurses have a more intensive theoretical background regarding the HIV virus. It seems that older nurses may have adequate coping strategies related to stress and prejudiced behaviour due to their years of experience. It seems that nursing training programmes may have focused on the knowledge component of HIV/AIDS; however, according to this study, the focus needs to be directed towards educational interventions that will help to address and deter negative attitudes. Further research is therefore needed to assess the course work of nurses.

Once we have written the conclusion and discussion sections of a research report, we can write its abstract (see Section 10.3.2). For this reason you can now do Activity 10.2.

ACTIVITY 10.2

Read the answers given above together with Case Studies A, B, C, D, E, F, and G in Appendix D on page 306.

QUESTION

Write an abstract of not more than 120 words of each report (taking the answers to Activity 10.1 above into account).

ANSWER

case study a

The results of an investigation into attitudes towards and knowledge of AIDS in a group of 74 South African health professionals are described. The researchers attempted to determine the degree to which attitudes towards AIDS correlate with knowledge of AIDS, and the degree to which such attitudes correlate with attitudes towards the sexual practices of a high-risk group, namely prostitutes. It appears that attitudes towards AIDS correlate more significantly with attitudes towards prostitution than with knowledge of AIDS. The implications are that educational programmes in South Africa should also focus on prostitution, and particularly on their sexual practices, if more objective attitudes towards AIDS are to be brought about.

case study b

The effect of a role induction procedure on goldsmith apprentices was investigated by means of a 10-minute video summary of Bernard's (1979) supervision model. The role induction procedure was applied to 20 apprentices on three occasions during their training period. The apprentices' attitudes towards the supervision process were evaluated by means of a self-description scale. Results showed that apprentices evaluated supervision more negatively in the period after role induction than before the role induction.

case study c

In order to evaluate a training course for first-line supervisors regarding their knowledge of management principles, a research design consisting of an experimental and control group was used. The sample consisted of 40 first-line supervisors at a South African agricultural corporation who were randomly drawn from a population of 60. The subjects' knowledge of management principles was measured with an hour-long written test before and after the training. The course significantly improved the knowledge of supervisors in the experimental group, while the control group's knowledge remained constant.

case study d

The relationship between preparation and performance in public speech-making was investigated by videotaping the speeches of 49 students from four technikons who had completed seven speech-making assignments. Speech quality was rated on a five-point scale and its relationship with the subjects' preparation time (measured as the total number of minutes spent on different activities) and degree of anxiety (measured on an existing 21-item self-evaluation questionnaire) was calculated using the product moment correlation. Speech quality and preparation time had a high positive correlation, while anxiety did not show a relationship to speech quality. It appears, therefore, that with a group of technikon students there is a positive strong relationship between preparation and performance in public speech-making.

case study e

This research investigates whether bankrupt small businesses in Tshwane (formerly Pretoria) exceeded their bank overdrafts limits significantly, and experienced more cash flow problems than non-bankrupt small businesses during a two-year period. Thirty-six bankrupt and 36 non-bankrupt small businesses indicated their bank overdraft usage and the extent to which they experienced cash flow problems on a questionnaire. The results showed that bankrupt small businesses exceeded their bank overdraft limits significantly and experienced serious cash flow problems. Future research should use a more representative South African sample.

case study f

The purpose of the investigation was to compare the innovative problem-solving styles of entrepreneurs and managers of big businesses. An accidental sample of 222 business people was used, consisting of 112 entrepreneurs and 110 managers. The level of innovation of the respondents was measured using the KAI scale. According to the results, the entrepreneurs obtained a significantly higher mean on the KAI than the managers. The research hypothesis can be accepted as true, but the sampling did not take into account the different strata, and the sample was not representative. Consequently, one cannot confidently generalise the results in respect of all business people in South Africa.

case study g	pling. As far as the results are concerned, four important
The purpose of this qualitative explorative study was to establish the attitudes of nurses towards HIV/AIDS patients and whether there exists a difference between the attitudes of older and younger nurses. A qualitative case study design was used and the data were collected by means of unstructured in-depth interviews. Twenty respondents were selected by means of purposive sam-	themes were identified by means of qualitative analysis: fear of contracting AIDS; discriminatory behaviour; stress; and mixed feelings such as doubt, fear, sympathy, and empathy. It seems that nurses' attitudes towards patients were more negative than positive and that younger nurses were much more negatively inclined towards patients than older nurses.

10.3.9 The list of references

A research report should include a **list of the sources** (see Section 3.4) to which reference is made in the report. The purpose of the list is to enable the reader to consult these sources. Only sources that have been consulted and that have been referred to directly in the report, should appear in this list.

In textbooks, such lists are often substituted by bibliographies in which it is permissible also to list sources that have not been cited directly but that may have influenced the author's way of thinking.

There are different systems according to which the list of references may be compiled and none of them is necessarily more correct than the others. However, the important point is that whichever system we choose, we should apply it consistently (see Chapter 3).

10.3.10 Appendices or annexures

Material such as tests, questionnaires, and stimulus materials designed specifically for the research project and that may detract from the main line of thought of the report, may be placed in **one or more appendices** immediately after the list of references.

These materials are made available to enable other researchers to evaluate the research project properly and even to replicate it, if they should care to do so. Due to the restriction on their length, journal articles generally prefer to avoid appendices. Usually, a note is included for the benefit of readers, indicating where material or apparatus used in the study may be obtained (for example from the author).

Nonetheless, the research report should form a self-contained source in itself so that it should not be necessary for readers to consult the appendices or even the author(s) themselves to gain clarity on the methods and procedures used. As indicated (see Section 10.3.8), a few examples of items of a self-developed questionnaire, for instance, should be given in the procedures section.

10.4 Conventions, grammar, and style

10.4.1 Conventions

We can follow several conventions when we write a research report. Although it is not necessarily incorrect to deviate from such conventions, adherence to them does suggest a measure of insight. Moreover, it facilitates the editing of articles that are accepted for publication and displays courtesy towards the editor.

(a) Headings and titles

In a journal article section titles (such as "Participants") usually appear on the left-hand side of the page and section headings (such as "Method and Procedure") in the centre of the text. In the case of dissertations and theses it will be presented as shown in the example box on the next page.

EXAMPLE   **ACADEMIC JOURNAL ARTICLE**

THE INTERRELATIONSHIP BETWEEN JOB SATISFACTION AND ACADEMIC
ACHIEVEMENT OF DISTANCE EDUCATION STUDENTS

JC WELMAN & PA BASSON

ABSTRACT

In terms of the ....
....

The aim of this study .... etc.

Experiential learning

There appear to be ....
.... etc.

METHOD AND PROCEDURE

Participants
One hundred students .... etc.

EXAMPLE   **DISSERTATION/THESIS**

CHAPTER 2

LITERATURE REVIEW

2.1 Experiential learning .... etc.

(b) Person, voice, and tense

It is customary to use the past tense when we describe the research of previous researchers and the procedures they used, and when we discuss the results and implications of the research on which we report.

(c) Abbreviations

When such a name or word appears for the first time, we should write it out in full and place its abbreviation between brackets (parentheses) immediately following it. Compare the use of the abbreviation for Statistics South Africa (Stats SA) in Section 7.7.

(d) Gender

The use of male nouns and pronouns when both sexes are referred to is seriously discouraged. Usually this problem may be avoided by using the plural form.

FOR EXAMPLE Instead of saying:

> *After each individual has completed his or her questionnaire.*

we may write:

> *After all individuals have completed their questionnaires.*

When our intention is indeed to emphasise individuality, *he or she* or *him or her* may be used, provided that this is done sparingly and preferably not more than once or twice in the same sentence. In all contexts in which males are referred to as men (rather than gentlemen), females should be referred to as women (rather than ladies).

10.4.2 Grammar and style

(a) Accuracy

Remember that the scientific approach requires accuracy, also as far as writing of the research report is concerned. Regardless of how ingenious or creative researchers may be in planning and executing their research, if they are not capable of conveying its importance and implications to the scientific community, they cannot do justice to their research. Editors may edit a manuscript so that it is grammatically correct. However, if there is something amiss with the content, there may be no way of detecting it.

(b) Clear yet concise

When we write the report on the completed research, we should bear in mind that the meaningfulness and appropriateness of the entire research project will be judged solely on the basis of the report.

Apart from all the grammatical rules and conventions, the most important aspects to bear in mind when committing anything to paper are:

▶ accuracy
▶ optimal clarity
▶ unambiguity.

Keep sentences as short as possible. This will make the text more readable and reduce the chances of ambiguity. Sentences with more than 30 words should preferably be shortened. This can be done by either rephrasing the text or by breaking the sentence up into two shorter sentences.

On the other hand, short staccato-like sentences may be adequate in only the most simple material. Where appropriate, the length of sentences should thus preferably be varied. Moreover, the use of short sentences may go a long way in achieving clarity, but may not prevent ambiguity entirely.

As soon as a sentence has to be read more than once to determine its meaning, it is usually an indication that it should be rewritten.

NOTE: Good advice is to file the report for at least a week after it has been completed before rereading it.

(c) Logical flow

There should be a logical train of thought from one sentence to the next and from one paragraph to the next.

FOR EXAMPLE It is advisable to vary the choice of words. Instead of saying:

> *…A has found something, B has found something, C has found something,…*

we can replace the word *found* with words such as *maintain, suggest,* or whichever best conveys the author's contribution.

It may be worthwhile to take note of the manner in which the news media alternate the word *beat* (in *the one team beat another* at whatever margin) with *thrash, defeat,* and so on, when they report sports results.

The contents of a paragraph should preferably focus on a single idea, but paragraphs containing a single sentence should be avoided. An exception occurs when different points are enumerated, each of which is regarded as important enough to warrant a separate paragraph.

(d) Adjectives and adverbs

Adjectives and adverbs such as *only* should appear next to the word or phrase to which they refer. Thus, in the following two sentences almost opposite meanings are conveyed by placing this word in different positions:

It took only five minutes to complete the first test.

It took five minutes to complete the first test only.

When pronouns such as *this*, *that*, *these*, *those*, and *there* are used, it should be clear what their referents are. Consider the following:

A correlation was computed between the violence ratings of workers' favourite television programmes and their aggressiveness.

From this formulation it is not clear whether the second variable was the aggressiveness of the television programmes or the aggressiveness of the workers. One way to avoid this problem would be to replace *their* with the word *workers'*.

Publication manuals generally recommend that *while* should not be used as a synonym for *although*, *whereas*, *and* or *but*, but that it should be restricted to references to time.

10.5 Evaluation criteria for a research report

In Table 10.2 we provide a brief collection of questions in terms of which researchers may evaluate their research reports. This checklist mainly draws on Tuckman (1990) and Zuber-Skerritt (1998). In respect of each of these questions, scores may be assigned where appropriate, as shown in the table on pages 294–295.

Table 10.2 Evaluation criteria for a research report

Key to score:

N	Not applicable
1	Unacceptable and leaves much room for improvement
2	Has much merit; leaves a little room for improvement
3	As good as possible

Checklist questions	Scores			
The title:	N	1	2	3
• is a true reflection of the contents of the report. • is not too long, yet descriptive. • contains the important variables.				
The statement of the problem:	N	1	2	3
• is formulated clearly and understandably. • is formulated adequately in terms of defined concepts relevant to the topic and field of study. • does not relate to something trivial, but is of scientific, theoretical, and/or practical significance (so that it holds the prospect of an expansion of subject knowledge). • clearly describes the theory, practical problem or previous research from which it proceeds logically. • explicitly sets out different points of view and assumptions.				

The statement of the problem (continued):	N	1	2	3
• is congruent with the title as well as the aim of the study (addresses the same issue/s). • culminates in research hypotheses or research questions which are formulated clearly in terms of the relationship between the important variables.				
The literature review:	N	1	2	3
• is relevant to the aim and problem statement of the study. • is sufficiently comprehensive and uses essential information sources. • offers a logically organised and integrated summary (in the researcher's own words, of course). • notes theories relevant to the aim of the study. • presents previous research technically correctly and provides justified criticisms of flaws in it.				
The research design:	N	1	2	3

• is appropriate for the problem in question (survey or experimental or case study design, and so on).
• is described clearly in respect of the following aspects (so that it is replicable):
  i) sampling procedures (so that, for example the experimentally accessible population is clear);
  ii) the way in which the respondents will be classified or the participants are to be assigned to groups; and
  iii) interventions (if appropriate) and/or measuring instruments administered to subjects.
• takes care of threats to internal validity (for example nuisance and third variable problems, pre-existing differences between groups, and so on).
• takes care of threats to external validity (for example the generalisability of the results from the sample to the target population and/or to other situations, and so on).				

The measuring instrument's:	N	1	2	3
• contents are described briefly. • administering and/or data-collection procedures are described. • reliability is discussed. • validity is discussed.				
The analytical/statistical techniques:	N	1	2	3
• are appropriate for the given problem (descriptive and/or inferential). • have been applied properly.				
The results:	N	1	2	3
• are clearly and properly presented. • are interpreted correctly.				
The discussion:	N	1	2	3
• provides necessary and valid interpretations and conclusions. • covers appropriate and reasonable theoretical and/or practical implications. • is unbiased and considers whether or not alternative explanations of the obtained results are appropriate. • takes unforeseen restrictions on the internal and external validity into consideration.				

The write-up of the report in its entirety:	N	1	2	3
• follows a logical structure and train of thought. • is concise without being ambiguous or foregoing clarity and readability.				

SUMMARY

As indicated in this Chapter, a research report should have a clear, simple writing style and clearly defined sections so that the reader of the report finds all the information readily accessible. Spelling and grammatical errors should be avoided.

TEST YOURSELF

Question 1: Self-evaluation question

(Some answers appear in Appendix A on page 299.)

1.1 Evaluate any research article published in any professional journal in the human behavioural sciences in terms of the checklist given in Table 10.2. An article (Welman & Basson, 1995) is hereby provided for this exercise.

APPENDIX

THE INTERRELATIONSHIP BETWEEN THE WORK EXPERIENCE OF DISTANCE EDUCATION STUDENTS, JOB SATISFACTION, AND ACADEMIC ACHIEVEMENT

JC WELMAN & PA BASSON

In terms of the cooperative education strategy of technikons, students are expected to do subject-relevant work in the industry/commerce to gain practical experience. The degree of subject-relevant work performed by 166 distance education students, and the way in which this is related to their academic performance, was investigated. It was found that, in contrast to older Afrikaans- and English-speaking male students, it was mainly students who speak a black language who did not gain subject-relevant work experience, had minimal job satisfaction, and did not earn high marks in the third-year subject (Organisational Behaviour). It is suggested that the State integrates the issues of work provision, education, and training for the success of cooperative education in South Africa.

INTRODUCTION

The aim of this study, supported by the background provided by the various perspectives on cooperative education, is to explore and confirm the implications of cooperative education for third-year students studying *via* distance education at technikons.

If the goal of cooperative education is to equip the student to attain occupational competence and economic independence, how is this goal accomplished in distance education, where the academic institution is not in a position to offer real work experience?

Given the differences that exist between cooperative and non-cooperative jobs and their relation to achieving learning objectives (Stern, Stone, Hopkins, McMillion & Cagampang, 1992), and keeping in mind that there are many elements in the cooperative experience that are vital to success (Laycock, Hermon & Laetz, 1992), the question arises as to how the participation of the academic institution in cooperative education will be affected if students are unemployed or hold non-cooperative jobs. Examined in more detail: how will the employed student's extent of academic subject-related work experience (Kaupins & Warberg, 1992) and job satisfaction influence his or her academic achievement?

PERSPECTIVES ON COOPERATIVE EDUCATION

There appear to be different perspectives concerning cooperative education in South Africa (Du Plessis, 1994). These are as follows:

1. The student and industry are partners alongside each other on a horizontal plane, with the academic institution playing some part in preparing the student for efficient service.
2. There is a symmetrical relationship between the student (the important partner), the academic institution, and the student's employer.
3. The State, as a fourth partner, acts as mediator for industry/commerce and the academic institution with the aim of ensuring that each individual has knowledge about the manufacturing process.
4. The academic institution helps to bring about contact between the student and employer.

According to Du Plessis (1994), the role of the academic institution in the first three perspectives mentioned above is limited to the period of academic training and culminates in the delivery of the career-mature student as an employee to industry/commerce. It is only in the last (fourth) perspective mentioned that the academic institution fulfils its contribution to cooperative education.

In ascertaining whether the academic institution satisfies the expectations of the market (Coldstream, 1988), graduation rates (progress, drop out, and completion rates), overall placement rates (employability), and career achievement of graduates can be used as indicators. The employer's role in this process is, *inter alia*, to provide job descriptions, criteria, job specifications, and other requirements for inputs, processes, and outputs of the education system (Van Wyk, 1993).

PROBLEM STATEMENT AND RESEARCH HYPOTHESIS

At Technikon SA, due to the limitation that distance education places on the above-mentioned role, the onus rests on the student to make contact with (potential) employers. For that matter, it is assumed that students are employed while studying towards a specific and specialised career (Tothill, 1993a). Bearing this problem in mind, what are the implications of cooperative education within a distance education environment such as Technikon SA?

Given that the general supportive and facilitative environment of the academic institution influences what is accomplished in terms of academic, personal, and vocational gains (Davis & Murrell, 1993) and that work factors are related to the failure rate for part-time students (Snelgar, 1990), students whose jobs are not in the field in which they are studying may well not have suitable facilities in their place of work to acquire practical experience (Aslanian, 1993).

In this regard Laycock *et al.* (1992) found that the student's perception of the job is not related to his or her overall perception of the quality of the cooperative education experience. This may be so because cooperative education jobs (which are often first learning experiences in a professional setting) do not contain all the dimensions of a highly motivating position.

The perception of employees of how well their jobs provide for and meet their expectations has an effect on their attitude towards the job. Employees who are satisfied with their job may, for example, feel that they are being treated well and are being rewarded with a good salary – and so have a positive attitude towards the job (that is, the work, the boss, and/or co-workers) (Luthans, 1992).

In examining the outcomes of job satisfaction, it seems that low job satisfaction leads to high employee turnover and absenteeism, while high job satisfaction results in fewer on-the-job accidents, work grievances, and less time required to learn job-related tasks (Luthans, 1992).

THE FOLLOWING RESEARCH HYPOTHESIS WAS EXAMINED:

There is a significant positive relationship between the extent of subject-related work experience of distance education students (degree of academic subject-relatedness), job satisfaction, and academic achievement.

METHOD

SUBJECTS

One hundred and sixty-eight (168) students in Personnel Management III (Organisational Behaviour) at Technikon SA participated in the study. These students had submitted the required two out of three assignments containing exercises and questionnaires used to sample the data needed for this study. Two (2) students were unemployed and their data could not be used, since it was based on previous jobs they had held.

INSTRUMENT

In the exercises, which formed part of the assignments, the students had to complete questionnaires presented in the prescribed book by Luthans (1992). One of these questionnaires was used as an instrument in this study, namely the Minnesota Satisfaction Questionnaire (MSQ), on which the students rated the extent to which they are satisfied with various aspects of their present job.

THE MINNESOTA SATISFACTION QUESTIONNAIRE

The Minnesota Satisfaction Questionnaire (MSQ) is a rating scale for measuring job satisfaction. The rating scale used in this study is a short form of the MSQ consisting of 20 items, that is, the items with the highest factor loadings on each of the 20 subscales of the MSQ. It provides a detailed picture of the specific satisfactions and dissatisfactions of employees (Luthans, 1992).

The MSQ measures satisfaction and dissatisfaction with ability utilisation, achievement, activity, advancement, authority, company policies and practices, compensation, co-workers, creativity, independence, moral values, recognition, responsibility, security, social service, social status, supervision – human relations, supervision – technical, variety, and working conditions (Gillet & Schwab, 1975).

Gillet and Schwab (1975) reported validity coefficients (by using multitrait-multimethod analysis) of four scales of the MSQ ranging from 0,49 to 0,70 (Kerlinger, 1986, p. 424, describes a value of 0,53 as "fairly substantial"). Using a South African sample of 1 791 professional people, Kaplan (1990) examined the validity of the instrument and found the factors of the short-form MSQ to be conceptually meaningful and distinct. Kaplan reported a reliability coefficient of 0,90 for the sum of the 20 items.

Since the instrument was administered only once in the present study, it was decided to examine the reliability of the instrument (its accuracy or precision) by means of Cronbach's alpha coefficient. This method was used to determine the internal consistency of the instrument (the homogeneity of the 20 items of the instrument).

Unfortunately the construct validity of the instrument could not be determined by way of factor analysis because the sample size was too small (Kerlinger, 1986).

PROCEDURE

ACADEMIC ACHIEVEMENT

All Personnel Management III students at Technikon SA were required to complete two of three assignments (consisting of case studies and exercises). If a student submitted all three assignments, the two highest marks were used to calculate the average which represented the student's year mark. A student had to obtain a minimum of 40% to write the two open book examinations (comprising a case study problem to be solved with the help of the prescribed textbook) in November 1993. The final mark was calculated (as indicated in the Calendar of Technikon SA) as the sum of 40% of the year mark and 60% of the examination mark.

CRITERION GROUPS

The students were categorised into nine (9) groups according to how closely their area of work experience was related to the academic subject area (Organisational Behaviour). This was done by comparing the extent to which the aspects covered by the syllabus for Organisational Behaviour were present in the student's job title and work experience (the exercises that the students had to do as part of their assignments consisted, *inter alia*, of writing down their present job title and what work they were doing).

THE SYLLABUS OF THE SUBJECT ORGANISATIONAL BEHAVIOUR COMPRISES THE FOLLOWING UNITS:

Introduction to organisational behaviour; Job satisfaction; Motivation; Change in organisational behaviour; Informal organisation; Conflict; Leadership; Communication; Decision-making; Organisational development.

The rated area of work experience of group 9 was closely related to the syllabus content of the subject Organisational Behaviour and involved management and administration of organisational behaviour, while the rated area of work experience of group 1 was not related at all (it involved no participation in or experience of organisational behaviour). A typical member of group 9 would be the Personnel Manager in charge of organisational development in a big corporate organisation, while a night watchman is a good example of a member of group 1. The distribution of participants according to this rating is presented in Table 1.

Table 1 Distribution (frequency) of the students in terms of subject-related work experience

	Work experience group									
	1	2	3	4	5	6	7	8	9	Total
Number of students	19	32	39	17	31	12	11	3	1	166
Percentage of total	11	19	23	10	19	8	7	2	1	100

STATISTICAL TECHNIQUES

Descriptive statistics (frequency distributions, central tendency, and variability) were used to compile a student profile. The Product Moment Correlation was used to examine the relationship between the variables and to establish whether the hypothesis was acceptable (Huysamen, 1990).

Cronbach's coefficient alpha was used to examine the reliability of the Minnesota Satisfaction Questionnaire (MSQ). The computer package SPSS for Windows (release 6.0) was used for the calculations.

RESULTS

To construct a student profile, the following variables with alpha codes and values were included in the study:

AGE: Age group of the student at enrollment for the subject (0 = 17–23 yrs, 1 = 24–30 yrs, 2 = 31–44 yrs, 3 = 45+ yrs)

SEX: Sex of the student (0 = female, 1 = male)

LANGUAGE: Home language of student (0 = Afrikaans, 1 = English, 2 = Other, 3 = North Sotho, 4 = South Sotho, 5 = Swazi, 6 = Tsonga, 7 = Tswana, 8 = Venda, 9 = Xhosa, 10 = Zulu)

Values for the item choices of the Minnesota Satisfaction Questionnaire (MSQ) were coded as follows: "Very dissatisfied" was assigned the value 1, and items ranged as far as "Very satisfied", which was assigned the value 5. The minimum and maximum scores that any respondent could obtain were 20 and 100 respectively.

MEANS AND STANDARD DEVIATIONS

Table 2 shows that students in the subject-related work experience groups (groups 5 to 9) obtained relative high marks in the subject. It seems that the older students and more male than female students had more closely subject-related work experience (groups 6 to 9).

From Table 2 it seems that the majority of students in all language groups except Afrikaans and English had work experience not closely related to the academic subject (groups 1 to 3).

Table 2 indicates that the students with the more academic subject-related work experience had a higher degree of job satisfaction.

In brief, the means and standard deviations of the variables presented in Table 2 show that students with closely subject-related work experience obtained higher marks in the academic subject, are older, male, tend to be Afrikaans- and English-speaking, and experience a high degree of job satisfaction.

Table 2 Group means and standard deviations of variables

			Variables				
Group	*n*		MARK	AGE	SEX	LANG	SATS
1	(19)	$\overline{X}$	47,42	1,00	0,58	4,42	66,26
		s	19,59	0,58	0,51	4,02	14,51
2	(32)	$\overline{X}$	53,00	1,09	0,50	1,38	73,84
		s	15,91	0,53	0,51	2,54	13,09
3	(39)	$\overline{X}$	53,13	1,49	0,64	1,90	73,18
		s	10,38	0,68	0,49	2,86	14,18

Group	n		Variables MARK	AGE	SEX	LANG	SATS
4	(17)	$\overline{X}$	56,88	1,53	0,76	1,41	72,41
		s	6,53	0,80	0,44	2,69	17,49
5	(31)	$\overline{X}$	58,32	2,03	0,71	1,41	75,77
		s	7,73	0,66	0,46	2,61	14,63
6	(13)	$\overline{X}$	58,31	2,08	0,85	0,77	74,62
		s	9,35	0,86	0,38	2,20	13,40
7	(11)	$\overline{X}$	61,18	2,09	0,91	0,27	73,00
		s	10,78	0,70	0,30	0,47	12,73
8	(3)	$\overline{X}$	55,67	2,33	0,67	0,33	90,67
		s	13,50	0,58	0,58	0,58	6,43
9	(1)	$\overline{X}$	73,00	2,00	1,00	0,00	65,00
		s	0,00	0,00	0,00	0,00	0,00
Total	166	$\overline{X}$	54,91	1,56	0,67	1,72	73,29
		s	12,68	0,77	0,47	2,89	14,37

$\overline{X}$ (read "X-bar") is the symbol representing the arithmetic mean, or average, of the sample (n).

s is the symbol representing the standard deviation expressed in the same units as those of the original measurements.

n is the symbol representing the group size.

CORRELATION MATRIX

The intercorrelation matrix presented in Table 3 confirms what was shown in Table 2 and indicates that there is a positive relationship between the rated work experience (degree of academic subject-relatedness), job satisfaction, and academic achievement. It also shows that students who experience high job satisfaction obtained higher marks in the academic subject.

Table 3 Intercorrelations between all variables in the study

Variable	MARK	AGE	SEX	LANG	SATS
GROUP	0,29°°	0,51°°	0,22°°	−0,28°°	0,14°°
MARK		0,11	0,00	−0,39°°	0,18°°
AGE			0,24°°	−0,09	0,03
SEX				−0,03	0,03
LANG					−0,22°°

°$p<0,05$ for one-tailed significance.
°°$p<0,05$ for two-tailed significance.

RELIABILITY OF THE MEASURING INSTRUMENT

An alpha coefficient of 0,9233 for the Minnesota Satisfaction Questionnaire (MSQ) was found. Each of the 20 items contributes not less than a coefficient of 0,9169.

CONCLUSION

There is a positive relationship between the rated work experience (degree of academic subject-relatedness) of students studying *via* distance education, job satisfaction, and academic achievement.

The cooperative education experience differs for the rated different work experiences and thus different employers. This makes a cooperative education programme (where administrators and placement staff of the academic institution perform support functions in developing practical experiences for students) invaluable if cooperative education is to succeed as an educational strategy in South Africa or any other part of the world.

From the research results it seems clear that a student who had work experience that is closely subject-related obtains a high mark in that academic subject and experiences a high degree of job satisfaction. However, it seems that it is mostly older, male, Afrikaans-speaking and English-speaking (home language) students who had the closest subject-related work experience.

Young black-language speaking students therefore need subject-related work experience opportunities.

In order for students to make a link between theory and practice, cooperative education is the answer. Academic institutions are, of course, obliged to ensure the vocational relevance of their courses (Tothill, 1993b), but if organisations (potential employers) continue to scale down and/or restrict their recruitment to "experienced" candidates in order to be internationally competitive in the short term, cooperative education in South Africa will not succeed.

Policy decisions about the practical role of industry/commerce in employing students who have no work experience must be considered a priority by the Government of the "new South Africa". In this regard it may be necessary to stipulate the role of the academic institution (in conjunction with the State department of Manpower) in having the power to, and taking the responsibility for the administration (or coordination) of the placement of students, in legislation. Perhaps an amalgamation of the areas of employment, education, and training into a single State department of "Higher Education and Employment Services" is the answer.

REFERENCES

Aslanian, C.B. (1993). Organizations as students – the challenge for education. *Industry and Higher Education*, **7**(2), 98–103.

Coldstream, P. (1988). Industry finds its voice – and higher education an unexpected ally. *Higher Education Quarterly*, **42**(4), 370–377.

Davis, T.M. & Murrell, P.H. (1993). A structural model of perceived academic, personal, and vocational gains related to college student responsibility. *Research in Higher Education*, **34**(3), 267–289.

Du Plessis, W.S. (1994). Die ko-operatiewe onderwysstrategie. *Suid-Afrikaanse Tydskrif vir Hoër Onderwys*, **8**(1), 57–60.

Gillet, B. & Schwab, D. P. (1975). Convergent and discriminant validities of corresponding Job Descriptive Index and Minnesota Satisfaction Questionnaire scales. *Journal of Applied Psychology*, **60**(3), 313–317.

Huysamen, G.K. (1990). *Introductory statistics and research design for the behavioural sciences: Volume I* (2nd ed.). Cape Town: H&R Academica.

Kaplan, R.A.L. (1990). The career anchors, job involvement and job satisfaction of professional people. Unpublished doctoral thesis, University of Cape Town, Cape Town.

Kaupins, G. & Warberg, W. (1992). Course prerequisites for personnel cooperative education students. *Journal of Cooperative Education*, **28**(1), 48–55.

Kerlinger, F.N. (1986). *Foundations of behavioral research* (3rd ed.). New York: CBS Publishing.

Laycock, A.B., Hermon, M.V. & Laetz, V. (1992). Cooperative education: Key factors related to a quality experience. *Journal of Cooperative Education*, **27**(3), 36–46.

Luthans, F. (1992). *Organizational behavior* (6th ed.). New York: McGraw-Hill.

Snelgar, R. J. (1990). Stress and the part-time student: Work factors associated with failure rate. *South African Journal of Psychology*, **20**(1), 42–46.

Stern, D., Stone, J.R., Hopkins, C., McMillion, M. & Cagampang, H. (1992). Quality of work experience as perceived by two-year college students in co-op and non-co-op jobs. *Journal of Cooperative Education*, **28**(1), 34–47.

Tothill, A. (1993a). Distance education in the workplace. *People Dynamics*, **11**(8), 27–32.

Tothill, A. (1993b). Higher education and employment in the OECD: Lessons for South Africa? *Africa 2001*, **2**(1), 40–45.

Van Wyk, J.J. (1993). The role of the employer in curriculum development and quality assurance. *Pro Technida* (Port Elizabeth Technikon), **10**(2), 51–64.

The research proposal

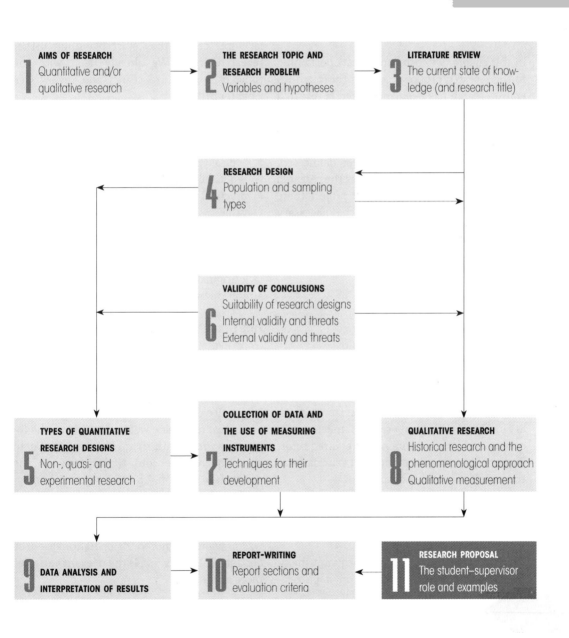

1 AIMS OF RESEARCH
Quantitative and/or qualitative research

2 THE RESEARCH TOPIC AND RESEARCH PROBLEM
Variables and hypotheses

3 LITERATURE REVIEW
The current state of knowledge (and research title)

4 RESEARCH DESIGN
Population and sampling types

6 VALIDITY OF CONCLUSIONS
Suitability of research designs
Internal validity and threats
External validity and threats

5 TYPES OF QUANTITATIVE RESEARCH DESIGNS
Non-, quasi- and experimental research

7 COLLECTION OF DATA AND THE USE OF MEASURING INSTRUMENTS
Techniques for their development

8 QUALITATIVE RESEARCH
Historical research and the phenomenological approach
Qualitative measurement

9 DATA ANALYSIS AND INTERPRETATION OF RESULTS

10 REPORT-WRITING
Report sections and evaluation criteria

11 RESEARCH PROPOSAL
The student–supervisor role and examples

LEARNING OUTCOMES

Between conceptualising a specific research project and conducting the research it is often, in fact, almost always, required that we draw up a research proposal. This should be done in order to meet the requirements of a tertiary institution or to obtain funding for the project.

After studying this chapter, you will be able to:
- plan a research project
- list the sections of a research proposal
- write a research proposal relevant to your study field.

11.1 Introduction

In this chapter we focus on aspects pertaining to the research proposal. After a thorough literature search has been conducted, a research topic is identified. Ideally research on this topic should add value to the existing literature and should be topical.

Once the research area has been delineated, we can proceed with the design of the research project. In designing a research project there are various aspects to which the necessary attention should be paid. These include the following:
- variables – independent, dependent, and nuisance variables
- sampling procedures
- collection of data
- measurement instruments
- statistical analysis of the results.

Once this stage has been completed, a research proposal can be compiled either for funding purposes or to obtain permission from a tertiary institution. The proposal must meet certain criteria and should contain the required information. These requirements and criteria form the main focus of this chapter.

11.2 Requirements of a research topic

Prospective researchers should acquaint themselves with previous research on a particular topic before they start planning further research on it. We already dealt with the topic of a literature search and review (see Chapter 3).

The research topic should meet the following requirements:
- originality
- topicality (actuality)
- replicability
- practical feasibility
- value-free topics.

(a) Originality

We could easily recognise that some topics lack originality in that they immediately elicit a reaction of "So what?"

FOR EXAMPLE Consider the difference in psychological adjustment of individuals whose bedroom windows face north and south respectively.

Previous research projects are seldom repeated in practice unless there is convincing evidence to suggest that there was something methodologically wrong with them. However, researchers frequently set out to **improve** on the design (see Section 4.3.5) or statistical analysis (see Section 9.4) of previous researchers. Rather than simply duplicating these projects, they may examine the role of a variable that was previously ignored, or operationalise (see Sections 2.4, 6.1 & 6.2.4) the relevant variables more adequately.

FOR EXAMPLE We have shown (see Section 6.2.3.3) how the findings of one project on the relationship between television-viewing and feelings of safety were put in a totally different perspective by an investigation in which the residential area of the participants was taken into consideration.

We can also consider repeating a research project on a different population. Technically speaking, this does not result in a simple duplication, but might lack originality.

Especially in the case of doctoral research, the prospective research is usually required to represent a meaningful contribution to the particular field of study. Doctoral students, in particular, should realise that using a research problem suggested by a lecturer provides less room for demonstrating originality.

NOTE: A word of caution: if you plan a project with an overly grandiose scope, the chances are that it may prove to be practically unfeasible (compare the requirement of practical feasibility), or you may have to abandon it for some or other reason. The topic should preferably be sufficiently limited in scope without being trivial (compare the requirement of topicality).

(b) Topicality (actuality)

Research is often undertaken simply because data collected for another purpose (typically psychometric test data) are available. The research topic is then formulated to fit the available data, rather than the other way around. The problem with such pre-existing data sets is that data on key variables necessary for investigating topical and interesting problems may be lacking. As a result, the researcher is restricted to the available information, a situation that may be likened to putting the cart before the horse.

Formulating hypotheses and questions of scientific merit require **experience** and a **sound knowledge** of research development in the area involved. As a superficial indication of the topicality of the proposed research, the dates of the references (see Section 3.4) are often checked to determine how recent the majority of them are. Naturally, not all references need to be of a recent publication date.

(c) Replicability

The core feature of scientific research is its **controllability** or **replicability**. By this we mean that future researchers should be able to repeat the proposed research administering the same operationalised variables (see Sections 2.4, 6.1 & 6.2.3) to a new sample from the same population (see Section 4.2). In some cases the intervention (see Section 5.2) cannot be recreated on purpose, for example earthquakes, the El Niño effect, the collapse of the share markets (stock exchanges) or riots. In such an event, however, the data collected originally should be available for possible re-analysis (see Section 9.4).

(d) Practical feasibility

When we choose a research topic for a master's degree or doctorate, certain practical considerations should be taken into account.

- **Feasibility**. The problem should preferably not be so comprehensive that it cannot be investigated in a single project. It is often advisable to study only a single aspect of an extensive research problem.

    FOR EXAMPLE It would have been impossible to investigate Latané and Darley's research into the helping behaviour of bystanders (Research Example VI, see Section 6.2.4.1, page 118).

- **Sample**. A sufficiently large sample of the required subjects should be available without incurring exorbitant costs.

    FOR EXAMPLE It would be impractical to compare a large group of South African companies over 50 years in existence with a control group if only a few such companies are readily available to the prospective researcher.

- **Time**. We should be certain that we can complete the proposed research within the time available or permitted. Obviously, a longitudinal study (see Section 5.4.3) extending over five years would be less suitable for a master's dissertation.

Apart from the time required for the execution of a research project, the writing, technical preparation, and editing of the report (see Chapters 3 & 8) usually require much more time than we originally anticipate.

▶ **Costs**. We should budget for costs that will be incurred by the following:
- hiring staff (research assistants, typist)
- the procurement of the necessary literature (computer searches, photocopying, translating in the case of sources in foreign languages)
- the purchase or even development of apparatus (for operationalising variables)
- telephone accounts (in telephone surveys)
- travelling expenses (for visiting participants)
- computer time and translation (if applicable)
- duplication and binding of the report (project report, dissertation or thesis).

▶ **Ethical considerations**. We must also consider the feasibility of the proposed project in the light of possible ethical objections (see Section 7.9) and the prevailing political climate.

▶ **Personal factors**. Finally, we should take into consideration our own preferences, training, skills, and limitations. It would serve little purpose to select a topic with which we cannot identify and/or for which we lack the necessary training and skills.

FOR EXAMPLE If a student has no training and experience in the application of statistical methods, the choice of a topic requiring multivariate statistical techniques (see Section 9.4), may prove to be disastrous.

A researcher conducting a study on the incidence of emotional outbursts among middle-aged male managers may possibly be accused of considering the lives of middle-aged male managers of greater importance than those of middle-aged female managers.

If someone develops a programme to improve the assertiveness of disabled employees, it may be seen as an indication that this kind of behaviour is regarded as desirable.

When an application for funding is made, there are specific factors which should be taken into consideration:

▶ **Budget**. A detailed budget is required and the details regarding costs serve to convince the funding organisation that the researcher knows what is at stake and that he or she is the right person to be funded for the research. The expenditures which might be questioned, must be justified especially carefully.

▶ **Practical requirements**. It should be clear that the facilities (laboratories, apparatus, and so on) and the assistance necessary for the execution of the project, are available.

▶ **Value of research**. Furthermore, some research institutions have to be persuaded of the practical value of the eventual results so that funding will not amount to a waste of their money. They wish to be satisfied that the project will yield dividends for their expenditure. We should thus point out possible practical applications of the expected results.

▶ **Relevance of research**. In addition, we should be sure to point out how the proposed research relates to matters of interest to the funding organisation. If the funding organisation favours certain topics because of particular sociopolitical considerations, we should keep this in mind.

(e) Value-free topics

It is difficult to conceptualise instances of entirely value-free research. Values may prejudice researchers to such an extent that their ability to examine phenomena without bias is impaired.

11.3 Designing a research project

After we have identified a general research area and delineated a more limited research problem, we have to **plan** or **design** a project to investigate the relationships we postulated in the research hypothesis(es) or research question(s) (see Section 2.4). In this regard, we should bear in mind that statistical techniques (see Section 9.4), however sophisticated, cannot compensate for inept theorising (see Section 2.3.1), design flaws (such as inadequate operationalisation of variables – see Sections 2.4, 6.2 & 6.2.4) or for unsatisfactory data (see Chapters 5, 6 & 7).

(a) Statistical analysis

We could correct faulty statistical analysis (see Section 9.4) by means of re-analysis, but no statistical analysis can compensate for, or rectify the omission of key variables in the collection of data, for example. The research design (see Chapter 5) occupies a **central component** in the proposal that is planned at this stage.

(b) Defining the variables

In planning a research project, we must operationally define (see Sections 2.4, 6.2 & 6.2.4) the **relevant variables** (for example independent and dependent variables (see Section 2.3) in experimental research) and identify possible **nuisance variables** (in experimental research – see Section 5.2.1) or third variables (in survey research – see Section 6.2.3). Therefore, if we plan an experiment, we must decide which **manipulations** (interventions), if any, are required to create the independent variable appearing in the research hypothesis (see Section 2.4). As we indicated (see Section 6.2.4), it is usually desirable to consider ways in which variables have been operationalised in previous research. If the variables in the research hypothesis cannot be defined operationally, it means that the research hypothesis cannot be investigated empirically.

In the case of a single qualitative independent variable, the minimum number of levels that are required is usually dictated directly by the research hypothesis.

FOR EXAMPLE Suppose the research hypothesis states the following:

> Typists learn to type faster by means of a computer program method than with a written manual instruction method.

We have to include at least these two methods in the experiment (see Figure 11.1).

We do not determine the appropriate number of levels of a quantitative independent variable by means of the research hypothesis only, but in the light of:

▶ previous research
▶ the researcher's experience.

Kerlinger's (1986) recommendation that the variance (see Section 9.3.1) of the independent variable should be maximised is probably relevant in the case of quantitative independent variables only. In terms of this recommendation, it will be advisable to use values that are spread across the widest possible range of the quantitative scale, rather than values that are close to each other.

FOR EXAMPLE The practice schedules used in Research Example I (learning in a distributed fashion versus massed learning – see Section 1.2.1.5, page 4) should not differ in terms of hours only, but also in terms of weeks.

NOTE: It is not the role of research hypotheses to make value judgements. For instance, in Research Example I (see Section 1.2.1.5, page 4), the research hypothesis did not suggest that one practice schedule was better than another, but simply that it would result in a higher addition proficiency. Therefore, the researcher did not make any value judgements.

Refer to Figure 11.1 for an explanation of the difference between qualitative and quantitative independent variables.

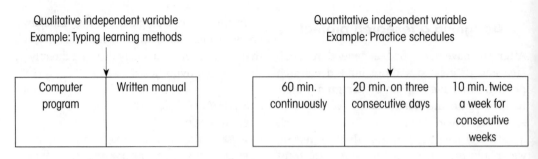

Figure 11.1 *The difference between qualitative and quantitative variables*

(c) Nuisance variables

If we should find that there are one or more nuisance variables that may be relevant in a proposed experiment, we should consider ways of **eliminating or controlling** them. In this regard, the literature survey (see Chapter 3) may suggest nuisance variables that previous researchers in the particular area have considered necessary to control as well as the method used to achieve this. In the discussion of their findings, previous researchers also may have indicated nuisance variables that should be taken care of in future research in the area involved.

As we have indicated before, there are various ways in which we can keep nuisance variables at bay, including:

- matching groups (see Section 6.2.8)
- creating blocks (see Section 9.3.2.3) of individuals who are homogeneous in terms of such variables
- randomly assigning participants:
  - to all levels of the independent variable (see Section 6.2.7) or
  - to all possible combinations of the levels of two or more independent variables (see Section 9.4).

If the research hypothesis deals with the effect of repeated exposure to a task or stimulus, such as in solitary confinement studies, and if there are no non-additive sequencing effects, the repeated measures design (see Section 9.3.2.3) may be considered to control

nuisance variables pertaining to differences among individuals.

(d) Dependent variable

If the dependent variable is a physical attribute, such as weight or blood pressure, the operational definition of its measurement does not present insurmountable problems.

However, the operational definition of the dependent variable (see Sections 2.4 & 7.3) usually does not follow directly from the research hypothesis.

There is no obvious measurement of dependent variables such as *creativity* or *leadership*. In other cases, again, there may be more than one measure of the dependent variable.

FOR EXAMPLE There are at least five methods to measure the retention of verbal learning. (The recall method, for example, requires that subjects reproduce the material they have learnt, whereas the recognition method requires them to select from among several items the one which is the response which they have learnt.)

(e) Measuring instruments

If reliable and valid measuring instruments (see Chapter 7) of the relevant variables are commercially available, we should obviously consider using them.

FOR EXAMPLE It would be unwise to construct a test of job satisfaction in view of the various job satisfaction tests currently available in South Africa. (See the list of Internet sites on page 302.)

Of course, we should ensure that the **reliability coefficients** (see Section 7.5) reported in the test manual of published tests have been determined for a group similar to the one we intend using. If we plan to use an instrument for a group for which no such information is available, the reliability of the instrument should be investigated for such a group, or for a similar one.

We should also ensure that the available instrument is valid for the purpose for which we want to use it (see Section 7.4). A measuring instrument that has been found to be valid for one particular purpose need not necessarily be valid for measuring the particular dependent variable in the research hypothesis.

If a questionnaire or attitude scale is translated from another language into English, Brislin's (1970) **backward translation procedure** is recommended. In this procedure, two people translate the material into English, independently of each other, and then two other individuals translate the resulting version back into the original language. Differences between the original and the translated versions may be eliminated through discussion.

Measuring instruments should neither be too difficult nor too easy if the intended intervention is supposed to increase or decrease scores respectively.

Suppose an instrument is too easy, so that all participants obtain relatively high scores. In this case, it may be impossible for the treatment group whose scores are intended to be raised, to obtain even higher scores than the other group(s). This phenomenon is known as the **ceiling effect**.

The **floor effect**, on the other hand, occurs when the test is so difficult that all participants obtain relatively low scores. In this case, we cannot discern any differences between groups if a group has been subjected to a treatment designed to lower scores.

11.4 The research proposal

The main objective of a research proposal is to convey the plan in terms of which our proposed research is going to be carried out clearly and unambiguously. Therefore, the two main questions that should be answered by a research proposal are:

▶ Which problem is going to be investigated?
▶ How is this problem going to be investigated?

A research proposal furthermore has the following purposes:
▶ clarifying and organising ideas
▶ convincing the audience
▶ making a contract with a "client"
▶ being practically possible.

A research proposal is obligatory, especially if researchers apply for funds from a research institution. University and technikon authorities usually require master's and doctoral students to submit a research proposal before they are permitted to begin their research.

NOTE: In all these instances, prospective applicants (researchers and students) should acquaint themselves thoroughly with the precise conditions with which their applications should comply. Often, postgraduate students do not obtain a research problem directly from theories, everyday observation or practical problems (see Section 2.3.1). A lecturer, for example, (who has obtained it directly from one of those sources) may suggest it to them.

It should be kept in mind that when a research proposal is evaluated by a funding organisation, it is done on the basis of the proposal exclusively. Considerations such as the limited time that proposal writers had at their disposal, or that the latter's competence should ensure that any problems cropping up during the research process will be dealt with, cannot be taken into consideration. The evaluators are restricted to what they have in print in front of them and this should be the deciding factor. Researchers should also bear in mind that the project will not be evaluated in terms of its good intentions (for example to eradicate poverty, and so on) but on the basis of the manner in which it intends to achieve such admirable objectives, whatever they may be.

Even if a research proposal is not required for official or formal reasons, it remains an essential element in the research process because it represents the blueprint or ground-plan for the proposed research. We can compare it to an architect's plan for the construction of a new building. The saying "well begun is half done", applies perfectly to this blueprint. Regardless of how ingeniously the plan may have been conceived and how carefully it may have been planned, it cannot anticipate all unforeseen complications.

Similar to an architect's drawing, the following aspects should be taken care of:

▶ Our aim should be so **unambiguously formulated** and detailed in the research proposal that someone else should be able to execute the proposed research without having to consult with its compiler.

▶ All questions that may possibly occur to the potential reader should be anticipated and dealt with.

As far as the requirement of explicitness is concerned, researchers planning to use one of the open designs (see Chapter 8) may be in a less favourable position than those who intend to use one of the more conventional designs (see Chapter 5).

To use the analogy of an architect's plan, such researchers in effect ask the reader to trust them, because they will decide:

▶ how deep the foundations should be dug when they have acquainted themselves with the soil formations and

▶ what the slope of the roof should be once they have learnt more about the average annual rainfall.

Since open design proposals cannot provide preliminary plans as discussed above, we can

understand why funding organisations are less inclined to provide financial support for such proposals.

Naturally, the research proposal should have a **title** that concisely yet unambiguously identifies the exact topic of the proposed research. In other words, the title should not reflect the general field of study in which the research is to be carried out, but the exact topic. In the case of experimental research, at least the independent variable (and preferably the dependent variable, too) (see Section 2.3) should be reflected in the title.

11.4.1 Sections of a research proposal

A research proposal should contain (at least) the following sections:

▶ a **background** to the study which should contain reference to the relevant research literature (see Chapter 3) as well as motivations as to the importance of the proposed research

▶ the statement or formulation of the **research problem** (hypotheses, research questions or propositions) (see Sections 2.3 & 2.4)

▶ the proposed **method** (see Chapter 7), research **design**, operationalisation of terms, procedures (see Chapter 5) and **statistical analyses** (see Section 9.4)

▶ a list of **relevant references** (see Chapter 3 and Section 10.3.9).

11.4.2 The background (scope)

The objective of the background is to inform the reader of the value of the proposed research. The importance, meaningfulness or relevance of the proposed research, in other words, the justification for the research should be spelled out clearly.

To achieve this, it may be necessary to provide a critical and analytical review of the relevant literature in which we refer briefly to the theories or research from which the intended research proceeds. If an extended literature survey has already been completed, it is sufficient to include a meaningful summary of the literature that is directly relevant to the proposed research and that will enhance understanding of the formulation of the objectives of the research project. As a guide, this section can be subdivided into the following subsections:

▶ Problem statement
▶ Purpose of the study
▶ Significance of the study
▶ Limitations of the study.

NOTE: The library is no longer our only source of information. The development of the Internet, electronic publishing and its effect on research supervision, peer review of publications, and general communications capabilities have all changed the way in which researchers work. (See the list of Internet sites on page 302.) Furthermore, most tertiary institutions have access to a wide range of databases where students can access the latest academic journals.

FOR EHAMPLE The Researchers Networking Database is published with the Nexus Database System. It contains biographical profiles of individual researchers in South Africa, including their fields of interest and areas of specialisation in the social sciences and the humanities. Visit the web site at: http://stardata.nrf.ac.za.

This will provide you with a list of experts in various fields. You can also view the TALK conference database.

11.4.3 The statement or formulation of the research problem

Here we should identify the variables (see Section 2.3) and specify the target populations (see Section 4.2).

The formulation of the research problem, research hypothesis(es) or research question(s) (or central thesis in the case of analytical studies – see Section 2.3.3 and Chapter 6) should follow from the introduction.

The problem statement may take the form of:
▶ a testable research hypothesis
FOR EHAMPLE Typists learn to type in a shorter period of time by means of Method A than by Method B.
▶ an exploratory question.
FOR EHAMPLE To investigate to what extent the top management success of junior managers may be predicted by means of matriculation achievement, intelligence, and achievement motivation.

If there is more than one research hypothesis or research question, we should state them all and clarify the rationale of each, as it arises from the concise literature survey. As we have indicated (see Section 2.4), such a hypothesis or question deals with the relationship between variables in one or more population(s) (see Section 4.2).

11.4.4 The proposed method, procedures, and statistical analysis

11.4.4.1 RESEARCH METHOD AND PROCEDURES

The research procedures by means of which we intend to investigate the stated problem should be scientifically well-founded and should describe the following aspects:
▶ the population(s) (see Section 4.2) from which the participants will be obtained
▶ the number of participants and the way in which these will be obtained
▶ the number of groups and the way in which these will be formed
▶ the way in which the data will be collected and the specifications of any apparatus (see Chapter 7) including:
  • in the case of experimental research, the manipulations (interventions – see Section 5.2.2) intended to create the independent variables (see Section 2.3)
▶ the measurement and operationalisation of the variables (see Chapter 7)
▶ the statistical methods for processing and analysing the data obtained (see Chapter 9).

The description of the above-mentioned points should clarify the way in which the proposed course of action will assist in finding answers to the formulated problem. If new or modified methods are proposed, these should be justified. It should be clear to the reader that the proposed research methods are the most appropriate for the intended research.

11.4.4.2 STATISTICAL ANALYSIS (SEE SECTION 9.4)

In respect of the statistical methods, it will not be sufficient to simply state that the data will be analysed by means of some computer program (for example SPSS, BMDP, SAS or MoonStats on the CD-ROM included on the back cover of this book). We should not only identify the name of the statistical technique(s) but also the variables to which they are to be applied. In the case of multiple regression, we should similarly identify the predictor variables (see Section 5.4.4) and the criterion variable.

FOR EXAMPLE If we are going to use the t-test for independent groups, we should identify the two groups (including the unit of analysis) and the dependent variable:

The t-test for independent groups will be used to investigate whether the experimental group of workers has shown significantly more aggressive responses than the control group.

By indicating the reason for and the method of the proposed statistical procedures, the candidate aims to convince the reader that he or she understands why a particular statistical technique is going to be used.

11.4.5 The list of references

We conclude the research project with a list of relevant and key references. The required number of references would be dictated by the audience of the proposal, as well as specific department or university requirements. The conventions related to compiling such a list are indicated in Chapter 3.

Finally, the entire proposal should be well-thought-out, logically coherent, and grammatically flawless. The evaluators (of the proposal) should be convinced that the researcher (prospective student) has mastery over that particular study field, both as far as terminology and methodology are concerned, and that he or she should be able to complete the project successfully.

11.5 Evaluation criteria for a research proposal

In this section, there is a brief collection of questions in terms of which supervisors and prospective students (researchers) may evaluate their research proposals. This checklist mainly draws on Tuckman (1990), Zuber-Skerritt (1998), and Saunders *et al.* (2003). In respect of each of these questions, scores may even be assigned, where appropriate, as follows:

Key to score:

N	Not applicable
1	Unacceptable and leaves much room for improvement
2	Has much merit; leaves a little room for improvement
3	As good as possible

Checklist questions	Scores			
The title:	N	1	2	3
• is a true reflection of the contents of the report. • is not too long yet descriptive. • contains the important variables.				
The statement of the problem:	N	1	2	3
• is formulated clearly and understandably. • is formulated adequately in terms of defined concepts relevant to the topic and field of study. • does not relate to something trivial, but is of scientific, theoretical and/or practical significance (so that it holds the prospect of an expansion of subject knowledge). • clearly describes the theory, practical problem or previous research from which it proceeds logically. • explicitly sets out different points of view and assumptions. • is congruent with the title as well as the aim of the study (addresses the same issue/s). • culminates in research hypotheses or research questions which are formulated clearly in terms of the relationship between the important variables. • notes theories relevant to the aim of the study. • includes keywords/concepts used in a computer literature search with a copy of its results.				
The literature review:	N	1	2	3
• is relevant to the aim and problem statement of the study. • is sufficiently comprehensive and uses essential information sources. • offers a logically organised and integrated summary (in the researcher's own words, of course).				
The research design:	N	1	2	3

• is appropriate for the problem in question (survey or experimental or case study design, and so on).
• is described clearly in respect of the following aspects (so that it is replicable):
  i) sampling procedures (so that, for example, the experimentally accessible population is clear);
  ii) the way in which the respondents will be classified or the participants are to be assigned to groups; and
  iii) interventions (if appropriate) and/or measuring instruments administered to subjects.
• takes care of threats to internal validity (for example nuisance and third variable problems, pre-existing differences between groups, and so on).
• takes care of threats to external validity (for example the generalisability of the results from the sample to the target population and/or to other situations, and so on).				

The measuring instrument's:	N	1	2	3
• contents are described briefly. • administering and/or data-collection procedures are described. • reliability is discussed. • validity is discussed.				

Checklist questions	Scores			
The analytical/statistical techniques:	N	1	2	3
• are appropriate for the given problem (descriptive and/or inferential).				
The proposal:	N	1	2	3
• is limited to 10 typed pages. • includes a time schedule for the writing of different chapters.				

Thus, the research proposal should satisfy the following criteria:

1. The purpose of the research (see Section 2.3.2) should be clearly defined.
2. The overall "fit" of the proposal should be indicated, showing that the methods flow from the research questions, which arise from the literature.
3. The research procedure (Chapters 4, 5, 7 and/or 8) to be used should be described in sufficient detail to permit another researcher to continue or repeat the research.
4. Possible flaws in procedural design and an estimate of their effects upon the research findings should be reported (compare Chapter 6).

The acceptability of a research topic for study purposes may be judged by giving consideration to its feasibility and value. **Feasibility** involves the following aspects:

- availability of, and access to, information or data
- opportunity to pursue a particular research design
- time needed to complete the research
- technical skills needed
- financial support.

Value entails demonstrating a measure of research competence or problem-solving ability (see Chapter 1) and, to a lesser degree, adding to the body of knowledge in a field of science.

11.6 **The student–study supervisor role**

The first step in designing a research project is to prepare a research proposal for approval by your study supervisor (study leader) or promoter. The supervisor/promoter must have the necessary insight and understanding to lead you and help you reach a high standard in your research.

The role of the supervisor is NOT to:

- choose your topic for you
- find the relevant literature
- do the critical thinking for you
- develop research questions/hypotheses
- decide the most appropriate methodology
- perform data analysis
- teach you statistics
- act as your language editor
- rewrite your work
- correct your referencing technique.

Figure 11.2 *Student–study supervisor relationship*

Rather, the role of the supervisor is to guide, mentor, and provide constructive advice and feedback on YOUR research work.

Ultimately it is your responsibility to do the following:

▶ select the research topic
▶ develop a proposal
▶ execute and manage the research project
▶ write the research report.

Supervisor/Study leader	Student
Be available at specified times	Initiate contact and explore study field
Have in-depth knowledge of study field	Follow up guidelines given by the supervisor
Help student to plan research	Plan research
Provide support in the development of the research proposal	Develop the research proposal
Guide the student's thinking and provide feedback on submitted work	Obtain new perspectives
Be involved and show interest in student	Show flexibility and dedication
Provide constructive criticism	Follow up on suggestions and ideas
Provide guidelines and support on the structure and form of the research report	Develop the research report and follow the provided guidelines
Provide support and suggestions regarding: • obtaining the sample selection; • the questionnaire application; • doing fieldwork; and • analysing the results.	Has to: • draw the sample; • administer the questionnaire; • do the fieldwork; and • analyse the results.
Ensure availability and access to research facilities	Use the available research facilities and explore new ones if necessary
Should terminate the candidature if student does not make progress	Should terminate the relationship if personal conflict occurs
Provide advice on prerequisites of publication acceptance	Take full responsibility for grammar and spelling
Encourage	Be enthusiastic

11.7 Research proposal evaluation example

In this example the research proposal by a prospective master's degree student in Human Resource Management is presented. Normally it would be followed by the comments and evaluation by the supervisor but, in order to show and compare these comments in connection to the relevant sections of the prospective student's proposal, both scripts are presented in two columns (this way of supervising can be followed if the student's draft is available on disk, email, or the Internet).

PERCEPTIONS ON TRADE UNION INVOLVEMENT
IN AFFIRMATIVE ACTION PROGRAMMES

by

U. WILLBESORRY

RESEARCH PROPOSAL

submitted in preliminary fulfilment
of the requirements for the

MAGISTER TECHNOLOGIAE

Human Resource Management

TECHNIKON BEPREPARED

Supervisor: Dr C. Youhavenot
Co-Supervisor: Dr U. Haveto

April 2002

NOTE: This should be a full page – the first page of the proposal.

General comments

Dear student

Your research proposal is, in general, well structured. You have obviously considered the structural elements in the development of a research proposal. In addition, there is definitely a need for this study, and you deserve recognition for having identified the importance of considering trade union perceptions of affirmative action. However, due to serious shortcomings with regard to methodology and content, you will have to do some more work and then resubmit this proposal. The following general comments are therefore pertinent:

- Your proposal (draft) is based on an overdependence on secondary sources. You should do further reading on studies by leading South African corporate and academic South African experts such as L. Human, M. van Wyk, K. Hofmeyr, E. Charoux, and P. Madi. In addition, you should consult scientific journals such as the *Industrial Relations Journal of South Africa* and the *SA Journal of Labour Relations* in order to enhance the scientific value of your proposal and, ultimately, your master's manuscript itself.
- You make no reference to the Employment Equity Act. You should study this Act in detail and identify its impact on the field of study.
- Furthermore, you should attempt to obtain policy documents and position papers on affirmative action published by trade unions and union federations. You should also read the union views in the *SA Labour Bulletin*. See also Patel (in Innes, 1993) in your presented list of sources (references).

- You should specify the limitations of the study and indicate how these limitations will be addressed.
- The conceptual framework of your research proposal is not well developed. Your proposal raises many questions that need further clarification. The how, what, why, where, when, and who need to be addressed during the planning phase of this study in order to prevent problems during the research process.
- The discrepancy between the current title and the content of your research proposal is highly problematic. You could either change the title or amend the content of the proposal in order to ensure congruency.
- You should correct the spelling and grammatical errors.

NOTE: The prospective student's research proposal appears in the left-hand column of the table as well as on the following pages. The supervisor's comments appear in the right-hand column, and will usually be presented in the form of a letter to the student.

In order for one to read the proposal, several general comments by the supervisor are presented here first, as well as after the proposal in the form of an evaluation form (checklist) including the 'conclusion' section of the letter.

	SPECIFIC COMMENTS FROM THE SUPERVISOR
1. TITLE "Perceptions of Trade Union involvement on Affirmative Action Programmes"	Another suggested title that may be suitable for the topic to be studied may be presented here.
2. INTRODUCTION Affirmative Action began in America in the early 1950s as a basis for formal equality in education, employment and welfare. However, this was not a guarantee for equal treatment because it could not eradicate inequalities deriving from economic, cultural and environmental factors. In Australia, representation can be achieved by a legally registered union. In colonial Africa, it is noted that whenever Africans took over higher posts without the necessary experience and qualifications, productivity would be very poor as has been the case in Ghana, Angola and Guinea. In the Sub-Sahara, Zimbabwe has never precisely formulated or implemented Affirmative Action. In the South African context various factors affecting success and failures of Affirmative Action as a reactive process to address discrimination in job need to be analysed and this is the basis for the research.	Your fleeting reference to a few isolated countries is neither correct nor complete. Although not a legal requirement, affirmative action (AA) has been, and still is being, practised by large companies in Zimbabwe. See Strachan (1993) and Gatherer & Erickson (in Innes, 1993) which you consulted according to your list of sources (references). What are the various factors you referred to?

	SPECIFIC COMMENTS FROM THE SUPERVISOR
3. MOTIVATION FOR THE INVESTIGATION Affirmative action is an issue that continues to arouse interest and demand attention and deliberations in the content of a changing South Africa. To date, much has been debated and written on the issue, particularly on the philosophy of the policy and the implementation. However, these arguments and deliberations have focussed primarily on the need to address imbalances emanating from the apartheid era, as Griffin (1990:25) contends. Ironically, the South African society is engaged in a multiparty democracy with diversified political persuasions. It is this dichotomy that arouses interest in the project since their viewpoints on affirmative action differ significantly. The practical and fundamental importance of the study, therefore, is to attempt to evaluate whether or not external consultancy has a bearing on the quality of people employed and the resultant production. The assumption is made that rationalization necessitates union involvement as a result of the Government's open-door policy.	The purpose of this paragraph is not clear. It does not form part of the motivation for the research. It is not clear why external consultancy is considered important. Why does rationalisation necessitate union involvement?
4. AIMS OF THE RESEARCH While affirmative action is a major focus in the 1990s, Innes (1993:1) sees it as a priority which will pave the way for a truly democratic society. The main aim of the investigation is to establish perception concerning the role of trade unions on affirmative action. This aim may be supported by secondary aims in an attempt to explain why people join the unions. These objectives may be considered as indirect methods of maintaining the welfare of union members. At the end of the research, it will be clear to everybody that on a macro level, addressing the imbalances of the past is the ideal objective, but such efforts should not be executed in a dogmatic manner without taking cognisance of the practical implications.	There is no link between these two sentences. In addition, why do you want to establish perception concerning the role of trade unions on affirmative action? What is the significance of this? How can organisations benefit from the research? The secondary aim must also relate to the title of the research. This statement does not make sense. Phrases such as " … it will be clear to everybody … " are too sweeping. Yes, it is important to consider the practical implications. At this stage, can you identify some of these?

	SPECIFIC COMMENTS FROM THE SUPERVISOR

5. THEORETICAL GROUNDING OF THE INVESTIGATION
Theoretical grounding of the investigation should emphasise the following themes:
• An explanation of the concept affirmative action as well as its operation. Affirmative action is best described by Rosenfeld (1991:42) as an attempt to bring members of under represented groups, that have suffered discrimination into a higher degree of participation in some beneficial programme.
   – Beneficiaries: This is a controversial issue as beneficiaries are described in political and racial overtones.
   – Moral, political and constitutional arguments for and against affirmative action
• An explanation of the concept Trade Union.
   – Section 25 of the New Labour Relations Act (LRA) 66 of 1995 provides for workers representation in the workplace.
   – Why workers join trade unions (Finnemore & Van der Merwe 1992: 95–97).
	Consider South African definitions of affirmative action, especially by the Department of Labour. Rosenfeld's definition is not the best one. The phrase '… some beneficial programme' is vague. Give your own interpretation of the term after you have provided a formal definition.
	   In addition, your theoretical basis for terms such as 'beneficiaries' is not clear. Be specific. Who are the beneficiaries? Please read the Employment Equity Bill. What is the relevance of moral, political and constitutional arguments for and against affirmative action? The fact that affirmative action will need to be compatible with the Constitution and the above-mentioned Bill makes some of these issues somewhat irrelevant. Also, the concept trade union is not explained. Yes, the Labour Relations Act (LRA) makes provision for worker representation in the workplace, but you should indicate the relevance of this for your study.
	
	Why do workers join trade unions – relevance?

6. AN OVERVIEW OF RELATED STUDIES There is not enough literature to address issues related to affirmative action.	This statement is incorrect. There is a vast amount of literature available on issues related to affirmative action. According to the Human Sciences Research Council, more than 100 theses are being written on affirmative action.
Available literature with regard to this current issue can be categorised as follows: • Studies that are generally well executed: Some books written within an American context are generally well executed. In the American context, affirmative action was aimed mainly at blacks (Qunta, 1995:29). Nevertheless, there are some American indicators for the South African situation. For example, the book by Conrad P.J. and Maddur R.B. sets a comprehensive and practical guidelines about equal employment and affirmative action which may well be executed in South Africa.	Your discussion of available literature is inadequate. You are not required to do book reviews. Rather, take the most relevant literature and indicate how your study will build on it. In addition, when criticising other studies, make sure that your criticism is valid, objective, and well-substantiated from a scientific perspective.

	SPECIFIC COMMENTS FROM THE SUPERVISOR
• The second category are those studies with some shortcomings which invalidate findings: Some books written within the South African context are marred by shortcomings. For instance, Maphai seems to be biased against other racial groups in dealing with beneficiaries for affirmative action while Hugo favours the whites. It is therefore, a matter of black and white syndrome. Test samples are taken from their respective communities and they rely on their empirical observation and subjective interpretation of important issues. Books written under these circumstances cannot depict a clear and objective picture of employment problems in South Africa.	
• Areas where little or no systematic knowledge exists: Klug (1993:25) is of the opinion that all along the National Party (NP) has been practising affirmative action.	Klug's statement bears no relevance to your topic.
• Well conducted studies: Christine Qunta's book, Who is Afraid of Affirmative Action is unique regarding the provision for worker representation in the workplace.	Your review of Qunta's book does not relate to the topic of your research either. Yes, the author does focus on the role of the black professional, but how will you integrate this with the perceptions of trade unions?
7. STATEMENT OF PROBLEM AND ITS PRACTICAL RELEVANCE The research problem can be formulated as follows: "To what extent will trade unions have an effect on affirmative action programmes?" This problem may be elucidated by the following hypotheses: H_0: There is no significant difference in the perceptions of government-, trade union and academic respondents that trade unions must be involved in affirmative action programmes. H_1: There is significant difference in the perceptions of government-, trade union and academic respondents that trade unions must be involved in affirmative action programmes.	The problem statement is not well formulated. Check your grammar as well. Elaborate more on the problem in a paragraph or two prior to formulating your hypotheses.

	SPECIFIC COMMENTS FROM THE SUPERVISOR
Rationale: Affirmative action will pave the way for racial integration. This means that the traditional rule that certain jobs are reserved for Whites will disappear. Unions will no longer be aggressive towards the management.	Your rationale does not relate to the hypothesis. The hypotheses must flow logically from the theoretical rationale and review of the literature.
Problems facing civil service centre around the following: • Psychological and symbolic level (Hugo & Scheire, 1990:133). The September Commission of Cosatu in Kempton Park exposed deep rooted mistrust between the government and COSATU (Adler, 1997: 38). • The economic role of civil service (Walton & Handy, 1997: 210) • On political level, civil service is strongly partisan and top echelon in the civil service should represent a major political power block.	What is the relevance of the mistrust between the government and COSATU? Please explain. What do you mean when you state that the civil service is strongly partisan and should represent a major political power block? The emphasis you place on the civil service gives the impression that you intend to focus your study on the civil service, but this is not explicitly mentioned anywhere in your proposal.
8. THE INVESTIGATION The investigation will be carried out, very broadly in the following way: **8.1 Method** According to Huysamen (1993:26) the survey method is generally used when the researcher wishes to elicit opinions. Since the objective of the research will be to measure perceptions concerning the impacts of trade union on affirmative action, the survey method is deemed to be most appropriate. It will also be practically impossible to exercise control over the variables. As a sensitive project, participants will be able to voice their opinions without being recognized.	
8.2 Test samples The target population for this research will be the top management in the Government service, Trade unionists and the academics. This will be done by approaching informants in a simple random sample. The number required for the whole exercise will be one hundred and fifty (150). The said procedure will be conducted irrespective of age distribution, level of education, socio-economic status, gender or creed. Data collected will be used to test the hypothesis.	Why are academics to be included, which academics are going to be included, and from which institutions or departments? Which trade unions will be used? What problems do you foresee? Will all groups complete the same questionnaire, and if so, how many questionnaires for each group? Have you considered alternative data-collection methods and sampling procedures?

	SPECIFIC COMMENTS FROM THE SUPERVISOR
8.3 Measuring instruments It is important that measuring instruments used should ensure some measure of reliability and validity. Most appropriate measuring instruments are survey questionnaires. According to Huysamen (1993, p.128) these are used to obtain information from respondents about biographical particulars (age, educational qualification, etcetera) typical behaviour (what they favour) opinions and attitudes. Structured and unstructured questionnaires and these will conform to the Likert Scale.	More information is needed on your questionnaire. What do you plan to include in the questionnaire? How and where will the questionnaires be administered and distributed? How will reliability and validity be ensured? Why have you referred to structured and unstructured questionnaires? How will the Likert scale be used?
8.4 Statistical analysis An appropriate statistical technique is the t-test. Illustrations in the form of diagrams will be demonstrated.	Why is the t-test appropriate, and how and where will this analysis be done?
9. EXPECTED RESULTS It is expected trade unionists will favour dominating role in affirmative action involvement whereas the majority of top management in the public service will favour no role of trade unionists because of frequent conflicts with the government policies. The academics will not favour any trade union involvement. In fact, affirmative action should pave the way for equal opportunities	How do these statements relate to your hypotheses? What is your rationale for stating that academics would not favour trade union involvement?
10. A LIST OF EQUIPMENT AND FACILITIES THAT WILL BE REQUIRED A computer is most appropriate to analyse data in this regard.	This statement does not constitute a list. Which computer package will be used? Any other equipment and facilities?
11. PROGRAMME/SCHEDULE Progress reports will be submitted per chapter per month after 1st March 2002 until the whole project is completed.	A detailed research plan is required. When will the literature study be conducted? When will the survey instrument be compiled? When will it be distributed? When will data be collected and analysed? When will results be discussed? When will language editing be done? When will the manuscript be typed? When will the final product be completed?
12. THE POSSIBLE IMPACT ON INDUSTRY AND/OR COMMUNITY Affirmative action practice has a bearing on national economic reconstruction issues. Production by well satisfied and qualified employees will result in increased production and subsequent economic increase. Economics often shudder at the costs affirmative action will demand to compensate for the inefficiencies that are likely to follow from some irregular affirmative action initiatives.	This paragraph is one of the most important parts of your proposal. You should clearly indicate the value of your study for industry and the community. Once again, this discussion should be directly related to your topic.

	SPECIFIC COMMENTS FROM THE SUPERVISOR
13. LIST OF SOURCES ADLER, GLENN. 1977. Cosatu's Fine Balancing Act. *Mail Guardian*.19–25 September: 38. CONRAD, P.J. & MADDUX, R.B. 1988. *Guide to Affirmative Action: A Primer for Supervisors and Managers.* Menlo Park: CA Crisp. FINNERMORE, M. & VAN DER MERWE, R.1992. 3rd ed. *Introduction to Industrial Relations in South Africa.* Johannesburg: Lexicon. GRIFFIN, R.W. 1990. *Management.* Boston: Hougton. HUGO, P. & SCHRIRE, R. 1990. *Affirmative Action in the Public Service: Critical Choices for South Africa – Agenda for the 1990's.* Cape Town: Oxford. HUYSAMEN, G.K. 1994. *Methodology for the Social and Behavioral Sciences.* Halfway House: Southern. INNES, D. 1993. Affirmative Action: Issues and Strategies. IN Kentridge, M. & Perold, H. (Eds). *Reversing Discrimination Affirmative Action in the workplace*: 4–21. Cape Town: Oxford. KLUG, H. 1993. Affirmative Action in Action. *Suid-Afrikaan*: 20–25.May/Jun. ROSENFELD, M. 1991. *Affirmative Action & Justice – A philosophical and Constitutional Enquiry.* London: Yale. QUNTA, C. 1995. *Who's Afraid of Affirmative Action.* Cape Town: Kwela Books. ROGENFELD, M. 1991. *Affirmative Action and Justice – A Philosophical and Constitutional Inquiry.* London: Yale. WALTON, M. & HENDY, J. 1997. Individual Right To Union Representation in International Law. *International Law Journal,* **26**(3) 207–210. SEPT.	There are a number of mistakes in your list of references (you named it "sources"!), for example incorrect dates, the omission of subtitles, and incorrect alphabetical sequence.

Key to score:

N	Not applicable
1	Unacceptable and leaves much room for improvement
2	Has much merit; leaves a little room for improvement
3	As good as possible

Checklist questions	Scores			
The title:	N	1	2	3
• is a true reflection of the contents of the report.		X		
• is not too long yet descriptive.			X	
• contains the important variables.			X	
The statement of the problem:	N	1	2	3
• is formulated clearly and understandably.		X		
• is formulated adequately in terms of defined concepts relevant to the topic and field of study.		X		
• does not relate to something trivial, but is of scientific theoretical and/or practical significance (so that it holds the prospect of an expansion of subject knowledge).				X
• clearly describes the theory, practical problem or previous research from which it proceeds logically.		X		
• explicitly sets out different points of view and assumptions.		X		
• is congruent with the title as well as the aim of the study (addresses the same issue/s).		X		
• culminates in research hypotheses or research questions which are formulated clearly in terms of the relationship between the important variables.		X		
The literature review:	N	1	2	3
• is relevant to the aim and problem statement of the study.		X		
• is sufficiently comprehensive and uses essential information sources.		X		
• offers a logically organised and integrated summary (in the researcher's own words, of course).		X		
• notes theories relevant to the aim of the study.		X		
• includes keywords/concepts used in a computer literature search with a copy of its results.		X		
The research design:	N	1	2	3
• is appropriate for the problem in question (survey or experimental or case study design, and so on).		X		
• is described clearly in respect of the following aspects (so that it is replicable):		X		
i) sampling procedures (so that, for example, the experimentally accessible population is clear);		X		
ii) the way in which the respondents will be classified or the participants are to be assigned to groups; and		X		
iii) interventions (if appropriate) and/or measuring instruments administered to subjects.		X		
• takes care of threats to internal validity (for example nuisance and third variable problems, pre-existing differences between groups, and so on).		X		
• takes care of threats to external validity (for example the generalisability of the results from the sample to the target population and/or to other situations, and so on).		X		
The measuring instrument's:	N	1	2	3
• contents are described briefly.		X		
• administering and/or data-collection procedures are described.			X	
• reliability is discussed.		X		
• validity is discussed.		X		

Checklist questions	Scores			
The analytical/statistical techniques:	N	1	2	3
• are appropriate for the given problem (descriptive and/or inferential).		✗		
The proposal:	N	1	2	3
• is limited to 10 typed pages.				✗
• includes a time schedule for the writing of different chapters.		✗		

CONCLUSION

In the light of the above comments it is evident that you need to redevelop your research proposal. By taking cognisance of the comments and suggestions made, the scientific quality of this proposal will be improved and you will get a clear picture of the research plan and its implications.

A well-developed research proposal will not only guide you during the research process, but will also prevent frustration when problems do occur. It will make it easier for you to achieve the objectives of your study and complete the dissertation.

Please reconsider answering the following questions in rewriting your research proposal:
• What is the central question or problem?
• Why is this problem important and worthy of research?
• What research methods will you use and why?
• What is the time structure for each stage of your proposed research methods and writing process?

ACTIVITY 11.1

Evaluate the following research proposal according to the example above and the checklist (Section 11.5.)

RESEARCH PROPOSAL

by

X.X. WHYBESOBER

submitted in partial fulfilment of the
preliminary requirements for the

MASTER'S DEGREE IN COMPUTER SCIENCE

UNIVERSITY OF NOT SO STUPID

Supervisor: Dr C. Omputer

April 2004

NOTE THE FOLLOWING: This should be a full page – the first page of the proposal.

RESEARCH TITLE

A description of Object Oriented design implementation problems in the software engineering industry.

MOTIVATION

Due to the difficult nature of the software engineering industry there is a constant move to new methods for solving design problems. More specifically there is a move towards the Object Oriented (OO) methods, presumably because of the various advantages offered in terms of maintainability, and changeability of code produced this way.

As with various other aspects of the software industry there are, however, also problems encountered in this transition and lessons to be learned from the experience of companies who have already performed this change.

The aim of this study therefore is to know what these problems are and how to avoid them in order to make a success of Object Oriented (OO) projects, so that the advantages offered by OO can indeed be utilised. Also, before making this change, it is useful to find out if indeed the change should be made to OO and if there are not even newer options available.

PROBLEM

The research done will look at the general change in methods, but will concentrate on two areas:

- where change was undertaken from a previously structured design to an OO design; and
- where informal or no design principles were previously used.

POSSIBLE CONTRIBUTION TO STUDY FIELD

The final report will provide guidelines for companies who are currently contemplating a change to the OO methodology, covering important issues one should know about prior to this change.

It will also summarise the problems faced in the transition so far, the reasons for these problems and suggest possible solutions.

PLANNED APPROACH AND PROPOSED SOLUTION

The target population that the study will concentrate on is the situation in the South African market place.

While researching this transition, a questionnaire will be developed and circulated to selected companies, in conjunction with interviews addressing the following issues:

- the role of CASE tools
- budget size of the project undertaken, number of people involved as well as company size (according to taxable profits) and area of work (military, banking, and so on)
- skills base of developers used (years of experience and qualifications), permanent or contracting, in house skills, consultants, and so on
- specific method used the past two years, if any, and reasons for specific choice of method
- influence of the need for obtaining ISO 9000 or similar accreditation within the same department or company

- cost and time implications of existing method
- resistance faced internally when changing methods
- the role of cost effective software project management
- the situation companies in South Africa face, in contrast with the global situation: is there anything to be learnt from the development done overseas.

Depending on the results obtained, some of the above areas will be studied more carefully, if it is found to have an important influence on the progress of projects.

DRAFT WORK PLAN

The following chart demonstrates the tasks and their proposed duration during 2004:

Plan of action	Feb–Mar	Apr–May	Jun–Jul	Aug–Sept	Oct
Literature study	✗				
Data collection		✗	✗		
Interviews		✗	✗		
Data interpretation			✗	✗	
Interim report		✗	✗		
Evaluation				✗	
Final report					✗

LITERATURE STUDY

A literature search and review will be conducted to find out what work has already been done in this research area, and what type of data will need to be collected. Where possible data from the Internet will be collected and all other possible resources will also be explored.

UNITS OF ANALYSIS

The emphasis throughout will be on South African companies and projects, since the constraints are often localised, and may be different from those experienced overseas.

It is important to note that the word transition is used in this proposal to refer not only to the change made from other methods (such as structured methods) but also to refer to those situations where no design method was previously used. Companies that fall in the latter category will therefore also be included in the study.

DATA COLLECTION

A list of companies will be compiled. Selection will be done such that all the main business sectors are covered, including banking, retail, military and mining, using stratified sampling procedures. Selection will also be done in such a way that the entire range from small to large enterprises is covered. Questionnaires will be sent to all the selected companies that are willing to assist in the research, ensuring a high response rate.

INTERVIEWS

Once the questionnaires have been sent out, interviews will be arranged and conducted with the selected companies to discuss the questionnaire (either telephonically or personally), as well as any additional information these companies can supply that could be of assistance.

DATA INTERPRETATION

Data collected will be interpreted to find any similarities between design methods and the companies that use it.

The data acquired will be evaluated in conjunction with all other information acquired *via* resources such as the Internet and literature available, followed by suggestions. This will include profiles of companies that made the transition.

In addition, the transition process that takes place will be classified to determine what was or is a successful or unsuccessful method of change.

EVALUATION

Once all the necessary data have been obtained and evaluated, the results will be interpreted and written up and possible guidelines formulated.

REQUIREMENTS AT THE UNIVERSITY

For the literature study and data collection, the library facilities as well as access to the Electrical Engineering network will be required.

Costs involved in the research include photocopying, fax and telephone costs, as well as the cost of travelling to the various companies.

ACTIVITY 11.2

Do Activity 3.1 and the self-evaluation exercise given at the end of Chapter 10.

NOTE: See page 49 for a information regarding access to academic journals (periodicals) that contain mostly good articles that may be used as information sources for the literature review (introduction) of your research proposal.

SUMMARY

In general, the research proposal refers to the preconceived plan for the envisaged investigation of the research hypothesis or research question/central theme. This proposal contains a background to the study, the statement of the research problem, an explanation of the proposed method, research design, and statistical analysis, as well as a list of references. It also describes the number of units of analysis, the way in which these units should be formed, data-collection methods, as well as the methods of analysis which are to be used.

Appendices

Appendix A ANSWERS TO TEST-YOURSELF EXERCISES

Please note that answers for all the multiple-choice and true/false questions are provided, but only for certain self-evaluation questions.

Chapter 1   The aims of research

Question 1 Multiple-choice questions
1.1 d   1.2 c   1.3 a   1.4 d

Question 2 Self-evaluation questions
2.1 lay person's (non-scientific) knowledge; accidental observation
2.2 lay person's (non-scientific) knowledge; authority

Chapter 2   The research topic, project title, and research problem

Question 1 Multiple-choice questions
1.1 c   1.2 b   1.3 d   1.4 b   1.5 b
1.6 d   1.7 a

Question 2 True/false questions
2.1 T   2.2 F   2.3 T   2.4 F

Question 3 Self-evaluation questions
3.1 There are more cars with GP registration numbers than any other registration numbers on that route. Consequently, one may expect more careless drivers with GP registration numbers than with other numbers on this route.
3.2 There may be other reasons which play a role in a decision to go to university, such as social pressure of parents or peers.
3.4 a) sex, race, and ability of applicant
    b) success of application

Chapter 3   Literature review

Question 1 Multiple-choice questions
1.1 b   1.2 d   1.3 b   1.4 c   1.5 c

Chapter 4   Population and sampling types

Question 1 Multiple-choice questions
1.1 b   1.2 c   1.3 c   1.4 d   1.5 c
1.6 c   1.7 b

Question 2 True/false questions
2.1 T   2.2 T   2.3 T

Chapter 5   Types of quantitative research designs

Question 1 Multiple-choice questions
1.1 c   1.2 d   1.3 d   1.4 c   1.5 b
1.6 b   1.7 b

Question 2 True/false questions
2.1 T   2.2 T

Question 3 Self-evaluation exercises
3.1 a) experimental research
 b) field study
3.2 a) pre-experimental research
 b) premeasurement and postmeasurement design
3.3 interrupted time-series design
3.4 interrupted time-series design
3.5 a) non-experimental research
 b) correlational design
3.8 panel study

Chapter 6   Validity of conclusions

Question 1 Multiple-choice questions
1.1 b   1.2 d   1.3 d   1.4 d   1.5 c

Question 2 True/false questions
2.1 T

Question 3 Self-evaluation exercises
3.1 This design would be regarded as internally valid to the extent that an increase in assertiveness may be unambiguously ascribed to the assertiveness training programme rather than anything else. Possible threats include: historical events possibly occurring concurrently with the programme, spontaneous development of assertiveness as students become more familiar with their new environment, measurement reactivity, and the regression effect.
3.2 None of the threats under 3.1 applies.
3.3 Lecturers are usually older than students. Poorer vision is associated with increasing age. Those with poorer eyesight probably sign their names larger than those with better eyesight.
3.4 Population validity is suspect because only employees of a particular insurance company were used. These employees are not necessarily representative of all individuals with an unhealthy Type A behaviour.

Ecological validity is hampered due to the artificiality of the situations to which subjects were exposed in a specially-equipped room.
3.5 Because the students were aware of the fact that they were participating in an experiment, their behaviour possibly might not have been representative of their behaviour in similar real-life situations of spatial crowding.

Chapter 7   Data-collecting methods and measuring instruments in quantitative research

Question 1 Multiple-choice questions
1.1 a   1.2 a   1.3 c   1.4 d   1.5 d
1.6 d   1.7 d   1.8 d   1.9 c   1.10 d

Question 2 True/false questions
2.1 F   2.2 T   2.3 T   2.4 T   2.5 T
2.6 F   2.7 T   2.8 T   2.9 T

Question 3 Self-evaluation exercises
3.1 a) interval (approximately)
 b) ordinal
 c) nominal
 d) nominal
3.3 semantic differential
3.8 Again there is a difference of opinion. It could be argued that it is difficult to see how someone's dignity could be impugned if neither the person whose dignity is so affected nor the person who does this to him or her, is familiar with the former's identity.
3.9 Construct validity of the operationalisation of the independent variable is suspect because of the possibility of subject effects (the so-called control group does not meet the definition of such a group) and experimenter effects (raters know which of the subjects were in the experimental group and which were in the control group).

Chapter 8   Qualitative research designs

Question 1 Multiple-choice questions
1.1 c   1.2 c   1.3 b   1.4 a   1.5 c
1.6 a   1.7 d   1.8 a

Question 2 True/false questions
2.1 F   2.2 T   2.3 F   2.4 F   2.5 T
2.6 T   2.7 T

Chapter 9   Data analysis and interpretation of results

Question 1 Multiple-choice questions
1.1 d   1.2 c   1.3 d   1.4 c   1.5 b
1.6 a   1.7 b   1.8 d   1.9 c   1.10 d
1.11 b   1.12 b

Question 2 True/false questions
2.1 F   2.2 T   2.3 T   2.4 T   2.5 T
2.6 T   2.7 T   2.8 T

Appendix B INTERNET RESOURCES

(All Technikon SA Students have automatic access to UNISA's excellent library. You can access the library online by visiting http://www.unisa.ac.za/ and clicking on "library". Individuals with specific research requirements and who are not students at UNISA or Technikon SA can contact the library for information regarding gaining access to the collection.)

General sites

Visit the first site for a general overview of research. Use the other addresses to access information for specific purposes, as indicated by the headings. (Note: Although all these addresses were correct at the time of going to press, web sites and Internet addresses are subject to change.)

SPECIFIC IMPORTANT ISSUES IN CONDUCTING RESEARCH

African Digital Library – access to about 8 000 full text books for people living in Africa.
http://africaeducation.org/adl/
NetLibrary – an online library that offers access to a variety of electronic books, journals, and reference resources.
http://www.netlibrary.com

BURSARIES AND FUNDING – NATIONAL RESEARCH FOUNDATION

http://www.nrf.ac.za/funding/guide/

BUSINESS ABSTRACTS/INDEXING

Provides access to more than 150 databases and thousands of electronic journals.
http://search.epnet.com/login.asp?site=ehost
User ID: technikon   Password: ebsco

BUSINESS CREDIT NEWS

http://www.creditman.co.uk

BUSINESS DAY

http://www.bday.co.za

CODE OF STANDARDS FOR SURVEY RESEARCH IN THE UNITED STATES

http://www.casro.org/

CONFERENCES DATABASE

http://stardata.nrf.ac.za
http://www.apa.org/science/lib.html

EMERALD (MCB) LIBRARY

More than 20 000 full-text management articles
http://www.emerald-library.com/EMR/EMR.html

Username: tsa1	Password: bird
tsa2	ant
tsa3	fly

ETHICS, TEACHING THEREOF IN RESEARCH

http://ethics.ucsd.edu

GENETICS – RESEARCH FOR THE US HUMAN GENOME PROJECT, 1998–2003

http://www.ncbi.nlm.nih.gov/genome/guide/human/

GENETICS – BIOMEDICAL RESEARCH

http://www.ornl.gov/sci/techresources/Human_Genome/home.shtml

GOVERNMENT WEB SITE

http://www.polity.org.za

GUIDELINES FOR POSTGRADUATE TRAINING IN DOING RESEARCH (UNITED KINGDOM)

http://www.esrcsocietytoday.ac.uk/ESRCInfoCentre/
http://www.esrcsocietytoday.ac.uk/ESRCInfoCentre/How/For%5FPostgrad%FFStudents

HARVARD METHOD OF REFERENCING

http://www.lib.uct.ac.za/infolit/bibharvard.htm

HUMAN – LIFE IN SOUTH AFRICA – BIO-INFORMATION

http://www.sanbi.ac.za/Dbases.html

HUMAN RESOURCE MANAGEMENT PRACTICE – PROFESSION'S STANDARDS

http://www.sabpp.co.za

INTERNET RESEARCH

http://www.nrf.ac.za/yenza

LABOUR, SA DEPARTMENT OF

http://www.labour.gov.za

LIBRARIES ONLINE

http://AfricaEducation.org/adl/
http://www.sabinet.co.za
http://oasis.unisa.ac.za/search/
http://www.lib.ouhk.edu.hk/
http://www.emerald-library.com/EMR/EMR.html

Username: tsa1   Password: bird
         tsa2   ant
         tsa3   fly

MANAGEMENT ARTICLES MCB LIBRARY

More than 20 000 full-text management articles
http://www.emerald-library.com/EMR/EMR.html

Username: tsa1   Password: bird
         tsa2   ant
         tsa3   fly

METHODS OF RESEARCH – THE NATIONAL RESEARCH FOUNDATION

http://www.nrf.ac.za/methods/archmeth.htm

MONETARY ISSUES – EUROPEAN

http://www.cfp-pec.gc.ca/english/emu.htm
http://www.ecb.int/home/html/index.en.html

NATIONAL ACADEMY OF SCIENCES' BOOKLET ON BEING A SCIENTIST

http://books.nap.edu/catalog/4917.html

NATIONAL RESEARCH FOUNDATION (NRF)

Tel. (012) 481-4000; email (info@nrf.ac.za).
http://www.nrf.ac.za

NEXUS – CURRENT & COMPLETED RESEARCH IN SOUTH AFRICA

77 000 projects listed.
http://www.hsrc.ac.za/
http://stardata.nrf.ac.za

OPEN UNIVERSITY OF HONG KONG

1 000 databases & 500 000 volumes of books.
http://www.lib.ouhk.edu.hk/

POLITICAL INFORMATION – SOUTH AFRICA

http://www.idasa.org.za/

POSTGRADUATE GUIDELINES – ECONOMIC & SOCIAL RESEARCH COUNCIL (UNITED KINGDOM)

http://www.esrcsocietytoday.ac.uk/ESRCInfoCentre/
http://www.esrcsocietytoday.ac.uk/ESRCInfoCentre/How/For%5
FPostgrad%FFStudents

PROGRAMME EVALUATION

Proposal – writing of the research proposal from the NRF's workshop kit.
http://www.nrf.ac.za/yenza/research/proposal.htm

QUALITATIVE RESEARCH

http://www.qualitativeresearch.uga.edu/QualPage/

QUALITATIVE RESEARCH CONJUNCTIONS AND DIVERGENCES WITH QUANTITATIVE RESEARCH

http://qualitative-research.net/fqs/fqs-eng.htm

QUALITATIVE RESEARCH COMPUTER PACKAGE – ATLAS.TI

http://www.atlasti.de

REFERENCE TO INFORMATION SOURCES

The Harvard method:
http://www.lib.uct.ac.za/infolit/bibharvard.htm

The APA (American Psychological Association) method:
http://www.apa.org

Online citing sources:
http://www.quinion.com/words/articles/citation.htm

RESEARCHERS IN SOUTH AFRICA – PROFILES, INTERESTS & SPECIALISATION

http://stardata.nrf.ac.za

RESEARCH PROPOSAL WRITING FROM THE NRF'S WORKSHOP KIT

http://www.nrf.ac.za/yenza/research/proposal.htm

RESEARCH TOPIC/TITLES REGISTERED WITH THE HUMAN SCIENCES RESEARCH COUNCIL

http://stardata.nrf.ac.za

Username: ztsa   Password: tsa5

SABINET HIGH QUALITY DATABASE

http://www.sabinet.co.za

SOUTH AFRICAN ACADEMIC JOURNALS

http://www.nrf.ac.za/yenza/research/sajourn.htm

STATISTICS SOUTH AFRICA – FOR INFORMATION AND RESULTS OF CENSUS 1996 & 2001/OTHER

http://www.statssa.gov.za/

STATISTICAL PACKAGE MOONSTATS

http://www.moonstats.co.za

http://www.kalahari.net

SURVEY RESEARCH

South African and international (SADA):
http://www.nrf.ac.za/sada

Commercial in the USA:
http://www.casro.org/

TEXTBOOKS ON RESEARCH METHODOLOGY – REVIEWS

http://www.nrf.ac.za/yenza/research/reviews.htm

THESES AND DISSERTATIONS

African Universities – database:
http://www.aau.org./datad/

Australian – full text from seven universities:
http://adt.caul.edu.au/

WORKSHOPS – RESEARCH AND ACADEMIC DEVELOPMENT

http://www.radct.co.za/

WORLD KNOWLEDGE PORTAL LINKS RELEVANT TO CULTURAL HERITAGE, WATER RESOURCES, AND DISTANCE LEARNING

http://www.unesco.org

Search engines

GLOBAL SEARCH ENGINE

There are many search engines – two examples are listed:

http://www.google.co.za/

http://www.yahoo.com

SOUTH AFRICAN SEARCH ENGINES

There are a number of search engines – two examples are listed:

http://www.aardvark.co.za

http://www.anazi.co.za

Appendix C TABLE OF RANDOM NUMBERS

97	76	75	66	21	32	99	04	37	80	15	28
49	70	78	25	05	11	26	50	66	42	58	76
61	80	34	80	70	02	75	34	24	33	34	12
82	93	22	90	42	38	44	22	38	22	56	73
92	50	70	65	59	62	39	79	17	89	67	54
80	80	56	13	73	21	69	27	36	73	36	90
11	04	24	07	26	93	22	97	78	98	04	89
80	01	79	63	68	41	29	09	84	27	47	34
00	55	27	65	42	68	32	75	57	70	46	79
02	76	38	45	26	52	76	84	20	59	88	65
74	08	77	92	54	91	64	60	81	48	15	56
56	06	25	94	43	07	51	42	95	88	35	82
74	49	24	99	77	72	37	73	02	55	63	50
04	30	44	90	42	36	38	97	41	73	71	41
66	39	34	52	01	40	28	04	76	15	47	98
05	95	21	69	18	87	63	89	67	00	81	26
97	80	04	01	64	71	50	61	14	28	99	09
46	20	02	29	59	89	03	12	42	43	99	04
74	56	71	17	63	21	61	74	92	86	94	76
99	51	13	12	58	36	93	28	27	13	74	81
26	43	21	34	14	77	30	87	51	24	41	81
79	60	42	11	85	11	97	82	17	62	29	89
20	62	87	64	01	31	74	64	22	48	73	96
93	22	94	63	28	98	38	46	31	66	28	19
14	91	17	79	20	05	46	31	70	42	06	66
20	40	63	12	03	14	55	95	78	08	61	85
48	13	42	32	11	79	75	36	34	80	29	38
73	17	45	12	65	79	90	24	34	83	64	03
90	92	43	30	91	67	88	19	19	42	31	48
79	94	51	57	78	53	13	01	89	20	02	27
19	33	26	50	70	66	63	80	11	48	16	66
85	73	73	84	43	99	85	30	41	80	09	29
02	95	49	36	71	02	68	85	98	24	67	04
55	11	76	51	21	61	79	21	13	88	53	70
06	42	96	94	01	58	37	00	65	86	54	59
27	87	75	66	22	35	12	58	40	15	13	98
29	30	22	58	48	65	53	34	23	32	86	20
81	99	59	59	27	27	15	40	06	76	21	95
00	12	71	18	69	53	92	78	38	22	39	76
87	19	27	91	03	95	42	93	80	40	40	10

(Adapted from Huysamen, 1989a.)

Note: Compare Section 4.3.2.2 as well as the random number generator on the CD-ROM attached to the back cover of this book and page 326 (Random number calculator).

Appendix D CASE STUDIES

Case Study A

AIDS: Knowledge and attitudes of a group of South African health professionals

INTRODUCTION

Over the last decade there has been growing concern about the rapid spread of acquired immune deficiency syndrome (AIDS) throughout the world. AIDS was first diagnosed in South Africa in 1982 and is spreading steadily. By December 1990, 613 full-blown AIDS cases had been diagnosed positively. The number of AIDS cases in South Africa doubles every 11,4 months (Ijsselmuiden, Steinberg, Padayachee, Schaub, Strauss, Buch, Davies, De Beer, Gear & Hurwitz, 1988). There is, therefore, an urgent need to continue with research and to plan for the management and prevention of the syndrome.

This study is an attempt to investigate attitudes towards AIDS among a group of South African health professionals. Since doctors and nurses are often the first-line staff who deal with AIDS cases, their attitudes towards these patients are meaningful for treatment and prevention purposes.

One of the greatest obstacles in the case of AIDS is the moral censure and prejudice surrounding the syndrome. As the high-risk groups that have been identified, namely homosexuals, prostitutes, and users of intravenous drugs, tend to be stereotyped negatively, they have influenced the general social perceptions of AIDS sufferers (Levi, 1987). We must understand these attitudes if we want to implement effective educational programmes (Ijsselmuiden et al., 1988).

It was widely accepted that effective education about AIDS involves teaching people the facts about the syndrome, and that this knowledge is adequate to eliminate the prejudices and misconceptions regarding the virus and its sufferers. However, recent psychological research (Furnham, 1988) suggests that knowledge of AIDS is perhaps not the main determinant of attitudes towards AIDS. Educational initiatives may therefore be necessary to pay attention to the dominant attitudes towards high-risk groups and provide information at the same time. This study investigated the relationship between attitudes towards AIDS and knowledge of AIDS, as well as attitudes towards the sexuality of an observed high-risk group, namely prostitutes.

The study investigated the extent of correlation between a measurement of subjects' attitudes towards AIDS and the following two variables:

▶ knowledge of AIDS
▶ attitude towards prostitution.

METHOD

Subjects

Permission was obtained to conduct the study in a general hospital that served mainly white and coloured population groups. Participation in the study was voluntary. In total, 80 subjects were approached to participate in the study, and 74 completed the questionnaire on which the analysis was based.

Of the 74 subjects:

▶ 43 were nursing sisters and 31 doctors
▶ 48 were female and 26 male
▶ 61 were white, 7 were coloured, 4 were Indian, and 2 were black
▶ the ages ranged from 22 to 64 years (an average of 38 years).

Instrument

The questionnaire used in this study was based on a scale developed by McManus and Morton (1986). This scale incorporates three basic areas of involvement: knowledge of AIDS, attitude towards AIDS, and attitude towards prostitution. The three sections of the questionnaire contained the following broad dimensions:

1. Knowledge of AIDS (18 items):
   1.1 General knowledge of AIDS, for example: AIDS was first diagnosed in the previous decade.
   1.2 Questions on transmission, symptoms, and appearance of AIDS, for example: one must assume that all people with antibodies against HIV are infected.
   1.3 Questions on AIDS in the South African context, for example: the occurrence of AIDS is highest among prostitutes in South Africa.
2. Attitudes towards AIDS (12 items):
   2.1 Moral judgement, for example: AIDS is a punishment for immoral activities.
   2.2 Prejudice based on fear, for example: AIDS patients must be avoided if possible.
3. Attitude towards prostitution (12 items):
   3.1 The normality or deviation of prostitution, for example: prostitution is a psychological disturbance.
   3.2 Moral judgement, for example: prostitution is immoral.
   3.3 The rights of prostitutes, for example: prostitutes must have job opportunities.

The first part of the questionnaire comprised 18 knowledge questions and the last part contained the 24 attitude items in random order. It took approximately 30 minutes to complete the questionnaire. Knowledge questions required a true/false or correct/incorrect answer, while the attitude questions were evaluated on a five-point Likert scale, from *do not agree at all* (1) to *agree fully* (5).

PROCEDURE

A pilot study was done to ensure that the questionnaire was effective. After small amendments, the questionnaire was given to the subjects individually. Subjects were assured that the questionnaire was confidential and they were encouraged to answer as honestly as possible. The data were collected over a period of two weeks in 1988.

The questionnaires were marked individually and then analysed statistically. Each question was analysed individually in terms of validity, content, and the frequency of responses. In addition, Pearson's product moment correlation was used to calculate the correlation between the three dimensions of the questionnaire.

Correlations were based on the average score of each subject for each of the three sections of the questionnaire which concerned the variables being studied.

RESULTS

Only the correlative data are given below, since they were the most convincing for the article. The correlations between the three variables are illustrated in Table A.

Table A Correlative findings

	Attitude towards AIDS	Attitude towards prostitution
Knowledge of AIDS	0,22	0,03
Attitudes Towards AIDS		0,60

REFERENCES

Furnham, A. 1988. *The relationship between knowledge of, and attitudes to AIDS.* Unpublished manuscript. London: Department of Psychology, University College.

Gottlieb, M. 1987. AIDS in Africa: an agenda for behavioural scientists. In N. Miler & R.C. Rockwell (Eds). *AIDS in Africa: The Social and Policy Impact.* Queenston: Edward Mellen.

Ijsselmuiden, C.B., Steinberg, M.H., Padayachee, G.N., Schoub, B.D., Strauss, S.A., Buch, E., Davies, J.C.A., De Beer, C., Gear, J.S.S. & Hurwitz, H.S. 1988. AIDS and South Africa – towards a comprehensive strategy: Part I–III. *South African Medical Journal*, **73**: 455–467.

McManus, I. & Morton, A. 1986. Attitudes to and knowledge about the acquired immune deficiency syndrome: Lack of a correlation. *British Medical Journal*, **293**: 67–71.

Case Study B

The effect of role induction on goldsmith apprentices' perceptions of supervision

INTRODUCTION

Supervision over goldsmith apprentices is essential because the incorrect use of precious metals and stones in the creation of jewellery leads to large financial losses. However, the supervision is often stressful, partly because of the apprentices' lack of knowledge of the supervision process (Cohen, 1980; Schauer, Seymour & Green, 1985). Goldsmith apprentices receive theoretical and applied training, but there are few training programmes that prepare apprentices in any way for the supervision experience. It therefore limits the effectiveness of the supervision interaction.

It is clear that if apprentices were better informed of what supervision entails, the period of adaptation could be shorter and less stressful, and the quality of the supervision relationship could therefore be improved.

Role induction (by showing a video) is one method of informing apprentices of the supervision process. The current investigation examined the effectiveness of a role induction procedure during the adaptation process of goldsmith apprentices. The role induction procedure is designed to provide the apprentices with a conceptual framework to understand the roles, expectations, and objectives of the supervision process. For the specific role induction, the apprentices were shown a video of Bernard's (1979) supervision model. This model defines the supervisor role (for example advisor) and the objectives of supervision (for example to improve diamond setting skills). The ideal is that the apprentices' needs determine the choice of the supervision objective and the supervisory role that must be fulfilled.

Two hypotheses were investigated in the study. The first hypothesis was that if no role induction is offered, the apprentices' evaluations of supervision will become increasingly negative over time. This hypothesis is based on the belief that the apprentices' lack of understanding of the expectations and roles of supervision will lead to confusion, stress, and increasing dissatisfaction with the supervision interaction. The second hypothesis was that the implementation of the role induction procedure will lead to a more favourable evaluation of supervision.

METHOD

Subjects

The subjects were 20 goldsmith apprentices with no previous experience of supervision, and who were enrolled for a course in goldsmith work at a large jewellery firm. Of the 20 subjects:

- 10 were women and 10 were men
- six were white, seven were black, and seven were coloured
- nine were 19 years old, eight were 20 years old, and three were 21 years old.

Role induction

For the role induction procedure, the subjects studied a 10-minute video recording describing Bernard's (1979) supervision model. The video briefly outlined the objectives of supervision, such as improving goldsmith skills in various areas. The skills dimensions were described in order to explain the concepts. After the presentation of the goldsmith skills areas, a brief overview was given of the supervisors' roles.

The subjects were told that the video had been compiled to promote communication in the supervision process. The video was shown in a small-group situation during an ordinary scheduled practical class.

Questionnaire

The semantic differential (SD) was used as a measure of the subjects' attitudes towards supervision. The questionnaire comprised six bipolar word pairs where subjects had to indicate their associations with the key concept "supervision". Osgood (1952) indicated test-retest correlations of 0,85 for group averages in the SD.

PROCEDURE

All the subjects completed the questionnaire (SD) on three occasions. The questionnaire was given to all the apprentices at the beginning of the training period to obtain a baseline measure of attitudes towards supervision before the process was begun. The second and third evaluations were done immediately before the role induction (screening of the video) and one week after role induction. It was assumed that differences in the subjects' responses that became evident between the first and second evaluations could be attributed to the effect of time on supervision. It was also assumed that differences in subjects' responses from the second to the third application reflected changes stemming from the role induction procedure.

All the apprentices received group and individual supervision by licensed and different supervisors during the entire training period. None of the individual and group supervisors was aware of the aim or nature of the role induction intervention.

RESULTS

All 20 subjects in the sample completed the questionnaire from which data on the early, middle, and late role induction groups were obtained. This data were used to make compar-

isons between the first and second application (changes as a result of time in supervision) and between the second and third application (changes as a result of role induction). Table B summarises the averages and standard deviations for the dependent measures over the three evaluation periods.

Table B Averages and standard deviations over time for the semantic differential (SD)

		Time 1	Time 2	Time 3
Evaluation of	$\bar{X}$	2,76	3,24	3,19
supervision	s	0,73	0,83	0,96

NOTE: Higher scores on the SD reflect more negative evaluations.

REFERENCES

Bernard, J. 1989. Supervision training: A discrimination model. *Education and Supervision*, **2**(19): 60–68.

Cohen, L. 1990. *The new supervisee views supervision*. New York: Wiley.

Osgood, C.E. 1952. The nature and measurement of meaning. *Psychological Bulletin*, **49**: 197–237.

Schauer, A.H., Seymour, W.R. & Green, R.G. 1993. Effects of observation and evaluation on anxiety in apprentices. *Journal of Development*, **6**(3): 26–47.

Case Study C

Evaluation of a training course in management principles for first-line supervisors at a South African agricultural corporation

INTRODUCTION

Since unskilled supervisors often learn negative behaviour that is difficult to change, it is important that supervisors learn the skills of supervision before they are introduced into supervisory situations (Jacobs, 1985). To emphasise the urgency of offering evaluated management courses, Nortjé and Crous (1990) point out that supervisors in southern Africa must be trained to meet the increasing challenges and higher expectations.

According to Heunis (1981), it is important that when time and money are invested in training needs, training interventions are not launched without the necessary evaluation. Flippo (1981) supports this thought when he mentions that the only answer to the evaluation of management courses lies in the scientific evaluation of training results.

The aim of this research study is therefore to evaluate the above management course for first-line supervisors on a scientific basis with regard to their knowledge in order to determine the effectiveness of the course for the agricultural corporation.

Problem statement

The problem, according to the formulation of the aim of this study, is whether a significant increase in the knowledge of first-line supervisors will occur as a result of their attendance of a management course.

METHOD

Subjects

An experimental group and a control group were used. The sample group consisted of 40 supervisors (experimental $n = 18$, control group $n = 22$), randomly drawn from a population of 60 supervisors working for the agricultural corporation from the following provinces and distributed as follows:

▶ Free State: 9
▶ Mpumalanga: 6
▶ North West: 14
▶ Northern Cape: 11.

Measuring instrument

The measuring instrument consisted of a one-hour written test that was used to evaluate the knowledge of management principles of the experimental and control group in the pre- and postmeasurement phases.

PROCEDURE

A non-equivalent control group design was used in this study. The researcher trained a group of first-line supervisors in management principles. These principles included study objectives such as leadership skills, the presentation of a programme and schedule, organisation of planned actions, guidance, and control. The evaluation was carried out before and after the training course to evaluate the nature of the changes in knowledge.

RESULTS

The results of the experimental and control groups were compared with regard to the two phases of evaluation. In Table C the results of the total group in respect of knowledge (scores on the test presented in percentages) are compared before and after the course was offered to the experimental group.

Table C Differences in averages between the experimental and control group before and after the training intervention

	Knowledge test scores	
	Before training	After training
Experimental group	57%	78%
Control group	58%	56%

REFERENCES

Flippo, E.B. (1981). *Personnel management*. 5th edition. Auckland: McGraw-Hill.

Heunis, D.F. (1987). *The task of the first-line supervisor in the South African public service*. Unpublished master's dissertation, University of Port Elizabeth, Port Elizabeth.

Jacobs, W. (1985). Training of supervisors. *Human Resource Management*, **1**(1): 35–36.

Nortjé, J.D. & Crous, M.J. (1990). *The changing role of management*. Bloemfontein: University of the Orange Free State.

Case Study D

The relationship between preparation time and actual performance in public speech-making

INTRODUCTION

Public speech coaches have long taken for granted that there is a positive relationship between preparation time and actual performance in public speech-making. They stress the importance of preparation to their students; but what about the student who reports spending hours in preparation and yet makes a poor speech? What about the student who admittedly does very little preparation but is a superb speaker? Hayes (1978) found, for example, that good speakers had lower anxiety levels – this is a factor outside the realm of preparation.

A survey of public speech-making students (Hayes, 1978) showed that nearly all perceived a positive relationship between the time they spent preparing for a speech and the quality of the speech that followed. Reisch and Ballard (1985) encourage coaches of speakers to emphasise practice; they note that "practice at any time, in any place will do more to bolster the self-confidence of a novice speaker than any other factor" (p. 13).

One factor that may diminish the effectiveness of preparation is the amount of anxiety that the speaker feels. Students in basic communication courses who experience speech anxiety reported being more concerned about audience size and speech length than preparation procedures (Hayes & Marshall, 1984).

Research questions

This study examined the relationship between preparation time and speech anxiety with respect to the quality of public speaking. Two specific questions were addressed:

1. What is the relationship between speech quality and total preparation time?
2. What is the relationship between speech quality and speech anxiety?

METHOD

Subjects

The subjects in this study were 49 students from four technikons and they were distributed as follows:

- Cape Technikon: 15
- Technikon Natal: 9
- Technikon Free State: 8
- Technikon Pretoria: 17

The subjects' ages ranged from 18 to 48, with a mean age of 23.

All subjects had completed seven speech-making assignments prior to the final video-taped speech upon which this study is based.

PROCEDURE

Speech preparation time

The subjects were asked to indicate, in minutes, the time they spent on the following activities: discussion with coach, library research, audience analysis, preparation of speaking notes, silent rehearsal, oral rehearsal, and other activities. The times were added to obtain the total time spent in preparation.

Speech quality

A speech rating scale was used to measure the following: the introduction, conclusion, overall organisation and structure of arguments, eye contact, gestures and movement, voice usage, energy, and enthusiasm. Each of these eight elements was evaluated on a five-point scale: done exceptionally well (5); done well (4); average (3); done poorly (2); not done well at all (1). The values were added to obtain a total score for each subject.

Speech anxiety

Speech anxiety was evaluated with a questionnaire developed by Booth and Gould (1986). The questionnaire consists of 21 items pertaining to the subject's general feelings of anxiety about communication. Subjects assign values for all items (for example, "I am short of breath before I begin a speech") on a four-point scale ranging from 1 (almost never) to 4 (almost always). The responses were added to obtain a single speech anxiety score for each subject.

Data analysis

The data were analysed with the Statistical Package for Social Sciences (SPSS). The product moment correlation was used to determine the relationship among variables.

RESULTS

Table D displays the results of this study. It is a summary of the results as they relate to the two research questions.

Table D Correlations between speech quality and other variables

	Speech quality
Speech preparation time	0,75
Speech anxiety	0,03

Booth and Gould (1986) used Cronbach's coefficient alpha as a reliability estimate for the communication anxiety questionnaire and reported a coefficient of 0,89.

REFERENCES

Booth, S. & Gould, M. (1986). The communication anxiety questionnaire. *Communication Quarterly*, **34**, 194–205.

Hayes, B.J. & Marshall, W.L. (1984). Generalization of treatment effects in training public speakers. *Behavior Research & Therapy*, **22**, 519–533.

Hayes, D.T. (1978). *Nonintellective predictors of public speaking ability and academic success in a basic college-level speech communication course*. Unpublished doctoral thesis, University of Missouri, Missouri.

Reisch, R.J. & Ballard, D.S. (1985). *Coaching strategies in contest persuasive speaking: A guide to coaching the novice*. Paper presented at the annual meeting of the Speech Communication Association, Denver.

Case Study E

The role of bank overdraft usage and cash flow problems in the prediction of bankruptcy

INTRODUCTION

From the claims records in judicial courts ("Third of claims", 1992), it appears that the non-availability of cash is still the predominant cause of bankruptcy in all small businesses in South Africa. Research on possible contributory causes of bankruptcy therefore remains of the utmost importance.

Friedman and Rosenman (1974) came to the conclusion that risk factors for bankruptcy (such as poor credit control and debt collection) were predictors of fewer than half the cases of bankruptcy. According to these authors, businesses that exceed their bank overdraft run a greater risk of becoming bankrupt.

During the eighties, the findings on the importance of bank overdraft usage as predictor of bankruptcy were contradicted in several prominent investigations, and enthusiasm for this topic waned. These investigations tended to consider bankruptcy in terms of bank overdraft usage without taking other risk factors, such as cash flow problems into account.

Levy (1998) believes that, statistically, bank overdraft usage is a less important predictor of bankruptcy than management skills, and that there is a mutually operative relationship between bank overdraft usage and management skills in this regard. As a possible explanation of the data they obtained in investigating the opinion of Levy above, Kreitler and Brunner (1997) suggest that "a business where management skills such as co-ordination of enterprise functions is highly developed ... tends more to business where management skills such as co-ordination of enterprise functions is highly developed ... tends more to make use of bank overdrafts as a means for controlling cash flow problems" (p. 493).

There are various means by which management skills and cash flow problems might combine with bank overdraft usage to give rise to bankruptcy. Accordingly, overextension of bank overdraft need not represent a risk on its own; it can become a risk only if it is linked to specific levels of other variables (Maticek, 1998). Thus, bank overdraft usage and cash flow problems do not have to be played off against each other regarding their ability to predict bankruptcy, because this ability to predict is in fact increased by viewing these factors jointly.

The purpose of the present research therefore was to investigate the role of bank overdraft usage and cash flow problems in predicting bankruptcy status (bankrupt versus non-bankrupt).

METHOD

Subjects

The names and telephone numbers of small businesses that employed between 40 to 60 employees that had been declared bankrupt in the preceding two years were obtained from the Receiver of Revenue in Pretoria. The owners of small businesses situated in Pretoria were contacted by telephone to secure their co-operation in completing the questionnaire. Only three refused to participate in the project. Appointments were made with 36 owners, during which they were given the questionnaires and told how to complete them. A control group of an equal number of small business owners who were prepared to participate in the project of corresponding sizes (number of employees) and comparable business sectors (for example bakeries, second hand car sales, and so on) but without any record of bankruptcy completed the questionnaire in the same manner.

The average size of the bankrupt group was 50 employees and that of the control group was 49.

Procedure

Apart from the business owners having to indicate the size of the small business (number of workers employed) as well as the busi-

ness sector to which they belonged, they also had to indicate the amount by which they exceeded their overdraft limit on average per month. They furthermore had to indicate on a four-point scale the extent to which they are/were prone to having cash-flow problems by marking the letters F (completely false), f (more false than true), t (more true than false) or T (completely true). T was scored 4 (four).

Bankruptcy was scored 1 (one) and non-bankrupt 0 (zero).

RESULTS

The correlations between the predictor variables and bankruptcy-status (bankrupt/non-bankrupt) are provided in Table E.

Table E Correlation matrix of variables

	Bank overdraft usage	Bankruptcy
Cash-flow problem	0,83	0,94
Bankruptcy status	0,45	

Bank overdraft usage (reported amount by which bank overdrafts were exceeded) correlated significantly high ($r = 0,94$) with bankruptcy status and also showed a significantly high positive correlation of 0,83 with cash-flow problems. Cash-flow problems showed a correlation of 0,45 with bankruptcy status (bankrupt/non-bankrupt).

REFERENCES

Third of claims (1992, 18 December). *The Star*, p. 8.

Levy, H.J. (1998). The perspective importance of management skills, bank overdraft and interaction effects for the genesis of bankruptcy. *Management skills and small businesses*, **9**, 453–464.

Friedman, M., & Rosenman, R.H. (1974). Association of bank overdraft usage patterns with increase in bankruptcy. *Journal of the American Business Association*, **44**, 525–553.

Maticek, R. (1998). Synergetic effects of bank overdraft, cashflow problems and risk factors in bank overdraft usage. *Financial Business Skills*, **34**, 267–272.

Kreitler, S. & Brunner, D. (1997). The relation of bank overdraft to financial risk factors for bankruptcy. *Management Skills and Small Businesses*, **12**, 487–495.

Case Study F

The differences in innovative problem-solving styles of entrepreneurs and managers of big businesses in South Africa

INTRODUCTION

Research conducted on the skills of business people has recently shifted to an examination of entrepreneurs' cognitive styles and innovative abilities in terms of problem-solving. It also focused on the differences in management styles of managers and entrepreneurs.

Begley and Boyd (1986) found, for example, that entrepreneurs exhibited a higher risk-taking propensity than small business managers. In a comparison of the decision-making approaches used by entrepreneurs and managers of larger firms, Smith, Gannon, Grimm and Mitchell (1988) found that the managers used a more rational approach than did entrepreneurs. Swayne and Tucker (1973) argued that entrepreneurs are more innovative than managers in seeking ways to expand their business or start new ones.

Research by Sexton and Bowman-Upton (1986) shows that entrepreneurship students tend to be more innovative than other business administration students. Similarly, the research of Chaganti and Chaganti (1983) suggests that entrepreneurs will be more innovative than managers.

A theoretical framework for identifying problem-solving styles is the Kirton Adaption-Innovation (KAI) theory (Kirton, 1987). Kirton (1976) developed a measuring-instrument (KAI scale) based on the above-mentioned theory.

The purpose of the current study was to compare the innovative problem-solving styles, as measured by the KAI scale, of entrepreneurs and managers of big businesses.

METHOD

Respondents

A sample of 222 business people was used in the research project. They were located in the following way:

A sample of 300 respondents (entrepreneurs) located in Gauteng and the Western Cape was selected from two entrepreneurial networking groups. An introductory letter was sent to each respondent inviting him or her to participate in the research project. One hundred and sixty respondents returned the response forms, indicating their willingness to participate in the research project. The KAI measurement questionnaires were mailed to the 160 respondents and 112 completed questionnaires were returned. The 112 respondents (entrepreneurs) consisted of:

▶ 100 males
▶ 12 females.

The average age of the entrepreneurial group was 28.

A sample of 300 respondents (managers) of 30 large companies located in Gauteng and the Western Cape was also selected. An introductory letter was sent to each respondent, inviting him or her to participate in the research project. One hundred and thirty respondents returned the response forms, indicating their willingness to participate in the research project. The KAI measurement questionnaires were mailed to the 130 managers and 110 completed questionnaires were returned. The 110 respondents (managers) consisted of:

▶ 70 males
▶ 40 females.

The average age of the group of managers was 42.

Measuring instrument

The measuring instrument used in the project to measure the difference in the innovative problem-solving styles of the respondents was the Kirton Adaptation-Innovation Scale (KAI scale). The KAI is a 32-item self-report measuring instrument with scores ranging from 32 (lowest level of innovation) to 160 (highest level of innovation).

RESULTS

For the purpose of the study, the mean KAI score for the entrepreneurs was compared with the mean KAI score for the managers. The KAI scores for the two groups are as follows (Table F):

Table F Mean scores and standard deviation scores of managers and entrepreneurs on the KAI scale

	Mean scores on KAI	Standard deviation
Managers	96,0	13,0
Entrepreneurs	113,9	13,2

The results of the *t*-test comparing the means of the two groups indicated that the entrepreneurs were significantly more innovative than the managers.

REFERENCES

Begley, T. & Boyd, D. (1986). Psychological characteristics associated with Entrepeneurial Performance. In *Frontiers of Entrepreneurship Research*, (red.) R. Ronstadt, J. Hornaday, R. Peterson, & K.Vesper, Wellesley, Mass.: Babson College, Center for Entrepreneurial Studies, 146–166.

Chaganti, R. & Chaganti, R. (1983). A Profile of Profitable and Not-so-profitable Small Business. *Journal of Small Business Management*, **21** (July), 26–31.

Kirton, M. (1976). Adaption and Innovation: A description and Measure, *Journal of Applied Psychology*, **61** (October), 622–629.

Smith, K.M., Gannon, M., Grimm, C. & Mitchell, T. (1988). Decision making behaviour in Smaller Entrepreneurial and Larger Professionally Managed Firms, *Journal of Business Venturing*, **3** (Summer), 223–232.

Sexton, D. & Bowman-Upton, N. (1986). Validation of a Personality Index: Comparative Entrepreneurial Analysis of Female Entrepreneurs, Managers, Entrepreneurship Students and Business Students. In *Frontiers of Entrepreneurship Research*, (red.) R. Ronstadt, J. Hornaday, R. Peterson & K. Vesper, Wellesley, Mass.: Babson College, Center for Entrepreneurial Studies, 40–51.

Swayne, C. & Tucker, W. (1973). *The Effective Entrepreneur*. Morristown, N.J.: General Learning Press.

Case study G

The attitudes of nurses towards patients who suffer from HIV/AIDS

INTRODUCTION

Attitudes can be described as any general evaluations people that have of others, themselves, and other issues and they are manifested in feelings of like, dislike, favour, and disfavour (Petty, 1995). Some attitudes have an ego-defensive function by protecting people from threatening truths about themselves or to enhance their self-image. Attitudes can be either negative or positive. Discrimination follows from negative attitudes (prejudice) and it can be described as a display of negative behaviour reflecting negative thoughts and feelings (Bremer & Byrne, 1991).

People reduce the complexity of the social world by demarcating similarities and differences between people – a strategy called social categorisation. Groups sharing similarities with the person who holds the attitude are classified as "in-groups", and "out-groups" consist of those people who are perceived as "different". Socially undesirable victims were initially held responsible for AIDS. The mass media quickly labelled AIDS the "homosexual" plague or the black African disease and this stigmatisation caused prejudice towards the minority group to increase (van Dyk, 2001). Devine (1995) reported that self-esteem is enhanced by maintaining negative attitudes towards "outgroup" members such as HIV/AIDS patients. When people are confronted with HIV/AIDS patients, their reaction is often one of disapproval, fear, prejudice, as well as condemnation.

These negative attitudes are carried into the healthcare environment and lead to prejudices towards HIV/AIDS patients amongst nurses. Although the causes of AIDS are known, many nurses are locked in the negative and emotive feelings associated with the initial stage of AIDS. Nurses therefore also adopt discriminatory behaviour towards HIV/AIDS patients by avoiding such patients in the implementation of care. Although overt and direct forms of prejudice have decreased, prejudiced feelings have not been reduced and overt forms of prejudice have been replaced by covert and subtle forms of prejudice.

The aim of this investigation was to investigate the attitudes of nurses towards HIV/AIDS patients at a specific hospital in South Africa and to establish whether there is a difference in attitudes towards HIV/AIDS patients between younger and older nurses.

METHOD

Subjects

The target population consisted of a convenience (purposive) sample of nurses at a public hospital in South Africa. The nurses had to meet specific criteria and should have had at least two years' experience in the care of HIV/AIDS patients. The respondents consisted of two groups of female nurses. One group consisted of 10 nurses between the ages of 20 and 30 years and the other group of 10 nurses were between the ages of 30 and 50 years. The

age categories were used to establish whether differences in attitudes exist. The average education level of the younger nurses was matric plus two years' training and the average level of the older nurses was Grade 10.

Measuring instrument

The respondents were interviewed individually by means of unstructured in-depth interviews and field notes were taken by the researcher. The questions related to the differences in treatment of patients affected with HIV/AIDS and interpersonal relations with and behaviour towards HIV/AIDS patients.

PROCEDURE

Respondents were provided with a case study which reflected on nurses' interpersonal relations and implementation of care towards a patient with HIV/AIDS. By viewing this situation from a distance, respondents could express feelings that they would not have been able to express if they were in the situation. Respondents were also presented with a cartoon of a nurse caring for an HIV/AIDS patient as a stimulus to which they had to respond. The respondents were asked to explore possible responses on the part of the nurse presented in the sketch. This method provided a much richer understanding of attitudes than abstract questions.

Permission was obtained from the appropriate authorities to carry out a project of such a sensitive nature. The respondents were made aware that there were no correct or incorrect responses and that confidentiality would be maintained.

The purpose of analysing the field notes was to identify the most important themes (keywords or sentences) by means of coding. The codes were used to attach meaning to the descriptive information that had been collected during the field work. They were used to retrieve and organise the chunks of text that had been categorised according to the particular themes within the original raw data or field notes.

RESULTS

The frequencies and percentages of answers per age group of the four themes identified by means of the analysis of the field notes are displayed in Table G2. The number/frequencies of the responses from the respondents are displayed in the spreadsheet (matrix) in Table G1.

Table G1 Spreadsheet for analysing interviews

Theme	Age
1	1
1	1
1	1
1	1
1	1
1	1
1	1
1	1
1	2
1	2
1	2
1	2
1	2
2	1
2	1
2	1
2	1
2	1
2	2
2	2
2	2
3	1
3	1
3	1
3	1
3	1
3	1
3	1

Theme	Age
3	1
3	1
3	2
3	2
3	2
3	2
3	2
3	2
3	2
4	1
4	1
4	1
4	1
4	1
4	1
4	1
4	1
4	1
4	1
4	2
4	2
4	2
4	2
4	2
4	2
4	2
4	2
4	2

Table G2 Frequencies of answers per theme and age group

Themes	Age group	Number of responses	Percentage
Fear of contracting HIV/AIDS	20–30 years	8	40%
	30–50 years	6	30%
Discriminatory behaviour towards patients	20–30 years	5	25%
	30–50 years	3	15%
Experiencing stress in nursing patients	20–30 years	9	45%
	30–50 years	7	35%
Experiencing mixed feelings (doubt, fear, sympathy, empathy, uncertainty)	20–30 years	10	50%
	30–50 years	10	50%

REFERENCES

Bremer, A.T. & Byrne, D. (1991). *Understanding human behaviour*. London: Allyn & Bacon.

Devine, P.G. (1995). Prejudice and outgroup perception. In A. Tesser (ed.) *Advanced Social Psychology* (pp. 467–524). New York: McGraw-Hill, Inc.

Petty, R.E. (1995). Attitude change. In A. Tesser (ed.) *Advanced Social Psychology* (pp. 195–255). New York: McGraw-Hill Inc.

Van Dyk, A. (2001). *HIV/AIDS care and Counselling. A multidisciplinary approach*. Cape Town: Pearson Education.

MoonStats user guide

1 Introducing MoonStats

MoonStats© is a stand-alone statistical software program that operates in Windows 95 or higher. It is designed for novice and advanced computer users and provides the statistical tools for data exploration and data description. Users can gain experience in the most commonly used statistics with the aid of an intuitive user interface. All statistical routines are complemented by graphs to enhance the user's visual understanding of the statistic. MoonStats enables students, researchers, and professionals to develop a solid foundation in statistics, and to manage basic statistics with confidence.

MoonStats allows for data entry of numeric values into a data sheet of up to 100 variables and 1 000 cases (units of analyses). It performs the standard descriptive statistical computations as well as a selection of bivariate descriptive and inferential statistics as listed below:

Descriptive statistics: mode, median, mean, standard deviation, the 95% confidence interval for the mean, minimum, maximum, range, skewness, kurtosis, and frequency tables.

Graphs: bar charts, pie charts, histograms, and scatterplots.

Bivariate statistics: cross-tabulation with chi-square, Pearson's product moment and Spearman's rank order correlations, and t-tests for independent and dependent groups.

Each statistic is accompanied by *result-specific comments* on the interpretation of the statistical result, and provides suggestions on how to report the results. The program also incorporates a *pseudo-random number calculator* to generate sampling lists.

2 System requirements

▶ A Pentium level personal computer.
▶ Windows 95 or higher.
▶ 32 Mb RAM.
▶ At least 3 Mb of hard disk space.
▶ A CD-ROM driver.

3 End-user licence agreement

3.1 Read the terms and conditions of the licence carefully before installing this program. By using the MoonStats software the user acknowledges that he/she has read and accepts the following terms and conditions of the MoonStats software and the "MoonStats User Guide". This is an agreement between the user and the MoonStats Close Corporation (hereafter MoonStats CC). If you do not agree with the terms and conditions, do not install, open or use the MoonStats software.

3.2 MoonStats CC grants the user a non-exclusive licence to use one copy of the enclosed software programme solely for the user's personal or business purpose on a single computer (whether a standard computer or a workstation component of a multi-user environment). This licence to use the software is conditional upon the user's compliance with the terms of this agreement. The software is in use on a computer when it is loaded into temporary storage (RAM) or installed into permanent memory (hard disk, CD-ROM or other storage device). The user agrees to only copy the software into any machine-readable or printed form as necessary to use it in accordance with this licence or for backup purposes in support of the user's use of the software.

3.3 MoonStats CC is the owner of all rights, title, and interest, including copyright of the software recorded on the CD-ROM or storage device, and copyright of the "MoonStats User Guide" supplied as an Appendix in the textbook *Research methodology* (3rd edition) by J.C. Welman, S.J. Kruger & B.C. Mitchell, published by Oxford University Press Southern Africa (hereafter referred to as "the textbook"). Ownership of the MoonStats software and the "MoonStats User Guide" and all proprietary rights relating thereto remain with MoonStats CC. MoonStats CC reserves all rights not expressly granted in this licence.

3.4 The only licensed user is the legal owner of the textbook described in the previous section (hereafter referred to as "the

licensee" or "the user"). The licensee may make only one copy of the MoonStats software for backup or archival purposes, or transfer the software to a single hard disk. The licensee may not (a) rent or lease the software, (b) copy or reproduce the software through a LAN or network or other system, or (c) modify, adapt, decompile, disassemble, reverse engineer, translate, or create derivative works based on the software. Any attempt to do so (whether or not successful), terminates this licence to use the software without refund of any fees paid. The licensee may transfer the software and user documentation with the textbook on a permanent basis provided the transferee agrees to accept the terms and conditions of this agreement and the previous owner retains no copies of the software nor of the "MoonStats User Guide".

3.5 The software media (CD-ROM) is warranted for a period of 60 days from the date of the original purchase of the textbook with MoonStats only. If the CD-ROM is damaged and Oxford University Press Southern Africa receives notification of defects in the CD-ROM within the warranty period and valid proof of purchase is supplied, Oxford University Press Southern Africa will replace the defective CD-ROM.

3.6 MoonStats CC, Oxford University Press Southern Africa, and the authors of the textbook disclaim all other warranties, express or implied, including without limitation implied warranties of merchantability, fitness for a particular use, and/or noninfringement of third-party rights, with respect to the software, the programs, the source code contained therein, and/or the techniques described in the textbook and the "MoonStats User Guide", and also do not warrant that the functions contained in the software will meet the user's requirements or that the operation of the software will be error-free. While every effort has been made to ensure that the program is virus-free, the onus is on the user to implement the latest computer virus protection. This software and accompanying written materials (including instructions for use) are provided "as is" without warranty of any kind. MoonStats CC does not warrant, guarantee, or make any representations regarding the use, or the results of use, of the software or written materials in terms of correctness, accuracy, reliability, currentness, or otherwise. The entire risk as to the results and performance of the software is assumed by the software user. If the software or written materials are defective, the software user (and not MoonStats CC or its dealers, distributors, agents, or employees) assumes the entire cost of all necessary servicing, repair, or correction.

3.7 MoonStats CC's and Oxford University Press Southern Africa's entire liability and exclusive remedy for defects in materials and workmanship shall be limited to replacing the software media by writing and returning the defective media with valid proof of purchase to: Client Services – *Research Methodology*, Oxford University Press Southern Africa, PO Box 12119, N1 City, Goodwood, 7463, South Africa. This limited warranty is void if failure of the software media has resulted from accident, abuse or misapplication. Any replacement software media shall be warranted for thirty days after postage to the user.

3.8 In no event shall MoonStats CC or Oxford University Press Southern Africa or the book editors or authors be liable for any damages whatsoever (including without limitation damages for loss of business profits, business interruption, loss of business information, or any other pecuniary loss) arising from the use of or inability to use the "MoonStats User Guide" and/or the software.

3.9 By using the software, the user acknowledges that he/she has read this limited warranty, understands it, and agrees to be bound by its terms and conditions. The user also agrees that the limited warranty is the complete and exclusive statement of agreement between the parties and supersedes all proposals or prior agreements, oral or written, and any other communications between the parties relating to the subject matter of the limited warranty.

4 Software support

For software questions and support visit our website at http://www.moonstats.co.za or email us at info@moonstats.co.za. Alternatively, you can write to us at the following address: Client Services – "MoonStats – Research Methodology", Oxford University Press Southern Africa, PO Box 12119, N1 City, Goodwood, 7463, South Africa. If your CD-ROM is defective and covered under the limited warranty, return the CD-ROM to Oxford University Press.

5 Installing MoonStats

▶ Insert the CD-ROM (label side up) into your CD-ROM drive.

▶ Select and click on "My Computer" on your Windows Desktop.

▶ Select and click on the drive that lists the MoonStats CD.

▶ Follow the instructions that appear on your screen. You must agree with the licensing agreement to install and use the program.

6 Getting started – a quick overview of MoonStats

MoonStats was designed to make data entry and data analysis on computer as simple as possible. The best way to become familiar with the program is to explore it by using the following easy steps.

Firstly, install the software as described in the previous section. Then start the program by clicking on the MoonStats icon on the Windows Desktop (or selecting MoonStats from the Windows Programs menu). Once the program is open (see Box 1), you can open any data set (such as the data set "BUS.MON") that was supplied with the program by clicking on the "Open a data set" button (see Box 2).

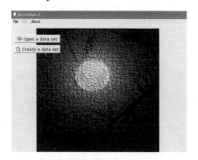

Box 1 *MoonStats start-up window*

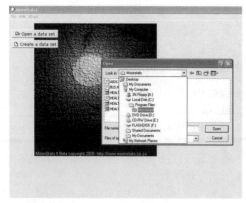

Box 2 *Open data set*

The first two screens which you will see when starting MoonStats and opening a data set are displayed in Box 1 and 2. MoonStats data sets work with *.MON (and *.MN1 for labels) or *.DBF extensions. Once you have opened a data set, the data will be displayed in the data sheet window.

If the software was installed on the hard drive (in most cases this will be local disk C:\), the example data sets can be found under the folder C:\ProgramFiles\Moonstats.

The upgrade of MoonStats ("MoonStats 2") consists of five window tabs:

1. A **Specifications window** to enter and edit labels.
2. A **Data window** to enter and edit data.
3. A **Univariate data analysis window** to select any of the single variable analytical procedures.
4. A **Bivariate data analysis window** to select bivariate analytical procedures.
5. A **Tools window** to calculate random samples and perform chi-square calculations.

You can move between these windows by clicking on the tabs labelled Specifications, Data, Univariate, Bivariate, and Tools.

7 Enter or edit data using the MoonStats data sheet

Data can be entered or edited using the data sheet.

7.1 What is a data sheet?

A **data sheet** is also called a **data matrix** or a **spreadsheet** and presents a clear and easy way of working with a large **data set**. Each data sheet consists of **columns** (running vertically from top to bottom) and **rows** (running horizontally from left to right).

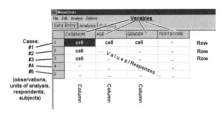

Box 3 *Detailed data sheet*

Each column is occupied by a **variable** that relates to an item or question in the data collection instrument (questionnaire/interview/ and so on) that was used to collect the data. In this instance the variables are as follows: *casenum, age, gender, testscore.*

Each row is occupied by a **case** or **unit of analysis**, also called an **observation, respondent**, **subject**, **individual**, or **element**. A case can be a person, household, school, and so on, depending on the research. There are five cases in this example, and these are numbered from case #1 to case #5.

The **cell** or box where each row and column meet represents the specific **response, value, score** or **datum** (datum is the singular of data) that the respondent or subject provided to the specific question or item. In this example the five rows and four columns result in 20 cells or values.

7.2 Open a data set in the data sheet

When the MoonStats program opens, you have the option to "Open a data set" or to "Create a data set". You can also find the "Open" and "Create" functions on the File menu. The default (the selection automatically chosen by the computer) extension of MoonStats data files is *.MON. You can open MoonStats data files (*.MON) or import data files in the widely available Xbase/Dbase format (*.DBF).

Note that MoonStats data files can contain *numerical* values only! You must therefore convert any *alphabetic* values (a, b, c, and so on) to numeric values (1, 2, 3, and so on) prior

to data entry and analysis. Open the desired data set or any of the data sets, such as "BUS. MON", provided with MoonStats, or incorporate your own data from other software programs such as Excel, Quattro Pro, SAS, SPSS, and so on, by converting them to Xbase/Dbase (*.dbf) and importing them to MoonStats.

7.3 Create a new data set in the data sheet

You can create a new data set by selecting the option "Create a data set" on the MoonStats start-up screen or by selecting "Create" from the File menu. You must remember that MoonStats data files can contain numerical values only and that you should convert any alphabetic values (a, b, c, and so on) to numeric values (1, 2, 3, and so on) before entering the values or doing data analysis. It is a good idea to make a note of the names that you assign to each variable and to keep track of your data entry process. You should use variable names that are descriptive of the question or item, as the variable names appear in the output tables and graphs. MoonStats allows a maximum of 10 characters for a variable name. You should therefore abbreviate long words to 10 letters or fewer.

7.3.1 DEFINE THE DATA SET

When you choose to create a data set, the "define a data set" dialog box (see Box 4) will appear. This box will contain the list of variables in your new data set. A few examples of variable names are provided by default, for example, REFNUM, SEX, AGE, but these can be changed to suit your needs. However, you should always have a REFNUM variable that corresponds to the unique number written on top of each data collection measure (questionnaire, interview, etc.). This will help you to check the data on the physical data collection measure (the questionnaire, interview, and so on) against the data entered for that case/ subject on the data sheet. A variable name can be changed by clicking on it and editing it. Additional variables can be added by selecting the "add variable" button. You will be prompted to supply a file name for the data set. The default (automatic choice) data set or file name will be "NEWSET.MON" unless you change it. Remember to use an appropriate name for your data set that accurately describes your research topic.

Box 4 *Define a new data set*

Once these steps have been completed, you can enter the data. If you wish to add another variable at a later stage, simply go to the specifications window.

7.3.2 ENTER THE DATA

Data entry is done by clicking on the first empty cell (case 1, variable 1) and typing in numeric data. MoonStats saves each data entry, while you are busy entering the data.

Box 5 *Enter the data*

When a question or item has not been completed by a respondent, you have "missing data". This happens when the question is not relevant to the person for a specific reason, such as sensitivity of the information, failure to complete the questionnaire, entry of an invalid code, and so on. MoonStats deals with missing data by excluding it from univariate analysis. In a bivariate analysis the case/person/unit of analysis is simply ignored as well.

If a value is missing, you can simply leave that cell in the data sheet empty. As MoonStats only recognises numerical values, all alphabetical values are also treated as missing values. If you have missing data you must not use a zero (0) as a missing value – zero is an actual value!

	REFNUM	AGE	SEX	EDUC	INCOME	BUSROUTE	BUSTIME
1	32	26	1	8	4900	1	5
2	28	26	1	5	4700	1	5
3	112	34	2	5	4500	1	3
4	44	29	1	4	4500	1	3
5	20	25	1	4	4500	1	4
6	86	26	2	5	4400	1	4
7	11	23	1		4400	1	5
8	88	28	2	5	4300	1	4
9	27	26	1	4	4300	1	4
10	22		1	5	4300	1	2
11	54	32	1	4	4200	1	5
12	24	25	1	4	4200	1	4
13	9	22	1	4	4200	1	4
14	36	27	1	4	4100	1	3
15	31	26		5	4100	1	3
16	101	31	2	5	4000	1	3
17	14	24	1	5	4000	1	5
18	13	23	1	4	4000	1	5
19	1	16	1	3	3900	1	4
20	39	27	1	3	3700	1	4
21	33	26	1	3	3600	1	4
22	3	20	1	3	3600	1	4
23	90	29	2	5	3500	1	4
24	91	29	2	4	3500	1	4
25	19	24	1	3	3500	1	3
26	7	22	1	3	3500	1	3
27	96	30	2	4	3400	1	3
28	43	29	1	3	3400	1	3

1=< grade 10 2=grade 10+11 3=grade 12 5=post grad 4=dipl/degree

Box 6 *Bus data*

TIP: MAKE BACKUP COPIES!
Remember to make a backup of your data on a memory stick, stiffy diskette or other removable storage media such as CD-RW. You need to have access to your backup data in case your computer breaks down or disappears. Always store two or more copies of your data in a safe place, preferably in a different venue away from the computer. If you consider what it will cost you in time, energy, and money to recreate the data set, you will realise the importance of backups.

---

8 Analysing the data

To perform statistical analyses you should go to the Univariate Analysis window (click on the Univariate window tab). Select one or more variables and then click on the various statistics.

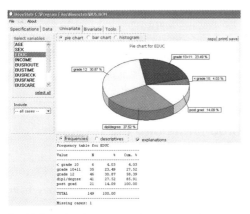

Box 7 *Univariate frequency statistics and pie chart*

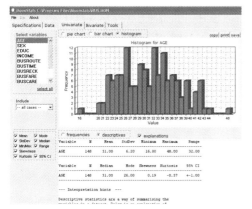

Box 8 *Univariate descriptive statistics and histogram*

You can calculate bivariate statistics by selecting two variables from the two drop-down lists on the left-hand side of the screen. A correlation (Pearson's product moment for interval/ratio data or Spearman's rank-order for ordinal data) provides the relationship between variables. The scatterplot provides a visual representation of the relationship between the variables.

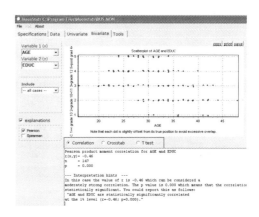

Box 9 *Bivariate correlation and scatterplot*

A cross-tabulation will provide a chi-square statistic for nominal and/or ordinal variables with a limited range. The bar chart provides a visual representation of the relationship between the variables.

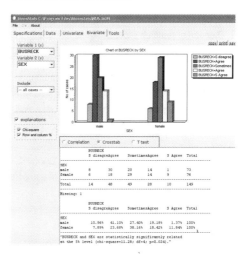

Box 10 *Bivariate tables and chi-square with bar chart*

The *t*-test is used to evaluate the differences in the means of two groups. Independent groups are randomly selected experimental/treatment and control groups. Dependent groups are based on related subject samples, for instance when a group of subjects is tested before and after an intervention to determine if there is an improvement in their scores. The bivariate chart provides a visual representation of the relationship between the variables.

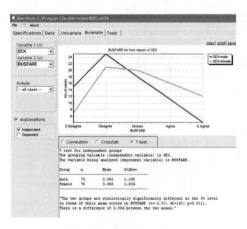

Box 11 *Bivariate t-test and line graph*

A random number calculator is available and can be accessed *via* the Tools tab. A list of pseudo-random numbers can be created, based on sampling without replacement. In such a list no numbers are repeated in the sampling list. The default setting is for a population of 110 (that is, your sampling frame or list of all possible cases) and a sample of 15 cases, but you can change these values as required.

9 MoonStats and the research phases

By now you are perhaps wondering how to start your research project, or you may have collected research data and need to analyse the results and write the report. The following table provides an overview of the research phases and indicates how MoonStats can help you. The stages of research, as discussed in the rest of the textbook, are indicated with an arrow (➔). The dark arrows (➔) indicate how MoonStats can assist you with the research.

Table 1 Overview of research phases

➔ Decide on a topic that you want to investigate (see Chapter 2).

➔ Conduct a literature review of the topic and consult key stakeholders (see Chapter 3).

➔ Define the research problem and objectives. Formulate hypotheses or exploratory questions (see Chapter 2).

➔ Develop a data analysis plan by deciding what statistic is to be used with each variable and for what purpose (see Chapters 2 and 9). Also develop an outline for your report to indicate what statistic will be reported in the appropriate sections of the proposal and report.

➔ Design data collection instruments (questionnaires, interviews, and so on).

➔ Decide on and draw the sample in terms of sampling frame/list.

  ➔ If the study requires RANDOM SELECTION, create a list of random numbers for the sample with the RANDOM NUMBER CALCULATOR.

Data entry and analysis with MoonStats

➔ CODE the data into numerical format and create a (hand-written) CODE SHEET on a separate page, and keep this page in a safe place.

➔ ENTER the data using the MoonStats Data sheet.

➔ CLEAN the data of errors and make data backups.

➔ EXPLORE the data using charts and descriptive statistics.

➔ UNIVARIATE STATISTICS:

  • Charts: bar chart, histogram, and pie chart.

  • Frequency tabulation.

  • Descriptive statistics: mode, median, mean, standard deviation, 95% confidence interval of the mean, minimum/maximum, range, skewness, kurtosis.

→ BIVARIATE STATISTICS:
  • Cross tabulation, Chi-square, and bivariate chart.
  • *t*-test for dependent or independent groups and bivariate chart.
  • Correlation and scatterplot.
→ Write report.
→ Disseminate report and implement findings.

9.1 Code the data into numerical format and create a Code Sheet

As we have mentioned before, MoonStats accepts only numerical data – therefore, if you have alphabetical data, you have to code your data to make it numerical. You may, for example, have a question which has response values that range from A to E, as is the case in the example in Table 2. This should be recoded in the following way: A = 1, B = 2, C = 3, D = 4, E = 5. You can then enter the numbers in the data sheet or spreadsheet, keeping in mind that a value of "1" on this variable represents an A, and a value of "5" represents an E.

Let us work through an example data set provided with MoonStats. The following questionnaire was used to collect the data in the "Bus Service" study (in the "BUS.MON" data file). This is a fictitious study of bus passengers' perceptions of their bus service, and was designed as an example data set to introduce users to MoonStats.

Table 2 Questionnaire used in the "Bus Service" study (see "BUS.MON" data file)

Dear Sir/Madam   Please help us improve our bus service by completing the following anonymous questionnaire. Write your answers or indicate with a cross on the appropriate answer to what extent you agree or disagree with the statements.
Reference number for administrative purposes:
1. What is your age? ....
2. Indicate your gender.   [(1) male / (2) female]
3. What is the highest educational level that you have completed successfully?   [(1) Below Grade 10 / (2) Grade 10 and 11 / (3) Grade 12 (Matric) /   (4) Post-matric Diploma or Degree / (5) Postgraduate degree]
4. Indicate your monthly income   R........................ per month
5. What bus route do you normally use? [(1) Rietvlei ..../ (2) Kwa-Thema ....]
6. Our local buses are usually on time.   [(a) Strongly disagree / (b) Disagree / (c) Sometimes / (d) Agree / (e) Strongly Agree]
7. Our local bus drivers are reckless.   [(a) Strongly disagree / (b) Disagree / (c) Sometimes / (d) Agree / (e) Strongly Agree]
8. Our local bus fares are too high.   [(a) Strongly disagree / (b) Disagree / (c) Not sure / (d) Agree / (e) Strongly Agree]

9. Our local bus services care for their passengers [(a) Strongly disagree / (b) Disagree / (c) Not sure / (d) Agree / (e) Strongly Agree]	
10. Would you like to add anything about the bus service?	
Thank you. Your participation is greatly appreciated!	

9.2 Create your own CODE SHEET for the "Bus Service" data set

A code sheet provides a summary of the questions or items in the data-collection instrument (questionnaire/interview/and so on), the names of the variables in the data set, the coding or meaning of values, the minimum and maximum values, the range, and the measurement levels. A code sheet can be made using pen and paper.

Some of the questions in the questionnaire (Table 2) have numeric responses (1, 2, 3, ...) and others have alphabetical responses (a, b, c, ...). As MoonStats accepts only numeric data, you must convert the alphabetical values to numeric values. Therefore, we strongly encourage you to work out a detailed CODE SHEET of your data set on a piece of paper.

The following code sheet relates to the questionnaire in the previous section on the "Bus Service" study (in the "BUS.MON" data file).

Table 3 Code sheet for the bus study

CODE SHEET				
Data set: BUS.MON *				Date: 1/10/2005
Question/item and variable name	Coding	Minimum – Maximum	Range	Measurement level
Reference number of questionnaire completed by passenger (refnum) **	Unique number on each questionnaire	1–150	149	Ratio (could be zero)
Age (age)	Exact age as supplied by respondent	16–48	32	Ratio (could be zero)
Gender (gender)	1 = male 2 = female	1–2	1	Nominal/ categorical
Monthly income level (income)	Exact income as supplied by respondent in Rands	500–4900		Ratio (could be zero)
Educational level (educ)	1 = Below Grade 10 2 = Grade 10 and 11 3 = Grade 12 (Matric) 4 = Diploma/Degree 5 = Postgraduate degree	1–5	4	Ordinal
Bus route (busroute)	1 = Rietvlei 2 = Kwa-Thema	1–2	1	Nominal/ categorical

CODE SHEET

Data set: BUS.MON *

Date: 1/10/2005

Question/item and variable name	Coding	Minimum – Maximum	Range	Measurement level
Our local buses are on time (bustime)	Likert scale *** a = 1, b = 2, c = 3, d = 4, e = 5	1–5	4	Ordinal (but can be treated as interval for practical purposes)
Our local bus drivers are reckless (busreck)	Likert scale a = 1, b = 2, c = 3, d = 4, e = 5	1–5	4	Ordinal (but can be treated as interval for practical purposes)
Our local bus fares are too high (busfare)	Likert scale a = 1, b = 2, c = 3, d = 4, e = 5	1–5	4	Ordinal (but can be treated as interval for practical purposes)
Our local bus services care for their passengers (buscare)	Likert scale a = 1, b = 2, c = 3, d = 4, e = 5	1–5	4	Ordinal (but can be treated as interval for practical purposes)
Open-ended question: Would you like to add anything about the bus service? (busadd)	These themes were identified after the data were collected and the following codes were assigned to each theme: 1. The bus service is very good. 2. The buses don't wait for passengers. 3. Do something about the reckless driving of the bus drivers. 4. Start a bus service at 21h00 when we work late. 5. The bus drivers make detours to pick up their friends and then we are late for work.	1–5	4	Nominal/categorical

*   You don't have to type in the data of this research – just open the file "bus.mon".

**   Variable names in MoonStats are limited to 10 characters or fewer. In this case *reference number* (15 characters) is reduced to the variable name *refnum* (six characters) in the data set.

*** The Likert-type item responses were worded as follows: a = Strongly disagree, b = Disagree, c = Not sure or sometimes, d = Agree, e = Strongly Agree.

NOTE: The Code Sheet is not on the MoonStats programme or CD-ROM – you will have to create the code sheet on your own on a separate sheet of paper!

9.3 Clean the data set

Most data sets contain some errors initially. These errors could be due to typing errors, misreading the raw data, computer errors or other human errors. It is vital that you "clean" the data before doing statistical calculations. If the data have errors, your statistical output will reflect these errors. In computer terminology this is called *gigo* (garbage in – garbage out). It is therefore imperative that your data are "clean" and 100% correct before you start doing statistical analyses!

You can follow these steps to clean the data:

▶ Compare the original questionnaires with the data in the data sheet.
▶ Check the minimum and maximum values.
▶ Look out for outliers, that is, values in the data set that are substantially different from the other observations. They are much higher or lower than the bulk of the values in the distribution.

9.3.1 COMPARE THE ORIGINAL QUESTIONNAIRES WITH THE DATA IN THE DATA SHEET

Select a random sample of 10% to 15% of the original questionnaires or interviews. Compare these against the data entered in the data sheet, using the reference number to trace the original questionnaire on the data sheet. (When you enter the data, you should always write a unique reference number on top of each questionnaire, and enter this number in the first column of the data sheet. In MoonStats the first default variable "refnum" is supplied automatically for this very reason.)

One way to select the random sample is by selecting, for instance, every seventh (or every *n*th number – this will lead to a sample of between 10% and 15%). Then take the sample of questionnaires and double-check that the correct values for each variable have been entered in the data sheet. If you encounter errors, you should fix them.

It would be prudent to try and determine why these errors occurred (that is, did a specific person make the same errors or do poor quality work? Are the errors always on a specific place in the data set?). You need to consider what the chances are that there are many of these errors in the remaining 85% or 90% of the questionnaires that you have not checked. You need to be 100% sure that the data are error-free and clean before you start with any statistical analysis, otherwise you will have *gigo*! If you find that the data have been unreliably entered you have the option to either re-enter all the data correctly, or to check each and every value in the data sheet against the original questionnaire. When the data have been cleaned in this way, you should make backups before continuing.

9.3.2 CHECK THE MINIMUM AND MAXIMUM VALUES

The following procedure will produce an output window with minimum and maximum values, which you can then compare to the minimum and maximum values as indicated on the code sheet that you have created:

After entering the data (and making backup copies of the data set), go to the "analysis" window in MoonStats. Now use the "univariate statistics" function and select all the variables by clicking "select all". Then click on the "descriptive statistics" button. The output window will appear and show the variable names, means, standard deviations, minimum, and maximum values.

Carefully study the descriptive statistics in the output window. Some of the invalid data can be detected here because their values are outside the permissible range of minimum or maximum values. Invalid values are lower than the prescribed minimum value or higher than the prescribed maximum value on the data set code sheet that you created (see previous page for an example code sheet). If you find invalid values, you must return to the data sheet (click on the "data sheet" window), and search the variables for the incorrect value. You can do this by going to the top menu, selecting "edit", and scrolling down and selecting "find". Find and then delete the invalid value and replace it with the correct value by referring to the original questionnaire.

9.3.3 OUTLIERS

An outlier is a score/observation/value that is substantially different from the others. Outliers can be a result of: (a) incorrect data entry; (b) an extraordinary event that can be explained (in which case you should decide whether it is representative of the sample or should be ignored); (c) an extraordinary event that cannot be explained (again you should decide whether to include or ignore the data); and (d) observations that fall within the ordinary range of values on each of the variables but are unique in their combination across the variables (Hair, Anderson, Tatham & Black, 1998; Howell, 1989; Terre Blanche & Durrheim, 2001; Welman, Kruger & Mitchell, 2005).

Some outliers which were the result of incorrect data entry will have been fixed in the previous section by checking the minimum and maximum values.

The remaining outliers are most easily detected in MoonStats by using the appropriate graphical methods of representation, that is, bar charts, pie charts, histograms, scatter plots or *t*-test group histograms. These are described in the next section. Within each of these methods you should look for exceptionally high bars or plots, or clearly isolated bars or plots to the left or right of the distribution. If you find outliers, you should return to the data sheet (click on the "data sheet" window), and search the variables for the outlier value (go to the top menu, select "edit", and scroll down and select "find"). Compare the outlier values with the values on the original questionnaire by matching the unique reference number on the questionnaire to the value in the *refnum* variable. If the outliers are invalid due to data entry errors, you can now correct them.

> **TIP: MAKE A BACKUP COPY OF THE CLEANED DATA!**
> After spending some time and energy to clean the data, it is the ideal time to update the backups of the data you made on diskette or other removable storage device! Store the updated backups in a safe and accessible place.

9.4 Univariate statistics

The univariate statistics available in MoonStats include the following:

- **Mode**: The most common occurring value or score.
- **Median**: The score corresponding to the point in the exact middle of the values, so that 50% of the values are below it when the scores are arranged from low to high.
- **Mean**: The average value obtained for a variable by adding all the values and dividing by the number of values.
- **Standard deviation**: The standard deviation – an indication of how closely values are clustered around the mean. Approximately 68% of the values lie between one standard deviation below and one standard deviation above the mean. The variance is the squared standard deviation.
- **95% Confidence Interval (95% CI)**: If you are working with a sample, there is a 95% probability that the actual mean of the larger population from which your sample was drawn lies within the range indicated by this value – either above or below your sample mean.
- **Minimum**: The smallest value obtained for a variable.
- **Maximum**: The largest value obtained for a variable.
- **Range**: The distance from the lowest to the highest values. Obtained by subtracting the lowest from the highest values.
- **Skewness**: Indicates whether the distribution of values is symmetrical or not. A negatively skewed distribution has a mean that tends toward the higher values.

▶ **Kurtosis**: Kurtosis measures the "peakedness" of a distribution by looking at the flatness of the tail-ends of the distribution. If the kurtosis is high, then the distribution has a heavy-tailed distribution with a large number of scores that are very high and very low. If the kurtosis is low, then the distribution is more "peaked" and has relatively few values that are very high and very low.

▶ **Frequency tables**: A table listing the values or scores and the frequencies with which they occur.

The following graphs can be used with univariate statistics:

▶ **Bar chart**: A graph in which disconnected rectangles are used to represent frequencies of values.

▶ **Pie chart**: A graph in which the slices of a circle are used to represent frequencies of values.

▶ **Histogram**: A graph in which connected rectangles are used to represent frequencies of values.

Univariate statistics, frequency tabulation, and charts can be classified according to the measurement level of the variable as listed in Table 4.

Table 4 List of univariate descriptive statistical techniques and measurement level for MoonStats

| | Categorical | | Continuous/Quantitative | |
	Nominal	Ordinal	Interval	Ratio
Descriptive statistic	Frequency tables	Frequency tables	Frequency tables	Frequency tables
	Min-maximum	Min-maximum	Min-maximum	Min-maximum
	Mode	Mode	Mode	Mode
	–	Median	Median	Median
	–	–	Mean and standard deviation	Mean and standard deviation
	–	–	95% confidence interval of the mean	95% confidence interval of the mean
	–	–	Skewness and kurtosis	Skewness and kurtosis
Graphical method	Pie chart	Pie chart	Pie chart	Pie chart
	Bar chart	Bar chart	–	–
	–	–	Histogram	Histogram
Examples of variables	Gender, marital status, work status, disability status, province, city, day of week, month, cultural group, home language.	Social class, attitudes, any ranking of high/ middle/low, or junior/ mid-level/senior.	Attitudes, calendar time, scores of abilities (verbal, numerical, 3-dimensional insight, memory, artistic, writing, empathy).	Age, cost, exact income, number of children, exam result as a percentage.

9.5 Bivariate statistics

The bivariate statistics available in MoonStats are as follows:

▶ A **cross-tabulation** shows the number of cases with particular values on one variable that have particular values on another variable. If you ticked the "percentages" box, you will also see tables showing these frequencies as row and column percentages. You can also select a chi-square statistic for nominal and/or ordinal variables with a limited range (no more than 25 categories in MoonStats). The chi-square test shows whether there is a relationship between two categorical variables. Simply look at the *p*-value to see if the relationship is statistically significant. The bivariate chart provides a visual representation of the relationship between the variables.

▶ A **correlation** (Pearson's product moment for normally distributed data or Spearman's rank-order for not-normally distributed data or when the distribution is unknown) describes the relationship between variables. The *p*-value provides an indication of the significance of the relationship. The scatterplot provides a visual representation of the relationship between the variables. Correlations are relatively sensitive to outliers.

▶ The **t-test** is used to evaluate the differences in means between two groups. Randomly selected experimental/treatment and control groups are examples of independent groups. Dependent groups are based on related subject samples, for instance when a group of subjects are tested before and after an intervention to determine if there is an improvement in their scores. The bivariate chart gives a visual representation of the relationship between the variables. The *p*-value reported with a *t*-test represents the probability of error involved in accepting the research hypothesis about the existence of a difference in the means. The *t*-statistic assumes normality of the group distributions or variance. However, if the variances are unequal, a different formula is used to perform the *t*-test.

10 Write report

Each output window has a copy and save option. You can copy and paste the results and charts to a word processor, or save the results and then import them into the word processor. After clicking on the "copy" button in the output window, simply go to your word processor (MS Word, Wordpad, Word Perfect, and so on) and use the "edit" and "paste" functions on the top menu bar (or Ctrl + V on the keyboard). You may need to resize charts by dragging the size larger with the mouse (refer to your word processor help documentation for more information). If the statistical tables lose their alignment, ensure that the font is any Courier type as this will return the alignment of rows and tables of numbers.

11 Export MoonStats data

To export a data set from MoonStats to other programs, you should save the data set as a XBase (DBase) file. After opening the relevant data set in MoonStats, use the menu option "file" and "save data set as" and "Xbase file". You can then open the newly saved XBase file in the spreadsheet or other statistical software of your choice in DBase format.

REFERENCES

Hair, J.J., Anderson, R.E., Tatham, R.L. & Black, W.C. (1998). *Multivariate data analysis* (5th ed.). New Jersey: Prentice-Hall International.

Howell, D.C. (1989) *Fundamental statistics for the behavioural sciences* (2nd ed.). Massachusetts: PWS-Kent.

MoonStats (2001, 2005). *MoonStats User Manual*. Typeset Document. Pretoria.

Terre Blanche, M. & Durrheim, K. (Eds). (2001). *Research in Practice*. Cape Town: University of Cape Town Press.

Welman, J.C., Kruger, S.J. & Mitchell, B.C. (2005). *Research Methodology* (3rd ed). Cape Town: Oxford University Press Southern Africa.

References

Africa research on nevirapine "hides flaws". (2004, 14 December). *Daily News*, p. 2 (http://www.iol.co.za/index.php?set_id=1&click_id=31&art_id=vn20041214103252350C723627, 25/08/2005).

Ancer, J. & Sapa-AP. (2004, 11 February). Nevirapine poses risk for moms – study. *The Star*, p. 1 (http://www.iol.co.za/index.php?set_id=1&clicl_id=31&art_id=vn20040211042328587C559058, 25/08/2005).

Arnold, D.O. (1982). Qualitative field methods. In R.B. Smith & P.K. Manning (Eds), *A handbook of social science methods, Vol. II: Qualitative methods*. Cambridge, Mass.: Ballinger.

Atkinson, P. (1991). Supervising the text. *Qualitative Studies in Education*, **4**(2), 161–174

Babbie, E. & Mouton, J. (2001). *The practice of social research*. Cape Town: Oxford University Press.

Bachrach, A.J. (1981). *Psychological research: An introduction* (4th ed.). New York: Random House.

Bailey, K.D. (1987). *Methods of social research* (3rd ed.). New York: The Free Press.

Bem, D.J. (1986). Writing the research report. In L.H. Kidder & C.M. Judd (Eds), *Research methods in social relations* (5th ed.). New York: CBS Publishing.

Bless, C. & Higson-Smith, C. (1995). *Fundamentals of social research methods*. Kenwyn: Juta & Co.

Bluen, S.D. & Goodman, E.R. (1984). The stigmatization of ex-political detainees in employment practices. *South African Journal of Psychology*, **14**, 137–139.

Botha, J. (1987, 3 May). VSA se ergste TV-reekse ook hier uitgesaai [Worst USA TV series also broadcast here]. *Rapport*, p. 3.

Botha, M.P. (1990). *Televisieblootstelling en aggressiwiteit by hoërskoolleerlinge: 'n Opvolgondersoek oor vyf jaar* [Television exposure and aggressiveness among high-school pupils: A follow-up study over five years]. Unpublished doctoral thesis, University of the Free State, Bloemfontein.

Bracht, G.H. & Glass, G.V. (1968). The external validity of experiments. *American Educational Research Journal*, **5**, 437–474.

Brislin, R.W. (1970). Back translation for cross-cultural research. *Journal of Cross-cultural Research*, **1**, 185–216.

Campbell, D.T. & Ross, H.L. (1968). The Connecticut crackdown on speeding: Time-series data in quasi-experimental analysis. *Law and Society Review*, **3**, 33–53.

Cannell, C.F. & Kahn, R.L. (1986). Interviewing. In G. Lindzey & E. Aronson (Eds), *Handbook of social psychology* (2nd ed.). Reading, Mass.: Addison-Wesley.

Carley, K. (1990). Content analysis. In R.E. Asher (Ed.), *The encyclopedia of language and linguistics*. Edinburgh: Pergamon.

Carlsmith, J.M. & Anderson, C.A. (1979). Ambient temperature and the occurrence of collective violence: A new analysis. *Journal of Personality and Social Psychology*, **37**, 337–344.

Christensen, L.B. (1985). *Experimental methodology* (3rd ed.). Boston: Allyn & Bacon.

Cleaver, G. (1988). A phenomenological analysis of victimization. The experience of having one's house attacked and damaged. *South African Journal of Psychology*, **18**, 76–83.

Cook, T.D. & Campbell, D.T. (1979). *Quasi-Experimentation: Design and analysis issues for field settings*. Chicago: Rand McNally.

Coolican, H. (1992). *Research methods and statistics in psychology*. London: Hodder & Stoughton.

Denzin, N.K. & Lincoln, Y.S. (Eds) (1994). *Handbook of qualitative research*. California: SAGE Publications.

Department of Labour. (2000). *Employment Equity Act*. http://www.labour.gov.za/docs/legislation/eea/forms/eea3-eng.htm.

Dillman, D.A. (1978). *Mail and telephone surveys*. New York: Wiley.

Doob, A.N. & MacDonald, G.E. (1979). Television viewing and fear of victimization: Is the relationship causal? *Journal of Personality and Social Psychology*, **37**, 170–179.

Feather, N.T. (1964). Acceptance and rejection of arguments in relation to attitude strength, critical ability, and intolerance of inconsistency. *Journal of Abnormal and Social Psychology*, **69** (2), 127–136.

Fontana, A. & Frey, J.H. (1994). Interviewing. The art of science. In N.K. Denzin & Y.S. Lincoln (Eds). *Handbook of qualitative research*. California: SAGE Publications.

Gerbner, G. & Gross, L. (1976, April). The scary world of TV's heavy viewer. *Psychology Today*, 41–45.

Ghauri, P. & Gronhaugh, K. (2002). *Research methods in business studies: A practical guide* (2nd ed.). Harlow: Pearson.

Glass, G.V. (1968). Analysis of data on the Connecticut speeding crackdown as a time-series quasi-experiment. *Law and Society Review*, **3**(1), 55–76.

Gottschalk, L. (1969). *Understanding history: A primer of historical method*. New York: Knopf.

Green, J. (2005, 18 July). Most mothers develop drug resistance – study. *Cape Times*, p. 5 (http://www.iol.co.za/index.php?set_id=1&click_id=31art_id=vn2005071806 2759119C261241, 25 August 2005).

Haertel, E.H. (1987). Review of 'Foundations of behavioral research' (3rd ed.) by F.N. Kerlinger. *Contemporary Psychology*, **32**, 249–250.

Hays, W.L. (1988). *Statistics for the social sciences* (4th ed.). New York: Holt, Rinehart & Winston.

House, E.R. (1991). Realism in research. *Educational Researcher*, **20**(6), 2–9.

Huysamen, G.K. (1989a). *Introductory statistics and research design for the behavioural sciences*, Vol. II. Bloemfontein: Author.

Huysamen, G.K. (1989b). *Psychological and educational test theory*. Bloemfontein: Author.

Huysamen, G.K. (1990a). *Introductory statistics and research design for the behavioural sciences*, Vol. I. Bloemfontein: Author.

Huysamen, G.K. (1990b). *Psychological measurement: An introduction with South African examples*. Pretoria: Academica.

Huysamen, G.K. (1991). Steekproefgroottes in plaaslik gepubliseerde psigologiese navorsing [Sample sizes in locally published psychological research]. *Suid-Afrikaanse Tydskrif vir Sielkunde*, **21**(3), 183–190.

Huysamen, G.K. (1994). *Methodology for the social and behavioural sciences*. Halfway House: Southern.

Huysamen, G.K. (1997). Parallels between qualitative research and sequentially performed quantitative research. *South African Journal of Psychology*, **27**(1), 1–8.

Kaestle, C.F. (1997). Recent methodological developments in the history of American education. In R.M. Jaeger (Ed.). *Complementary methods for research in education*. Washington, D.C.: American Educational Research Association.

Kahn, R.L. & Cannell, C.F. (1957). *The dynamics of interviewing: Theory, technique, and cases*. New York: Wiley.

Kemmis, S. (1985). Action research. In T. Husen & T.N. Postlethwaite (Eds), *The international encyclopedia of education*, Vol. I. Oxford: Pergamon.

Kerlinger, F.N. (1979). *Behavioral research: A conceptual approach*. New York: Holt, Rinehart & Winston.

Kerlinger, F.N. (1986). *Foundations of behavioral research* (3rd ed.). New York: CBS Publishing.

Kidder, L.H. & Judd, C.M. (1986). *Research methods in social relations* (5th ed.). New York: CBS College Publishing.

Kotler, P. (1997). *Marketing management* (9th ed.). Englewood Cliffs, NJ: Prentice-Hall

Latané, B. & Darley, J.M. (1968). Group inhibition of bystander intervention in emergencies. *Journal of Personality and Social Psychology*, **10**, 215–221.

Lazarus, S. (1985). Action research in an educational setting. *South African Journal of Psychology*, **15**, 112–118.

Lofland, J. (1971). *Analysing social settings: A guide to qualitative observation and analysis*. Belmont, CA:Wadsworth.

Mathibela, J. (1996, 1 Apr.). The starts in black management [Letter to the editor]. *Sowetan*, p. 12.

Miles, M.B. & Huberman, A.M. (1994). *Qualitative data analysis*. California: SAGE Publications.

Murphy, K.R. & Balzer, W.K. (1989). Rater errors and rating accuracy. *Journal of Applied Psychology*, **74**, 619–624.

Naude, C.M.B. (1990). Execution patterns in the USA and South Africa in terms of race of offenders, types of crimes committed, race and gender of victims, and sentences commuted. *Acta Criminologica*, **3**(2), 5–10.

Neumann, W.L. (2000). *Social research methods* (2nd edition). London: Allyn & Bacon.

Oakley, A. (1981). Interviewing women: A contradiction in terms. In H. Roberts (ed.), *Doing feminist research* (pp. 30–61). London: Routledge.

Osgood, C.E., Suci, C.J. & Tannenbaum, P.H. (1957). *The measurement of meaning*. Urbana, IL: University of Illinois Press.

Page, B. (1976). *Reactions to disaster: Two studies in South Africa*. Grahamstown: Rhodes University.

Pedhazur, E. (1982). *Multiple regression in behavioral research: Explanation and prediction* (2nd ed.). New York: Holt, Rinehart & Winston.

Perold, S. (1983, 31 Oktober). Reg in die kol! [Right on target!]. *Rapport*, p. 11.

Piliavin, I.M., Rodin, J. & Piliavin, J.A. (1969). Good samaritanism: An underground phenomenon? *Journal of Personality and Social Psychology*, **13**(4), 289–299.

Preston-Whyte, E. (1982). Why questionnaires are not the answer. In South African Labour and Development Research Unit (SALDRU) (Ed.), *Questionnaires are no short cut*. Cape Town: SALDRU, University of Cape Town.

Psychological Association of South Africa (PASA). (1987). *Guide to authors*. Pretoria: SAPA.

Raimond, P. (1993). *Management projects: Design, research and presentation*. London: Chapman & Hall.

Rhoodie, N.J. (1986). Die wortels van wit-swartkonflik in Suid-Afrika vanuit die perspektief van John Galtung se teorie oor revolusionêre aggressie [The roots of white-black conflict in South Africa from the perspective of John Galtung's theory on revolutionary aggression]. *Suid-Afrikaanse Tydskrif vir Sosiologie*, **17**, 117–133.

Robson, C. (2002). *Real world research* (2nd ed.). Oxford: Blackwell.

Ryan, G.W. & Bernard H.R. (nd). *Techniques to identify themes in qualitative data*. http://www.analytich-tech.com/mb870 (19/07/2001).

Saal, F.E., Downey, R.G. & Lahey, M.A. (1980). Rating the ratings: Assessing the psychometric quality of rating data. *Psychological Bulletin*, **88**, 413–428.

Saling, M., Abrams, R. & Chester, H. (1983). A photographic survey of lateral cradling preferences in black and white women. *South African Journal of Psychology*, **13**(4), 135–136.

Saunders, M., Lewis, P. & Thornhill, A. (2003). *Research methods for business students* (3rd edition). Harlow: Pearson.

Schuman, H. & Presser, S. (1981*). Questions and answers in attitude surveys*. New York: Academic Press.

Smith, L.M. (1992). Ethnography. In M.C. Alkin (Ed.), *Encyclopedia of educational research, Volume 2* (pp. 458–462). New York: Macmillan.

Spector, P.E. (1981). *Research designs*. Beverly Hills, Cal.: Sage.

Stainback, S. & Stainback, W. (1984). Broadening the Research Perspective in Education. *Exceptional children*, **50**, 400–408.

Stake, R.E. (1997). Case study methods in educational research: Seeking sweet water. In R.M. Jaeger (Ed.), *Complementary methods for research in education*. Washington, D.C.: American Educational Research Association.

Statistics South Africa. Census 2001. http://www.statssa.gov.za/census01/html/default.asp (5/08/2005).

Stevens, S.S. (1951). Mathematics, measurement and psychophysics. In S.S. Stevens (Ed.), *Handbook of experimental psychology*. New York: Wiley.

Stewart, D.W. & Shamdasani, P.N. (1990). *Focus groups: Theory and practice* (Applied Social Research Methods Series, Vol. 20). Newbury Park, CA: Sage.

Strümpfer, D.J.W. (1980, September). *Een honderd-en-een jaar na Wundt* [One hundred and one years after Wundt]. Paper presented at the National Psychological Congress, Johannesburg.

Strümpfer, D.J.W. (1989). Do white South African managers suffer from exceptional levels of job stress? *South African Journal of Psychology*, **19**, 130–137.

Te veel bier lei tot tydelike impotensie [Too much beer leads to temporary impotence]. (1991, 8 Nov.). *Die Burger*, p. 15.

Tuckman, B.W. (1990). A proposal for improving the quality of published educational research. *Educational Researcher*, **19**(9), 22–25.

Twentieth World Conference on Open Learning and Distance Education. (2001). [CD-ROM] Fern Universität Hagen, Germany.

Tyack, D.B. (1976). Ways of seeing: An essay on the history of compulsory schooling. *Harvard Educational Review*, **46**(3), 355–389.

Tyson, G.A. & Turnbull, O. (1990). Ambient temperature and the occurrence of collective violence: A South African replication. *South African Journal of Psychology*, **20**(3), 159–169.

Valle, R.S., King, M. & Halling, S. (1989). An introduction to existential-phenomenological thought in psychology. In R.S. Valle & S. Halling (Eds), *Existential-phenomenological perspectives in psychology*. New York: Plenum.

Van Maanen, (1979). The fact of fiction in organizational ethnography. *Administrative Science Quarterly*, **24**, 539–611.

Webb, E.J., Campbell, D.T., Schwartz, R.D. & Sechrest, L. (1966). *Unobtrusive measures: Nonreactive research in the social sciences*. Chicago: Rand McNally.

Weitzman, E. & Miles, M. (1995). *Computer software for qualitative analysis*. London: Sage.

Welman, J.C.,& Basson, P.A. (1995). The interrelationship between the work experience of distance education students, job satisfaction, and academic achievement. *Journal of Industrial Psychology*, **21**(1), 14–17.

Wolcott, H.F. (1990). *Writing up qualitative research*. San Francisco: Sage.

Zelger, J. (1991). GABÉK – a new method for qualitative evaluation of interviews and model construction with PC-support. In E.A. Stuhler & M.O. Suileabhain (Eds.) *Enchanting human capacity to solve ecological and social-economic problems* (pp. 14–35). München, Germany: Rainer Hampp Verlag.

Zietsman, P.H. (1990, 19 Des.). *"Oriëntering" disorienteer* [Brief aan die redakteur]. ["Orientation" disorientated (letter to the Editor)] *Beeld*, p. 14.

Zuber-Skerritt, O. (1998). *Postgraduate research training and supervision* (Workshop notes). Gordon's Bay: Centre for Higher and Adult Education – University of Stellenbosch.

Zweigenhaft, R.L. (1970). Signature size: A key to status awareness. *Journal of Social Psychology*, **81**, 49–54.

Index